AN INTRIGUING LOOK
AT THE RELATIONSHIP BETWEEN
TWO ARTISTIC PROCESSES

What happened when Anthony Burgess's *A Clockwork Orange*, a novel narrated in a weird futuristic language called Nadsat, was made into a film by controversial director Stanley Kubrick? When D. H. Lawrence's challenging novel *Women in Love* became Ken Russell's extravagant movie, a film filled with frequently bizarre camera angles and with the dark Oliver Reed cast in the role of the Nordic Gerald?

Did these films capture the power and impact of the original work? Or, like *Ragtime*, did they miss the beat? And how do our expectations and readings of the novel affect our response? *Double Exposure* provides a fascinating view of the complex interactions among reader, novel, viewer, and movie, and of how the rich and multi-faceted language of film can be used to translate the language of literature.

Joy Gould Boyum is Professor of English and Communication Arts at New York University. Formerly the film critic for *The Wall Street Journal*, she currently reviews film for *Glamour* magazine and National Public Radio. She is a member of the New York Film Critics Circle and the National Society of Film Critics. Her previous works include *Film as Film: Critical Approaches to Film Art*.

DOUBLE EXPOSURE

FICTION INTO FILM

Joy Gould Boyum

A PLUME BOOK

NEW AMERICAN LIBRARY

NEW YORK AND SCARBOROUGH, ONTARIO

PERMISSIONS ACKNOWLEDGMENTS

From THE PROUST SCREENPLAY by Harold Pinter with
the collaboration of Joseph Losey and Barbara Bray.
Copyright © 1977 by Harold Pinter.
Reprinted by permission of Grove Press, Inc., New York.

From Dylan Thomas, POEMS OF DYLAN THOMAS.
Copyright © 1952 by Dylan Thomas.
Reprinted by permission of New Directions Publishing Corporation.

 PLUME TRADEMARK REG. U.S. PAT. OFF. AND FOREIGN COUNTRIES
REG. TRADEMARK—MARCA REGISTRADA
HECHO EN HARRISONBURG, VA., U.S.A.

SIGNET, SIGNET CLASSIC, MENTOR, PLUME, MERIDIAN
and NAL BOOKS are published *in the United States*
by New American Library, 1633 Broadway, New York, New York 10019,
in Canada by The New American Library of Canada Limited,
81 Mack Avenue, Scarborough, Ontario M1L 1M8

Library of Congress Cataloging in Publication Data
Boyum, Joy Gould, 1934-
    Double exposure.

    Bibliography: p.243
    1. Film adaptations—History and criticism.
2. Moving-pictures and literature.   I. Title.
PN1997.85.B69   1985b   791.43'09   85-13848
ISBN 0-452-25722-0

First Printing, October, 1985

1 2 3 4 5 6 7 8 9

PRINTED IN THE UNITED STATES OF AMERICA

For Heather

Contents

Preface   ix

PART ONE
In Defense of Adaptations

1: Biases and Preconceptions   3
2: Film as Literature   21

PART TWO
Adaptation as Interpretation

3: The Viewer as Reader: Varieties of Interpretation   43
4: The Filmmaker as Reader: The Question of Fidelity   63

PART THREE
The Rhetoric of Adaptation

5: Point of View   85

   The Innocents: Point of View as Puzzle   91

   The Great Gatsby: The Breakdown of Distance   98

   The French Lieutenant's Woman: Dual Perspectives   104

   Apocalypse Now: Misguided Journey to the Heart of Darkness   110

6: Style and Tone   118

Women in Love: Style as Daring   124

Ragtime: Missing the Beat   132

Tess: Romantic Strains and Tragic Rhythms   138

Daisy Miller: The Loss of Innocence   145

7: Metaphor, Symbol, Allegory   154

A Clockwork Orange: Viddying Metaphor   162

Lord of the Flies: Boys Will Be Boys   169

Wise Blood: Wise Choices   175

Death in Venice: The Seductiveness of the Sensual   182

8: Interiors: Thought, Dream, Inner Action   189

Slaughterhouse-Five: Pilgrim's Progress through Time and Space   197

Under the Volcano: Looking Outward   205

The Day of the Locust: Hollywood as a State of Mind   212

Swann in Love and *The Proust Screenplay:* Proust Outside and In   219

Afterword *The Magnificent Ambersons:* Reversing the Bias   230

BIBLIOGRAPHY   243

NOTES   255

INDEX   269

Preface

This book sets out not only to explore the art of adaptation but also to defend it. Its sources are many, but chiefly it derives from what I tend to think of less as "my brilliant career" than my somewhat schizophrenic one—from the fact that for the greater part of my professional life I have been a teacher of literature and a professional film reviewer, both an academic approaching film as art and a journalist immersed in film as news and commodity. This dual and often contradictory perspective has been crucial in shaping my view of film and fiction and their interrelationship.

It's important, I think, that I came to criticism from academia, from literature to film, and not the other way around. For this should help make clear that when, in the opening chapter of this book, I discuss the biases and preconceptions brought to bear on film by the literary establishment, I know whereof I speak. At one time or another, there probably wasn't a single one of these biases I myself didn't share. I don't mean by this to suggest that I didn't always love movies, but rather to indicate (or perhaps confess) that they were originally, at least, one of my guilty pleasures. Moreover, unlike many of my colleagues in the film world, I didn't grow up in my local Loews, nor was it the American genre film that first persuaded me of film's authentic value and excitement. Since my intellectual coming of age happened to coincide with the great resurgence of European film in the fifties and since I was also raised in New York City where foreign films were widely available, I came to my deeper passion for movies and my sense of their aesthetic possibilities (dubiously, some cineastes would argue) through the European art film. Ironically, I began to function as a reviewer (in 1971) just at the time that the European art film was beginning its decline and when, by and large, the excitement that was to be found in the movie scene came nearly exclusively from American films—films whose energy and sheer professionalism I came more and more to admire.

Still, whether it was *The Seventh Seal* or *Easy Rider*, it was clear to me very early on that there was a vitality in film, a spontaneity and intensity in the interest it generated, that was simply not to be found in the other arts. Certainly, all through college and graduate school and later, though none of us was studying film, my friends and I tended to talk more frequently and argue more vehemently about movies than about any other works of art. I recall that my husband and I had one of our most serious arguments about *Jules and Jim*, and that the merits and demerits of *Bonnie and Clyde* became the exclusive subject of conversation at a dinner party for eight, not one of whom (myself included) was involved in film in any professional way.

But whatever my involvement with film, as an academic trained in literature and literary theory, I tended to take a proprietary attitude toward books and brought that attitude with me to my first years of reviewing. I may have loved movies, but I accepted the received view of how they differed from books and regarded the adaptation especially as a suspect form. (Actually, the first piece of film criticism I ever wrote—for a college paper—was a vitriolic attack on adaptations, excited by my discovery that *My Foolish Heart*, a movie I recalled as utter tripe, had been based on my beloved J. D. Salinger's "Uncle Wiggily in Connecticut.") But much in the manner of a child who just can't keep his tongue away from that somewhat painful loose molar, I remained fascinated with the process all the same and with the interrelationships between literature and film in general. I found that, whatever I had believed at first, my increased exposure to film kept impressing on me to a greater and richer extent the continuities rather than the differences between these two extraordinary narrative forms, just as it also did the possibilities rather than the limitations of adaptations. From *A Clockwork Orange* to *The Man Who Would Be King*, from *The Godfather* to *One Flew Over the Cuckoo's Nest*, from *Barry Lyndon* to *Tess*, I couldn't help but be struck by the fact that an extraordinary number of the most compelling films I saw were adaptations. And my views began to change.

Another factor in encouraging that shift in attitude was a course I developed in literature and film at New York University—a course devoted to exploring contrasts and continuities in the two media chiefly through a study of literary works and their adaptations. Writing criticism is certainly one way of forcing you to clarify your views—of finding out what you actually think—but there's nothing quite like teaching for learning. And whether the film in question was *Tom Jones* or *The Rocking-Horse Winner*, *La Symphonie Pastorale* or *Great Expectations*, *Diary of a Country Priest* or *Lady with a Dog*—the shared exploration of the challenges of translating book to film and of the various strategies used to meet them made the possibilities of adaptation seem richer and richer still and the theory that emphatically denied those possibilities seem more and more mistaken in turn.

I also became increasingly sensitive to the enormous role of prior experience and expectations in shaping responses to adaptations. Having been both the student and colleague of Louise M. Rosenblatt, an early proponent of what has come to be called reader-response theory, I had long subscribed to the view that a literary work has no mode of existence in itself—that it comes into being only as a partner in a cooperative venture with a reader who inevitably brings to bear an entire constellation of past experiences, personal associations, cultural biases and aesthetic preconceptions. And I had also long recognized that theory's very particular application to film. Together with my friend and colleague Adrienne Scott, I assembled a text centered on that view back in 1970, *Film as Film: Critical Approaches to Film Art.* But I began to see more clearly the extraordinary complexity of that transaction between viewer and film in the context of the adaptation, where the viewer's response to a given film was so frequently preceded and controlled by a prior response to the literary work on which that film was based. I also began to perceive with greater clarity the special nature of the biases adaptation tends to elicit—biases that, in my own case as well, had often skewed perception and interfered with appreciation. And I became persuaded at the same time of how enriching to one's understanding of the nature of both media the study of adaptation could be.

In short, over the years, my view of adaptation evolved and, I suppose, is evolving still. But at some point, one has to stop and take stock. That is what I've tried to do in this book—just as I've attempted something else as well. For if my tenure as a critic has coincided with a period of enormous vitality in American film, it has also come at a time when the view of the director as supreme film artist has been dominant and when film itself has grown increasingly conscious of itself as a visual art and further away from a concern with narrative—and not simply to its detriment but even to tragically wasteful results. *Heaven's Gate* alone can make the point: however massive Michael Cimino's gifts as director, breathtaking the film's images, and potentially fascinating its subject, all foundered for want of a strong and substantive script—for want, that is, of a writer's touch. My argument in support of adaptations is implicitly, then, also an argument for film as collaborative art and a reminder of its storytelling powers. Put another way, it's an attempt to redress the balance.

* * *

As for my selection of films for discussion, throughout it has been determined to a great extent by how well the particular movie illustrates the point at hand—though, of course, I also tended to opt for movies I had taught and in some instances for those I had written about before. (In several instances—*A Clockwork Orange* and *Daisy Miller*, for example—my discussions build on reviews originally written for the *Wall Street Journal*.) I also attempted to concentrate on English-language films based on English-language works, partly because both films and books were likely to be better known; partly as a way of avoiding getting involved in the tricky task of examining a translation of what for most of us at least is also a translation itself; though mostly, I suppose, because the European film, even when an adaptation, tends to elicit less bias than does its American or English counterpart. Where the film in question was especially apt to the issue being discussed—as it was in the case of *Death in Venice* and *Swann's Way*—I did, however, make an exception to the rule. I also tried wherever possible to choose an adaptation to which I could bring a somewhat fresh approach. Thus the omission of certain films traditional to the canon—*The Grapes of Wrath*, *Great Expectations*, *The Rocking-Horse Winner*—and of certain special favorites, such as *Tom Jones*, written about elsewhere not only eloquently but also from a vantage point similar to the one I myself would have taken.

I'd like to take this opportunity to express my gratitude to New York University for granting me a sabbatical leave which allowed for the completion of this manuscript; to my students, on whom I tested so many of these ideas over the years, and to Frank Brady particularly, who shared with me not only his collection of videotapes but his materials on Orson Welles and *The Magnificent Ambersons*; to Paramount, Universal, Columbia, United Artists, and Warner Brothers for their generous loan of prints and especially to Paramount's William S. Kenly for providing me with materials from his own collection and for sharing with me his arcane knowledge of the movie past. I am also extremely grateful to the friends and colleagues who read this manuscript at various stages: Adrienne Scott, whose early encouragement was crucial to the development of this book; Gordon Pradl, who searched an early draft for inconsistencies and inaccuracies; Deirdre Levinson, who gave my arguments consideration despite her disagreements; and Marjorie Rosen, with whom I have exchanged so many opinions and ideas about movies and who read through these pages with her sharp eye for jargon and pedantry. I also want to thank Arnold Dolin of New American Library for his patience, his helpful editorial advice, and above all, for his kindness and good will. To the members of my family, I am hugely indebted: to my husband, Asmund, for his unfailing support in this and all my endeavors; to my son, David, for challenging me with his exacting sense of logic and argument; and to my daughter, Ingrid, especially, for willingly serving as guinea pig, for carefully reading through and questioning this manuscript at various stages, and for her consistently wise suggestions. I also want to acknowledge all I owe to the late Heather Livingston Barbash to whom this book is dedicated and who, for the more than thirty years of our friendship, shared with me her wit, her insight, her taste, and her love of literature in all its forms.

J.G.B.

DOUBLE EXPOSURE

FICTION INTO FILM

PART ONE

In Defense of Adaptations

1

Biases and Preconceptions

Hollywood has never been noted for its literacy. Yet from its very beginnings, it has turned to literature for inspiration and persisted in the practice of translating books to film. Our first and greatest film artist, the man who is variously credited with "inventing Hollywood" and with forging film's distinctive language, typically based his movies on poems, plays, short stories, and novels. True, D.W. Griffith's most famous films are taken from the kind of works which hardly classify as "literature" at all: Thomas Burke's story "The Chink and the Child," which served as the basis for *Broken Blossoms;* Adolph D. Ennery's sentimental melodrama *The Two Orphans*, which he translated into *Orphans of the Storm;* and most notoriously, Thomas Dixon's racist bestseller *The Clansman*, which was both the source and original title of *The Birth of a Nation.* But Griffith—who was evidently more well read than most of his followers and is said to have arrived on the set each day carrying one or another of Dickens's novels—also frequently made use of the classics. He adapted Tennyson in *Enoch Arden*, Browning in *Pippa Passes*, Thomas Hood in *The Song of the Shirt*, Jack London in *The Call of the Wild*, and, in *The Cricket on the Hearth*, his beloved Dickens, whose work is generally credited with inspiring the innovations—the use of the close-up, parallel editing, montage, and even the dissolve—which helped earn Griffith the epithet "father of film technique."

Griffith, however, wasn't the father of adaptation. In bringing classic literary works to the screen, he was merely following the lead of French and Italian filmmakers who had looked to literature for story material as early as 1902. That was the year that Georges Méliès filmed his *A Trip to the Moon* which, loose as its connections to its literary source may have been, still had its origins in a Jules Verne novel, as did Méliès' later film *Twenty Thousand Leagues under the Sea.* More serious attempts at adaptation were made just a few years later: 1908 saw the formation of the Société Film d'Art, a French company formed for the express purpose of translating

3

prestigious literary works to the screen, mostly dramas but also novels by Hugo, Balzac, and Dickens. The Italians, for their part, were attracted to historical works—novels such as Edgar Bulwer-Lytton's *The Last Days of Pompei* and Henrik Sienkiewicz's *Quo Vadis*, which in 1908 and 1912 respectively made for some of the earliest adaptations, as well as for the movies' first superspectaculars.

What's interesting is that, primitive as these adaptations were in every respect—after all, what can one expect of a five-minute silent version of Zola's *L'Assommoir* or a one-reel *Ben-Hur* shot with static camera against a painted backdrop?—they were generally greeted with praise, if not for their aesthetic value, at least for their educational potential. For, like early movies in general, such films were aimed primarily at the lower classes and so were perceived as a promising means of providing these viewers with a share in "the great tradition." Writing in *The Moving Picture World* in 1911, critic Stephen Bush carried such sentiments even further, making the introduction of the literary classics to the masses the very mission of the motion picture:

> It is the masterpiece of the ages that especially invites filming, and the reason for it is very plain. An epic that has pleased and charmed many generations is most likely to stand the test of cinematographic reproduction. . . . After all, the word "classic" has some meaning. It implies the approval of the best people in the most enlightened times. The merits of a classic subject are nonetheless certain because known and appreciated by comparatively few men. It is the business of the moving picture to make them known to all.

"The business of the moving picture" being primarily "business" itself, it's doubtful there were many moviemakers who shared Bush's messianic view. Here and there, a director might have felt drawn to a classic out of some passionate involvement with it, but for the most part, literature attracted filmmakers back then for the same reasons it does today. On the most practical of levels, it supplied motion pictures with a much-needed source of plots and characters. And if the work in question also happened to be either a "masterwork of the ages" or a popular play or novel, it also made for that most valuable of screen assets—the proverbial "proven property." There was another factor at work too: such classic sources gave movies—that suspect, vulgar form which even Griffith had at first held in contempt and which right from the outset suffered from a sense of inferiority regarding its status and respectability—their own touch of class. For to adapt a prestigious work was to do more than merely borrow its plot, its characters, its themes: in the eyes of the movie industry, it was—and in fact still is—to borrow a bit of that work's quality and stature.

Certainly, this is one of the reasons that adaptations have always held such a privileged place in the movie industry and why at the Academy Awards, it's the adaptation more than any other kind of film on which the industry bestows its honors. Take that stellar movie year 1939, when nearly every competing film was an adaptation—*Wuthering Heights, The Wizard of Oz, Of Mice and Men, Goodbye, Mr. Chips*, and of course, *Gone with the Wind*—and when even the winner of the year's award for best short subject was an adaptation, Disney's version of Hans Christian Andersen's "The Ugly Duckling." Take almost any year in fact, since a list of the movies which have either won or at least been nominated for Best Picture sounds startlingly like a library catalogue: *The Way of All Flesh, All Quiet on the Western Front, Mutiny on the Bounty, Arrowsmith, A Farewell to Arms, David Copperfield, The Informer, A Midsummer Night's Dream, Pygmalion, The Grapes of Wrath, The Magnificent Ambersons, For Whom the Bell Tolls, The Ox-Bow Incident, Hamlet, Henry V, Great Expectations, All the King's Men, The Heiress* (from Henry James's *Washington Square*), *King Solomon's Mines, A Place in the Sun* (from Dreiser's *An American Tragedy*), *Ivanhoe, From Here to Eternity, A Streetcar Named Desire, The Rose Tattoo, Cat on a Hot Tin Roof, Room at the Top, Elmer Gantry, Sons and Lovers, To Kill a Mockingbird, Beckett, Zorba the Greek, Dr. Zhivago, Romeo and Juliet, Tom Jones, A Clockwork Orange, Barry Lyndon, One Flew Over the Cuckoo's Nest, Apocalypse Now* (inspired by Conrad's *Heart of Darkness*), *Tess, Sophie's Choice*, and so on. Not to mention such films as *Women in Love, The Prime of Miss Jean Brodie*, and *Being There*, whose stars won awards for Best Performance (outstanding novels, as well as outstanding plays, apparently offering actors equally outstanding opportunities for characterization), or *The Garden of the Finzi-Continis, The Tin Drum*, and *Mephisto* (among other adaptations which have won in the category of Best Foreign Film, first instituted in 1956). What is more, since the industry approval implicit in these awards not only reflects a given film's "quality" but also its popularity—the latter being one of Hollywood's crucial yardsticks of the former—it's fairly clear that in most instances, audiences have also been responsive to these movies.

But if the adaptation has had its supporters, it has also had its detractors. And since most of these have come from the ranks of neither moviemakers nor ordinary moviegoers but of academics, theorists, and latter-day critics—or in other words, from those who tend to put their ideas into print—the fact is that despite occasional early support, most of what has been set down about adaptation has been set down firmly against it. Rumblings were heard even back in those early optimistic days. There was Vachel Lindsay who, passionately taken with this new form and bent on championing "film as art," argued against adaptation on the grounds that it worked against the film medium's uniqueness. Virginia Woolf likewise expressed the view that the "alliance" between cinema and literature was "unnatural" and "disastrous" to both forms, though her language makes it clear that she believed it a good deal more disastrous to one than the other and that, unlike Lindsay, her concern was less with the future of movies than with the future of books. Railing against the adaptation, she wrote of books as the "prey" and "unfortunate victim," movies as a "parasite" which feeds on them with "immense rapacity," and the movie audience itself (presumably in contrast to the audience for books) as "the savages of the twentieth century."

Lindsay and Woolf were both, of course, writing in the silent days—he in 1915, she a decade later. And though we see in the stance of each the lines along which subsequent arguments against the adaptation have been drawn, these positions were not to become either truly solidified or widespread until movies began to talk and until they also went through a series of dramatic changes in their aesthetics and in their economic and social structures in the years immediately following World War II.

When one considers that the silent film had a lifespan of a mere thirty-five years, its accomplishments are staggering. Still, even in the hands of a Griffith or an Eisenstein, it remained extremely limited as a storytelling medium. For its narrative and dramatic possibilities to be in any way fulfilled, film clearly demanded sound. And sound also brought with it, as moviemakers struggled to come to terms with its use, a host of other technological and stylistic advances. So enormous were the changes that film underwent during the first decades of the sound era (that is, during the thirties and forties) that reviewing them in his essay "The Evolution of the Language of Cinema," André Bazin could go so far as to declare: "the filmmaker . . . is, at last, the equal of the novelist." In the eyes of those who, unlike Bazin, took literature as their primary concern, this hardly seemed the case, but one thing was certain: the filmmaker had become the novelist's competitor. And it wasn't simply that the movies now quite literally had the language of literature at their disposal; it was also that during the first decades of the sound era, movies had become an extraordinarily pervasive medium which now numbered among its audience, together with the uneducated lower classes, members of the middle and upper-middle classes as well.*

Movies, moreover, weren't the only mass medium that had come to the fore in this period: the thirties and forties were also the golden age of radio and the era in which comic books and picture magazines like *Life, Look,* and *Coronet* flourished. Thus, by the early 1950s, when the great growth spurt of television began, defenders of traditional culture began to panic. (Actually, they had begun to panic earlier, but more important issues, chiefly World War II, distracted their attention for a while.) Culture was divided up and categorized: into avant-garde and kitsch; highbrow, middlebrow, and lowbrow; mass-cult and mid-cult; the traditional arts and the popular ones; art and entertainment. The aesthetics of the popular arts were explored, the effects of mass culture were investigated; and nearly everywhere with the implicit aim not simply of salvaging the genuine from the ersatz, of rescuing good taste from the onslaught of bad, but indeed of saving culture itself. For thanks to the media (or so certain critics claimed) not only couldn't Johnny read, but with the entertainment industry voraciously feeding on genuine works of art, transforming and making them digestible, there seemed a very real danger that the books he might read (if he could) might themselves be eaten up and destroyed. Such were the fears expressed by numerous defenders of high culture—among them Hannah Arendt, who put the matter this way:

> The entertainment industry is confronted with gargantuan appetites, and since its wares disappear in consumption, it must constantly offer new commodities. In this predicament, those who produce for the mass media ransack the entire range of past and present culture in the hope of finding suitable material. This material, however, cannot be offered as it is; it must be prepared and altered in order to become entertaining. . . . The danger is . . . precisely that it may become very entertaining indeed; there are many great authors of the past who have survived centuries of oblivion and neglect, but it is still an open question whether they will be able to survive an entertaining version of what they have to say.

It's Virginia Woolf all over again—only a good deal stronger—the metaphor having shifted from the biological one of the "parasite" (which, whatever damage it does to its host, at least has the virtue of proceeding quietly)

---

*During the thirties and forties, the American movie industry recorded as many as 85 million admissions to the movies per week out of a total population of 130 million. Even taking repeat viewers into account (as well as the industry's notorious inaccuracies), it's clear that an extraordinary percentage of Americans of that time were regularly going to the movies.

to the much more strident one of war. On the one side we have the "ransacking" hordes of mass culture; on the other the defending troops of high culture fighting for their very life; with the adaptation emerging as the convenient emblem of the conflict. Why the adaptation? Because, as Arendt suggests, it is here that the gold of art is transformed into the dross of entertainment, and refined, legitimate culture is pummeled into its vulgar mass form. The biases underlying this view are hard to miss: that a work of literature (or anything truly worthy of the name) is by definition a work of complexity and quality which is addressed to an educated elite; that movies, in contrast, are mere entertainment, directed at anyone and everyone; and that to adapt a book to film is thus of necessity to adjust it, not so much to its new medium as to its audience. That is, to the uneducated, undifferentiated mass, with its inevitably limited comprehension and predilection for the homiletic sentiment. Adaptation, in Arendt's view, is synonymous with betrayal.

— It hardly seems a coincidence that it was precisely at this time (1957) that the first major study of adaptation appeared—George Bluestone's *Novels into Film*. Nor should Bluestone's conclusions—that despite superficial similarities, the movie and the novel are essentially antithetical forms and that a film adaptation will, even at its very best, be a lesser work of art than its source—seem particularly coincidental either. Writing during a period of great concern with the effects of mass culture on high culture, a period in which (as he himself states) there was an increased trend toward adaptation, Bluestone was also looking at movies at an unfortunate time for movies themselves, at least in the United States. Threatened by the loss of their audience to television and devastated by the Supreme Court ruling that forced the studios to divest themselves of their theatres, movies were in fact at their absolute nadir—both economically and aesthetically. Not that Bluestone was concentrating on fifties films, but it was hard to escape the aura and attitudes created by the spate of 3-D horror films, Biblical spectaculars, and beach-blanket teen-flicks currently being released.

Bluestone had also chosen to focus solely on American studio products, though a similar trend toward adaptation was simultaneously asserting itself abroad (in England and France especially) and with decidedly different results from those that obtained on this side of the Atlantic. It's interesting to speculate just how different his conclusions might have been had he based his study not on the likes of Vincente Minelli's *Madame Bovary* or William Wyler's *Wuthering Heights*, but on David Lean's films of Dickens (*Great Expectations* and *Oliver Twist*), on Carol Reed's of Graham Green (*Odd Man*

Out, The Third Man, The Fallen Idol) and Conrad *(An Outcast of the Islands)*, on Jean Delannoy's version of Andre Gide's *Symphonie Pastorale,* on Robert Bresson's *Diary of a Country Priest* (based on the novel by Bernanos). Instead of stating that when a filmmaker presumes to adapt a work of substance and significance, "destruction is inevitable," he might have agreed with the then still-untranslated André Bazin that it's possible for an intelligent and sensitive adaptation to achieve "an almost dizzy height of fidelity." This is fairly unlikely, however, since it's not simply the particular films he deals with that force Bluestone to his point of view. Nor is it only his belief that an art addressed to a mass audience will by that very fact be more limited than an art addressed to an elite one. Implicit throughout his discussion is the crucial assumption that words, rather than images, make for the superior medium.

We hardly need a Marshall McLuhan to tell us that defenders of high culture have always shared Bluestone's bias. That's one of the reasons that some quarter of a century after the publication of *Novels into Film,* and after the release of dozens of infinitely more sophisticated adaptations than those he deals with, no study of adaptations has come along to replace it.*\ It's one of the reasons too that—such complex works as Eric Rohmer's *The Marquise of O* and Stanley Kubrick's *Barry Lyndon* notwithstanding—the view still prevails in the literary establishment that the adaptation is a variety of classic comic and that film itself (despite its Ingmar Bergmans and Alain Resnais') is a lesser form. However seemingly sophisticated the works created from it, the "language" of film is still held by many to be an essentially transparent and crude one when contrasted to the "language" of literature. (While everyone has to be taught how to read, we are reminded, no one really has to be taught how to see a movie.) And if the medium isn't simplistic, where are the works that reflect its complexity? Where are the masterpieces of cinematic art? Where are the films, as one defender of high culture asks, that can stand comparison with "the main works of Aeschylus, Sophocles, Euripides, Aristophanes, Homer, Virgil, Dante, Shakespeare, Moliere, Goethe . . ."? So *Citizen Kane* is one of the greatest films ever made. Can the film enthusiast really claim that its symbolism is

---

*There have been several studies of the interrelationships between literature and film and several anthologies containing articles on individual adaptations. But except for Geoffrey Wagner's *The Novel and the Cinema*—which, despite disclaimers to the contrary, comes to much the same conclusions as Bluestone—there has been no sustained work at all on the adaptation of novels to film.

"in the same league as the iconography of Amiens, the images in Dante's *Commedia* or even the lesser number in *Moby Dick* or *Ulysses;* that the portrayal of a man in *Citizen Kane* is even to be compared with that say in *Le Rouge et le Noir* or *The Great Gatsby"*? So Fellini is one of the great filmmakers. "Is [he] really such an observer as Joyce?"

But I suspect there's a more pressing reason yet that film tends to be dismissed. In the time since Bluestone's study was written and Hannah Arendt expressed her fears concerning the imminent death of art at the hands of entertainment, the threat that film seemingly poses to literature has become a good deal stronger. It's more than Johnny who doesn't read, it suddenly seems to be almost everyone, with the literary establishment confronting defectors from its very own ranks—and not simply the venerable Shakespeare professor from Toronto, Marshall McLuhan. "Nearly everyone I know would rather see a movie than read a book," writes novelist and critic Alfred Chester, significantly enough in the context of a book review; while literature professor Leslie Fiedler—who recently authored a tome grimly entitled *What Was Literature?*—has similarly remarked that the sight of a stack of new novels excites in him not the desperate desire to read, but "a desperate desire to sneak out to a movie."

To "sneak out" of course suggests the notion of slumming. Movies appeal, then, Professor Fiedler implies, not in their likeness to that stack of novels on his desk, but in their difference from them: in the extent to which they stand outside the boundaries of traditional culture, lack the respectability of books, and—to use the term popularized by Pauline Kael—constitute low-down "trash." Could it be that we have here the ground for still another argument against adaptation? Could it be that those who contend that much of the contempt directed at adaptation follows from an effort to keep movies in their place, to keep them from being uppity, to keep them at the level of "kitsch," really do have a point? Perhaps. For in the same period that literature has seemingly gone more and more into decline, movies have in fact grown more and more uppity. No longer content to be mere entertainment—and certainly not to be trash—they've now asserted themselves as "art." And this has not only created a whole new set of aesthetic problems, but given rise to a whole new set of arguments against the adaptation.

As the writings of Vachel Lindsay make clear, there were those who regarded movies as a legitimate and significant aesthetic enterprise from the very outset. Still, it wasn't until the late fifties and early sixties that, in this country at least, such a view really took hold. In large part, this reevaluation of film was a function of developments abroad. Immediately after World War II the various European industries began to recover; Italian Neorealism and the French New Wave developed, and suddenly we were importing a type of complex, challenging, even puzzling work that looked like art, felt like art, and was consequently dubbed the "art film." Even more important to this revised perception of film, however, was a development at home—television. Television may have helped spur criticism of mass culture in which movies were inevitably included, and it may have worked economic havoc on the movie industry, but in stealing away movies' great mass audience, it helped to make movies themselves more elite. Moreover, once the studios had sold off their old libraries to this new medium, television suddenly made available the whole of Hollywood's past, evoking a great deal of nostalgia on the one hand, and an enormous amount of serious rethinking and reevaluation on the other.

So we find that during the fifties and sixties, movies began to make a major effort to reshape their image and to reshape it very distinctly in the mold of art. They changed their name, dropping "motion picture" altogether (as in "Academy of Motion Picture Arts and Sciences") and opting for the more connotatively cultivated labels: "film" (as in the newly constituted American Film Institute) and even "cinema." They found a forum at prestigious cultural institutions like Washington, D.C.'s, Kennedy Center and New York City's Lincoln Center. They gave rise, in place of the old fan magazines, to seriously intended publications such as *Film Culture* and *Film Comment*. Their "reviewers" were magically transformed into "critics."* More important yet, they began to make major inroads behind the walls of ivy.†

But if changing status is one thing, feeling secure about it is another. And

---

*As evidence consider that when the collected journalism of James Agee was published in 1958, it was called *James Agee on Film: Reviews and Comments*, but that when the journalism of Otis Ferguson was collected in 1971, it was entitled *The Film Criticism of Otis Ferguson*.

†According to *The American Film Institute's Guide to College Film Courses* (later entitled *The AFI Guide to Courses in Film and Television*), the number of film courses offered in American universities during the period of 1964–70 increased by some 84 percent and nearly doubled from a total of 1,669 in the academic year 1970–71 to 2,392 in 1971–72. By the end of the decade, the number had grown to 3,991, with an additional 3,657 courses in television and other media. The figures are particularly impressive in that the AFI survey is far from complete.

film in its efforts to be accepted as art has had to deal not only with such obvious extrinsic burdens as its blatant commercialism and the inescapable trashiness of so many of its products; it has also been plagued with certain intrinsic problems deriving from its very nature. Arguing for film as art, Vachel Lindsay felt it necessary to put forth a case for film's uniqueness, and theorists since his time have felt similarly impelled. But try as they might to isolate qualities truly special to the form, these theorists simply haven't been able to come up with any—beyond, that is, the facts that film is a machine art, depending on mechanical equipment for both its creation and reception, and that it relies on illusion, on our acceptance that pictures are actually moving when of course they aren't.

One problem with determining the "essence" of film is that it's not only an art (like poetry or music or painting), but also a medium like print—and one that, among its other uses, can serve to record the other arts. (You can film a ballet, an opera, a theatre performance; you can even, if you wish to—and as movies used to do in the old days—photograph the words to a song.) As an art, moreover, it can function as essay, devoting itself to exposition or persuasion (as in such "nonfiction" films as *The River, Nanook of the North, Triumph of the Will*). It can operate as lyric or "pure" image (as in the works of Stan Brakhage, Kenneth Anger, and Maya Deren). It can photograph drawings as in animation or dispense with photography altogether, etching images directly on the filmstrip itself and becoming painting-in-motion (as in the works of James Whitney and Norman McLaren). Most of us though, and most theorists as well, tend to identify film with the form it most frequently assumes, and in which we usually experience it—that is, the fictional narrative.

Yet, even when limited to art rather than medium and to the fictional narrative, film still proves elusive to the theorist who would isolate its defining qualities. As Susan Sontag puts it, "Cinema is a kind of pan-art." It can make use of, even absorb, just about every other art, while there isn't a quality it has that isn't also found in one or another of these arts. Film shares its visual aspect with painting, its dependence on movement with dance, its ability to produce kinetic and emotional effects with music, its reliance on performance and spectacle with theatre, its technological basis with architecture. But the art with which film (or at least narrative film) clearly shares most—from its use of plot, characters, setting, dialogue, and imagery through its manner of expressing theme to its tendency to manipulate space and time—is literature. And so it follows that the effort to assert film's uniqueness involves distancing it from no art so much as the one to which it seems so intimately related.

Here, of course, lies the basis for much of the antipathy cineastes hold toward the adaptation. It's also the basis, significantly enough, for a common approach to the evolution of film itself, one which views film as having struggled throughout its history to free itself from the yoke of literature and its dependence on literary models. It was very much because he saw them as "writer's films," for example, that the young critic François Truffaut took issue with the French films of the postwar period—films which constituted what was known as the "Tradition of Quality" and which were generally based on French classics. That Truffaut didn't criticize them on these particular grounds doesn't matter in the least. (He didn't mind an adaptation, he noted, when it was the work of a "man of the cinema" or, put another way, an *auteur;* while the fact is that when he himself became a filmmaker, he frequently turned to literary sources, whether the works of Henri-Pierre Roche in *Jules and Jim* and *Two English Girls* or of Ray Bradbury in *Fahrenheit 451* or of Henry James in *The Green Room.)* Truffaut's views have nonetheless contributed immeasurably to the negative attitude toward the adaptation—the adaptation being, in the minds of most, inescapably a "writer's film" or, to use a term of even greater opprobrium to cineastes, a "literary" one. An authentically "cinematic" film, in contrast—or so it's widely held—will be free of such roots and connections. It will be originated for the screen and not for the page; conceived in images and not in words; a work that is visual and not linear.

Such a film, as Truffaut proposed, will also be the creation of an *auteur;* and the *"politique"* that issued from this claim contributed in still another way toward the negative perception of the adaptation. For if one of film's difficulties in claiming that it is art lies in its inability to truly determine its cinematic essence, another rests in its peculiar status as a group production—as an art, that is, without an artist. Can such an entity be a work of art at all? The answer for many has been a resounding no. And so, together with the search for the uniqueness of its language and logic of representation, still another of cinema's projects has been to come up with a unique creator—someone conveniently supplied by the *politique des auteurs* in the person of the film director.

Certain films very easily accommodate this view; others, to the contrary, don't. And chief among these, once again, is the adaptation. Consider how much less difficulty there is in thinking of John Ford as the "auteur" of *Fort Apache* than of *The Grapes of Wrath*, where the shadow of Steinbeck looms so large; or in crediting John Huston as creator of *The Asphalt Jungle* than as the guiding sensibility behind *The Man Who Would Be King*. For much as the thriller might owe to W. R. Burnett's novel, it seems to us a good deal less than the classic adventure owes to Kipling. It follows then that in the canon of uniquely cinematic works created by the unique film artist, the likes of *Fort Apache* and *The Asphalt Jungle* would inevitably rank above films like *The Grapes of Wrath* and *The Man Who Would Be King*. And Hollywood's tendency to prefer the latter films to the former only serves to strengthen the auteurist position. Hollywood, after all, is still another of the difficult burdens film must bear in its effort to assert itself as art; and Hollywood's taste (as reflected in the Academy Awards especially) is judged at its very worst to be as vulgar as Hollywood itself, while at its very best, to be naive and misguided—to confuse seriousness of intent with meaningful accomplishment.

Admittedly, not all those who take film seriously subscribe to the arguments of the auteurists. And these arguments certainly don't sit well either with defenders of high culture, who, among other things, have considerable difficulty with the standard auteurist canon—including as it does westerns and thrillers, or, in other words, what is traditionally taken as pulp.* There is, however, one argument against adaptation with which nearly all— whether auteurist, nonauteurist, or member of the literati—agree, and which because of this consensus emerges as the most powerful of all: that the adaptation is a lesser form because it lacks originality. Certainly, this is the view that prevails in academia, while it's also the criterion a good number of serious filmmakers would subscribe to as well. "It's hard to think of a truly revolutionary film that was derived from a novel," writes George Linden in his text *Reflections on the Screen*; "I would not want to shoot the adaptation of a novel because . . . to make a film of it is a little like reheating a meal," remarks Alain Resnais; and Jean-Luc Godard notes rather coyly that the only way he could think of filming a novel would be to photograph it page by page. Forget that Godard has in fact adapted both Maupaussant (in an early short, *Une Femme Coquette)* and Moravia (in his

---

*The effects of the auteurist arguments are, however, widely felt in the film world, as is evidenced by the latest *Sight and Sound* critics' poll of the best films of all time. For here, together with such European art films (and thus such traditional choices) as Fellini's *8½*, Renoir's *The Rules of the Game*, and Michaelangelo Antonioni's *L'Avventura*, we now find such American genre films as John Ford's *The Searchers* and Alfred Hitchcock's *Vertigo*.

1963 feature *Le Mépris)*. Forget, too, that among the "revolutionary films" Professor Linden cites in support of his contention—"films that stand as examples, *par excellence*, of the medium"—are *The Birth of a Nation* (whose source in Dixon's *The Clansman* Linden overlooks) and *The Bicycle Thief* (which he also fails to note was derived from Luigi Bartolini's *Landri de Biciclette*). The idea is simply that if film is going to declare itself an art, it must find arguments in its favor. And ironically, perhaps, considering its emphasis on its uniqueness, it has found them not in the unique conditions of the medium, but in the traditional canon of art. Thus, the view that to be truly artful, a film must be the product of a single controlling sensibility; it must have a "language" and "content" of its own; and it must at all costs be a thoroughgoing original. It cannot, then, be an adaptation.

In short, nobody loves an adaptation. Not literary enough in that it proceeds through pictures, not cinematic enough in that it has its origins in words, it finds itself in a no-man's-land, caught somewhere between a series of conflicting aesthetic claims and rivalries. For if film threatens literature, literature also threatens film, and nowhere so powerfully, in either instance, as in the form of adaptation. What makes matters worse is that desperate as both arts are—film for status and legitimacy; literature for mere survival— both overstate their case. Defenders on both sides fail to see how many of their positions follow from doctrinaire notions about the nature and role of art, from simple bias toward one medium or the other, and from—dare one say it?—sheer hysteria.

Consider the Woolf-Arendt view of the adaptation as threatening to devour and/or destroy its literary source. It's a dramatic notion, but what does it really add up to? It can't be the literal survival of the work that's at stake. Even where a time-honored classic has been reduced to out-and-out kitsch—as in the case of Walt Disney's version of Sir James Barrie's *Peter Pan*, James Whale's adaptation of *Frankenstein*, or the Hollywood *Brothers Karamazov*—the original still exists on the library shelf for those who would read and savor it. Can it mean then, that having seen *The Brothers Karamazov*, the viewer will believe he knows Dostoyevsky's novel and never be led to read it? This certainly seems more possible, but it still doesn't follow. For the simple fact is that when a film is made of a novel, it tends to encourage reading rather than discourage it—just as the fact that we've read the novel encourages us to see the film. All any of us has to do is glance at a local paperback rack and the books themselves will make the point—all those reissued copies of E. L. Doctorow's *The Book of Daniel* or of Bernard Malamud's *The Natural*, with their respective cover photos of Timothy Hutton and Robert Redford. And this symbiotic relationship isn't a function of the current book-movie tie-in or paperback revolution. Back in 1939, when the film version of *Wuthering Heights* was released, more copies of the novel were sold than in the entire previous near-century of its existence.

Is it then, as Jean-Paul Sartre contends, that the film will somehow stand between us and the book—that if we read *The Natural* after seeing the movie, we will be stuck forever with the image of Robert Redford? This may be true in a sense, but only to the extent that both film and performance are powerful enough to control our reading, or conversely, when the book is not powerful enough to assert its own view. Consider this anecdote related by a thirties film critic who, getting into a taxi one day, noted that the driver was reading Robert Louis Stevenson's *Kidnapped*. The driver had been inspired by the recent movie, and now that he had "the real thing" in his hands, he was absolutely furious at the liberties producer Darryl Zanuck had taken. "There ain't no girl in the book," he informed the critic, "and this David Balfour was a lot older than Freddie Bartholomew." He went on to add, "Why, if I had any dough, I'd sue Zanuck for fraud. They have no right to put over stuff like that on the public." The point isn't to give this driver the last word on adaptation. It's rather to suggest that Sartre notwithstanding—he has been able to see beyond Freddie Bartholomew to the novel's very different image of David Balfour—to read, that is, in ways other than the movie had directed him. Thus even when we see the movie first and read the book after, we still often test the film by the book and not, as Sartre also implies, the book by the film. The novel has a way of remaining the authority.

If the adaptation, then, can't really be seen as destructive to literature, in what sense can it be seen as destructive to film? Does the fact that a film derives from a literary work actually undermine the medium's uniqueness? This could only be the case if it were possible to maintain that the "essence" of cinema lies in its difference from the other arts. But surely, the uniqueness of film, its distinctiveness and special quality, lies in something quite the opposite: in its "melting pot" nature, in the fact that it not only shares each and every one of its qualities with other art forms, but combines the effects of all of them. Looking at film this way—stressing the extent to which it combines the resources of literature, music, dance, painting—we come to understand something of its peculiar power, just as we also come to see there's really nothing that isn't appropriate to cinema or that isn't "cinematic." Not even a movie that's called "a writer's film," not even a "literary" film adaptation. And what is a "literary" movie anyway? Is it a nonstop talkie with not much more than a single set, like Howard Hawks's *His Girl Friday*? A film with a voice-over commentary, like Billy Wilder's *Sunset Boulevard*? A movie pervaded by the sensibility of its scenarist, like poet Jacques Prévert's *Children of Paradise*? Or is it merely a question of origins, of the source of any given film in the first place? Adapted from a Henri-Pierre Roche novel, and so originally conceived for the printed page, is *Jules and Jim* literary? Is Fassbinder's *Effi Briest*? Is even Eric Rohmer's nearly line-by-line rendition of Heinrich von Kleist's *The Marquise of O*? And are they any more "literary" than Bergman's *The Seventh Seal* or Antonioni's *L'Avventura*?

And to turn to that most crucial of the arguments against adaptation, just what constitutes originality in a work of art anyway, at least when we apply it as a criterion of value? It can't be a question of a work being the first of its kind—since in film, as in any art, being the first is far from synonymous with being the best or even with being merely good. (We're surely not going to claim that the 1930 *Little Caesar* was a better movie than *The Godfather*, or that the 1903 *The Great Train Robbery* was superior to *The Wild Bunch*—though these first films are much more "original" than those that followed them.) Nor can originality be a matter of mere invention, since a work can be highly inventive and great, or highly inventive and awful. Originality isn't even a matter of a work's materials, of an artist making up his own story or characters, of generating his own subject matter—if it were, we'd have to reject not only Verdi's *Otello* but even *Othello* itself and everything else of Shakespeare's. What it is a matter of instead—given that originality isn't a totally meaningless term and that some films do strike us as fresh, others in contrast as stale—is the way those materials are handled. What makes for the originality (and for the greatness as well) of Sir Laurence Olivier's *Henry V* is the way Olivier "staged" that play on film; just as what makes for the originality of Fellini's *8½* is the manner in which the maestro mounted his fantasies.

It's evident, then, that an adaptation can be as original or unoriginal as any other kind of movie. Can one also claim, however, that an adaptation is equally *necessary*? Why bother to adapt a fine novel in the first place? The only reasonable answer to such a question, it seems to me, is why not? An artist has the right to look anywhere for his materials—and if he finds his stories and characters in books rather than life, if he finds his *donnée* on a printed page rather than in a glimpse of a painting or an overheard piece of conversation, so be it. Besides, there's a natural impulse to want to vivify a work of literature that has moved us and mattered to us. It may even be this challenge itself that excites the filmmaker and that, more often than is generally acknowledged, has inspired him to reach for new techniques, discover new strategies, expand the narrative and psychological possibilities of his art. Indeed, the history of film suggests that adaptations have frequently been quite as revolutionary in their techniques—if not more so—than other types of film.

The history of film also suggests that whatever the limitations of certain current-day adaptations—whether highly controversial and ambitious ones like Stanley Kubrick's *Barry Lyndon* or modest and generally neglected ones like George Roy Hill's *The World According to Garp* or Sidney Lumet's *Daniel*—their flaws and insufficiencies have little to do with those of the *reductio ad absurdum* adaptations of the old days: with the likes, that is, of the Hollywood *War and Peace*, of Martin Ritt's *The Sound and the Fury*, of Minelli's *Madame Bovary*. For movies have done more than change their image: movies themselves have changed, and so have adaptations right along with them. The literary establishment seems not to have noticed, however, given that so many of the arguments it puts forth against adaptation (and against movies themselves) are really arguments about film-as-it-was, rather than about film-as-it-is; about film when it was synonymous with Hollywood and had to submit to the taste of the moguls, the strictures of the star system, and the censoring eye of the Hayes office; about film when it was more of a mass medium than it is today and, consequently, operated with very different notions as to the nature of its audience. Today, most moviegoers may be young; but the few adults among them tend, as moviemakers clearly are aware, to be more educated and sophisticated than the population at large. As such, they no longer demand the traditional Hollywood sop—among other things, bowdlerizations and happy endings.

And it's not only film's sociology and structure that have changed; its very aesthetic has as well—though once again you'd never know it from those who rail against adaptation. Ignoring the radical artistic changes of recent years, their arguments are about movies before they began to incorporate the innovations of avant-garde filmmaking, the French New Wave, the Italian Neorealists, and other contemporary arts as well. They also tend to be about film before technological developments altered its shape and texture: from the widespread use of color, the development of handheld cameras, and the emphasis on location shooting to the increased pace and tempo of editing.

Earlier, talking about the silent film, I noted the impressive extent of its accomplishments given its very brief lifespan. The same holds true for film in general, whose growth over the mere century of its existence is astonishing. Certainly, the distance between Edwin S. Porter's *The Great Train Robbery* and *Bonnie and Clyde*, between Méliès's *A Trip to the Moon* and *2001* is greater than that between a Greek tragedy and the plays of Ibsen, between the statues of Praxiteles and those of Rodin. And though the distance between adaptation then and adaptations now isn't nearly as huge, it's nonetheless considerable. Made today, *The Grapes of Wrath* could have retained the novel's devastating ending. A modern-day version of the Laurence Olivier–Merle Oberon *Wuthering Heights* would clearly have avoided the use of pasteboard sets and most likely, too, the inclusion of an insistent and saccharine score. A film of *A Farewell to Arms* in the 1980s wouldn't have to marry off Catherine and Frederick. And given the decline of the star system, *Madame Bovary* wouldn't have been forced to feature a Jennifer Jones, *Moby Dick* a Gregory Peck, *The Sound and the Fury* a Yul Brynner (thus sparing it, among other things, the need to transform Jason into a Cajun).

This isn't to dismiss all adaptations made prior to 1960, or to assert that what's new, wide, in color, and sexually explicit is necessarily more effective than what's old, black and white, and implicit. There were worthy adaptations around even in the silent days, just as there are totally miscarried adaptations now.* My point is merely to suggest that a great deal of what has always troubled us about adaptations in the past and a good deal, too, of the so-called theoretical talk about them is very much a matter of issues like these—blatant omissions, ludicrous revisions, absurd miscarriages. It's also to say that what may trouble us about the film versions of *The Bostonians* or *A Passage to India* or the 1984 *1984* is on another aesthetic plane altogether.

What all this adds up to is the basic contention of this book: that ideas about what film can't do that literature can, about differences in the structure and effects of the two media, and above all, about the process of

---

*Wuthering Heights, for example, was in fact remade not long ago (in 1971) and, despite its color and authentic moors, to much less effect. (The Wyler *Wuthering Heights* is also a considerably better realized adaptation than Buñuel's 1953 version.)

adaptation itself are very much in need of revision. For one thing, there are the prejudices that have prevailed; for another, there are the changes that have taken place in the nature and situation of film. There's also the fact that—since adaptations are likely always to be with us and since film tends to be extremely sensitive to its audience—the more sophistication we as viewers bring to the process, the more effective these adaptations will tend to be. But perhaps the most pressing reason for rethinking these issues and reconsidering this curiously controversial form lies in the essential absurdity of seeing film and literature as mortal enemies. Indeed when the din and dust of the battle die down, when the bias toward print is removed and the need to assert cinema's uniqueness quelled, what becomes manifest is something quite the opposite: that far from being literature's antagonist, film is in a very real sense a form of literature itself. Not simply sharing the very qualities that make literature literature, but making for a system of narration that unites the power of words with the potentially even greater power of the images they aim to create, it might even be considered a natural next step in literature's evolution—a form that Flaubert and Dickens and other writers had somehow envisioned in their mind's eye and, through Griffith, Eisenstein, and other filmmakers, actually helped to create.

2

Film as Literature

The writer uses words; the filmmaker uses pictures. So begins all traditional argument against adaptation. And there's no doubt about it, words and pictures *do* make for very different currency. To borrow the terminology of the semiologists: words are arbitrary signs or "symbols" which are meaningless in themselves, signifying only by conventional agreement. Pictures, in contrast, are generally thought of as natural signs or "icons" which represent things on the basis of some sort of inherent resemblance to them and which, in the case of the photographic image, give the illusion of being almost identical to what they signify.* It follows, according to this reasoning, that to the extent literature is dependent on the one and film is rooted in the other, each communicates through a different "language"—that is, if film can be considered a language at all.

"Language in the strict sense," as Susanne Langer tells us, "is essentially discursive; it has permanent units of meaning which are combinable into larger units; it has fixed equivalences that make definition and translation possible; its connotations are general, so that it requires non-verbal acts, like pointing, looking, or emphatic voice-inflections, to assign specific denotations to its terms." Film, as we know, displays few of these defining qualities. It has no permanent vocabulary; it has no fixed grammar; and though its syntax is characterized by certain rules of usage, it can't, in the manner of verbal language, be referred back to any preexistent code. Film also—addressing the senses directly, giving us "an incredible wealth and detail of

*This is, of course, a massive oversimplification. On another level, literature and film can both be seen as containing symbolic and iconic signs; while the relationship between iconic signs and what they represent is a much more intricate one than the above would indicate. I cite this simple distinction here only as a way of getting at what is generally held to be the most basic difference between "images" and "words" as signifiers—the immediately recognizable quality of the one; the highly encoded nature of the other.

information" all at once—constitutes what Langer, in contrast to "linguistic" or "discursive" forms, calls a "presentational" one.

How then is it possible to argue that film is a species of literature? Isn't language—verbal language, that is—the raw material of literature, just as sound is of music? And doesn't the distance between the verbal and the visual, between linguistic systems and presentational ones, make for an unbridgeable gap between the two media? There is a gap, of course. But an unbridgeable one? Far from it, as I hope to demonstrate. For though words and pictures may be inherently different classes of signs, the simple fact is that both *are* signs. They are also both components of larger systems of signification that are, in turn, part of the entire complex of human communication, part of our total manner of making meaning. And *meaning* is the key term here. For whether or not film contains "permanent units" or "fixed equivalences," or is even "*essentially* discursive," it is capable, in the way that other "presentational" forms aren't, of a coherent and reasoned treatment of a subject. It can inform, it can explain, it can persuade, and it shares with verbal language the function that makes such discourse possible: it can create a "text," otherwise known as a movie. Thus, though film may not be a language in the strict sense, it is nonetheless a language in some sense and a language which, metaphoric or not, is in its function and effect like no language so much as the language of literature.

To begin with the obvious, film isn't simply a language of images. A medium that makes use of various systems of signification, film is also a language of sounds—whether natural sound, music, or, as in the case of literature, words. Not that the image isn't primary. Remove the soundtrack from a film and you still have a movie; remove the visuals and you have something on the order of radio. Still, the image is not only far from being film's exclusive means of making meaning, it's also frequently (if not always) dependent on sound to specify and anchor its sense. Garbo's face, as Roland Barthes suggests, may indeed be an "icon." But even that highly expressive icon is unable, without the support of words, to communicate a message as precise as "I want to be alone." Humphrey Bogart's dangling cigarette, bemused expression, and white dinner jacket may hint at Rick Blaine's hard-edged personality. But his line of dialogue "I stick my neck out for nobody" doesn't merely hint, it tells. Even silent films found it difficult to rely solely on the image—thus, their use of music and intertitles. Moreover, though it's generally held that music and words are mere additives to image in film, that as Erwin Panofsky asserts, "sound, articulate or not, cannot express any more than is expressed by visible movement," this simply isn't the case.

Take an instance involving natural sound—the final sequence of Antonioni's *Blow Up,* in which our hero-photographer comes across a group of mimes pretending to play a game of tennis without a ball. On the sound track, the sound of that "invisible ball" is heard, a sound which serves to alter our understanding of that image to such a degree that it's almost as if another image entirely had been imposed upon it. Or consider films in which music plays a similar role: *Easy Rider,* for example, where song for song, the music interprets and comments on the action for us, giving us information far beyond that which is communicated by the images alone; or the "Dawn of Man" segment of Kubrick's *2001,* where the "World Riddle" theme from Strauss's *Thus Spake Zarathustra* both determines the attitude we are to assume toward that great mysterious slab and supplies the most meaningful clue we have as to how we are to make sense of it.

Articulate sound, quite naturally, has even greater expressive capabilities. Consider such instances as Francis Coppola's *The Conversation,* a film about a professional eavesdropper whose drama lies not in what is seen but in what is heard and in what those sounds evoke in the eavesdropper's imagination (and in our own as well); or Louis Malle's *My Dinner with André* where, restricted to the sight of Wallace Shawn and André Gregory sitting at a restaurant table, our interest is focused almost entirely on the odd couple's conversation; or Bibi Andersson's extended monologue in Ingmar Bergman's *Persona* where through words and words alone—since the camera remains fixed on Andersson's face—the highly charged story of an orgy is conveyed to us.

These examples show incontrovertibly how words carry meaning in film, but they also suggest the extent to which, in certain instances at least, film's mode of communication may be virtually identical with that of literature. It's not even true that whereas in film we experience simultaneously the sight of the eavesdropper and his tapes, the lean face of André Gregory and the round one of Wallace Shawn, Bibi Andersson's voice and her shifting expressions, in literature, we would be given words and words alone. For literature is not merely equivalent to literature in print. Before there was a Gutenberg, it found other formats for its expression and of course still does. Dylan Thomas's "Poem in October" as it exists on my Caedmon recording and "Poem in October" as printed in my *Selected Writings of Dylan Thomas* are both equally poems; while whatever distinctions one can make between the text of *Oedipus* and *Oedipus* performed, the latter isn't any less a work of "literature" than the former. (If anything, it would seem more so, given that no less an authority than Aristotle included in the defining elements of tragedy both spectacle and song, neither of which can exist except in the context of performance.) Of course, the poem read aloud and the play performed make for very different experiences from either encountered on the page: Dylan Thomas's highly expressive voice dramatically alters the force of his poem, contributing as much to my sense of his words as Bibi Andersson's voice does to hers. The question is to what extent I must call Thomas's voice a mere additive, something extraliterary, despite its being (especially if I've never *read* but only *heard* the poem) an inextricable part of my literary experience. Is print really a purer literary medium than the human voice? Is film purer when silent? Rudolph Arnheim contends that it is, but his view seems beside the point: it's been a long time since film was simply a moving picture or merely a language of images. Like literature, it is also a language of words.*

It's also a language whose mode of apprehension is very similar to that of literature, and not only in so far as it's dependent on verbal language. "In the cinema, one extracts the thought from the image; in literature, the image from the thought," André Levinson wrote some fifty years ago, helping to establish the opposition between the perceptual bias of imagery and the conceptual bias of words which many theorists have accepted as making for "the root difference" between film and literature. But, as numerous experiments have indicated, perception is itself a cognitive activity, involving the separation of field from ground, the interpretation of visual stimuli, the resolution of often seemingly contradictory signals. Put another way, just as we have to make sense of the little black marks that make up letters and words, we also have to organize the lines, the shapes, the colors, and the optical patterns that make up any cinematic image. And there's considerable evidence that, appearances to the contrary, the process is far from an intuitive one. Anthropologists have demonstrated that primitive tribes shown a motion picture for the first time are literally unable to see it, unable to synthesize the lights and shadows on the screen—which not only suggests that some degree of cultural training has gone into our own ability to see a movie, but also gives the lie to those who claim that because film is

---

*This isn't to say that some film artists may not choose to omit words or even sound altogether. Again, it's an issue of potential and capabilities.

capable of replicating the world with such fidelity, the process of perceiving an object on screen is no different from perceiving it in actuality.

Furthermore, though it's evident that once the primary organization of lines and marks takes place, reading entails at least one more mental step than viewing—it requires, in the case of the words "golden collie" or "Lassie," let's say, that we ourselves perform the act of visualization, whereas in the case of the image, the golden collie Lassie is visualized for us—in each instance, the subsequent step seems very much the same. Whether it's word or picture that's involved, we must inevitably construct a mental image of what we have "perceived." If we didn't, psychologists tell us, we couldn't "see" at all, since an image impressed on the retina disintegrates; but we know this to be the case even without the help of science. If we didn't fix "Lassie" mentally as much in the process of viewing as in that of reading, not only would we be unable to recall the movie after the fact, we wouldn't even in the course of watching the film be able to recognize Lassie when she came home.

All of this suggests that once one goes beyond the easily described distinction between image and word—the fact, that is, that visual imagery tends to the iconic, that words tend to the symbolic—differences between the languages of the two media begin to be a good deal harder to come by than likenesses. Image and word both "mean," both involve perception and cognition, and both also involve what has recently come to be known as the process of "decoding." More than merely perceiving a cinematic image, we have to link that perception to prior perceptions, to previously gained knowledge and experience. And since even a single shot in film tends to have an extraordinary complexity (considerably more, one might add, than a single word) the mental effort involved in making these applications, if perhaps different in kind from that demanded for the decoding of language, certainly can't be different in degree. Think about how much translation we perform when, in watching a black-and-white film like *Top Hat*, we "see" Ginger Rogers's white hair as blonde and of a different hue (although on screen it isn't) from Fred Astaire's tuxedo shirt; or of the even greater effort involved in perceiving that when Citizen Charlie Kane walks in on his wife's singing lessons, the figure we see standing at the door isn't smaller than the figure at the piano, but simply farther away.

Images in film, then, require for their decoding a certain awareness of pictorial conventions. They also demand a considerable degree of completion—something generally thought to be asked of us only by verbal language. Let's say I see a triangular green shape on film and I identify it as an evergreen. In order to do so, I must supply a third dimension, tactile qualities, even a fragrance. Yet these qualities are presented no more directly in the image of the evergreen than they are in the word. Depending on the context, I may also bring to bear on my perception of that evergreen on film a host of ideas and sensations—Christmas, happiness, presents, bright lights, or perhaps snow, skiing, cold. And whether for word or image, if the context is similar, so will the associations be, though they are not more explicit in the one than they are in the other.

Another way of saying all this is that, like words in literature, images in film are capable of carrying both denotations and connotations, that they not only signify entities other than themselves in the literal sense but also have a way of calling up feelings surrounding them. What's particularly interesting here is that though all theorists generally agree that the image carries stronger denotative force than the word, they tend to disagree rather markedly on the relative value of connotation. Gerald Barrett—taking his cue from Virginia Woolf, by the way—argues that film has much lesser connotative capacity than verbal language; while other theorists, Christian Metz for one, contend that the "cinematographic" image is much richer in connotative possibility than the word, in fact much richer than in denotation. I think that Metz is probably closer to the truth than Barrett, but that it's more than the image alone that allows film its greater connotative charge. It's the combination of image with word with music instead; while the mélange of elements probably also accounts for film's lesser control over the range of those connotations.

To speak of denotations and connotations, of literal meanings and emotional ones, is to broach the question of the relation of words and images to the intellect and emotions—the resolution of which is often taken to point to still another root difference between the two media. As Ingmar Bergman puts it:

> The written word is read and assimilated by a conscious act of the will in alliance with the intellect, little by little it affects the imagination and the emotions. The process is different with a motion picture. . . . Putting aside will and intellect, we make way for it in our imagination. The sequence of pictures plays directly on our feelings.

There's considerable irony in the filmmaker who gave us not only that sequence in *Persona* but a body of film that is among the most strikingly intellectual we have telling us that we put aside "intellect" in the process of viewing a motion picture. There's irony too in that, though Bergman's films bear indisputable relations to literature (and, in their ambiguity, symbolism, and psychological probing to modernist works especially), he also contends that "film has nothing to do with literature." Still, Bergman does have a point. For at least in their inherent potential, literary and cinematic languages are markedly different in their emotional and intellectual charge. Communicating through several means at once, film naturally addresses the feelings more immediately, directly, and powerfully than does literature. Nevertheless, whatever the inherent potential of film's mixed language of sights and sounds, as Bergman himself must know, a filmmaker is perfectly capable of underplaying and even totally undercutting it.

Consider these remarks on the matter by Susan Sontag:

> Some art aims directly at arousing the feelings; some art appeals to the feelings through the route of intelligence. There is art that detaches, that provokes reflection. Great reflective art is not frigid. It can exalt the spectator, it can present images that appall, it can make him weep. But its emotional power is mediated. The pull towards emotional involvement is counterbalanced by elements in the work that promote distance, disinterestedness, impartiality. Emotional involvement is always, to a greater or lesser degree, postponed.

Making a distinction not unlike Bergman's, Sontag is more judgmental: she is partial to art that is "reflective," that is indirect in its emotional appeals. Still, it isn't her preference that concerns us so much as it is her point of reference, for the "indirect" art that Sontag is describing here isn't the work of a literary artist but that of a filmmaker: Robert Bresson.

Bresson, moreover, isn't the only filmmaker committed to creating "art that detaches." Take the work of Jean-Marie Straub—*The Chronicle of Anna Magdalena Bach*, let's say—in which the director, keeping his camera static, repeating shots over and over again, having various historical documents read to us at length, quite literally drains his images of feeling, forcing us in this way to take an intellectual stance toward them. Or think of the films of Jean-Luc Godard—*La Chinoise*, for example, in which a series of Brechtian devices (among them, Godard's choice to have the actors address the audience directly and thus to break the dramatic illusion) compel us to *think* about what we're seeing, rather than to respond emotionally. There are countless moments in much more conventional films too—from the reading of a letter in an ordinary melodrama or the realization of the key to a mystery in a thriller to such decidedly more heady stuff as the philosophical debate in *My Night at Maud's*—which clearly are "assimilated by a conscious act . . . of the intellect" before they affect the emotions.

And if the language of film needn't always be addressed primarily to the emotions, neither is the language of literature always directed first and foremost to the intellect. Though frequently overlooked by those like Bergman, who press for differences between film and literature and who lump all verbal language together, words work differently in a poem than in an instructional manual or philosophic discourse. Unlike the language of exposition, literary language calls attention to itself, emphasizes its own formal qualities. It's language that is charged with emotion, language in which connotations, rhythm, and sound are put into play and given primary stress. Reading "I caught this morning morning's minion, king / dom of daylight's dauphin, dapple-dawn-drawn Falcon," how can one avoid responding first to the sensuous qualities of the language and only afterward to whatever conceptual content Gerard Manley Hopkins's lines might carry? Similarly with Dylan Thomas's "Do not go gentle into that good night, / Old age should burn and rave at close of day; / Rage, rage against the dying of the light," where the words would seem inevitably to "play on our feelings first" and only then make their way to the intellect. Obviously, there is some process of intellection in both instances—reading Hopkins silently, we must translate the printed words into sounds in our inner ear; we must first comprehend something of the denotative sense of Thomas's "rage" before we can grasp its emotional tenor. But is the process really all that different from the one we must go through in order to register the sensuous qualities or emotional force of a visual image, where at least *some* perceptual organization, *some* cognitive process is demanded before feeling and sensation can be experienced? And while the specific language of novels and plays is rarely either so intensely emotive or sensuous as that of poetry, the total effect of these works often is. Novels and plays are, after all, works of art, which means almost by definition that they carry emotional import and that their formal texture is central to their effect. It also means that, whatever the differences in their ultimate capacities, the language of film and the language of literature share the same crucial ability: to address both intellect and emotions, to make us feel and make us think, and sometimes to do both at once.

Still another similarity between cinematic and literary languages lies in their mode of construction—in the manner, that is, in which they tend to arrange their signs. Film of course may choose to communicate various "messages" simultaneously, while literature has no such capability. Film also, as we've suggested, has no grammar and so no predetermined rules for its construction. Nonetheless, in the manner of verbal language, film does tend to order its signs successively, cumulatively, discursively, adding one to the other in some logical relational sequence in order to make for meaning. In *Psycho*'s famous shower scene, for example, where some fifty-two separate shots make for some forty-five seconds of film, we see (among other things) the head and bare shoulders of a woman, a shower head spraying water straight at the camera, shower head and woman's head together, a figure vaguely perceived through a shower curtain coming through a door, a huge knife, the shower curtain being ripped open, the woman's face contorted in pain, blood streaming down a drain, the woman herself sliding down the shower wall and on to the floor. Never once do we see the knife enter the woman's body. But the images or signs themselves, the order in which they've been presented, and the implicit relationship between them, all force us to the conclusion that she has been stabbed.

Sergei Eisenstein, who was one of the earliest theorists to argue for the similarities between film and literature, used examples of this in order not simply to illustrate the principle of montage but also as a way of demonstrating that word and image share a mutual "concreteness." Citing Japanese ideograms ("a dog + a mouth = 'to bark'; a mouth + a child = 'to scream' "), he went on to state that this "is exactly what we do in cinema, combining shots that are *depictive*, single in meaning, neutral in content—into *intellectual* contexts and series." Applied to a hieroglyphic system like Japanese, Eisenstein's views as to the mutual concreteness of word and image make perfect sense; but their meaningfulness for Western languages has generally been discounted. The word "dog," the argument goes, is a much more abstract and general sign than either the hieroglyph or the film image; while what is true of such individual signs is taken to be true of the media themselves. Film is seen as a system of signification tied to the concrete and specific, literature as a system imbedded in the abstract, and consequently these forms are judged to have vastly differing capacities for generalization. We are frequently reminded that in film it is impossible to say: "Happy families are all alike; every unhappy family is unhappy in its own way" or "It is a truth universally acknowledged, that a single man in possession of a good fortune, must be in want of a wife."

But this is nonsense. Not only can film make these statements as easily as literature can, film can do so through the very same means: that is, through words, whether spoken (as are Olivier's generalizing remarks at the outset of his *Hamlet* that what we are about to see is the tragedy of a man who could not make up his mind) or written (as in the title cards that in the old days often rolled over the screen by way of introduction). Moreover, it isn't really any less characteristic of the one medium to make statements of this kind than it is of the other. For though it's true that verbal language is capable of generalization in a way that visual language isn't, and that both of the "generalizations" cited form the opening of two of our greatest novels—*Anna Karenina* and *Pride and Prejudice,* respectively—it's still the case that literature doesn't typically communicate in this way. It tends toward the specific and detailed, aspiring, in a very real sense, to the concreteness of film. It also tends, in the manner of film, to build its generalizations indirectly. Dostoyevsky doesn't articulate his themes—his views on murder, family, society, religion—any more than does Francis Coppola, but encourages us to come to an understanding of them through the drama he sets before us. And even if Tolstoi and Jane Austen do present us with "universals," those universals have no independent existence but come to life and gain meaning in the very same way they would were they to preface a film—through character and action. And here we arrive at the most crucial likeness between the two languages: their very special capacity to create those characters and actions, to situate them in time and place, and ultimately then to bring us into fictional worlds. The novel may indeed be, as Jean Mitry claims, "a narrative which organizes itself in a world; the film, a world which organizes itself in a narrative." Nevertheless, in both instances, narrative and world are created.

Significantly, it is precisely this capacity—rather than its raw material, verbal language—that theorists put forth as literature's distinguishing characteristic. Verbal language, as we know, has countless other uses besides the creation of literary works. What makes literature literature instead, as theorists no less traditional than René Wellek and Austin Warren suggest, is its "fictionality." "Fictionality" is, of course, also precisely what makes narrative film narrative film. Thus, whatever the differences in their raw materials, the two forms again display more than mere affinity; they even share the same decisive defining quality.

Could one really come up with more persuasive grounds for contending that film is a variety of literature—an argument which in its logic turns out to be not all that different from the one that allows us to accept film's system of signification as a species of "language"? We know that film isn't literally a language, or at least that there's much about its mode of communication that distinguishes it from verbal systems. Still, because it bears so many striking similarities to the verbal, because it is capable of the same discursive function, it is not simply a convenience to think of it in these terms, but an inevitability. Similarly, we know that the "texts" this language serves to create aren't literature in the traditional or historical sense. But art forms have a way of evolving, of adjusting to alterations in the world around them, of taking advantage of technological change. Music altered its sense of itself and its possibilities with the invention of complex recording mechanisms and the electronic synthesizer. Architecture vastly altered its possibilities with the enlargement of the range of usable raw materials and the development of highly sophisticated engineering procedures. Gutenberg invented movable type, and (coincidentally?) the novel developed. Edison (and others) constructed a Kinetograph, and the movies developed in turn.

How is it we can situate the Parthenon and the Empire State Building, Buckminster Fuller's geodesic dome and a stave church in Scandinavia, all as instances of "architecture"—their appearance and raw materials being just about as distant from one another as words are from moving images? Essentially, through function rather than form, through a recognition that each is a structure in which man may take shelter, work, or pray. How then to identify narrative film as a species of literature? Through function as well, through a recognition that like poems, drama, short stories, and novels, film is qualified by the fact that it can tell stories and make reference to "imaginary worlds." And to situate film in the context of the literary arts isn't in any way to diminish it. Rather, it's to emphasize its continuity with a medium that has yielded a content and excellence that are unassailable. It's also to suggest that film's ability to combine the traditional matter and appeal of literature with its own unique mode of realization may just be where its quite extraordinary power lies. Which may go a long way in explaining why film has emerged not only the dominant narrative medium of our century, but—as cultural historian Arnold Hauser would have us believe when he dubs the twentieth century "The Film Age"—its dominant artistic form.

Film and literature do more than share the distinction of being storytelling arts; both come to this propensity naturally. Unlike music, architecture, and dance, both tend to be fundamentally representational arts which have a natural tendency to reflect the world-out-there. The camera, of course, has a very rare and special ability to do so—in Siegfried Kracauer's phrase, to "redeem reality"—and film is indisputably the most extraordinary means man has yet discovered for reproducing his perceptions of nature and for re-creating the world in its own image. (It's because of this that film has managed to achieve almost instantaneously, as André

Bazin points out, what painting struggled to realize all throughout its more-than-2,000-year history.) Still, film from the outset veered away from such direct recording of life and toward a very different variety of "realism"—a variety much more consistent with the "realism" of imaginative literature, in which not life but its fictional representation is rendered truthfully, credibly, "realistically." Film also from the outset veered away from abstraction, which for literature—even for poetry, the least essentially representative of literary forms—would seem to be an outright impossibility. Words tend to make meaning even when syntax is destroyed (think of the failed efforts of French poet Stéphane Mallarmé to produce "pure," nonobjective poetry), just as syntax does in itself even when "words" aren't words at all (as in Lewis Carroll's "Jabberwocky").

As the abstract works of various avant-garde filmmakers have demonstrated, it's a good deal easier to achieve nonobjectivity in film. But not only are movies made up totally of abstract images more difficult to produce than those which present us with a recognizable reality, they also tend to carry with them inbuilt restrictions as to length. There are limits to our toleration of abstraction on film, and it's these limits—much more than any crass commercialism—that chiefly explain just why such nonobjective works have remained emphatically on the fringes of cinema. The urge toward narrative is a very basic human impulse and one that has tended to assert itself in all forms that contain the inherent potential for realizing it. And in film and literature both, this potential has much to do precisely with the matter of duration—or, put another way, with the fact that both are temporal arts. Whether ninety minutes or three and a half hours in length, whether one page or 1,001, both require time to reveal themselves. This differentiates them sharply from other representational arts like painting and photography and also suggests just why such static visual forms, though they may contain narrative elements, aren't truly capable of narrative. Narrative requires sequential development, and even in those huge Renaissance frescoes in which the various scenes and thus "stories" from the life of Christ are depicted, or in the Sistine Chapel which illustrates countless Biblical themes, everything is given to us at once. Time may be involved in a viewer's assimilation of those frescoes but time isn't involved in their presentation. Moreover, though the order in which the various elements are viewed in either instance may be guided by the work itself (our eye naturally traveling from left to right, at least in Western culture), the work can never totally control it. This is distinct from the way in which the various constituents of narrative proper come to us—element by element and in a sequence fully determined by the work itself. (Of course, I can run a film backwards and read a novel last page first—but in those instances, I'm aware that I'm performing the kind of violation on the "text" which I wouldn't be if, while standing beneath Michaelangelo's God and Adam, let's say, I were to view the fresco from Adam to God rather than from God to Adam.)

As in almost all proper narratives, there are also in most films and works of literature two different time frames at work: the time of the telling itself (the ninety minutes the film lasts; the 347 pages of the novel) and the time of the story. The latter may be twenty-four hours, it may be twenty-four years; whichever, it usually tends to be a time span longer than that involved in the story's telling. Both literature and film, then, must of necessity be capable of ellipsis. Both forms are also capable of summary, and though literature generally has an easier time of it, film has its own distinctive pictorial means. In *Citizen Kane*, for example, the disintegration of Charlie Kane's marriage to Emily is summarized for us in mere moments through a montage which shows us several scenes in rapid succession of the two at the breakfast table, growing older in look, colder in tone, and more distant from each other as the table itself grows wider.

Both forms are also capable of stopping time—the novel, for example, with long descriptive passages or philosophical commentaries; film with the freeze frame or, as in a movie like *Barry Lyndon*, simply with the long take. Film and literature can also both manipulate several time frames within a given narrative at once, as Faulkner does in *The Sound and the Fury*, and as Francis Coppola does in the more accessible and traditionally structured *The Godfather, Part II*. Similarly, within a given time frame, both are also able to manipulate parallel actions. Film, in part, derived its famous crosscutting technique (as in *The Birth of a Nation*, where shots of the Klan racing to the rescue are intercut with those of the Little Colonel's poor family trying to hold off their villainous darky attackers) from the novel, particularly from Dickens.

As for the two forms' comparative ability to handle tenses, it's generally maintained that film, unlike literature, only has one tense available to it— that, as Susanne Langer puts it, film "creates a virtual present." But though we *do* experience everything we see on film, even events that are presented as taking place in the "past," as immediately present, this is equally the case in literature. When I read "Jack and Jill fell down the hill," I may know— thanks to the signal of the verb—that this action took place in an earlier time frame. But as I construct the image, I see it now, just as I would in the case of film. Verb tenses are no less mere conventions used to situate and order our immediate perceptions than are the parallel strategies that serve similar ends in film—whether it's the cut or fade which tends to modify time; the positioning of the camera into long shot or close-up, high angle or low angle which modifies space; or whether it's any of the other host of cinematic strategies that shape and determine meaning. Furthermore, just as we learn the syntactical properties of verbal language through exposure and usage, so do we also learn the "syntax" of film, and whether or not we're conscious of it, we continually apply this knowledge while watching it. When Sam Spade is shown sipping his cocktail and the shot suddenly goes out of focus, we don't start shouting up to the projectionist that something's gone wrong with the machinery. We accept the "signal" that Sam Spade is losing consciousness, even deducing on the basis of the context that his drink has probably been spiked. It's a similar comprehension of the syntax of cinema that allows us to shift a present action into the past. When at the end of *The Godfather II,* for example, we cut from Michael, "now" darkly alone, to shots of Michael and his brothers sitting around their dining-room table talking and laughing, of course we are seeing the scene *in the present.* But surely—in part because Michael looks younger; in part because we are aware that those brothers are dead; and mostly because we've been "trained" to understand that a close-up of a character will often signal movement into consciousness and memory—we're aware that what we see is taking place in an earlier time and view it with a certain distance. And I find it hard to accept that a sentence like "Years ago, he recalled, they all sat around laughing and talking," communicates that sense of distance any more precisely or intensely.

Still another frequently cited difference between the two media's modes of expressing chronology derives from the view, first expressed by Erwin Panofsky, that film has the tendency and unique capacity to "spatialize time"—or, otherwise translated, to create the illusion of moving through time by actually moving through space. The novel, in contrast, is generally seen as creating "the illusion of space by moving from point to point in time." To the degree that film is a spatial art as well as a temporal one, whereas literature occupies only one of these dimensions, the distinction holds; and in film, spatial movement is indeed a characteristic means of expressing temporal movement. Still, this is far from its only means. Film is perfectly capable of rendering the passage of time while keeping its cameras absolutely static, by simply fading out and in on the very same scene—as movies habitually did in their pre-explicit days, for example, to suggest an offscreen love scene. (A couple embraced, the camera moved discreetly away from them to a bedroom window, outside of which the stars shone brightly; fade-out and then fade-in to that same window with the sun now shining brightly.) Moreover, the ability to spatialize time may be special to film, but it isn't unique to it. Certain writers disrupt the novel's natural temporal flow and replace it with a spatial organization of events on the order of that of film. One automatically thinks here of Joyce, Virginia Woolf, Dos Passos—novelists, that is, who can be said to have been influenced by film form—but the tendency is asserted even in such precinematic writers as Flaubert (to wit, the famous fair passage in *Madame Bovary).*

But whether proceeding from point to point in time or from point to point in space, both film and literature organize their materials in a logically determined sequence or, in other words, they develop "plots." Generally considered a higher, more sophisticated form of narrative organization than story, plot has been distinguished from story in several different ways, but it's E. M. Forster's formulation that is one of the most widely accepted and certainly the most succinct: " 'The king died, and then the queen died' is a story. 'The king died, and then the queen died of grief' is a plot."

Though film and literature generally do provide such causal connections between events, it's important to realize that in neither case is it always essential to the storytelling process that they do. And still another parallel between the two forms lies in the shared tendency of their more avant-garde works to do away with the requirements of logic, necessity, and probability, all of which are basic to the classical plot: thus, the seemingly disordered novels of Joyce, the circular plays of Samuel Beckett, the episodic films of Federico Fellini. What even such works as these find harder to do away with, however, is character. For though we certainly don't need to know why either the king or queen died to have a story, we at least need the king and queen—character being as essential to narrative as event, whether it assumes the guise of animals (as in a fable by Aesop or a Disney cartoon) or that of inanimate objects (such as the robots in *R.U.R.* or the computer HAL in *2001).*

This isn't to say that character hasn't been as much under attack in recent years as has plot—possibly even more so. But film, in general, has remained much more tied to nineteenth-century notions of character than has the novel: character, that is, as an entity defined through action and choice, through response to experience, through the manner in which any given individual behaves, through the content and style of his speech. The most frequent explanation for this is that film itself lacks the ability to create

the kind of psychological complexity necessary to illustrate the tension between inner self and social mask that tends to typify character in the contemporary novel. Film, the argument goes, is tied to the external rather
than the internal, unable to pierce through surfaces to whatever contradic-
tions they might conceal.

Yet, though film is of course bound to the visible and though it generally
does tend to create character through externals—through faces, bodies, expressions, movements, clothes, through reliance not simply on an actor's
physical presence but on his persona as well (Dietrich's exotic beauty is a
key element of any character she played, just as our sense of the towering Westerner played by John Wayne in *Red River* is largely determined
by our sense of Wayne himself)—film isn't bound by its very nature to restrict itself to these means, whatever theorists may tell us. In point of fact,
even the most ostensibly thoughtful and well-taken distinctions between
means of characterization in film and fiction—such as those proposed by
Leo Braudy in his otherwise highly perceptive study *The World in a
Frame*—don't really hold. Consider Braudy's contention that "the basic nature of character in film is omission—the omission of connective between
appearances, of references to the actor's existence in other films, of inner
mediation, in short of all possible other worlds and selves except the one we
see before us." True of film, this is equally true in literature, where the nature of the omissions may be different, but where there is omission just the
same. Recall Hemingway's famous remark: "I always write on the principle of the iceberg. There is seven-eighths of it underwater for every part
that shows. . . ." Braudy also suggests that whereas in fiction, a novelist
can always go beyond the "inscrutableness" or "ultimate blankness" of appearances, film must of necessity "collide" with it, "for nothing exposes the
literary crutches of a film more than explained action or heavily wielded
chunks of exposition." But surely "explained action" or "chunks of exposition" are hardly positive attributes of fiction either. Show us, don't tell us,
we advise the writer. Moreover, if film is committed to making character
visible, it still doesn't have to limit itself to externals. It can lend its propensity for the visible to dream and fantasy, giving imagistic form to internal
life as well.

Although it is generally maintained, it's not even true that film relies on
types whereas literature creates individualities. One could in fact argue just
the opposite. Embodied by an actor, a film character has a marked and inescapable particularity; while there are those who would maintain that it is
literature that operates chiefly through types, as does Northrop Frye: "All

lifelike characters, whether in drama or fiction, owe their consistency to the appropriateness of the stock type which belongs to their dramatic function. That stock type is not the character but it is as necessary to the character as a skeleton is to the actor who plays it." Agree or disagree, it's clear that the question of the typology of characters is complex, and probable too that literature and film demonstrate more likenesses here than differences. Ultimately, both tend to create character through a tension between the type and the individual, or once again, between the universal and the particular.

Still another element of narrative is setting, which, once again, serves similar functions whatever the medium. In either film or literature, setting can give us a sense of mood and atmosphere—lightning and thunder in Transylvania set us up for coming horror. It can add to a story's credibility—an accurately and realistically rendered Paris can help us to accept in turn the reality of the characters who populate it. And it can also help serve as a clue to characterization—a room or a house can tell us a great deal about the people who live in it. In both film and literature (and in the novel especially), these settings can be changed at will, thus reflecting the shared ability of both forms to move us as expansively in space as they do in time.

Some theorists, however, contend that there are critical distinctions in the two media's handling of scenic details. Seymour Chatman, for example, points out that whereas in a literary work a scene is "described"—built out of a highly selected number of details and filtered through a narrator—in a film, a scene is "depicted"—built out of an "indeterminate" number of details. But once again, though the statement seems at first glance well-taken, it breaks down in application. First of all, even if a scene in a film is built out of many more details than it would be in a novel, the very rapidity with which film moves (as Chatman himself recognizes) makes it unlikely if not impossible that we will be able to absorb anywhere near their total number. This means that, at least in our mental processing of film, there will inevitably be a high degree of selection—perhaps even more than there is in a prose description. And though it might seem that whereas in literature the narrator makes the selection for us, in film we make the selection for ourselves, this simply doesn't hold. Take the scene in *The Lady Vanishes* where villain Paul Lukas is trying to persuade our hero and heroine to drink from their tampered-with glasses. Here, the glasses are the dramatic center of the scene, and through the composition of the frame, the use of close-up, and even the device of constructing four-foot-high glasses as he was shooting that sequence, Hitchcock makes sure that our eyes are kept glued to them—and not to Michael Redgrave's moustache, to the scenery passing behind the train window, or to the monogram on Margaret Lockwood's scarf.

Second, as this example indicates, film is not presented to us directly, without intervention and guidance. In any given scene, the camera totally controls (if not absolutely dictates) our perceptions—determining our point of view, establishing our closeness or distance to figures and action, blurring our focus or sharpening it, selecting our angle of vision. And, not only telling us in this way what to see but also just how to see it, it does more than assume the function of a narrator: it becomes the equivalent of a narrator, a cinematic storyteller itself.

A drama is a story told to us without the intervention of a storyteller; a narrative is a story in which a teller always stands between us and the tale. Thus, narrative theory distinguishes between one storytelling art and another. Thus, too, film asserts itself less as the primarily *dramatic* form it might seem at first and as an essentially *narrative* form instead. Film may contain all of the elements of drama isolated by Aristotle: plot, character, diction, spectacle, and song. It may also, since it uses actors who impersonate these characters, share with it the quality of performance. But unlike theatre, where our eye is free to wander, to look anywhere or at anyone and in whatever order it pleases, film, by virtue of the presence of the camera-narrator, always mediates its materials and controls and directs our perceptions. So it is with the novel, to which film turns out to bear a good deal more resemblance than it does to a play.

Such a view would seem to run counter not only to appearances but to common sense. But there are crucial differences between theatre and film— and other crucial likenesses between film and prose fiction in turn. Some of the distinctions between theatre and film have to do with their manner of handling space—with the fact that in theatre, space is static; that its relationship to the spectator is fixed; that theatre is also, as Susan Sontag states, confined, in contrast to cinema, "to a logical or *continuous* use of space." Other distinctions are found in the matter of permanence—in the fact that where film (like the novel) has a fixed existence, theatre, existing only in performance, is fleeting and temporary. Still other distinctions are found in the relationships of screen and stage actors to their respective roles—a screen actor fusing more fully with his part than a stage actor, being in many instances indistinguishable from it. (The proof of this lies to some extent in the fact that if *Casablanca* were remade, an actor wouldn't simply be playing Rick Blaine, he'd also be playing Humphrey Bogart; though admittedly, when Robert Redford took on the part of Gatsby, he wasn't also playing Alan Ladd—no more than Jon Finch, playing Macbeth in Polanski's 1971 movie, was playing Orson Welles. Thus, one could say that such fusion only takes place either in the case of a truly striking performance or when a character is given its first memorable life on screen rather than on the page.)

But though all of these distinctions are significant and certainly worth more reflection than I've given them here, it seems to me that the most important one of all lies still elsewhere: and that is in the extent to which film and theatre traffic in very different kinds of fictional reality. In film, as Allardyce Nicoll suggests, we have a tendency to accept "what is given to us as the truth of life"; whereas when we sit in a theatre, "in every way the 'falsity' of a . . . production is borne upon us, so that we are prepared to demand nothing save theatrical truth." In theatre, we rarely lose ourselves completely or give ourselves up totally to fantasy. We remain conscious of the audience, conscious of the theatre as social occasion, conscious of the actors as actors, conscious of the actors' awareness of us, conscious finally of ourselves. Movies, in contrast, make for an infinitely more absorbing, more private experience. At a film, the social context, the theatre audience, all tend to disappear, and, thoroughly taken up with "the truth of life" up on the screen before us, we also disappear right along with them. We tend to lose all self-awareness while watching a film, which is why we are so often jarred and disoriented on leaving a movie theatre. ("What an uneasy feeling when the lights went on," writes Jean-Paul Sartre of his childhood experience at films. "In the street I found myself superfluous.") All of us have shared this sensation of let-down—because we feel the loss of an entire world, a world that has often seemed more vivid, more exciting, more romantic than the dreary actual one around us. The theatre can never quite give us this sensation. It's the distinction of the novel and the key to its close identity with film that it can.

Film and fiction thus share not only the same narrative forms and many storytelling strategies, they also share the very same basic appeal. Most of us have always gone to movies for the same reasons we read: for escape, for fantasy, for the opportunity to identify with—even to transform ourselves into—other human beings for awhile and vicariously participate in their lives. All of this accounts in part for this book's particular focus—for the fact that in the chapters that follow, the discussion of adaptation will center not on plays, but on prose fiction. There's another explanation, however. To stage a play on film isn't of necessity to *adapt* it—one can, if one wishes, simply photograph a theatrical performance whole, whether unimaginatively, as early movies did from the vantage point of a seat in the orchestra, or with a bit more filmic sense, as in the movies made of Peter Brook's *Marat/Sade* and Olivier's London stage performance of *Othello.* To bring a novel to the screen is something else altogether. For paradoxical as it may seem, though novel and film are closer than play and film in both form and function, to make a movie of a novel involves a great deal more in the way of translation. In fact, whatever the similarities between prose fiction and film and whatever the parallels in their languages, to translate page to screen, word to image, requires a major act of creative imagination. And as the chapters that follow should demonstrate, of interpretation as well.

PART TWO

Adaptation as Interpretation

3

The Viewer as Reader: Varieties of Interpretation

A chilly November evening in 1982. Five of us sit talking in a small New York City screening room. We are about to see the much-anticipated *Sophie's Choice*, which will be released in early December. No reviews have yet appeared, nor has any advance word been spread. Each of us sits then with only his or her own private set of expectations. The young man to my right, a casual acquaintance whom I have run into at other screenings, informs me that he has come tonight only out of "masochistic curiosity." He detests the novel and William Styron's "magnolia prose." In fact, he recently led a seminar on Styron at the New York Public Library for the express purpose of reexamining the author's "absurdly inflated reputation." He is interested, however, in seeing what the film will make of Styron's "phony heroine—that anti-Semitic Polish bitch." The young man's description disturbs the slightly older man sitting in front of us, a critic for a large-circulation New York magazine. He couldn't disagree more with this young man's evaluation of Styron and the novel. In his view, *Sophie's Choice* is one of the major works of our time, "a profound study of human evil, a brilliant study of guilt and retribution, a complex vision of the Holocaust." He also finds Styron an exquisite stylist. However, like the young man, he holds little hope for the movie. Adaptations in general displease him. Has there ever been a great movie made from a great book?

The guests I've brought are considerably more optimistic. One of them, an academic colleague of mine, hasn't read the novel, but is a frequent moviegoer whose appetite for the film has been whetted by both the book's reputation and that of Meryl Streep. The other is my seventeen-year-old daughter who, like the critic in the row in front of us, loved the novel, though her response to it was a good deal less intellectual and more intensely emotional. Stirred deeply by Sophie's wartime experiences, quite literally moved to tears at the point that this agonized mother was forced to make her horrible, dooming choice, she had also been enormously taken by what she perceived as the novel's "great romance." To her, Nathan seemed like a modernized Heathcliff. And so, the idea of the movie excited her enormously, so much so that she extracted a promise from me to take her to a screening of it even before it had finished production. Unlike either the critic or the young man, she is here tonight for the prime reason that many of us are attracted to adaptations: the promise they carry of allowing us to relive an experience we have found exciting, moving, absorbing. This is the usual reason we have for rereading a novel, though in the case of a film adaptation there are other factors at work: our desire to see that novel embodied and sometimes, too, our wish to see what someone else has made of the experience it offers. Like the young man, we too can be curious, but ordinarily not quite so morbidly; by and large, an adaptation of a book we found dull or off-putting simply won't command our attention.

In this case, I share most of these feelings—a desire to see the novel vivified; curiosity as to what kind of movie Alan Pakula (who wrote and directed it and whose work, especially in *All the President's Men*, I've admired) will make of it; a certain anticipation of reliving an experience similar, at least, to the one my reading of the novel offered. For though I was troubled by the extent to which Styron had forced the reader to identify Stingo, *Sophie's* narrator, with himself, finding the self-referential commentaries both self-conscious and somewhat self-aggrandizing, and though the novel also struck me as weighted with too much commentary in general, I responded strongly (as had my daughter) to Sophie and Nathan. Some reviewers at the time of the novel's publication had considered the concentration-camp sections the novel's most powerful. But for me, its present-tense world was most vivid: its vision of Sophie as sensualist, comedienne, masochist, sufferer, agonized mother, and tragic heroine; of Nathan as lover, madman, sadist, and even moral agent. To me, both characters were masterly creations, both lifelike and hugely, breathtakingly larger-than-life. As I sit in the screening room waiting, I wonder to what extent the screen will be able to contain them—if it will be able to contain them at all. But I find the casting choices, Meryl Streep and Kevin Kline, very much on the mark. In all, I am hopeful.

The five of us then each bring to this movie very different preconceptions, and so *whatever* appears on the screen when the lights go down, we are all bound to have very different responses. And, given the range in our ages, our past experiences, our personal associations, our aesthetic presuppositions, the fact that two of us are male and three of us female (among them, a mother and a daughter about to see a movie in which a mother, forced by a sadistic concentration-camp guard either to save the life of one of her children or to send both to their death, chooses the life of her son over that of her daughter), there's no possible way—whatever our expectations—that we can all even "see" the same movie in the first place.

And as true as this is of the five of us sitting before *Sophie's Choice*, it is also true of the fifty-five million viewing *The Birth of a Nation, Gone with the Wind*, or *E.T.* For the simple fact is that a movie, and by this I mean *any* movie, has no independent life of its own, no meaningful mode of existence as an isolated entity. It is only a parade of lights and shadows flickering on a screen, a mere series of noises of varying intensity, until a viewer comes onto the scene to perceive those sights and sounds, to organize and resolve them into symbolically charged patterns, to accord them sense and significance. This isn't quite the old "When a tree falls in the forest and there's no one around to hear it, does it make a sound?" issue. For whether that tree actually makes a sound or doesn't is in this instance beside the point. What's at stake is the significance of that sound, the fact that even if it booms and echoes for miles around, if no one is around to hear it, it has no importance as a sound, no human value, no *effective* existence. Thus a movie—like any work of art though perhaps more so, given the very particular context in which we experience it and which can't quite be duplicated seeing it again on videotape—can't be considered apart from our perception and recollection of it. To the contrary, the movie we describe, criticize, praise, argue about is *identical* with the movie we have experienced and brought into being. And to the extent that each of us is different, so will the movie we each create individually be different too.

I say "to the extent that we are different," because, of course, in certain ways we are sufficiently alike that if we happen to be sitting together and watching the same pattern of sights and sounds—if we are participating in a shared experience—our movies will also have a good deal in common. Moreover, whatever an individual viewer does see depends not only on his own situation and sensibility but on what is given up there on the screen. For if a movie cannot be meaningfully conceived of apart from our own individual perceptions of it, it can't be considered apart from the raw materials which stimulated those perceptions either. A viewer neither creates a film without some contribution from his own mind-set and emotions, nor does he create it out of nothing: it comes into being as a cooperative venture between a viewer and the lights, shadows, and sounds set before him.

So, whether I have a particularly strong set of emotional associations with the Brooklyn Bridge, and you have none at all, or whether still another of us once intended to be a bridge-builder himself, at the point in *Sophie's Choice* when an image of that bridge is projected on the screen, we will at least share the perception of it as a bridge and not see it as a house or a highway or a boat. And so will everyone else in the audience—except of course if among us were one of those primitive tribesmen referred to earlier who proved unable to decipher movie images. It's also fair to assume that we have significant perceptual and cognitive skills beyond this ability to perceive a bridge as a bridge: such capabilities as were discussed in the previous chapter to comprehend any given movie's syntactical signals, to figure out whether or not a change in shot also signals a shift in space and time, to determine whether the action before us constitutes a flashback, a flashforward, or neither. Film's language may not be highly encoded, but it is to a very large extent conventionalized. (If it weren't, the medium would be incapable of any communication at all.) Within a given range, then, a filmmaker can rely on universalized and fairly predictable patterns of interpretation. A richly colored close-up of Sophie sitting near the window of her Brooklyn room in the present, followed by a fade to a more distant shot of Sophie in another room, photographed this time in sepia tints, will be taken by almost all viewers as a movement into another time plane, even without the added guidance of her language.

Where our movies will begin to differ (at least most of the time) is at a higher level of organization: at the point where, once having decoded these images and sounds, we each individually organize them into a unity. They will differ in the degree to which, bringing to bear an entire constellation of psychological, attitudinal, and experiential factors, we call up associations and memories and end up identifying with the experience, being moved by it, and touched on a sensory level as well; and they will also differ in the way in which we interpret the totality of these interactions.

We're aware, of course, of the extreme variations of response and interpretation elicited by highly ambiguous films like *Blow Up* or *Last Year at Marienbad*—or even by films whose narrative is more straightforward but which are made up of volatile, highly charged materials. (*Sophie's Choice* is itself such an instance, touching as it does on such disturbing historical and moral issues as the Holocaust, on such unsettling personal matters as extreme varieties of sexuality.) But we tend to overlook the fact that we will find significant differences in interpretation even in the most transparent of movies: *E.T.*, let's say, which some viewers (the very young, for instance) might take as adventure pure and simple; which others (the over-readers among us, perhaps) might perceive as a Christian allegory, citing as evidence the fact that E.T. dies, is reborn, and then goes up to the heavens from which he descended in the first place; and which still others (the sentimental) might see as a celebration of a child's capacity for wonder and love.

This all may sound somewhat self-evident; yet it's something we frequently ignore in relation not only to the film experience but to other aesthetic experiences as well. It's only in recent years, for example, that literary theory has begun to take cognizance of the role the reader plays in shaping a text, in determining meaning, in bringing a poem or a novel into being. Prior to the advent of a group of critics whose work has elicited considerable attention of late and who, whatever the differences in their background and precise orientation, share an emphasis on the reader and his response, a New Critical view prevailed. Promoting a view of the literary work as an objective entity, as something existing outside and apart from any individual reader's realization of it, some New Critics even went so far as to assert that to focus attention on the reader's response was to become embroiled in an "Affective Fallacy," defined as "a confusion between the poem and its *results* (what it *is* and what it *does*). . . ." Reader-response critics, however, suggest that a poem *is* what it does, that the poem is in fact completely *inseparable* from its results.

And it wasn't only New Criticism that ignored the reader. As Louise Rosenblatt, one of the first of these recent critics to center a theory of literature on the reader's response, points out, this has generally been the case throughout the history of literary theory. Though emphases have tended to shift from a focus on the text (in formalistic criticism), to a focus on the author (in biographical criticism), and now and then to a focus on the text's relationship to the world (in historical or sociological criticism), always "the reader has tended to remain in shadow, taken for granted, to all intents and purposes invisible."

Rosenblatt's metaphor is a highly suggestive one—especially for film. Not that in the figurative sense the film viewer has in fact been invisible, suffering a neglect anywhere equal to the reader's. Perhaps it's because film's history is so short, or because New Criticism, with its elitist emphasis, paid no attention to it. Or maybe it's that as popular art and mass medium, movies almost by their very nature force attention on the viewer, or at least on their power to seduce and corrupt him. More likely though, it's that film, lacking the authority of literature, allows us a greater critical freedom and personalization of response. Joyce and Dostoyevsky, Lawrence and Virginia Woolf intimidate us: we may even tremble before them, assured that there is something we are supposed to get from their works, some implicit set of meanings, some carefully predetermined understandings. Not so in the case of movies, where we not only find ourselves standing fearless before even a Bergman or a Godard (not to mention a Hitchcock or a John Ford), but where some of us may often feel superior to them. Thus, we feel free to say what a work means in our particular view and whether we find it either worthless or worthwhile.

But I think there's still another reason that we find in film a stress on the first-person view—on the I/me response, that is—which is usually lacking in literature: the intensely personal and nostalgic nature of the experience film invites. In what other art is discussion so run through with an individual's autobiography? "Memories of movies are strand over strand with memories of my life," writes philosopher Stanley Cavell in his preface to *The World Viewed: Reflections on the Ontology of Film.* "Movies have been my landmarks. My first tragedy was James Dean's death. My first date, to see Danny Kaye in *Merry Andrew* . . .," notes Marjorie Rosen at the outset of *Popcorn Venus: Women, Movies, and the American Dream.* Whether nostalgic chatter, sociological argument, or abstruse semiological analysis, in most talk about movies, the viewer remains an emphatic presence.

Nonetheless, if he isn't metaphorically invisible, seated in a darkened auditorium, the viewer does remain quite literally unseen, and his peculiar physical situation creates the illusion of total passivity. (The reader at least is in the light with his book and must also turn the pages.) Thus, though film theory, in contrast to literary theory, has tended to include the viewer in its purview, it has rarely (if ever) given him the role of active participant. To the contrary, it has stressed his passivity instead, even going so far in some instances as to use that assumed state as the basis of a theory of film. Film becomes, from this angle of vision, an essentially voyeuristic art. Or, carrying the notion of voyeurism to its logical conclusion, an art, as Stanley Cavell would have it, whose "ontological conditions . . . reveal it as inherently pornographic." Or, in an even more intricate expansion of the notion of passivity, an inherently sentimental one. As Edgar Morin explains it: "the passivity of the spectator, his impotence, put him in a regressive situation. The theatre illustrates a general anthropological law: we become completely sentimental, sensitive, tearful when we are deprived of our means of action."

But even to the extent that film is in its essence voyeuristic, even to the extent that it has a way of tugging on our heartstrings more directly and insistently than any other art save music, this still doesn't mean that viewers are of necessity passive—not even in a physical sense. We've all felt our pulse quicken during chase scenes, like those in *The French Connection* or *Z;* had visceral reactions to fights in films, such as the bloody climactic battle in *On the Waterfront,* the even bloodier ones in *Raging Bull;* quite literally flinched and covered our eyes when a sword was unsheathed in *Yojimbo,* or when a razor sliced an eyeball in *Un Chien Andalou.* As I hope I've made clear, such physiological responses depend on considerable prior psychological and even cognitive activity, part of which is a matter of decoding the raw materials set before us, and even more of which is a matter of unifying, organizing, and interpreting them. We are anything but passive in watching a film: we are involved in a complex process of evocation.

It's significant that that process very much parallels the one involved in reading a work of imaginative literature—at least as described by those current theorists who conceive of literature as a lived-through experience in which the reader, actualizing the text before him, participates in the creation of the work of art. Indeed, given the terms in which several describe the literary experience—Louise Rosenblatt speaks of the poem "as an event in time"; Wolfgang Iser stresses the "inevitable omissions" or "gaps" in a text which the reader must of necessity fill; Stanley Fish claims the text is "no 'object' at all" and refers to literature as "kinetic art"—they might even be thought to be describing the film experience itself and more precisely even than the literary one. It's possible after all to think of a poem or a book as an empirical object existing in space; but a movie is inescapably an occurrence that takes place only in time. A movie—or at least a movie that is built in the traditional mode and so includes a considerable amount of editing—also contains more evident "gaps" (the space between one cut and another) than does a poem or a novel. And though Fish doesn't name film precisely, what more explicitly "kinetic art" is there save dance?

Clearly, the arrival of film on the narrative scene has enabled us to do more than perceive, as Robert Scholes suggests, "certain features of fiction more clearly because they are part of the narration in film while they have only been part of the reader's narrativity in fiction."* The arrival of film

---

*By "narrativity," Scholes means "the process by which a perceiver actively constructs a story from the fictional data provided by any narrative medium."

has allowed us to perceive even more clearly something of the essential nature of the literary experience itself. I would hardly argue for the direct influence of film on these various theorists; yet, it seems to me far from a coincidence that so many of their metaphors derive from film. (Fish, for example, speaks of "reading in slow motion"; Iser relates the opening of gaps in the text to "a cutting technique.") It seems even less of a coincidence that a stress on reader-response should arise in the film age.

But there's still another reason, aside from its analogical quality, for calling up the literary experience. For if we indeed resymbolize a text in the process of reading and consequently make it our own, and if we do the same in watching a film, consider the complexity of the process involved in watching a film of a book we have read—in other words, of crystallizing a new film experience out of the stuff of memory (which here includes the book on which that film is based) and thus interpreting on the basis of a prior interpretation the actual cinematic interpretation laid before us.

But let's return now to that screening of *Sophie's Choice* and consider the process at work—at least, in the case of the four people who have read the novel and for whom comparisons between the novel and the film will be inevitable. If we accept reader-response theory (which, at a certain commonsensical level, we must), it follows that the novel we will bring to bear on our film experience will not be precisely or exclusively Styron's, but one that has grown out of an encounter between the text and our individual sensibilities. In other words, each of us who has read the novel will in some way already have made the movie—our own movie—to which we're likely to have considerable commitment. This is one of the reasons, that we so often tend to be disappointed by the movie up there on the screen, and to express what we believe is a preference for the book itself over its adaptation. But what we are actually doing is announcing an allegiance to our own imaginative re-creation. Ultimately we are not comparing book with film, but rather one resymbolization with another—inevitably expecting the movie projected on the screen to be a shadow reflection of the movie we ourselves have imagined. Not only do we come to an adaptation with the hope of reliving a past experience, but we often tend to come with the hope of having the *same* experience—something that wouldn't even happen were we ourselves to reread a novel and consequently to imaginatively "reshoot" it.

Yet, though in a sense we do make our own movies, the metaphor may be somewhat misleading, since it implies that a powerful degree of visualization takes place in the act of reading. But despite the contentions of narrative theorists that much of our effort in reading goes toward visualization, and despite the avowed aim of novelists to make us see as well (Conrad says, in his preface to *The Nigger of the Narcissus*: "My task which I am trying to achieve is, by power of the written word, to make you hear, to make you feel—it is, before all, to make you *see*."), it's probably true that most of us in reading don't really *see* very much at all. (And the fault may not only lie in ourselves. I recall, after having assigned Conrad's "Youth" to a class, having a blind student come up to me and ask if Conrad himself had been blind, since his writing demanded so little in the way of imagined sight. It occurred to me then that it was in fact somewhat strange that a writer so bent on making us "see" should habitually give us scene after scene set in darkness on the deck of a ship, with little to "see" at all and with only Marlowe's voice to "listen" to.)

Still, even where a writer's work invites considerably more visualization than Conrad's, most of us don't pick up the cues, often leaving even such blatant images as the pink boardinghouse in *Sophie's Choice*, let's say, very vaguely sketched in the mind's eye. So what we get instead is the *illusion* of seeing, and one that becomes all the stronger when faced with a film adaptation. For an image on the screen has a way of somehow solidifying our impressions, giving us the sensation of having actually visualized that or another image for ourselves prior to the fact, sometimes even creating a sensation of déjà vu.

But if they aren't images, what then are the probable contents of these re-created novels that we bring to bear on an adaptation? Whatever else they might be, they certainly include a great number of emotions and sensations, some of which have hardened into evaluation, others of which remain tied not to any judgment but to the recollection of the immediate experience of reading. In fact, there are likely to be more of such feelings than anything else. For it's curious how much more strongly we often recall the quality or general texture of our experience rather than details of plot, conflict, or character. This is true even for books read in childhood, which tend to occupy a more secure place in our memories than books read later in life. One of my favorite novels as a child, one I recall reading several times, was *The Secret Garden*. Even today, I can summon up impressions of excitement and adventure, a feeling of entering into the spirit and world of the book, of identifying with the heroine, of seeing myself on what were (I think) the windswept Yorkshire moors. Try as I may, though, all I can recall of the precise details of the book are those moors themselves, a vague image of an overgrown, walled-in garden, and an even vaguer one of a pale, Indian-born little girl. The plot, other details of the heroine's character, other characters themselves, have long since vanished from my memory. The *Secret Garden* of my imagination consists then almost exclusively of feelings, and had I happened to see the movie that was made of that book (which I didn't), what I clearly would have expected of it above all was the duplication of those feelings. I suspect this is always what we chiefly expect even when, as in the case of *Sophie's Choice,* the novel will be much more fully filled out in our imaginations—given that there's no more than a three-year gap between our reading and our seeing of the movie tonight. For whatever details go into our individual resymbolizations, they will inevitably be overlaid with feeling. To the young man on my right, the novel—its setting, its characters—will include his irritation; for the critic in front of him, a sense of awe; for myself, some of the depth of sympathy I felt, some of the utter horror too; for my daughter, chiefly (I suspect) her feeling of being swept up in an intense and dark *Wuthering Heights* moved to Brooklyn.

The novel of each of us will also contain a great many very specific narrative elements. Built into it most likely is a strong sense of the overall story line, of the various time frames—the Holocaust past, the novel's present-day late-forties setting, the flashforwards to Stingo's future as a writer—and something of the manner of their interweaving. Each novel will also contain a number of very particular scenes, among which there will probably be considerable consistency—considering that there are in Styron's original several moments which are typically and rightly called "unforgettable." Included might be the scene in which Stingo surprises Sophie, finding her without her teeth; one or another of the various explicit sex scenes between Nathan and Sophie; one or another of Nathan's great outbursts of fury; certainly the moment in which Sophie makes her "choice." Possibly included too will be scenes like Stingo's meeting with Leslie Lapidus at Coney Island, his visit to her house, the picnic in the park, the meeting of Sophie and Nathan in the library. Less likely, though obviously included in my case, since I still remember them, are Stingo standing on a terrace in Greenwich Village and snatches of his recalled relationship with the Virginia girl whom we are to accept as the model for Peyton in Styron's own *Lie Down in Darkness.*

Sitting here now (some three years after reading the novel, more than a year after seeing the film), I'm struck by how few scenes I can recall which weren't also in the movie—and this observation speaks not simply to the greater freshness of the film experience, or just to the power of the film's images, but also, at least to my mind, to a certain aptness in their selection. For although there's no way that, watching a film, we can test its contents and sequence scene for scene—few of us have memories that sharp—we will, as the various scenes accumulate and the narrative thrust asserts itself, feel a certain anticipation and resolution, a certain satisfaction or frustration of our expectations. This is, the process we undergo watching any film at all, even one that isn't an adaptation, with one set of occurrences inevitably setting up expectations as to what will follow. (The stagecoach rattles over the plain, the Indians observe it from the top of a bluff—we don't need to have read the book or seen the movie before to know that an attack or a chase will ensue.) It's also the process that's central to the act of reading—as in the further dimension of retrospection, we reflect on events that have already occurred, granting them new meaning and significance in light of subsequent happenings. Wolfgang Iser contends, significantly enough, that it is by means of just this process of "anticipation and retrospection" that we animate a text, that our imaginative involvement is brought into plays; and that the stronger such anticipation, the more intense our interaction with the text in turn.

It follows that adaptations excite an extreme degree of participation from those familiar with the source. On the simplest level, there's our inevitable awareness of the sequence of events, of what is likely to occur in any given scene. Stingo walks into his room in the pink boardinghouse and we know that momentarily he will hear noises from the room above, that (we may recall) the ceiling fixture will rattle and shake. And when this in fact occurs on film, we are likely to feel confirmed—perhaps too confirmed, which is probably why Pakula's choice to show us that fixture in close-up was cited by some reviewers as indicative of the overly obvious and predictable quality of his direction. On a more complex and meaningful level, we bring an element of retrospection to events as they are happening, rather than merely after the fact. For example, we recognize, at the very moment they are enunciated, Sophie's early comments about her family and past—"My father was a civilized man"; "I think no child had a more beautiful father and mother and a more beautiful life . . ."—as the lies they actually are.

Watching an adaptation, then, everything comes to us framed in a double vision. There's our scene (roughly sketched as it may be) and there's Pakula's scene, which he will either superimpose strongly enough on our own so that there's a fusion, or fail to persuade us to accept so that a tension and distance remain. And the difference in outcome is likely to have a good deal less to do with the absolute consistency of the "facts" of any given sequence than with a continuity of the emotions elicited. For example, though I was aware of differences in the precise manner in which Nathan's brother revealed the secret of Nathan's schizophrenia in the novel and the way he revealed it in the film, this in itself didn't trouble me. What did was a sense of abruptness, a cloudiness, a lack of power in the scene which was totally unlike the strong feelings I recall having experienced at that revelation in the novel. And though I might have explained this loss of affect by the foreknowledge I brought to the film which I couldn't have brought to the novel, this seemed (even at the time) inadequate. More to the point was my lack of belief in the diagnosis on film—the movie's Nathan having failed to convince me that he was indeed "quite mad," that he was indeed "a paranoid schizophrenic." On the other hand, despite a similar foreknowledge, I had a totally opposite response to Pakula's handling of the scene where Sophie makes her nightmarish choice. I of course knew what constituted that choice; yet, in its darkness, in its fog-drenched atmosphere, in its reticence, Pakula's version struck me as one of infinitely more power than the much more dramatic (even melodramatic) scene I myself had envisioned—an effect explained only partly by the inherent force of the scene itself, and to a large degree by the greater skill with which the film handled Sophie and her secret in general. In other words, one revelation seemed so much more meaningful than the other on film because the character in question had been more fully and more movingly rendered.

The double vision we bring to individual scenes will also operate as we piece together the film's overall story line, a process in which we inevitably find ourselves searching out omissions, identifying interpolations—sometimes even doing some interpolating of our own. All of us can recall instances in which we "saw" in a given film scenes from the book that simply weren't there—Myrtle's accident in *The Great Gatsby*, for example, which occurs off-screen but which several viewers I've encountered recall distinctly having seen; the death of the horse at the outset of *Tess*, which is omitted in the movie version but which certain viewers again recall as part of the film. As such tricks of memory suggest, our first response to alterations will usually be to resist them—to be disoriented by such additions and inventions in *Sophie's Choice*, let's say, as the celebratory sequence on the Brooklyn Bridge or the montage at the amusement park in Coney Island; or conversely, to bemoan the omission of such scenes as the one in which Stingo discovers Sophie without her teeth—though in this particular instance I think that many viewers, like myself, might have forgiven its absence on the grounds that it seemed unfilmable.* On "retrospection," however, we may be persuaded by the rightness of the filmmakers' choice—though again this will frequently have as much to do with our prior commitment to the materials as with the filmmakers' mode of mounting them. (Take, for instance, my own experience. I suggested earlier that for me the novel had been weakest in the sections devoted to Stingo's ruminations, especially those relating to his writings, which were so inescapably Styron's own. And so quite predictably, the omission of such material in the film hardly struck me as a loss.)

A double vision will probably assert itself most forcefully, however, in our response to an adaptation's characters, since it's character—and especially in a novel like *Sophie's Choice*—that tends to figure more intensely in our individualized resymbolized novels than an overall sense of plot or a recollection of particular scenes. Typically, when we consider our conception of character, we tend to think once again of images, of pictures formed in the mind—of the way we have *seen* Sophie, Stingo, Nathan, Leslie Lapidus, or Yetta. But despite the impression of our having created distinctive mental images, it's probably true that, as with the novel in general, we don't really see literary characters with a great deal of precision. An exception to the rule lies in those cases where a series of illustrations are part and parcel of a text—those of Cruikshank for Dickens's novels, those of Tenniel for the works of Lewis Carroll. Now and then, even a drawing on a book jacket will work toward this end. But where we have no visual aids, our sense of a character's physical appearance will tend to be very generalized. So, even with a character like Sophie, who is described in such detail in Styron's novel—we all know she's blonde and beautiful and speaks with a Polish accent, but our sense of her looks, our feeling for her voice, probably isn't much more exact than that.

How explain then a response we will sometimes have to seeing a character embodied on the screen: but he (Robin Williams) isn't Garp; but she (Greer Garson) isn't Elizabeth Bennet. Flaubert, who surely would have violently disapproved not simply of Jennifer Jones as his Emma Bovary, but of anyone who tried to impersonate her, attempts an explanation. Refusing to allow his novels to be illustrated, he asserted, "A woman drawn resem-

---

*Actually, according to *The Boston Phoenix* (January 25, 1983), the scene was in fact filmed, with Streep using a gum plate. However, the filmmakers felt it should be cut. "They were afraid nobody would ever love Sophie again after that scene," Meryl Streep is quoted as saying.

bles one woman, that's all. The idea from then on is closed, complete. . . ." But is it really? Does a character really lose its universality through visual specification? How dare Michaelangelo depict for us, then, Moses or Mary, or Jesus or David, or God! How dare Picasso give us Don Quixote! How dare an actor embody Hamlet on the stage! How ever attempt to portray a character on screen?

Could it simply be then a matter of an actor's looks, the fact that he doesn't bear sufficient resemblance to the character as described? Sometimes, of course, this can be the case. Take Garp, to whom John Irving happened to give his own height and build, allowing us to perceive the character as a dead ringer for the author, much as Styron invites us to see Stingo as his younger self. And to the extent that Peter MacNicol doesn't look like the younger Styron, or that Robin Williams doesn't resemble John Irving, some small number of viewers at least (those, that is, familiar with Styron and Irving) will find their looks distracting. Mostly, though, within certain commonsensical limits—matters of age, height, girth, extremes of physical attractiveness—looks will play a surprisingly small role. My rejection of Greer Garson as Elizabeth Bennet in *Pride and Prejudice* has nothing to do with Jane Austen's descriptions. I have no recollection of Austen having told me precisely what Elizabeth looks like anyway. Moreover, there are instances in which I (and the rest of the moviegoing world) have willingly accepted a performer in a role, despite certain marked variations in appearance. The most obvious instance is the breathtaking Vivien Leigh as Scarlet O'Hara, who Margaret Mitchell had told us expressly, in the very first line of her novel, "was not beautiful."

But if it isn't appearance, what is it that prevents us from accepting an actor in a role—aside, that is, from blatant inadequacies in performance? First and foremost are the associations he calls up: associations built partly out of his public persona and partly out of the roles we have seen him play before. (By the time I saw Greer Garson as Elizabeth Bennet, I had already identified her as Mrs. Miniver and as someone decidedly too matronly for the heroine of *Pride and Prejudice*.) Secondly, there's his ability to submerge himself in a role—something which is, I suppose, part and parcel of an actor's talent, though some of our favorite movie stars never could perform such a disappearing act. Cary Grant was always Cary Grant; and if Bogart's range was a bit wider, he nonetheless was always Bogie. Thus, if we were unable to accept Gregory Peck as Captain Ahab it wasn't because he didn't look the part. It was rather because Gregory Peck in a little black beard is still Gregory Peck—only desperately working against type and looking a little bit silly. Similarly with our difficulty in accepting Yul Brynner as Dmitri Karamazov, since what we really saw up there on the screen was the King of Siam trying to pretend he was a Russian.

Moviemakers are obviously aware of the powerful personas certain stars project. And, since the decline of the star system, they have often (and frequently wisely) cast lesser-known performers in adaptations or at least opted for the chameleon-type actors around. (In the old days, interestingly, almost all of these, like Alec Guinness and Sir Laurence Olivier, tended to be British.) This has tended to be the case especially in the process of adapting highly popular works with strong characterizations like *Sophie's Choice*. Thus, one can assume, Pakula selected the relatively unknown Kevin Kline and Peter MacNicol. Thus, too, though he reportedly wanted a European actress to play the part, he was ultimately persuaded to accept Meryl Streep, who though neither classically beautiful (at least not in the way Styron's Sophie was), nor Polish, nor particularly sensuous, managed almost miraculously to transform herself into an almost transcendent Sophie. How so? Aside, that is, from her obvious gifts as an actress and the fact that she also possesses that extraordinary chameleon quality? (Like Olivier, she even *looks* different in each movie.) I'd suggest that the answer has to do with the extent that her own feelings about the character concurred with those of most readers. The point is that we clearly create characters in fiction in the very same way we build almost everything else, adding to traits, psychological tendencies, and actions the quality of our emotional response. Whatever the ambiguities, whatever the variations in the readings of *Sophie's Choice*, there is widespread agreement that Sophie herself and her experiences call up the classical emotions of pity and fear. And Streep, while certainly humanizing Sophie and supplying her with marvelous humor, still played her for that tragic grandeur, conveying a sense not simply of being Sophie, but of loving her, of sympathizing with her, of believing in her stature—a complex of feelings that I suspect helped to make her for so many viewers identical with their own Sophies. You can be sure, however, that she wasn't the Sophie of the young man sitting next to me. His, you might recall, was an "anti-Semitic bitch," and since Streep emerged as neither anti-Semitic nor a bitch, it almost goes without saying that he hated her in the role—as was likely to be the case with any reader-viewer similarly put off by Styron's creation. Consider Pauline Kael's evaluation: "Meryl Streep's work doesn't hold together here, but how could it? Sophie isn't a character; she's a pawn. . . ." Far from a judgment of

Streep, Kael's statement constitutes a judgment on Styron—which is precisely the point.

Neither Kevin Kline nor Peter MacNicol, to my mind, performed a similar feat of persuasion. I've already suggested one palpable (if not strictly aesthetic) reason why MacNicol failed for me; it's not quite as easy with Kevin Kline. He looked right and he certainly brought energy, a sense of romance, a feeling of heightened drama to the role. His Nathan also was credible—something which I suppose my Nathan, who was larger, madder, more brilliant, more of everything in fact, wasn't. But whether it was his performance itself—the extent to which, as an actor whose prior experience had been limited to the stage, he had deliberately selected to underplay this extraordinarily extravagant character—or the film's having diminished Nathan's role, or the inherently problematic nature of the character, Kline simply never managed to fuse with the Nathan in my imagination.

Thus far I've suggested that, heavily populated as our novels might be, their visual quality tends to be vague. Vague too, in most instances, is the quality of their language. It may be troubling to admit that we tend to have very weak recollections of any given novel's specific language, since it's widely held that a novel lives in its language—as, it's also claimed, do its characters, its actions, its themes. Indeed, there are some theorists who insist that such novelistic elements have no other meaningful existence. "Hamlet and Macbeth," we are told, "exist only as words on a printed page. They have no consciousness and they do whatever the dramatist requires them to do. The feeling that they are living people whose personalities determine the actions they perform is an illusion." But what is the end of literature itself but the creation of illusion—and an illusion which can exist nowhere but in a reader's mind? Moreover, the extent to which I am led to conceive of any given character not as a living person, but as a construct inextricably bound to words on the page is precisely the extent to which either those words themselves fail to set in motion or I myself fail to complete the creative imaginative act which is the whole point in the first place.

Quite simply, it makes no sense to claim that characters exist *only* as words. Language may be the raw material out of which they are constructed, the means of giving them existence in our imaginations in the first place, but characters manage somehow or other to free themselves from the symbols that contain them and to gain an independent mode of being. Indeed, it would seem to be precisely the ability of so many of its elements to release themselves from their context and attain an independent existence that is a salient characteristic of fiction, whether it comes to us in the form of literature or film. Fiction may be the one art which proves the exception to the rule that form and content are inseparable. To understand this better, you might try to think of a painting (*Guernica*, let's say) or a symphony (Beethoven's Fifth, for example). There is no way to recall them without their form, even if you don't recall the form entirely—which is one of the reasons that you can't make a symphony out of *Guernica*, or a painting out of Beethoven's Fifth, or a movie out of either. The most you can do is transfer both of them whole to the screen, form and content together, playing the symphony on the soundtrack and perhaps adding pictures in the manner of *Fantasia*, or photographing *Guernica* from a host of angles as you might in a documentary on Picasso. But so emphatically separable are elements of fiction from their context that I am capable of summoning up a Don Quixote without ever having had any experience of his original context at all. Which is why he can be moved not simply from the original Spanish into another linguistic system like English or French, but transferred without becoming unrecognizable into a totally different symbolic system altogether: he can be moved, that is, onto the stage or onto the screen.

This isn't to say that a reader might not retain, even long after his experience, some of the particular language of a novel. (The young man at the screening of *Sophie's Choice* who was so irritated by Styron's "magnolia prose" would probably have been able to provide me with numerous memorized examples.) Only the most striking instances, however—"Call me Ishmael," "Stately, plump Buck Mulligan," "Isn't it pretty to think so," and the like—are likely to stay with us sharply enough to allow us to test an adaptation by the degree to which it repeats verbatim the words of the original. And, though we can find a special pleasure in the recognition of a line taken directly from a novel, sometimes lines moved from one context to another will jar—especially in the instance of dialogue. The movie version of *The Sun Also Rises* made use of a great many of Hemingway's lines—dialogue which on the printed page had always seemed so strikingly lifelike. On screen, in startling contrast, it sounded mannered, artificial, lifeless. (Thus can an adaptation sometimes turn a discomforting magnifying glass on a novel, revealing, if not quite its flaws, at least the inaccuracy of our impressions. Hemingway's dialogue may have energy and precision. But lifelike? Clearly, it's anything but—whatever the great canon of Hemingway criticism has claimed.)

The Sun Also Rises notwithstanding, it's rare that we will find ourselves complaining of such literal transcription if we are committed to the original work. In the case of *Sophie's Choice*, for example, where the novel's language has been preserved to some extent both in the voice-over commentary and in the dialogue, those readers (like the critic at the screening) who found the novel brilliant will tend to praise the film for its attempts to adhere to the letter of Styron's prose, while those who found the same prose fulsome will have precisely the opposite response.

> In some ways [writes critic Stanley Kauffmann] . . . the film is better than the book. Primary benefit: we are spared almost all of Styron's grandiose prose. It is only when the unseen Josef Sommer, as the older Stingo, reads brief sections on the soundtrack, for commentary or transition, that we realize how lucky we are: whatever there is of merit in the book has been freed by the film from its prison of gummy rhetoric.

But if the specific language tends to be a key issue in adaptation only in such selected instances, the sense of style that language creates is another matter altogether. Style as it reveals itself in individual dialogue, in summarizing passages, and in the novel as a whole will tend to be a significant element in the novels we ourselves create in our minds. The question of how a film might translate that style is too complex to explore in this context and will be taken up in a later chapter. Suffice it to say here that in a film adaptation, it is only in very small part a matter of words.

Even more important than style, though, in most instances, and the factor on which all others in our re-creation of a novel tend to depend—whether it's our emotional response, our sense of its characters, our visualization of its world, our impression of its total flavor, our ultimate evaluation—is our interpretation, our ideas of what a novel's central themes are, of its central import. And each of us in that screening room that night had accordingly given to Styron's materials his or her own distinctive focus. So too had Alan Pakula who, as both director and scenarist, can rightly be considered the film's "author." Pakula had deleted much of Stingo's biography and personal story; he had cut away just about all of his historical and philosophical commentaries, his lengthy quotations from other writers; he had reduced much of Sophie's past, limiting his film to only a few snatches of her Cracow life and to restrained glimpses of concentration-camp existence. More than any of the novel's other materials he had retained those relating to Sophie and Nathan's relationship. Yet even here he had been highly selective: he had chosen to focus to a greater degree than did the novel on that relationship's humorous, passionate, and touching aspects, cutting back on its violence and fury; he had selected to concentrate more heavily than the novel on Sophie herself, underscoring, through extreme and extensive close-up, the rich expressiveness of Streep's features; and he had selected to bathe her and the present-tense portions of the film in soft colors, in the pastel hues supplied by Nestor Almendros's cinematography. He had added such lyric sequences as the amusement-park montage, and such poetic moments as the scene on the Brooklyn Bridge. In all, he had put forth a version of *Sophie's Choice* that muted its horror and pain and that was, inescapably, intensely romantic.

Such a view of the novel was, you may recall, distant from both that of the critic seated in front of me and that of the young man to my right, and not surprisingly both found the adaptation lacking. Although closer to my view, it was still far from identical with it. Nathan had been severely diminished and so had Stingo, and though I missed the former much more than the latter, the reduction of both had in turn reduced the material, making the film as a whole (while certainly moving and containing a Sophie of extraordinary stature) a lesser experience for me than the novel. The film in this way had also served as a commentary on the book, suggesting that whatever the problems presented by both these characters, they were still necessary to its balance and effect—more necessary than I had at first assumed. (Thus can an adaptation work not only to magnify faults, but also to reveal virtues.)

There was, though, one reader/viewer in the screening room that night whose perceptions the film approximated—my daughter—and it was she who consequently responded most deeply and fully to the film. She was, in a very real sense, its ideal viewer, the viewer implicitly inscribed in its text. To say this is to patronize neither her response nor her reading; nor is it to criticize the film itself, the relative success or failure of *Sophie's Choice* being (at this juncture at least) very much beside the point. At stake instead is the realization that there is inevitably an ideal viewer—and one, in the case of the adaptation, whose resymbolization of a particular novel will mesh with the resymbolized novel up there on the screen. In assessing an adaptation, we are never really comparing book with film, but an interpretation with an interpretation—the novel that we ourselves have re-created in our imaginations, out of which we have constructed our own individualized "movie," and the novel on which the filmmaker has worked a parallel transformation. For just as we are readers, so implicitly is the filmmaker, offering us, through his work, his perceptions, his vision, his particular insight into his source. An adaptation is always, whatever else it may be, an interpretation. And if this is one way of understanding the nature of adaptation and the relationship of any given film to the book that inspired it, it's also a way of understanding what may bring such a film into being in the first place: the chance to offer an analysis and an appreciation of one work of art through another.

4

The Filmmaker as Reader:
The Question of Fidelity

Story is that when Peter Lorre first came to this country and
did his first, successful picture, he was asked by the Big Boss
what he wanted to do next. He suggested *Crime and Punishment*. Boss said: "Gimme a one-page synopsis and we'll see."
Lorre looked around studio until he found a near moron working in the accounting office. Offered the man fifty bucks if he
could deliver a one-page synopsis of *Crime and Punishment* the
next day. Just skimming, hitting the high spots. Done. The synopsis read like an old-fashioned thriller (truth in that). Boss read
it and, in those days when the Industry was prospering and they
were making four or five times as many pictures as they do now
(though no more *good* ones), Boss says to get started. Picture
was almost finished before Boss got around to reading the
"property" and realized, raging, he had been had.

Such tales are legion in the annals of Hollywood. And so are instances of
adaptations which, whether or not in fact based on one-page synopses of
their sources, certainly could have been. How talk about the filmmaker as
reader then? Or perhaps more to the point, reader or not, how much responsibility does he have to his source anyway? If *Crime and Punishment*
can provide an exciting old-fashioned thriller plot, is there any reason for a
filmmaker to borrow, together with the bare outline of events, the novel's
rich thematic materials, its complex vision of good and evil, its depth of
characterization? Is there any reason for the Boss to think he's been had? Is
there any reason for us to feel—like the taxi driver who wanted to sue
Darryl Zanuck for including a girl in *Kidnapped* and making David Balfour
younger on screen than he was on the page—that so have we? Is it possible
that our recollections of a text on which a film is based make for little more
than a set of intrusive and distracting associations that serve merely to distort the film experience? Is the ideal viewer of a movie like *Sophie's Choice*
not the one we pointed to earlier, the viewer whose reading of the novel

coincided with that of the filmmaker? Could the ideal viewer instead be someone like the academic colleague I had also brought with me to that screening—a viewer who hasn't read the book at all?

Many would contend that such an "innocent" viewer is indeed the ideal one, that ideally novel and film should be regarded as independent entities. Whatever our associations and expectations, or so the argument goes, a filmmaker has no responsibility whatsoever to his source. And in a literal—or better, legal—sense, of course not. Once a novel is in the public domain, like *Crime and Punishment*, or once a producer has paid a novelist for the rights to his work, as in the instance of *Sophie's Choice*, he can do anything he wants with it. This is one of the reasons that many often react with such dismay when authors who have sold their works to the movies complain of the distortion and desecration they have undergone. After all, no one forced Bernard Malamud to sell the rights to *The Natural* or Isaac Bashevis Singer to accept Barbra Streisand's offer for *Yentl*. If they were fearful of what Hollywood would do to their creations, if they wanted them to remain strictly their own, they never should have taken the money in the first place. To complain after the fact seems hypocritical.

Yet, viewed from an aesthetic rather than a moral, legal, or financial vantage point, the issue of an adaptation's responsibility to its source becomes a different matter altogether and an infinitely more complicated one. Whatever the views of certain purists, an adaptation is by its very nature both work of art and palimpsest. Comprehensible without reference to the literary work on which it's based, it nevertheless stands in indissoluble relation to it, much in the manner of any reworking of preexistent materials—whether it's Marcel Duchamp's moustachioed and bearded version of the *Mona Lisa* or a jazz musician's arrangement of themes by Mozart or Bach.

There's a considerable difference, however, between a source that is a classic, or at least a work situated in the ranks of "literature," and the likes of an ordinary detective novel, a run-of-the-mill thriller, a category romance. Who really cares what Alfred Hitchcock did with Ethel Lina White's *The Wheel Spins* when he made it into *The Lady Vanishes*, or what John Ford did with Ernest Haycock's *Stagecoach to Lordsburg* when he transformed it into *Stagecoach*? Unless one is interested in a particular variety of source study or in investigating the creative process of either of these filmmakers, such works call up so little commitment on the part of the reader that they make aesthetic comparison seem beside the point. In fact, though such films might be included in any statistical count of adaptations, the original tends to be so insignificant we hardly respond to the movies based on them as adaptations at all.

Pulp fiction, then, allots the filmmaker an aesthetic freedom that substantive works simply don't. And it's here, rather than in any inherent affinity the film medium might have for such stuff, that one finds an explanation for a curious paradox—that lesser novels often make for fine movies whereas fine novels often make for lesser movies, a paradox that some have managed to turn into an aesthetic principle. Taking note of the fact that, for example, Truffaut's *Shoot the Piano Player* (based on David Goodis's slick crime novel *Down There)* is a better film than his *The Green Room* (inspired by Henry James), that Visconti's *Ossessione* (adapted from James M. Cain's *The Postman Always Rings Twice)* is a more successful work than his version of *The Stranger* (from Albert Camus's existential classic), they have concluded it's minor rather than major fiction which is most nourishing to the film medium.

But this is faulty reasoning, at best. All things being equal, of course a movie based on a work with greater thematic density and larger human significance will be more rewarding than a movie that remains tied in concept to a literary work whose materials are comparably thinner. John Ford's *Stagecoach* is an immensely entertaining movie, but drawn from an emphatically slight source to which Ford and scenarist Dudley Nichols added considerable wit and tension but little in the way of insight or depth of characterization, it emerges as a film with nowhere near the richness of Ford's version of *The Grapes of Wrath,* rooted as the latter is in Steinbeck's significant and emotionally charged materials. What provides the illusion that *Stagecoach* is a "better movie" (aside from its marvelous technique—the brilliant pacing and editing of the great chase scene across the plains, for example) is the fact that it's a genre film that manages within its own limited terms to fulfill its aspirations completely. Not so *The Grapes of Wrath,* which as an infinitely more ambitious work can be seen as falling somewhat short of its implicit intentions. But in the arena of art, the small perfect work of limited scope (such as a tale by Poe) has never seemed to us to have greater value than the imperfect but hugely ambitious one (like a novel by Dostoyevsky). So why should this be the case in film? A minor novel's only meaningful advantages for a filmmaker are that it controls him less and presents him with fewer challenges and, most important of all, that we ourselves will tend to bring to his "adaptation" nothing in the way of significant expectations.

In the case of a major work such expectations tend, as we have seen, to affect our responses to a considerable degree and are called into play not merely by our prior experiences but by the film itself. For once a filmmaker has chosen to adapt a substantive work to the screen, once he himself has thereby made reference to a previously existing work, he (and not we) has made it part and parcel of his film. He has, once he calls his movie *Sophie's Choice* and acknowledges Styron's novel in the credits, invited us quite explicitly to bring to bear on his movie our knowledge of the book—much as Joyce, deciding to entitle his great novel *Ulysses* rather than *Leopold Bloom in Dublin*, invites the application of our experience of Homer's *Odyssey*; much as E. L. Doctorow, naming his novel *The Book of Daniel*, asks us to associate the Biblical Daniel and his story with Doctorow's character and his. Neither Doctorow's *The Book of Daniel* nor Joyce's *Ulysses* is in any sense an adaptation; and the kind of reference each makes to a previously existing literary work is drastically different in kind from the reference the film adaptations of these very same novels (Sidney Lumet's *Daniel* and Joseph Strick's *Ulysses)* make to the novels themselves. Still, whatever the differences in kind, in each instance reference has been made and the reader has been granted the right—has in fact been called upon—to summon up the novel and make it part of his film. It's on these grounds, moreover, that one can maintain that the ideal viewer of any adaptation is not someone who hasn't read the novel, but someone who knows it very well indeed.

Consider the analogy of reading something on the order of T. S. Eliot's *The Waste Land.* Now presumably the poem is sufficiently self-contained so that whether or not the reader is acquainted with the various sources Eliot identifies in his notorious footnotes, the general sense of the work can still be grasped—though the point is clearly arguable. What isn't arguable is that the reader Eliot implicitly addresses is one with considerable erudition—a reader who has some familiarity with Jessie L. Weston's *From Ritual to Romance*, who knows Fraser's *The Golden Bough*, who has read Marvell, Dante, and Shakespeare, among others. What's also unarguable is that such a reader will almost of necessity have an experience of greater depth and dimension than one who can't bring such awarenesses to bear. It's more than a mere matter of being able to identify the various references: it's a question of the capacity to perceive the poet's ironies, his implicit intentions and methods, to comprehend his conception of the modern wasteland itself.

Most film adaptations (unless of a modernist work like *Ulysses,* which has at least as complex a skein of references as Eliot's poem) will hardly ask as much of us. But whether a poet makes reference to the entire history of

English literature or a filmmaker only to a single novel, the principle is the same. One text becomes part of another text, with the fullest knowledge of the one depending on the extent of one's knowledge of the other. Some critics argue (and I think rightly, even commonsensically) that all texts whatever their nature are read in a relational manner—though none, I should think, so inescapably as a "text" (read film here) which is also an adaptation. For if other texts (other movies, other books) provide a necessary "grid" for making any given work intelligible, what work would seem as essential to the intelligibility (or at least to the fullest and most meaningful grasp of the nature and quality) of an adaptation as the literary work on which it is based?

To say that the literary work from which an adaptation is drawn is inevitably inscribed in the cinematic text itself, and that so too is a viewer-cum-reader familiar with that work, isn't however also to claim that a film must adhere unswervingly to its source, that it must of necessity aim at replication. Not that certain films might not commit themselves to such an end, and not that such a view of adaptation hasn't been operative over the years. Indeed, if there are those who would hold that an adaptation carries with it no obligation whatever to its source, that film and book are independent entities, there are even more who hold just the opposite: that an adaptation of a work of literature is committed to a total and complete fidelity.

Yet, given that every reader creates his own individualized novel, and that every viewer brings into being his own particular film as well, what can the notion of "fidelity" actually mean? Faithful to whose Sophie? To Sophie the tragic heroine? To Sophie the anti-Semitic Polish bitch? To Sophie the masochist? To Sophie the towering romantic figure? And faithful to what aspects of any given literary work anyway? We all can think of numerous adaptations that have been "faithful" to the "facts" of a novel or play (dogged translations, for example, like many presented by "Masterpiece Theatre"—to wit, its six-part rendition of Dostoyevsky's *The Possessed* and its similarly lengthy treatment of Hardy's *Jude the Obscure)* and which have nonetheless struck many viewers as utter betrayals of the originals. Conversely, we can also cite certain adaptations that have altered these "facts" dramatically and have still struck many as startlingly faithful—the most telling instance being *Throne of Blood,* Akira Kurosawa's translation of *Macbeth,* which though altering details of story, setting, character, and time frame and preserving not a word of the Shakespearean original since the film is, of course, in Japanese, is still held to be one of the (if not *the*) greatest Shakespeare adaptations ever.

Quite simply, adaptations themselves reflect very different notions of "fidelity." And standing in enormously varying relationships to the books on which they're based, they also tend to set up different kinds of expectations and invite the application of different sets of criteria. Back in the thirties and forties, adaptations (at least of classic works) had a habit of beginning with a picture of the book itself: there was the book's cover, a process shot of the pages being flipped, a close-up of a line or two of the text ("Once upon a time, in a little village in Italy, there lived an old toymaker named Gepetto"), and then (especially if it was a Disney movie) another close-up of one of the book's illustrations (a picture of a quaint little Italian village on a starry night) that shortly was transformed into the movie's establishing shot. In this way, the film declared itself the equivalent of the book, or at the very least, an illustrated version of it. A viewer, then, was inevitably led to expect a literal transcription to follow—though, since it rarely did, he was usually left with a sense of betrayal.

Nowadays, such techniques of course seem dated, as does even such a directly illustrative stance itself. Take a filmmaker like Federico Fellini, who not only doesn't open his adaptations with images of books and turning pages, but even alters their titles, calling them not *Satyricon* or *The Memoirs of Jacques Casanova* but *Fellini Satyricon, Fellini's Casanova.* Thus the viewer is forewarned: What you are about to see may resemble these classic works; it may borrow some of their structures, may make use of some of their characters, scenes, concepts, and themes and so use these as a "grid"; but this is not Petronius and was never meant to be and it's not Casanova either; it's Petronius and Casanova refracted through the distinctive sensibility of the filmmaker.*

Adaptations other than those of Fellini are ordinarily a bit more discreet in their manner of informing us just how we are to take them. Nonetheless, as with his films, a change in title will often make a significant statement about the nature and extent of an adaptation's dependence on its source. If it's one thing to call your movie *An American Tragedy*, it's another to call it *A Place in the Sun*—the change immediately establishing a certain distance

*The explanation generally given for the title *Fellini Satyricon* is that Fellini's name was added to distinguish the film from another Italian adaptation of Petronius that was simultaneously in release. True or not, the fact doesn't in any way alter the *effect* of the title, nor does it serve to explain why Fellini subsequently decided to include his name in the title of his *Casanova*.

between the film and its source.* As with titles, a shift in time frame and locale will also affect our stance, as in such movies as *Bartleby*, in which, courtesy of director Anthony Friedman and scenarists Rodney Carr-Smith and George Bluestone, twentieth-century London is made to stand in for the nineteenth-century New York of the Melville original; or *The Bespoke Overcoat*, in which screenwriter Wolf Mankowitz performed a similar dislocation on a Gogol tale, this time updating and shifting the nineteenth-century Russian setting to that of contemporary England.

The fact that some films will effect such variations, while others will attempt to reproduce their sources as literally as possible, has prompted several theorists to attempt to classify adaptations, arranging them into "modes" or "types." They find their precedent, however, not in film or its theory but in literary theory instead—in particular, in a seventeenth-century treatise by John Dryden, proposing that all translations fall into one of three different categories:

> First, that of metaphrase, or turning an author word by word and line by line, from one language to another. . . . The second way is that of paraphrase or translation with latitude, where the author is kept in view by the translator, so as never to be lost, but his words are not so strictly followed as his sense, and that too is admitted to be amplified, but not altered. . . . The third way is that of imitation, where the translator . . . assumes the liberty not only to vary from the words and sense, but to forsake them both as he sees occasion; and taking only some general hints from the original, to run division on the groundwork as he pleases.

Thus Geoffrey Wagner in *The Novel and the Cinema* also divides film adaptation into three "modes": "the *transposition*, in which a novel is directly given on the screen, with a minimum of apparent interference" (two of Wagner's examples are William Wyler's *Wuthering Heights* and Vincente Minnelli's *Madame Bovary*); "the *commentary* . . . where an original is taken and either purposely or inadvertently altered in some respect" (instances cited: William Wyler's *The Heiress*, Mike Nichols's *Catch-22*); "the *analogy* . . . [which] must represent a considerable departure for the sake of making another work of art" (a key example: Bob Fosse's *Cabaret*). Gerald Barrett, for his part, divides adaptation into only two kinds. In

*Such changes, however, aren't always a reliable guide to intentions. Sometimes titles are altered out of commercial considerations alone. *A Place in the Sun*, after all, sounds a good deal more romantic than *An American Tragedy*—but then again so was the movie as a whole a good deal more romantic than Dreiser.

Barrett's view, it is impossible for an adaptation to be either a metaphrase (given the differences in cinematic and literary languages) or (for the same reason) to be precisely a paraphrase either. Adaptations are, he contends, always imitations, or "loose translations." At their very best, though, they also partake of the paraphrase, falling somewhere between the two modes.

This may be true. Still, I'm not sure that either the application of such categories, or the rule of thumb "evaluations" that follow from them, are particularly useful. Wagner has enormous difficulty slotting examples into his modes. As he himself admits: "There can be no neat pigeon-holes in this area. . . . Is Buñuel's *Belle de jour* commentary or analogy?" As for Barrett, his mode of classification ultimately leads him to reject any film in which "there is little or no attempt made to render a cinematic equivalent of the original," and thus without adequate means of distinguishing between the reductive likes of Big Boss's 1935 *Crime and Punishment* (which, despite the fact that it was directed by the gifted Josef von Sternberg, turned Dostoyevsky into little more than detective melodrama) and such equally "free" but emphatically sensitive "imitations" as Bresson's *Une Femme Douce* (after Dostoyevsky's "The Gentle Creature"); Bertolucci's *The Spider's Strategem* (after a story by Borges); or Maximillian Schell's *First Love* (after Turgenev).

But though neither categories nor criteria may be precisely to the point, the effort to distinguish between types of adaptations remains significant in principle. It's important to be reminded that there is no single type of correspondence between films and their literary sources, that while one film may aim at being as literal a version of its source as possible, another may attempt nothing of the kind, and to take such a work to task for altering plot, characters, even themes, is quite beside the point. Helpful, too, is the analogy with translation. For though adaptation is, of course, a very different kind of art, there are striking parallels nonetheless. Like the translator, the filmmaker who adapts is bent on a double task—he must demonstrate some sort of allegiance to a previously existing work of art (or why bother to use it as inspiration in the first place); and he must also, at the very same time, create a new work of art in his own particular language, the language of film. Like the translator, too, the filmmaker who presumes to adapt is first of all a reader and one who can either deal with his source naively and superficially, or with insight and intelligence. The filmmaker may not be able to come up with *the* sense of any given work (in the way that Dryden, for example, assumed his translator could); he will of necessity, however, come up with *some* sense. For the simple fact is that an adaptation always includes not only a reference to the literary work on which it's based, but also a reading of it—and a reading which will either strike us as persuasive and apt or seem to us reductive, even false.

And here, I think, we've come upon the only truly meaningful way to speak of any given film's "fidelity": in relation to the quality of its implicit interpretation of its source. This holds true for even the freest of adaptations, whose very omissions and rearrangements reflect on the nature of the filmmaker's insight into the work that inspired it. It isn't simply because it changes the plot that we find the 1926 *Moby Dick* absurd; it's because those particular changes reflect such little understanding of the essence and essentiality of certain plot elements. It isn't because it has deleted and altered characters that we find Martin Ritt's *The Sound and the Fury* such a betrayal; it's because of the *nature* of those changes, because in altering the blood ties between the central characters, the film has implicitly misconstrued the essence of the novel's tragedy—the fall of a family. In contrast, if we find Robert Bresson's adaptations of Dostoyevsky masterful, it's because, however dramatic the alterations, his selection and restructuring of Dostoyevsky's materials—in both *Une Femme Douce* and *Four Nights of a Dreamer*—seem to be based on intelligent readings of the original texts ("The Gentle Creature" and "White Nights"). In short, though a literary work can admit countless readings, the inescapable fact is that some readings are better than others.

How is it possible to maintain, on the one hand, that a literary work has no meaningful existence apart from an individual reader's experience of it—that out of the same raw materials, you create your novel and I create mine—and also to maintain, on the other, that one of these creations may have more validity than the other? Or, since our resymbolizations of a text are more or less equivalent to our interpretations of it, to maintain that though a work may admit a variety of such interpretations, some are more well taken than others? Only, it would seem, with great difficulty. For if we examine our responses to any given film, we inevitably find ourselves confronted with the challenge of assessing the validity of not just an interpretation, but an interpretation of an interpretation.

Yet, difficult as it may be to reconcile a pluralistic (and essentially open) view of the literary work with the notion that even pluralism has its limits, such reconciliation is far from impossible. Actually, there is a good deal less contradiction in maintaining these two positions than at first might appear. Consider the point made in relation to *Sophie's Choice:* that though a literary work may have no meaningful objective existence without the participation of a reader, such a work still serves as an objective reference against which that reader's experience can be tested. The text may spark countless interpretations, numerous individualized works of art, but it nonetheless places certain constraints on what a reader can sensibly, even commonsensically, do with it. There are linguistic norms which limit any statement's possible meanings; there are also various rhetorical conventions which are inevitably called into play. A reader, for example, may, on encountering William Blake's lines "Tiger! Tiger! burning bright / In the forests of the night," summon up an image of sunlit, treeless plains; but it's evident that if he does, he is refusing the conventionally accepted meaning of the words before him. He can also, if he wishes, perceive the tiger as literally on fire; but again, it's evident that he is failing to accept the poem's implicit invitation to apply the convention of metaphor.

So far so simple—but when one attempts to assess the validity of the reader's efforts to make sense of the poem as a whole, matters become more tricky. Yet even here there are evident constraints. For if the poem will admit many different readings, it still won't support any and all—certainly not one which sees it (given its references to the tiger's "fearful symmetry," "dread feet," and "deadly terrors") as a celebration of the gentleness, friendliness, and warmth of the animal (as a kind of *Born Free*, that is); or as a poem about passionate lovers (given the evident distance between the poem's tiger and its lamb). And herein lie some of the most basic principles at work in determining validity: that an interpretation must be consistent with the facts of any given text; that it must not break with linguistic conventions and must take account of the denotations and connotations of words and the total context that determines them; that it must be capable of support with evidence from the text itself.

Aside from blatant contradiction, there are still other criteria for assessing validity. For our reading of any text is guided and controlled by a certain knowledge not simply of linguistic and rhetorical conventions but of literary ones as well—by certain interpretive strategies and by a general notion of what we believe a literary work to be. For instance, we generally operate with the notion that any work carries within it certain implicit clues as to how we are to take it. And so, we expect any reading, if it is to be valid, to have some grasp of these immanent intentions. We also tend to conceive of substantial literary works, at least, as displaying a certain degree of complexity, a certain richness and suggestiveness. A valid reading in turn then would be one that reflected a recognition of this quality, that was sensitive to such riches and nuances, and that was somehow nuanced itself. Formal qualities also are seen as crucial to a work's effect, and consequently we expect a thorough reading to take account of certain aspects of a work's construction, to incorporate in its interpretation the contribution of a work's patterns, its point of view, its genre. Related to this is still another of our beliefs: that any literary work has an organic wholeness whereby each of its parts contributes to its total meaning and effect—though this is obviously more an ideal than a reality and more true in any case of a poem or play than of that frequently digressive and uneconomical form, the novel. Still, we expect a responsible reading to deal with the work as a totality, to account for most (if not all) of its various elements—its plot, its characters, its images, its tone, as well as its genre and formal aspects—and to unify them in a way consistent with the text's own logic. In fact, a valid reading will generally tend to be one that itself has a coherence and inner consistency.

What are the implications of this for adaptation? Even a filmmaker bent on literal transposition can never fully account for all the elements in his source, nor would he be likely to want to. And what of those filmmakers who select to reorder and alter certain key elements of a text (like the time frame and setting in the case of *Une Femme Douce*, like the ending in *The Natural*)? Wouldn't they of necessity be working against any given work's unity and wholeness, performing major violations on it? In a certain sense, of course, this is true. A filmmaker may be interpreting his source, but he is also at the same time creating his own work of art—inevitably his primary aim. And a reading of a literary work embedded in a film will in any case be of a different order entirely than one contained in a critical essay, and will certainly be less complete. But whether of a different order or not, whether partial or even totally fragmentary, the filmmaker's interpretation remains subject to many of the same criteria as those we've cited: consistency and coherence, sensitivity and nuance.

Still, though we may have some clue here as to what makes for validity in interpretation in film as well as fiction, we haven't broached the problem of the validity of *our* interpretation of that interpretation—or in other words of our response. In our discussion of *Sophie's Choice*, I noted that we tend to be responsive to an adaptation when and if its interpretation coincides with our own. And where this occurs—where the filmmaker's reading is my reading and where we each then affirm the other's—how then can we maintain that the interpretation lacks validity? To put the problem more precisely, let's consider not the silent *Moby Dick*, but the 1956 version, directed by John Huston from a script by Ray Bradbury. Unlike *Sophie's Choice*, it's a film based on a work whose aesthetic value has rarely been questioned. Similarly, unlike its silent counterpart, the film is "faithful" enough to the facts of the original and sufficiently intelligent in its interpretation to have excited some fairly positive response. First, the following by Edmund Carpenter:

> The film *Moby Dick* was in many ways an improvement on the book, primarily because of its explicitness. For *Moby Dick* is one of those admittedly great classics, like *Robinson Crusoe* or Kafka's *Trial*, whose plot and situation, as distilled apart from the book by time and familiarity, are actually much more imposing than the written book itself. It's the drama of Ahab's defiance rather than Melville's uncharted leviathan meanderings that is the greatness of *Moby Dick*. On film, instead of laborious tacks through leagues of discursive interruptions, the most vivid descriptions of whales and whaling become part of the action. On film, the viewer was constantly aboard ship; each scene an instantaneous shot of whaling life, an effect achieved in the book only by illusion, by constant detailed reference. . . . Unlike the book, the film gave a spare, hard, compelling dramatization, free of self-conscious symbolism.

In contrast, take these remarks by Brandon French, who concedes that the film is extremely "faithful" to the events of the novel, but goes on to complain:

> What Bradbury deleted are most of the documentary (whaling as a commercial occupation and industry) and the philosophical dimensions of the novel, leaving behind the adventure story with (as Bradbury himself has stated) "enough room here and there to be Shakespearean." . . . In the most general terms, these deletions cut the story loose from its moorings as "the real living experience of living men" in Ishmael's words, casting away the novel as allegory of the American nineteenth century capitalist spirit, as the balanced account of nature's epic adversaries . . . and as the adventures of the human soul in a chaotic universe of indeterminate morality. . . .

Thus in French's view, the Bradbury-Huston *Moby Dick*, rather than emerging as the "compelling dramatization" that Carpenter finds it, "ultimately founders."

The problem in coming to any conclusion as to whose "interpretation"—Edmund Carpenter's or Brandon French's—is more valid is compounded by the fact that both of their "interpretations" of Bradbury-Huston's "interpretation" are inextricably bound up with evaluation. Both have seen the same movie—they agree that the film omits the "discursive meanderings" or "documentary"; they also agree that it leaves out the "symbolism" or "allegory." (And this agreement is less self-evident than it might seem. For in bringing to bear his prior interpretation of the novel on the film, the viewer will often *impose* that interpretation on it, supplying the adaptation with the "symbolism" or "allegory," with the implicit layers of meaning, that is, found in the original; he will often tend to fill in the "gaps" overmuch. Not so in the case of these viewers.) Still, whereas Carpenter finds the omissions making for an apt and intelligent reading of *Moby Dick*, French considers them making for an inadequate one. Is there any way of deciding who's right?

On one level, no. If I think the greatness of *Moby Dick* lies in its philosophical implications and symbolic aura and you think these are instead its weaknesses, that the novel's greatness lies in the power of its narrative, who is to prove the one view more valid than the other? One might ask the same of our judgment of a musical performance, our assessment of a painting. If you think a performance is dull and I find it brilliant, if I find a painting pedestrian and you find it awesome, who is to say which view is the more apt? Yet, on another level, it's perfectly obvious whose is the more well taken: that of the listener with the better ear, the viewer with the sharper eye, that of whoever happens to be more trained and knowledgeable in either field. Lionel Trilling suggested that Art is not a democracy, and most of us will submit to the notion of expert opinion, to the idea that some listeners, some readers, even some viewers of film are more sensitive than others.

Another and perhaps more effective way of getting at this problem is to summon up a notion put forth by Stanley Fish—that of "interpretive communities." Fish, in contrast to the view suggested here, denies the text any objective status at all—as evidence, stimulus, or anything else. It is entirely, he argues, a function of our mental processes, with interpretive strategies never being "put into execution after reading," but rather constituting "the shape of reading" itself. We are the ones who create the literary "facts" used in support of our readings, and consequently those facts (or text) can never serve as a basis for deciding its acceptability or inadequacy. Yet, like other theorists with less extreme views, Fish admits that we do in fact have the right to rule out some interpretations, to judge some readings unacceptable. And what gives us the right is the institution of literature itself. There may be "no core of agreement *in* the text," but, he asserts, "there is a core of agreement . . . concerning the ways of *producing* the text. Nowhere is this set of acceptable ways written down, but it is part of everyone's knowledge of what it means to be operating within the literary institution. . . ." We've already discussed some of the "acceptable ways" by which we "produce" a text: the traditional literary conventions that allow us to detect a metaphor and that lead us to search out unity and coherence within the various elements in a literary work. There are other more subtle ones too—the allowance for a Freudian or Jungian approach to a work; for a Marxist or feminist or structuralist reading—all of which constitute the whole range of interpretive procedures by which we are enabled to arrive at any "acceptable" reading. Fish's concern, however, is less with the particular conventions themselves than with reminding us that they are indeed *conventions*—practices and ideas that are socially determined and ever-changing. Nonetheless, they are, he suggests, as binding at any given time to those involved in the process of interpretation as are the conventions as to how any language operates to those who would speak it.

What has all this to do with those contrasting evaluations of *Moby Dick*? A great deal if one considers, first of all, that Fish's interpretive communities are also evaluative communities and that they have construed *Moby Dick* as a work of great value, made of it, in fact, a classic. Second, one of the unwritten bylaws of the interpretive community is that any work of great value will tend to have a certain scope and insight, a certain complexity and depth of meaning. Thus, though there is certainly no consensus as to what *Moby Dick* means, no single interpretation of Ahab, the white whale, and their story, and probably never will be, there is consensus that they carry with them significant reverberations and that it is in their reverberations that the greatness of the text lies. From this point of view, removing the "implicitness" and "symbolism" of a work like *Moby Dick*, rather than releasing its "greatness," as Carpenter would suggest, drastically reduces it instead. It follows, then, that his interpretation of Huston-Bradbury's interpretation must inevitably seem less valid than that of Brandon French.

But this is not to find in Carpenter's view (as have some) evidence of a rampant "philistinism." It took a long time, after all, before readers got around to recognizing *Moby Dick*'s "symbolism" and "allegorical" implications in the first place, and who knows but that in some future time, our current perceptions of the novel might seem totally skewed. Moreover, I've had enough intelligent students over the years who found Melville's novel virtually unreadable to understand precisely where this interpretation is coming from. And how long can a classic remain a classic if fewer and fewer can get through its language? (Is there a—terrifying to some—implication for adaptation here? Is it possible that changing notions of values and literacy will mean that—even if adaptations themselves aren't destructive to classics—adaptations will nonetheless be the only exposure to them many will have? Is the accessibility that Carpenter implicitly argues for a greater value than the literary institution will currently allow? Have we come full circle to those early views about the mission of the adaptation—only now, not with the great unwashed mass as target audience, but with just about everyone?) The point is that we frequently face extraordinary difficulty in attempting to interpret the validity of any interpretation—that is, in attempting to assess the quality and degree of a filmmaker's fidelity to his source. And, among other reasons, because one must first ask a prior question: in the case of *Moby Dick*, just whose *Moby Dick* is the filmmaker being faithful to? Edmund Carpenter's great adventure or Brandon French's multileveled epic? Leslie Fieldler's Freudian novel or Newton Arvin's Marxist one?

This may seem all too relative, but there exists still another refinement of the notion of "fidelity." I've already suggested that a film might be considered faithful to its source to the extent that its implicit reading remained within the confines of that work's interpretive possibilities, to the extent that it neither violated nor diminished them. But in the case of a classic literary work, at least, there seems to be something else at stake: that an adaptation will be considered faithful to the extent that its interpretation remains consistent with those put forth by the interpretive community; with the interpretation (or possible interpretations) of that classic work, then, that made it a classic in the first place. In other words, every great work has been invested with certain distinctive qualities. It will have about it a particular aesthetic value, a certain degree of intricacy, a particular intensity, a given (but not necessarily limited) range of human qualities, a certain indeterminacy which allows for numerous (but not infinite) interpretations—all of which have worked to earn it its special stature. The reading of *Moby Dick* put forth by Carpenter notwithstanding, these are the very qualities the adaptor simply cannot ignore. And not just if he would be faithful, but much more importantly, if he would justify his art itself. Why adapt a great work if not because of its greatness and the chance it offers to replicate in another work of art some of the qualities that accounted for that greatness? Thus, the question of fidelity turns out to be more than one of an adaptation being responsible to its masterful source; it becomes an issue of making the adaptation a work that is masterful in itself.

* * *

Even if a filmmaker's reading is an enormously sensitive one; even if it operates according to the conventions and norms of the prevailing interpretive community; even if it takes into account those aspects of the work in question which have given it value—the filmmaker still faces the difficulty of transposing that interpretation to the screen. One obvious problem (at least most of the time) lies in the matter of compression and selection. For though a film can in actuality be any length at all—as long as von Stroheim's ten-hour *Greed* or Fassbinder's fifteen-hour twenty-one-minute *Berlin Alexanderplatz*—unless it is intended for television, its length must be guided by certain considerations and constraints. One is clearly commercial: the longer the film, the more difficulty it will have finding distribution and exhibition. Another has to do with the toleration of an audience, which can sit before a film for only so long. Still another, however, is strictly aesthetic, since it's probably the case that once a movie exceeds a length that allows for absorption in a single viewing, it sacrifices one of the medium's most crucial qualities: its immediacy of impact.

Thus, selection is a necessity. And while sometimes that choice will have an inevitability about it (the omission, let's say, of the "documentary" chapters in *Moby Dick*, the interchapters in *The Grapes of Wrath*, the extensive commentaries by Stingo in *Sophie's Choice*, even the revenge of Heathcliff after Cathy's death in *Wuthering Heights*), other times it's quite the contrary. How select from Tolstoi, Dostoyevsky, Dickens? More challenging yet, how select from someone such as Henry James, whose work has so striking a unity? Or better still, from Joyce or Proust, the vastness of whose great novels is so very crucial to their design and significance? Some would argue that selection from such works as these in itself constitutes betrayal; and admittedly, even a four- or five-hour film would be unlikely to reproduce their cumulative effect. But, given a sensitive and insightful selection of materials reflecting great insight into the works themselves, and a truly effective use of the movie medium's extraordinary capacity for compression, a film would be able to capture much more of their essential vision, obsessions, and art than one might imagine possible. (An example is Harold Pinter's *The Proust Screenplay*—a discussion of which is found in Chapter Eight.) In any case, the fact is that such titanic and densely packed literary works as *Ulysses* and *Remembrance of Things Past* are exceptions rather than the rule. Most novels lend themselves much more easily to cutting and condensation, making the problem of their length, if not a totally unimportant one, much less imposing than it might seem.

A more intricate problem lies in the transposition of a work conceived in another time into a contemporary context. It's commonly believed that all such works, having achieved a certain longevity, transcend their time and place. But while it's true that most classics do contain certain "universal" qualities, each in its own way also tends to be culture bound, rooted to the conventions, beliefs, even concepts of character of the age in which it was created—though some works more so than others. (I. A. Richards goes so far as to suggest that "far more of the great art of the past is actually obsolete than certain critics pretend," by which he means that the values and attitudes contained in them simply don't mesh with those of the present. *The Divine Comedy* is Richards's example.) When reading some of these works, we usually accept that they are products of another time, saturated with that period's sensibility, and thus suspend criticism of views that might otherwise strike us as untenable. But should that work be adapted to the screen, and those values carried along with it, our attitudes toward them change dramatically. Seeing them removed from the protective context of a dated poem or play or novel and embodied in a twentieth-century film, we tend to find them unacceptable. A filmmaker, then, must often omit certain elements, certain thematic strands which, though of central importance to a given work, simply cannot make the leap from their time to ours. A telling example here is the Tony Richardson–John Osborne adaptation of Fielding's *Tom Jones* which, as Fielding scholar Martin Battestin has observed, eliminates "a major intention behind Fielding's novel"—that is, its "moral seriousness." Nonetheless, celebrating the film as "one of the most successful cinematic adaptations of a novel ever made and, what is more, one of the most imaginative of comic films, a classic in its own right," Battestin finds the choice a well-advised one. For if there is anything in Fielding that has dated, he suggests, if there's anything that strikes the contemporary reader as naive, it's precisely that moral view. What proves congenial to the contemporary sensibility, in contrast, is precisely what Osborne and Richardson have preserved: the work's "essential spirit and manner."

The filmmaker must also find strategies through which to transform the purely verbal materials of the written text into the primarily visual matter of film. Sometimes, this may involve no more than the staging of a particular scene already dramatized in the novel, or the realization of a piece of description; other times (and perhaps more frequently), it will demand the dramatization of narrated passages, the dramatic translation of generalization and summary. In both cases, this involves a major imaginative act of transformation in which—again as Martin Battestin has observed, noting the battery of cinematic devices (fast-motion, flips, freeze-frames, exaggerated performance) used in the film of *Tom Jones* as equivalents for the novel's literary ones (amplifications, ironies, mock-heroics, parodies)—"analogy is the key." And here, whether it is transposition or commentary, whether it is literal rendition or free, we have what might be taken as the inescapable first principle of adaptation.

Compression and cutting, adjustment for temporal dislocation, the mutation of the narrative into the dramatic, of the descriptive into the presentational—all of these are essential to the process of adaptation and make for some of the key difficulties any adapter must face. There are other types of problems, however, which though less pervasive—tending to be special to particular works rather than characteristic of fiction in general— confront the adaptor with even greater challenges.

One of these is rendering and finding equivalents for a novel's focus of narration or point of view—in particular for the first person, an angle of vision not as readily available to film as third person. Yet, it's precisely the first-person narrator who prevails in many contemporary novels and the quality of whose sensibility determines what we see, how we see it, and ultimately what the novel is about. How does the adaptor convey such effects?

Another difficulty lies in capturing a particular novel's tone and its inseparable partner, style, both of which seem so inextricably bound to a novel's language as to make translation seem a near impossibility. What is more, tone is perhaps the most elusive of any given fiction's elements—the hardest to define and the element most capable of varying interpretation. It is also one of the most crucial to a novel's sense and effect. How does one first determine it and then find analogies for it?

The translation of literary works heavily dependent on metaphor and symbolism is also problematic for the adaptor—the verbal trope being one thing, the visual trope something else altogether. How, if at all, can film make such a figurative statement as (to use the most frequently cited example) "My luv's like a red, red rose / that's newly sprung in June" without resorting to words? How can film, which has a way of literalizing its images, grant them symbolic significance? What means does it have to let us know that if Moby Dick is an actual whale roaming actual seas, he is also a "great gliding demon of the seas of life"?

Finally, there's the difficulty the adaptor faces when attempting to render thought, dream, and interior action. Some theorists (such as George

Bluestone) have held that, committed to surfaces, limited to photographing exteriors, film is by its very nature incapable of revealing inner states of being, of "penetrating consciousness," as Bluestone phrases it. But though it seems to me that Bluestone is dead wrong, that film is as capable of "penetrating consciousness" as is the novel, it's still the case that it faces very special challenges in the attempt. For whereas the various novelistic strategies used to render inner life have a certain tradition behind them—for example, the stream-of-consciousness technique—the strategies available to film for reordering conventional reality tend both to be less codified and less easily accepted. Because of that, the filmmaker is often forced to reach for fresh strategies altogether.

Such problems as these demand extraordinary resourcefulness for their resolution, as will be made clear in the following chapters, where each will be explored in the context of selected adaptations. The "readings" of these films are, of course, my own and follow in each case both from my "interpretation" of the literary text in question and from my "interpretation of the interpretation." These films reflect what seem to me either successful, highly imaginative solutions to the challenge of translating problematic literary elements; or they illustrate precisely the opposite. But all the works discussed demonstrate unequivocally and it's that though narrative film can be seen as a branch of literature, though it may share with the novel similar aims and similar reasons for being, it remains embedded in a very different medium and makes use of a language which, however it might parallel that of the novel, is very different too. The rhetoric of fiction is simply not the rhetoric of film, and it's in finding analogous strategies whereby the one achieves the effects of the other that the greatest challenge of adaptation lies.

PART THREE

The Rhetoric of Adaptation

5

Point of View

Imagine *Sophie's Choice* narrated by paranoid-schizophrenic Nathan, or *Moby Dick* as seen through the eyes of the insanely obsessive Ahab, or *The Catcher in the Rye* as presented by an emphatically objective storyteller like the one we encounter in Hemingway's *The Killers*. Each of these narratives would become another work altogether. For there are few elements of fiction more crucial than narrative stance—the relation, that is, in which the teller stands to his tale, as well as the character and nature of that teller himself. There's no element either that has been more analyzed and debated by literary theorists in recent years—and that may be because it's precisely in the matter of narrative stance or, as it's otherwise termed, point of view, that prose fiction has changed most drastically.

Some would credit film itself with encouraging the change: they see movies and their distinctive strategies of narration as having stimulated the novel in discovering new strategies of its own. Most, however, situate the turning point elsewhere: in the works of Henry James, whose solution to the question of point of view was to present his stories through the re-stricted vantage point of a single character, to center the action in that indi-vidual's perceptions and make him serve, if not precisely as narrator, at least as the "window . . . of consciousness" through which the reader would then perceive the fictional world laid before him.

Not that prior to James one didn't encounter similar points of view. Pip tells his own story in *Great Expectations;* Nelly Dean tells the tale of Heathcliff and Catherine in *Wuthering Heights;* and though the heroine of Jane Austen's *Emma* doesn't tell her own story, we nonetheless see her ex-periences from her own point of view, her sensibility very much serving as our "window . . . of consciousness." But Pip and Nelly Dean are con-scious storytellers, commenting, intruding, and generalizing about their materials and reminding us that their stories are indeed *stories;* and if Emma's consciousness is our "window," there's still an ironic narrator standing behind *her* who can go well beyond her own perceptions and offer commentary she herself would be incapable of making. James's notion was to erase such authorial presence, and in the name of a greater immediacy of effect, an intensified illusion of reality, to create the impression that any given story was somehow telling itself. Since his time, such a narrative stance has tended to prevail, fiction having generally reshaped itself throughout the twentieth century according to his scheme.

Indeed, even where we do come across a self-conscious and fully dramatized storyteller in contemporary literature, his nature is quite different from such storytellers of old. The modern storyteller never quite admits to be creating a fiction in the manner of his predecessors, inviting us as they often did to sit down with them, as it were, by the fire, joining them in a game of "let's pretend." Nor does he claim omniscience—that godlike knowledge which allowed the likes of a Fielding or a Thackeray to know everything about everyone, to take us anywhere at all at any time they wished, to pop in and out of the minds of their characters at will. Whether the cause lies in our contemporary discomfort with omniscience, or in the attempt to create more intensely realistic effects, or simply in the effort to conform to the altered rhetoric of the novel, storytellers today inevitably admit to the limits of their knowledge, understanding, and perspective, frequently denying us any guiding comments at all. We are left on our own— forced to grapple by ourselves with the world created by the work, with the nature and quality of its speaker, and of course with its ultimate meaning. And this is not only because point of view is the most significant factor in shaping fiction itself; it's also because, the narrator's stance being our own stance, it's the most significant factor in guiding and controlling the reader's response.

It isn't only a question of distance, of how far or near we are situated in relation to a novel's action (or, in other words, of just how objective or subjective is the attitude we are invited to assume), or even of the way in which a narrator's sensibility colors our vision of the fictional world laid before us. It isn't even only that when the narrator is also a character in the story, his perceptions, his consciousness often become the very subject of the tale. It's that we inevitably enter into a relationship with the speaker and, if and when we can detect his presence, with the implied author standing behind him—our response to the work itself in large part being determined by our reaction to that narrative personality.

For example, do we find him clever or dense, sentimental or wry, or most important of all perhaps, do we find him trustworthy? In the old days, trust was never a question: one didn't doubt the omniscient, godlike storyteller. He knew anything and everything, and in any case the world before us was unmistakably his own creation. (That is, we tended not to hear another "voice" standing behind his own; we took him, in works like *Tom Jones* or *Vanity Fair,* to be virtually identical with the author.) But where the limited, subjective narrator is concerned, it's a different matter altogether, with the viewpoint of such a storyteller quite frequently open to suspicion. How can we trust a man like the narrator of Ford Madox Ford's *The Good Soldier* who keeps reiterating "I don't know; I don't know," who keeps telling us he knows "nothing—nothing in the world—of the hearts of men" and yet presumes to tell a tale of passion concerned precisely with those "hearts"? How are we to take the perceptions, the generalizations, the self-evaluation of a lunatic (or isn't he?) like *Lolita*'s Humbert Humbert?

The implications of all this for adaptation are far-reaching. For to translate any piece of fiction to the screen—and any work of modern fiction especially—one must obviously come to terms with its point of view and find filmic equivalents for it. Given not only much of contemporary literature's elusiveness, but the fact that film, as medium, would seem to be lacking in the rich rhetorical resources available to literature, this is clearly no mean task. Film lends itself with greater ease to certain vantage points than it does to others—some narrative strategies create the impression of straining the medium's possibilities, others of even going totally against its grain.* Heavily committed to surfaces, giving the illusion (at least) of recording events impartially, the medium does seem to have a natural disposition for the objective point of view, just as it also finds the omniscient stance a relatively easy one to assume. Like Fielding and Thackeray, film can range over vast periods of time, leap from one scene or setting to another, follow a great many different characters in the course of a single narrative, and keep its physical and/or emotional distance from all of them.

Subjective viewpoints seem much less a matter of course, and first-person perspectives especially tend to confront the medium with considerable diffi-

*Significantly, though many overlook the fact, literature too seems to find some points of view more congenial than others. The emphatically externalized and objectified descriptions of a novelist like Alain Robbe-Grillet strike some readers as so inappropriate to literature and so essentially "cinematic" as to lead them to wonder why Robbe-Grillet even "writes" in the first place. Why not simply make movies instead? Robbe-Grillet has, of course, made many films which, their ostensible "cinematic" vision notwithstanding, have proved as troubling to viewers as his novels have to readers.

culty. To present any action strictly and rigorously from the eyes of a first-person observer means excluding that observer from the scene—an effect which, if not totally unmanageable, can still seem very clumsy on screen. This isn't to say that the inability of the first-person narrator to actually observe himself, to include himself within his field of vision, can't also make for a certain awkwardness in literature. And similarly with the third-person restricted vantage point. Consider how often one comes across that inevitable (and inevitably weary) moment in which the narrator (or controlling consciousness) is suddenly found standing before his reflection, sizing himself up, commenting on the color of his eyes, the cut of his hair, and the like. ("Rosemary caught a glance of her reflection in the toaster"; "Berenice swung round in the barber's chair to face the mirror.")

In film, however, the viewpoint is decidedly more problematic yet. Whatever the difficulties that may arise in fiction due to the use of a restricted viewpoint, first-person point of view can still be signaled by no more than the simple use of the pronoun "I"; in film, it must be asserted through the camera, with "I" and the camera eye equated. Since in film just as in literature the narrator's position in relation to the action is our own, this means that we in turn must identify not with a character within the frame, a character whom we can see, but with the camera itself—an effect that can be totally disorienting.* The classic example here is Robert Montgomery's *Lady in the Lake,* a 1947 adaptation of a Raymond Chandler story in which the director (who also starred) attempted to make use of the first-person point of view throughout the film. As Philip Marlowe, the narrator-protagonist, Montgomery kept himself off-screen except at such moments as his reflection was caught in a mirror, and otherwise had the camera mounted on a helmet he wore throughout the shooting in order to maintain a subjective viewpoint. In conversation with him, then, the other characters found themselves addressing the camera directly—which in itself wasn't all that awkward. But when at one point the heroine (played by Audrey Totter) started moving toward the camera, beginning to embrace and kiss it, and when, in a fight scene, the attackers found themselves punching straight out at us, the results were ludicrous.

---

*Indeed, there are some—François Truffaut, for example—who would argue that more than being merely disorienting, such identification is in fact impossible. A truly subjective stance, Truffaut contends, requires audience identification with a particular character, something which demands in turn that the audience also *see* that figure.

A good deal more congenial to film is a stance approximating literature's third-person restricted vantage point—a stance in which our privileged glimpses into a character's thoughts, our restriction to his point of view, don't also involve the sacrifice of our ability to *see* him. In the case of film, the camera acts as third-person "narrator" while still establishing the controlling vision as a subjective one—identifying it as that of one of the characters shown to us on screen. It does this most obviously by the dramatic device of having that character present in each of a movie's scenes and restricting our knowledge to his own, never making us privy to what is beyond him. But it can also establish a character's perspective through its editing and cinematography—through the use of certain angles, lighting, variations in focus and lens, and most of all, through the point-of-view shot itself (the shot/reverse shot pattern in which the camera first focuses on a character, revealing his gaze as fixed somewhere off-screen, and then, via a cut, switches to an image from which that character is excluded). It also has various sound devices at its disposal: the voice-over or the use of subjective sound whereby we hear what a given character thinks or imagines he hears rather than what he really hears (as in Akira Kurosawa's *Dodeskaden*, where as we watch a retarded youth pretend that he is driving a trolley, we suddenly hear the actual sound of the motor and bells, signaling our entry into his consciousness).

All of this notwithstanding, there are those who contend that authentic subjectivity remains elusive in film. Whatever the angle, whatever the lighting, the argument goes, the camera is still a mechanical, impersonal observer, giving whatever it photographs an inescapably objective presence. How is it possible, then, not simply to assert a rigorous subjectivity but, more problematic yet, to indicate that a given set of perceptions is unreliable, actually a set of *mis*perceptions—or at least, how is it possible to do so without confusing the viewer? The question is troublesome, even more so in cases where film not only seeks to assert a subjective viewpoint, but to render thought, dream, fantasy—that is, subjective experience itself.

This is an enormous challenge to adaptation—and though related to that presented by the first person, of sufficient distinction and complexity as to warrant its own special discussion in Chapter Eight. Suffice it to say here that some of the devices used to assert the inner view, to dramatize dream and thought on film, are also those used to establish the outward-looking first person and that in both cases, similar arguments are raised against them. For instance, there are the claims that certain shots and devices are simply too disorienting (like the wide-angle lens used in *2001* to assert the perspective of HAL; like the jump cuts used by Godard in *Breathless)*; that they often make for near unintelligibility (like the disjointed editing in *Last Year in Marienbad* or *Providence)*; that other techniques are overly self-conscious (as in *The Graduate*, where, sharing Benjamin Braddock's perspective, we see the world at one point as if through a diving mask) or theatrical (like the expressionist sets used in *The Cabinet of Dr. Caligari)*; and that still others (the voice-over, for example) are too blatantly literary.

What's more, the argument continues, even if all these devices did seem more natural and inevitable to film than they do, true subjectivity would still remain elusive to it. One may be able to get away from the camera's impersonality, but one can't get away from its intervening presence. The camera lens simply isn't the eye, no matter how much it might pretend to duplicate its vision. The truth of this is incontrovertible; it's also beside the point—at least as regards adaptation. For one can also make the very same claim regarding literature, language constituting as much of an intermediary in establishing the first-person perspective as the camera. Perhaps even more so. Nor does it seem particularly true either—as some would contend—that whereas in the restricted third person in literature we sense a personality in the narrative voice and connect in some way to it, there is no such comparable teller in film with whom to relate. Just as such narrative personalities are created in literature through language—just as they in fact reside in language—so too do they reside in the camera in film. Surely, in any of Hitchcock's films, we sense in those often wry shots (the hand reaching out from the shadows to silence the singer in *The Lady Vanishes*, the huge glasses overwhelming the frame in that same film) the personality of the devilish creator of suspense; certainly, we sense too, in those often long-held images of mesas and buttes, of handsome men who ride tall in the saddle and serve as our heroes, the "voice" we've come to identify as that of John Ford. Just as in literature, moreover, the extent to which we find ourselves responsive to the works as a whole.

And let's say for a moment that we agree that film seems best and most fully suited to objectivity. Remember that once upon a time, when it too was a newly developed narrative form, this also seemed true of the novel, and that film may in some ways merely be repeating its history. (Susan Sontag, for one, claims that it is: "In D. W. Griffith," she writes, "the cinema had its Samuel Richardson . . .," while in the course of its development, she also points out, it's had "its Dickens, its Tolstoy, its Balzac, its Proust, its Nathanael West. . . .") Consequently, if we find various cinematic devices strained or more appropriate to literature, it may simply be a matter of habit—of our not being accustomed to their use or of their not yet being part of the accepted stock of cinematic conventions. Highly subjective fiction has also confounded most readers. The difference is that whereas many of us have been trained both to read and accept the likes of Virginia Woolf's *The Waves* and Faulkner's *The Sound and the Fury,* very few of us have had a similar education in film. It's also the case that young as film is, it hasn't come anywhere near exploring its rhetorical potential.

But even granted more possibilities than it's generally allowed, film still faces considerable challenges in its handling of point of view, and especially in handling first-person narration. It's not merely a matter of finding analogies for various literary devices in the repertoire of cinematic ones. It's understanding the function and significance of point of view in the particular novel the filmmaker would adapt in the first place: its role in shaping a story's structure, establishing meaning, determining attitude, creating emotional and psychological effects. And although that role is always decisive, it's admittedly more so in some instances than in others. There are some adaptations, as we'll find, whose very success or failure depends on the interpretation and rendering of point of view. These include such films as *The Innocents, The Great Gatsby, The French Lieutenant's Woman,* and *Apocalypse Now.*

The Innocents: Point of View as Puzzle

Henry James himself apparently didn't think much of *The Turn of the Screw:* he claimed it was a "potboiler," nothing more than a ghost story. "It is a piece of ingenuity pure and simple, of cold artistic calculation, an amusette to catch those not easily caught . . .," he wrote in the preface to the 1908 edition. But few readers today take James at his word. "Pure and simple"? This intricately constructed, highly suggestive story of a youthful and inexperienced governess who finds her two young charges haunted by demons she alone is able to see (and who therefore may or may not be mad) would seem to be anything but.

Indeed, it's one of the most ambiguous pieces of literature we have: a tale whose significance has not only been endlessly analyzed but whose very "facts" have been hotly debated. Not surprisingly, considering that the author is the very master of subjective narration, the story's difficulties arise from its carefully restricted point of view. Is the governess who tells the story in the first person a reliable narrator or isn't she? Has she actually seen the ghosts or are they merely figments of her imagination? Are the children innocent, or are young Miles and little Flora corrupt? Are they perhaps even evil? As for the ghosts, were their living counterparts—the valet Peter Quint, and the former governess Miss Jessel—given to horrible sexual depravity or weren't they? And what of Mrs. Grose, the housekeeper of Bly, the elegant country estate which serves as the story's setting? Does the answer to the puzzle lie in the hidden villainy of this seemingly straightforward and simple woman, or is it to be found instead in the dark and deeply neurotic sexual obsessions of the governess and indeed in the unconscious of Henry James himself?

Such questions have been raised over and over again and have been variously answered; the matter, though, remains unsettled. For the power (or as some contend, the problem) of *The Turn of the Screw* is that, given only the uncorroborated and inconsistent testimony of the governess, it's impossible to come to any final conclusion, to put forth any interpretation with absolute firmness. To some extent, the tale supports a literal reading of the ghosts; to some extent, too, it allows for a perception of them as hallucinatory; and it also in one way or another undercuts both readings. If the ghosts are real, how is it that no one but the governess can see them? If the ghosts are imaginary, how is it that though she has never seen the living Peter Quint, the governess is able to describe him perfectly? In short, however we might lean to one interpretation or another, we are invariably left with a sensation of discomforting but somehow tantalizing uncertainty.

It's precisely such a sensation that is also created by *The Innocents*—a generally overlooked and underestimated adaptation of James's story directed by Jack Clayton and written by Truman Capote and William Archibald (whose stage play both served as the film's most immediate source and provided it with its title). It's a graceful and remarkably intelligent film, and one that does more than reflect its makers' insightful grasp that ambiguity is at the core of the tale's effect. It also shows a literate understanding of the importance of a carefully restricted vantage point to the end of creating it. Not that the film makes any attempt to duplicate the novel's perspective precisely, or to mount a rigorous first-person perspective in the manner of *Lady in the Lake*. It uses no voice-over to establish the governess as teller of the tale and it does away completely with the novella's superinvolved opening section. Here, as a group of elliptically presented characters are found sitting about one Christmas Eve telling gruesome tales in an old country house, a man named Douglas asserts that he knows one which goes beyond all others for "uncanny ugliness and horror and pain"—that of a woman now dead some twenty years who was once his sister's governess and with whom, his listeners seem to suspect, he may possibly have been in love. She has left a manuscript in his keeping and, after sending down to London for it and setting the scene somewhat, he begins to read the tale, allowing her then to tell it herself.

Dispensing with this frame, the film establishes its ghost-story atmosphere with the title sequence alone: we are shown an eerie and exquisitely shadowy close-up of the face of the governess (Deborah Kerr) and then of her hands clasped in prayer, as she moans indistinctly, "All I want to do is save the children, not destroy them"—words and images both running under the credits. As for the film proper, it begins quite simply at the point that the governess herself begins in James's original: with her interview by a dashing gentleman (Michael Redgrave) who offers her a position caring for his orphaned niece and nephew. Ensconced at Bly, his country estate, the two are currently under the care of a housekeeper; it seems their previous governess has died.

Though the film doesn't establish the governess as narrator, it still makes clear that everything is being shown from her vantage point, that she is the film's informing consciousness. She's present in every scene; she's frequently seen in close-up; the camera consistently follows her gaze to establish her point of view; and her perspective itself is so rarely violated that here and there where we do assume a stance other than her own, we find it jarring. The few exceptions—as when the camera, positioned as if outside a window, shows us the little girl Flora smiling despite the fact that the governess is clearly not privy to the sight—tend to prove the rule here. The film thereby establishes a focus of narration that approximates the third-person restricted point of view. Its evident and highly effective solution to the challenge of rendering the story's first-person perspective was, then, to substitute one subjective vantage point for another.

The film also manages, almost from the outset, to assert the possible unreliability of the governess's perceptions. The ease with which it does so is striking, given that film has a tendency to validate what it shows us. One would have thought that to allow us to see the ghosts—as the film inevitably had to, once it had subscribed to the governess's point of view—would have granted them an undeniable reality. And all the more so because here to see is not only to believe, but also to be frightened, which means that our emotions might take over from the intellect completely, making doubt beside the point. *The Innocents* is frightening all right—I've seen it more than a half-dozen times and I still shudder at the moment when the ghost of Peter Quint appears to the governess at the window—and it's certainly much more frightening than *The Turn of the Screw*. (But then again, that kind of immediate involvement is part of the movies' special power. When was the last time you told anyone, "Don't worry, it's only a play"? Or the last time you shrieked from fright while reading?) *The Innocents*, however, manages to terrify without erasing doubt. Like the story, its achievement is, above all, to make us believe at the same time as we question that belief, and to make the uncertainty as to whether or not our perceptions are reliable somehow as frightening as those perceptions themselves.

How does the film call its vision into question? One obvious way is by having the governess (and us in turn) see and hear things that aren't perceived by others—sights like the ghosts, of course, and sounds like the thin voice heard calling out "Flora" on the very first day the governess arrives at Bly, which neither Flora herself nor the housekeeper seems to have heard. Another is through the exquisite modulation of its cinematography, the work of Freddie Francis, who invests some images with a suggestive haziness and others with an almost shocking clarity which in itself makes what we see vaguely unreal. The film is in black and white, and though it may sound like a rationalization—given that the film was shot in 1961 when color was still reserved mostly for musicals and historical epics—there's such a beauty and aptness to its visual texture that the choice seems truly deliberate. Appropriately, the moments in which we see the ghosts are among the most effectively rendered; certainly, they constitute the film's most visually elusive images. Take the scene in which the governess catches her first glimpse of Quint. As in the novella, she sees him at a considerable distance, standing on a tower. In the film, however, she finds herself also staring up into the glaring sunlight, with the film following her vision and shooting straight into the sunlight as well, giving the image a hallucinatory quality. As for her first sight of Miss Jessel, the film again follows the novella's design, showing the apparition from across a lake. Again, however, it also adds its own effect by encasing the sight in such a soft-edged, rainsoaked image that it's almost as if it weren't photographed at all but rendered in watercolors.

None of this would mean very much, however, if it weren't for the way in which the film makes the governess's nervous and unstable personality call her point of view into question. Nor would these techniques have been anywhere as effective if the screenwriters hadn't also chosen to alter somewhat the novella's events. For faithful as the film is to James's narrative line and effects, it's far from a slavish translation. It brings to bear its own interpretation. Unsurprisingly, considering that our age is less receptive to the idea of ghosts than that of James, and also considering the likelihood of the modern reader/viewer bringing psychological explanations to bear, that interpretation is fairly close to the Freudian one first proposed by critic Edmund Wilson.

In the very first scene, the film makes perfectly clear what the story only hints at: that the governess is in love with the uncle. We are given to understand that it's in large part because of this feeling that she has taken the job—a job that carries with it both the discomforting overtones of the previous governess's unexplained death and the peculiar condition that under no circumstances whatsoever is the new governess to disturb the uncle. The film also makes it clear, in the governess's first conversation with the housekeeper, that she brings romantic thoughts of the uncle with her to Bly. In contrast to the story, the governess is—one can assume for mere convenience' sake—given a name, Miss Giddens. And Deborah Kerr couldn't be more perfect in the role—especially gifted as she is at conveying a sense of repressed sensuality and hysteria, always on the verge of bursting out yet somehow also restrained. We can believe that such overstated propriety as hers might topple over into unintentional destructiveness, that such buried desires might lead to hallucination. Yet, at the same time, she's normal enough to invite our identification, to make us also suspect that the horror may in fact be real and that she's therefore more heroic than mad.

The film also reinforces its psychological reading by providing an answer to the crucial problem of how the governess was able to describe Quint so accurately. During a hide-and-seek game with the children Miss Giddens comes across a miniature of Quint in the attic, only moments before his second and closer appearance behind a window. Thus, her perceptions are given a possible psychological cause, as they also were in the earlier scene where she spies his ghost on the tower. Here, the governess is shown clipping roses in the garden, pulling back a branch, and coming across a hidden statue of a cherub, whose outstretched hands clasp another pair of hands, broken off at the wrists, and out of whose grinning mouth crawls a beetle. Startled, horrified, Miss Giddens turns to catch her first glimpse of Quint. Or, at least, she thinks she does.

The film also includes a great deal of suggestive imagery which, by the way, tends to be most blatantly Freudian when it derives specifically from James—the fact that Quint is first spotted on the tower, that Miss Jessel is seen at the pond (the phallic tower's feminine counterpart). The film's own inventions are: placing the boy Miles on the tower as well (playing with his pigeons); a scene of Miles riding his pony, perceived by Miss Giddens with an evident mixture of terror and sensuality; a suggestive dream montage revealing Miss Giddens's obsessiveness; emblematic use of flowers, especially white roses—the film is literally swimming with them, as in the early scene where the governess admiringly fondles some roses in a vase only to have their petals fall at her touch; and most telling of all, perhaps, having Miles at one point offer Miss Giddens a goodnight kiss that either is (or is perceived by her) as passionately sexual. (The mounting of this scene is extraordinary: we are given first an extreme close-up, almost romantic in texture, of Miss Giddens leaning over the boy, her hair in disarray, wisps hanging sensually around her face; then an even larger close-up of her startled, terrified eyes when she seems to sense the boy's amorous intentions; and finally, a still larger one yet of her ambiguously parted lips.)

But despite all this suggestive imagery, the film doesn't remove all doubts that the ghosts may in fact be real. Thus, it allows for still another of the tale's classical interpretations, in which the ghosts are seen as agents of evil and depravity and the governess as exorcist. The atmosphere of Bly itself, those sounds in the night, those candles blown out by mysterious blasts of wind, the chilling hide-and-seek game (another interpolation) played by the children and Miss Giddens, together create a sense of fear and forboding. The children too strike us as strange, in ways that seem to go beyond any skewed perception on Miss Giddens's part. Miles is startlingly self-possessed and flirtatious in a manner eerily elegant for a ten-year-old, and Flora, who continually hums the haunting refrain from Miss Jessel's music box, often seems purposefully, even smugly enigmatic.

Moreover, just as the film undercuts the reality of ghosts in some ways, it underscores their reality in others. For one thing, though many of their appearances have psychological explanations, others simply don't. There's the instance in which Miss Jessel's ghost abruptly shows up in the house one night. (In the novella, it's the ghost of Quint who makes such an appearance—the film evidencing a bit more logical consistency by keeping him always outside the house, as if attempting but unable to get in.) For another, although the ghosts are mostly seen from Miss Giddens's angle of vision, there are two instances in which this isn't the case. At the point that Miss Jessel appears in the schoolroom, the camera peers at her from behind

Miss Giddens, including Miss Giddens in the shot. In the final sequence, in which Peter Quint appears for the last time and Miles's heart gives out, we actually see Miss Giddens and Miles from the ghost's point of view, the camera looking down at them from over his shoulder. To share the ghost's vantage point is, of course, to allot him reality; as it also is to see his elusive figure or that of Miss Jessel together in the very same frame with figures whose existence is unquestionable. An even more persuasive piece of evidence for the spirits' actuality, though, and the film's most imaginative bit of interpolation, is the "tear" Miss Giddens finds on the desk after the appearance of Miss Jessel in the schoolroom. Is it in fact a "tear"? Is it the ghost's? It's impossible to say, and that's precisely the point.

What we have, then, is a film which, like the story on which it's based, is highly suggestive and ambiguous, resistant to any final, conclusive interpretation, and for the very same reasons—the impossibility of knowing whether or not to trust the vision of the governess. The movie isn't James precisely, but who would expect or want it to be? One is a work of fiction, the other is a film; one was written in 1898, the other made in 1961, a particular time lapse in which our sense of human personality has changed and also our feeling for the supernatural. Because of this, the alterations the film has made seem a necessity, since without the strong possibility of a psychological explanation, without an intensified ambiguity, it would become impossible for us to accept the tale, at least on a serious level. But if the film isn't precisely James, it does an extraordinary job of approximating his effects, and I'm not at all sure that it's any less good. After all, *The Turn of the Screw* isn't *The Ambassadors*. It's a tantalizing and very fine tale, just as *The Innocents* is a tantalizing and very fine movie.

There's an interesting footnote to all of this. At the time of the film's release, it was given far from generous reviews. Some critics complained that it made the ghosts mere psychological phenomena, others took it to task for entertaining the ghosts as actual phenomena; some found suggestions of incest in it, some of homosexuality, while still others complained of its Freudian overtones (as if the film had invented them). Pauline Kael, one of its few early defenders, suggests in her review (which is also something of a review of the statements of other critics) that the variations in interpretation themselves testify to the film's accomplishment—and certainly to the extent to which it has managed to mount a tale whose essence is ambiguity. What's more, since the responses to the film aren't really all that different from the original responses to the story—"a few readers were repulsed, some were charmed, most were mystified," as one James scholar tell us—

they also may testify to just how close the film has come to re-creating James's effects. Most revealing of all, though, is that the film has frequently been faulted for betraying James *precisely for those qualities found in the story itself.* (Take the following comment on the film, for example: "Perhaps the children . . . are possessed; and, on these perhapses, intelligent interest dissipates.") Is it that these critics haven't actually read James? Or that they haven't read him well? Or is it instead a matter of the extent to which, even among those whose primary commitment and concern is movies, a bias against film and in favor of literature prevails, ending up distorting vision?

The Great Gatsby:
The Breakdown of Distance

F. Scott Fitzgerald may have hated Hollywood; and Hollywood may not have thought much of Fitzgerald, at least when he tried his hand at screenwriting. But the Fitzgerald who wrote *Tender Is the Night, The Beautiful and the Damned, Babylon Revisited*—all of which, among others, were adapted to the screen—was something else altogether. Here was a writer whose works seemed to beg for cinematic translation, and none perhaps so much as his delicate masterpiece, *The Great Gatsby.* Filmed first in 1926, with Warner Baxter as Gatsby and Lois Wilson as Daisy, then again in 1948 with Alan Ladd and Betty Field, and after no less than two intervening television adaptations—one starring Robert Montgomery, the other Robert Ryan—it was given both its most extravagant treatment and its most glamorous Gatsby yet in the 1974 version starring Robert Redford.

What is it about *Gatsby* that has always held such appeal for moviemakers? There's the mystique of its central figure—the fabled and fabulous rags-to-riches hero obsessed with his dream of Daisy, the girl with the "voice full of money." There's the world of the novel—a world of glamorous wealth and garish wild parties, populated with people whose extraordinary riches have made them feckless, free, and different from the rest of us. There's the extent to which everything has been richly visualized: the novel is filled with striking individual images (the poster featuring the eyes of Dr. Eckleburg; the green light at the end of Daisy's dock) and marked by a strongly scenic presentation (the breeze-swept living room where Daisy and Jordan Baker lounge on a summer's afternoon; the "valley of ashes" where Wilson's garage is located). There's also Fitzgerald's prevailing mode of characterization—characterization not by lengthy summary or extended internal musing, but by speech (Gatsby's "old sport"; Meyer Wolfsheim's "I understand you're looking for a business *gonnegtion*") and action (Tom breaking Myrtle's nose; Daisy sobbing over Gatsby's beautiful shirts). And, lastly, there's the novel's slimness and economy of structure. There's little cutting or careful compression needed here. In fact, as more than one critic has noted, the novel reads much as if it were a scenario.

Why is it then that *The Great Gatsby* has managed to elude every attempt to translate it successfully to the screen, and why especially in the case of the 1974 adaptation? Certainly, no expense was spared and the filmmakers were far from studio hacks. British director Jack Clayton's previous work had been both intelligent and refined, and having made *The Bespoke Overcoat, The Innocents,* and *Room at the Top,* he had also proved himself especially gifted at adaptation. Scenarist Francis Coppola was at the time one of Hollywood's most promising talents—screenwriter for the award-winning *Patton,* director of *The Godfather* and *The Conversation.* What's more, as the film itself made evident, the filmmakers had attempted to be as faithful as possible to their source, following the novel scene by scene, almost page by page, here and there even line by line. Not that there aren't some changes: the omission of the figure of Dan Cody, Jay Gatz's original mentor; the alteration of the manner in which Nick first encounters Gatsby; the interpolation of several images and motifs—for example, the ring Gatsby gives to Daisy and ends up wearing himself and the addition of a brief coda in which Nick, seated in the tearoom of the Plaza Hotel with Jordan Baker, meets up with Tom and Daisy. But these alterations are both minor and minimal. And the Clayton-Coppola adaptation emerges, in spite of them, as one of the most literal adaptations ever made.

Nonetheless, the film was greeted, to borrow a phrase from Nick Carraway, with "unaffected scorn." Well, perhaps not totally "unaffected." The phenomenal publicity campaign that Paramount had mounted prior to the film's release—there were Gatsby fashions, Gatsby drinks, Gatsby haircuts, Gatsby pots and Gatsby pans, and an opening-night party featuring, among its other guests, hundreds of white doves—was bound to excite a good deal of critical resistance. But even viewed from the unsullied vantage point of the present, *The Great Gatsby* remains a misguided movie. It may seem much less a blockbuster of a bore than it did the first time around and a good deal more conscientious and sincere—there's something in its elegiac tone that touches you. Still, there's no getting away from the fact that the movie is a monumental failure.

As reviewers noted at the time, almost everything seems wrong with the film and out of sync with the novel to boot: its pacing is languorous, whereas the novel is tight and fast-paced; its look is consistently elegant, whereas in the novel much of what we see is characterized by an "ineffable gaudiness"; the parties are less wild and vulgar than they seem in the book and are populated not by a mix of nouveau-riche West-Eggers and elegant East-Eggers, but with all the same type of people. Its principals also seem miscast. While some have expressed dissatisfaction with Karen Black as Myrtle (with which I'd disagree, since she seems to me acceptably, even persuasively, vulgar), others with Bruce Dern (who as Tom comes across as insufficiently to the manner born), and still others with Sam Waterston (who, fine as he is on stage, emerges as far from scintillating on screen, at least in the role of Nick Carraway), the problem clearly lies above all with the casting of Daisy and Gatsby. Mia Farrow simply isn't compelling enough to explain Gatsby's single-minded devotion, while Robert Redford is both unconvincing and curiously lacking in the characteristic Redford charm. Given not only the weakness of the leads but the lack of clear definition of class, Gatsby's obsession consequently emerges as much less significant than it does in the novel—becoming merely a matter of unrequited love rather than one of the elusiveness and essential hollowness of the American dream.

But the film reveals an even more crucial flaw, and it's one that, although central to most of its other difficulties, has generally been ignored: that is, its mishandling of point of view. The film may open and close with Nick Carraway and even grant him more screen time than Gatsby; it may make clear that he is our storyteller, allowing him to comment in voice-over on the soundtrack. But it nevertheless fails to establish the perspective of the film as his own, to show us the world as if it were filtered through his eyes and consciousness. And as both the novel itself and the criticism that has grown up around it make clear, no one thing is more important to the novel's method and, in turn, to its significance and effect. For not only are we restricted here to what Nick sees and what Nick hears; not only are even his reports of what others have told him dominated by his sensibility; it's also that, however one reads Nick (and he's been read in many ways—as ironic narrator and hypocritical prig, or, a good deal more persuasively, as straightforward storyteller and true moralist), his perceptions and judgments stand at the story's very heart, not on its periphery. The entire progress of the novel lies in the development of his attitudes, the alteration of his vision. In the novel, Gatsby is one thing when we first meet him—a mysterious underworld character, an ostentatious social climber, a gauche and vulgar liar. He's something else at the end—a generous, idealistic man, run through with "romantic readiness" and bearer of an "incorruptible dream." So too with the Buchanans, who, arrogant and supercilious even from the outset, assert themselves as totally selfish, destructive, and cruel at the end. Importantly, it isn't these characters themselves who change; it is Nick's perception of them. Nick, in other words, isn't merely our window on the world; he is a self-conscious narrator, an authentic exemplar of the modern novel's distinctive emphasis, and the movements of his mind are the novel's dramatic center. Its development is his development—so much so that we can say the drama of the entire story becomes impossible to follow unless his vision is shared. And this is as true for the viewer as it is for the reader.

But Nick's point of view has still another function: it keeps us at a safe distance from Jay Gatsby himself—Fitzgerald's most quixotic, troublesome creation. From his speech—the manner of which, as Nick tells us, "bordered on the absurd," through his seemingly endless and startlingly sudden wealth, to his obsession with Daisy, his belief in the "green light," and his desire to "recreate the past"—there's something incredible about him. He's a fabulous character in the most literal sense of the word—more an emblem or type than an individualized personality. We accept him in the context of the novel, though, largely because we never see him directly: only as filtered through Nick.

And it's precisely this point of view that the film breaks down almost completely. Immediately after the scene in which Daisy sobs into Gatsby's shirts, Nick disappears from the screen altogether for a couple of reels, conveniently stepping aside to allow Gatsby and Daisy to renew their romance. No Nick overhears Gatsby and Daisy in awkward and strained conversation in Gatsby's bedroom; no Nick comes along while Daisy fingers copper molds in Gatsby's kitchen; no Nick sits on the sidelines as the two dance romantically by candlelight in Gatsby's ballroom. It's hardly a coincidence that these scenes are the most stultifying in the entire film, their only competition for dullness and distention being the sequence involving Gatsby's murder, which, significantly, also violates Nick's vantage point. (Here, we must drearily watch Redford climb into his suit, put on a record, leap into the pool, climb onto an air mattress, and awkwardly mutter "Daisy?" a couple of times before he's actually shot.) For whether it's Gatsby in love or Gatsby in death, we gain nothing and lose everything in seeing him directly, unprotected by Nick's viewpoint.

It's significant too that the montage of Gatsby and Daisy "in love" quite pointedly betrays the novel's thematic intentions. It's here more than anywhere, for example, that the film deprives Daisy of her suggestive power, transforming her into a literal love object rather than an embodiment of elusive "promises." It's here, too, that her original rejection of Gatsby is reduced from an insightful critique of class to emphatically simplistic sociology. "Why . . . why didn't you wait for me?" Gatsby asks. "Because . . . rich girls don't marry poor boys, Jay Gatsby," sobs Daisy, going on to repeat the line (as if we hadn't gotten it the first time): "Haven't you heard? Rich girls don't marry poor boys." This is perhaps Francis Coppola's single most damaging interpolation—one which works to both diminish the theme of the film and Gatsby's dream itself to the point where they lose all resonance.

The film also fails to subscribe to Nick's vantage point even when he *is* present. Nothing is tinged by his perspective, nothing seems perceived in a manner even close to the way he himself would have seen it—and this, of course, is key to why the film's vision so consistently strikes us as wrong. Nick Carraway, a struggling bond salesman, is often very wry about money ("I bought a dozen volumes on banking and credit and investment securities and they stood on my shelf . . . promising to unfold the secrets that only Midas and Morgan and Maecenas knew"), whereas the film seems to be consistently in awe of wealth. Douglas Slocombe's filtered cinematography bathes everything in a shimmery glow, with shot after shot focused on sparkling silver, glittering gold, luminous crystal. The pre-credit sequence itself has the camera tracking slowly and lovingly over Gatsby's lavish toilet articles, richly monogrammed sheets, and gilt-framed photos of Daisy. So wide-eyed is the film's vision, in fact, that we almost get the feeling we're sharing not Nick's point of view but Gatsby's—or at least we would if it weren't for the fact that everything is also mounted with extraordinary taste. Even Gatsby's house shares in this fastidious aesthetic. Imitated by an exquisite (if hugely oversized) Newport mansion, it's a far cry from the ersatz Normandy palace described in the novel. Still, such a house is suitable for the movie's Gatsby—though it makes him more unbelievable yet as a man who traffics with the likes of Wolfsheim. If the filmmakers had only paid more attention to the Gatsby Nick saw, they might have recalled that he was given to the gaudy and the vulgar, that what Nick saw was an "elegant . . . roughneck." In contrast the filmmakers apparently saw, and gave us, an archetypal WASP. Such a Gatsby is not only made doubly incredible; he is deprived at once of his outrageousness and his appeal.

Had the filmmakers read more carefully (and more insightfully as well), they also would have noticed that at the outset, at least, Nick also perceives Gatsby with "scorn," just as they would have understood how Nick's perceptions are later modified. In the film, however, everything is shown to us in precisely the same light at the end as at the beginning—and this is why the film has a strikingly static quality. Nothing changes in it. Daisy and Tom are utterly atrocious at the beginning, just as they are at the end; Jordan Baker is as vaguely bored and as bad a driver in the last shot as she is in the first; and Gatsby is elegized from the very first moment we see him. The cast even enunciates their lines in precisely the same tone throughout. The implication is hard to miss: the filmmakers failed to see that the drama of the novel lay in the development of Nick's moral vision and situated it in the novel's events instead. And since these events aren't really much—a party or two, a meeting or two, the hit-and-run killing of Myrtle (which takes place off-screen)—they've ended up with a movie that contains almost no drama at all.

They've also ended up with a Nick who is little more than mere reactor, a Nick who is undermined not only as storyteller but as character. He is neither moral prig nor "defunct arch-priest"; nor is he the somewhat pompous and proud young man who comes away from his experience with a new humility; nor a conscious ironist and balanced moralist. The Nick we see in the film is pretty much devoid of any character at all. Waterston has a thankless role—to smile vaguely here, to look a bit wide-eyed there, to listen, nod, and, of course, to offer an intermittent commentary on the soundtrack.

To make matters worse, his narration is delivered in the same measured, self-important tone throughout. Whether Nick is philosophizing about "the foul dust" that floated in Gatsby's dreams or simply telling us that he had known Tom Buchanan in New Haven, it all sounds the same. Much of his commentary is also made up of passages (taken verbatim from the novel) describing scenes or actions which, curiously enough, are visualized for us at the very same time, making Nick and his voice-over commentaries redundant. Must he, for example, tell us that "a corps of caterers came down with several hundred feet of canvas, and enough coloured lights to make a Christmas tree of Gatsby's enormous gardens" when we are being shown those caterers on screen? Must he tell us that "men and girls came and went . . ." when presumably we can see them? Clearly, although the film does attempt to use Nick as narrator, it reflects no understanding of how to give that narration any meaningful point.

Thus, in its muddling of point of view, the film has ended up both wasting Nick and diminishing Gatsby (ironically enough, in Gatsby's case, by showing him more distinctly and directly). Deprived of his mystery and distance, Gatsby has a reality his sketchy character simply cannot hold, and under the film's scrutiny, his obsession is reduced from tragedy to mere sentimentality. But how were the filmmakers to cast a superstar in a part and then keep him at a distance from the audience? One might argue that had the filmmakers truly grasped the nature of the novel they tried to adapt, they wouldn't have cast Redford as Gatsby in the first place. Indeed, had Jack Clayton and Francis Coppola fully understood the importance of point of view to Fitzgerald's novel—that *The Great Gatsby* is as much about the narrator as it is about Gatsby himself—they might have offered their superstar another role altogether. They might have invited him to play not Jay Gatsby, but to play Nick Carraway instead.

The French Lieutenant's Woman: Dual Perspectives

John Fowles's *The French Lieutenant's Woman* is a virtuoso literary performance—a novel of great originality and style. A classic Victorian romance run through with the form's characteristic drama and sweep, it is also a suggestive analysis of the genre, a reflection on the Victorian age as a whole, and a meditation on the art of the novel in general. The key to the book's richness lies largely in its rhetorical stance: in Fowles's choice to have his tale of the obsessive passion of a proper Victorian gentleman for a mysterious woman of questionable repute narrated by a speaker from our own age—and one who, though eminently Victorian in style, is emphatically modern in sensibility.

Knowing, chatty, with a wry sense of humor, he may intrude on his story whenever he wishes, generalizing about his characters and the period that produced them and comparing Victorian mores with our own. He may, like the Victorian novelist, affect a God-like stance, leaping about in time and space, offering all variety of insights and hindsights. Yet, like the modernist he is, he also admits to the limits of his knowledge. Of his heroine, the elusive French Lieutenant's woman, he asks: "Who is Sarah? Out of what shadows does she come?" only to answer, "I do not know." Also in the modernist manner, this narrator keeps playing games of illusion and reality with his reader, insisting on his characters as his own creation at the same time as he emphasizes their freedom from his control. He even goes so far as to play the greatest literary trick of all—he supplies his novel with alternative endings. One is typically Victorian, a happy ending that unites our star-crossed lovers and puts the world in order; another is inescapably contemporary: open-ended, frustrating, sad.

How does one bring such a novel to the screen? Indeed, so problematic was the translation that it took John Fowles eleven years to find a director and screenwriter willing to attempt it. Not that certain obvious solutions didn't present themselves—but each managed to bring with it equally obvious limitations. For example, though it would have been possible to omit the narrative frame and simply allow the Victorian tale to stand on its own, that would have telescoped the novel's stereoscopic vision and so the very source of its power. It also would have been possible to include the narrator himself as character—in the manner of *La Ronde,* Max Ophuls's film of the Schnitzler play, where a Master of Ceremonies guides us through the action and sometimes steps into it himself. Given the exceedingly talkative nature of Fowles's narrator, however, such a strategy might have struck the viewer as static and self-conscious.

The solution of director Karel Reisz and scenarist Harold Pinter is of another order altogether—and one so startlingly simple it seems curious (as Fowles himself suggests) that no one had thought of it before and which paradoxically is also so stunningly original as to make the film as much of a tour de force as the novel. Since the book is essentially a novel within a novel, reasoned Reisz—whom Pinter credits with the basic conception— why not, in translating it to screen, use the device of a movie within a movie? But there's a further twist yet. Since the frame of the novel is very much concerned with the process of writing a novel itself, we might have expected the frame of the film to be concerned in turn with the problems of moviemaking—something on the order of François Truffaut's *Day for Night,* let's say—but Reisz and Pinter opted to use it quite differently. They chose to tell not one love story but two: that of a contemporary actor and actress who are working together on a period movie, intercutting the tale of their affair with the period movie itself.

That period movie is, of course, *The French Lieutenant's Woman,* and though considerably condensed, it otherwise follows Fowles's story line quite closely. As in the novel, the action begins when Charles Smithson (Jeremy Irons), gentleman, amateur scientist, and Darwinian disciple, proposes marriage to the wealthy and charming Ernestina Freeman. Shortly thereafter, he catches a glimpse of the woman who will end up changing his life. Hooded, mysterious, standing mournfully on the quay at Lyme Regis—the English coastal town where most of the action is set—she is Sarah Woodruff (Meryl Streep), who, according to local gossip and her own account as well, has been seduced and abandoned by a worthless officer in the French navy and who so flaunts her shame and melancholy as to suggest she may be insane. Nonetheless, to Charles she becomes an obsession that intensifies: first, when he becomes her lover and discovers, to his total puzzlement, that he is the only lover she has ever had; and second, when she abruptly disappears, leaving him as desperate an outcast as she herself has been.

So goes the film within the film. As for the one that frames it, breaking into it only briefly and intermittently at the outset and more frequently and extensively toward the end, it too focuses on a love affair: between Mike, a young British actor who is portraying Charles in the film, and Anna, an American actress who is playing Sarah. Like Charles, Mike is committed to another woman—though she is not his fiancée but his wife. Like Sarah, Anna has a French lover—only this time an authentic one who seems totally committed to her. Like Charles too, Mike displays a passion that is obsessive; while like Sarah, Anna proves ultimately elusive.

Providing a double vision and an opportunity for a double ending—in the Victorian tale the lovers are united in the end; in the modern one, Anna runs off, leaving a despairing Mike behind her—the movie's framing device would otherwise seem so distant from that of the novel as to have another effect altogether. It's no surprise, then, that many viewers find themselves bewildered by it, troubled as to what to make of it and how to evaluate it. And all the more so in that the movie doesn't quite do justice to all of the novel's complex themes. Gone are the ruminations on the act of creation, on the artist as God-like manipulator. Gone too is the novel's rich fund of Victoriana. (Only at one point does the film make any effort to duplicate its historical texture—in an early sequence where, shown reading a book about Victorian England, Anna comments to Mike about the period's startling number of prostitutes.) Gone as well is much of the novel's emphasis on freedom and choice—the existential themes that some readers see as primary. Nor are there any of the narrative guideposts which give the novel its peculiar perspective—as for example the narrator's declaration that in those few "poised seconds" when Charles glimpsed Sarah on the Undercliff near the sea, "the whole Victorian Age was lost"; or his notation that though Charles himself knew nothing of it, as he strolled about Lyme Regis one afternoon, a "beavered German Jew" was busily working in the British Museum library, hastening to bring about a revolution.

But the movie withstands these losses, and offers its own thematic riches and rewards to boot—not least of these being the ironic interplay of the two stories and an enormous gain in immediacy. For charming and clever as Fowles's narrator might be, he interrupts too frequently, often with too much coyness. (Many readers in fact have complained of his inconsistency, of his "bad faith," and that he is little more than a "boring red herring.") There are times we couldn't care less what this chatty fellow has to tell us about the *nouveau roman*, about truth and reality in fiction—we just want him to get on with the story. It's already quite clear that this is all a fantasy and there's no need for him to belabor the point.

To its distinct advantage the movie avoids such overinsistence; it manages to assert its double vision and still bring us close to its characters and story, sweeping us up more fully than the novel in their passionate romance.* This is due in part to the change in medium itself—from the cooler vehicle of print to the more affective one of film—but it is also a function of the quality of this particular movie. The Victorian segments have been luxuriantly photographed in sepia tones that make the world of Lyme Regis a moody and passionate one and give extraordinary life and intensity to Fowles's own lush descriptions of nature. (The cinematographer here is once again the prodigiously gifted Freddie Francis.) The leading players—all the players in fact—are consummate performers: Jeremy Irons is thoroughly convincing both as Victorian gentleman and obsessed modern man; and Meryl Streep, with her Pre-Raphaelite beauty and suggestion of hidden depths, is a perfect embodiment of the puzzling Sarah. (Some, incidentally, have complained that you can see Streep thinking on screen—but what could be more strikingly apt for the intelligent, dissimulating Sarah?) Most importantly, however, and especially for a double romance, the two performers work extraordinarily well together. You truly believe in the characters' desire for one another and in the agony of their unfulfilled longings.

Director Reisz also presents the film-within-a-film segments without too many distracting reminders of what they are. Here and there, a sound

---

*The lessening of distance in *The Great Gatsby* was disastrous, but there's no contradiction here. Unlike Clayton and Coppola, Reisz manages to bring us close to Sarah without ever undermining her mystery. And it's important to note that every fiction—like every film— has its own demands.

bridge will pull us out of our reverie—as when, immediately before a shift to the present tense from the Victorian era, we hear a telephone ringing, or the sound of a helicopter or automobile. At another moment, immediately after watching Anna rehearsing a fall in the present, we cut (via a stunning edit) to Sarah executing that fall in the past, carrying overtones of what's happening in the present into our awareness of the past. And the first sequence of the movie—in which Sarah is shown walking out on the quay at Lyme Regis—is prefaced by the sight of a clapperboard reading "*The French Lieutenant's Woman*: Scene 1, Take 1." Mostly, though, Reisz restricts his direct assertions of the film's double vision to the modern segments. Mike is shown at lunch wearing Charles's makeup and costumes, whereas Charles makes no reference to Mike; Anna is shown selecting fabric for one of Sarah's dresses, whereas Sarah shows no awareness of Anna's existence; while in the final scene, Mike registers the loss of Anna in the very same room that only moments before served as the setting for Charles and Sarah's reconciliation. Thus, though the film certainly places its Victorian segments in quotation marks, we still watch them with only minimal interference—with the result that, rather than *experiencing* them as fantasy, we *reflect* on them as such only *after the fact*. It certainly helps us to become involved, too, that these segments take up almost three-quarters of the total film.

The effectiveness of the adaptation, however, doesn't lie only in its greater immediacy—in questions of losses and gains and trade-offs. As it turns out, more of the novel's themes and materials have been retained than it might seem on first impression. It's just that they exist in the highly compressed form typical not only of film itself but also of the work of Harold Pinter. Surely the contrast between the wild and needy Sarah and the more controlled and independent Anna carries much of the book's commentary on the Victorian woman, on her evolution into the modern. Surely, too, we can find embodied in the contrasting relationships of Charles and Sarah and Mike and Anna much of the novel's speculation on the differences in sexuality between past and present. Where Sarah is darkly, obsessively passionate, Anna is easy and untroubled in her promiscuity. ("They'll think I'm a whore," she giggles when Mike answers the phone in her room one morning, revealing that he has spent the night in her bed; "You just had me in Exeter," she laughs when Mike, seeing her off on a train to London, declares his desire for her.) And where Charles ends up sacrificing everything for Sarah—his engagement and his valued position in society—Mike sacrifices little (and certainly not his wife), and also proves himself to be very timorous. (Consider the sequence in which, when Anna's French lover answers the phone in her hotel room, he immediately hangs up the receiver like a frightened adolescent.) In other words, where Fowles's narrator *tells* us that perhaps in the modern era "we have, in destroying so much of the mystery, the difficulty, the aura of the forbidden, destroyed also a great deal of the pleasure . . . the greater force," the film *shows* us the very same thing.

The film's two endings also go beyond a mere recapitulation of the novel's device to convey some of its implications. As in the novel, the two endings allow us to perceive the differences between the conventions of fiction, past and present; between reality and fiction; and between the way we imagine things to happen in fantasy and the way they actually occur in life. While the novel hints at the extent to which we not only sometimes confuse illusion and reality but actually try to impose one on the other, the film makes the point explicit. At the end of the movie, Mike, seeing Anna drive off and out of his life, cries out, "Sarah." For him, quite clearly, art has become indistinguishable from life or, perhaps, preferable to it. And we can see why. The "illusory" ending that has preceded this discomforting "realistic one" was a good deal more optimistic, offering a soft, romantic image of Charles and Sarah together in a boat on a lake. No wonder then that director Reisz chose to place that image on the screen again, as if in response to Mike's wishes—and our own as well. In this way, we at least have a chance to choose a happy (if make-believe) ending, should that be our preference—and this is the same chance we have in the novel.

In short, the film's solution to the problem of the novel's troublesome point of view is extraordinarily effective. But there's yet another explanation for this adaptation's special power, and I think quite a significant one. For the solution that Pinter and Reisz chose reflects and exquisitely expresses a persuasive reading of John Fowles's novel. It's a commentary on art, yes. It's an analysis of the Victorian age as well. It's even an existential exploration. But *The French Lieutenant's Woman* is above all, in their view, "a love story" (Pinter's own words)—a novel about romance, about the complexities of passion, about the intricacies of male-female relationships, and about the mysterious and illusory power of women.

Their reading certainly won't please everyone. But it seems to me one which not only is well supported by the novel but which penetrates its intellectual veneer right through to its romantic heart—and especially to its intensely romantic vision of woman. (Consider that it is the mysterious Sarah herself who works the greatest change on Charles—much more than society or history does.) And what more brilliant metaphor for the French Lieutenant's woman—who indeed is always playing roles, of which "the French Lieutenant's woman" itself is one—than actress? Admittedly, it may confuse matters a bit that Charles emerges as actor, too, but his "role" is nevertheless a much more straightforward and transparent one—both in art and in life.

Significantly enough, Fowles called the framing device itself a "brilliant metaphor" for the novel. It's a telling description and one that has application beyond *The French Lieutenant's Woman.* Recall that Martin Battestin, in discussing Tony Richardson's *Tom Jones,* put forth as the central principle of adaptation: "analogy is the key." To suggest that metaphor is the key instead is, of course, only to carry the principle one step further. Yet, it may be a larger step than it seems at first: since to conceive of adaptation as metaphoric process is to underscore the form's imaginative possibilities, to suggest the extent to which adaptation at its very best can be, rather than mere re-creation, something nearer creation itself.

Apocalypse Now: Misguided Journey to the Heart of Darkness

Though inspired by Joseph Conrad's classic tale *Heart of Darkness,* Francis Coppola's *Apocalypse Now* is the kind of film we don't ordinarily think of as an adaptation. And not simply because of its change of title. It doesn't acknowledge its literary source in its credits—they simply read: "Screenplay by John Milius and Francis Coppola; Narration by Michael Herr." Its setting is the Southeast Asian jungle in the 1960s; Conrad's is the African interior in the 1890s. And given that many of its characters (such as the spaced-out young surfer played by Sam Bottoms) and many of its events (a USO show featuring Playboy bunnies) have no precedent in Conrad (to say the least), it's clear that the film doesn't make any attempt to be faithful to Conrad's narrative or even to present itself as that narrative's equivalent.

Yet, whatever its alterations, however distant it may seem at first glance, *Apocalypse Now* remains not only deeply indebted to Conrad's tale but not fully comprehensible without reference to it—especially in its climactic sequence. Taking the shape of a riverboat journey to the very outposts of civilization, it borrows Conrad's structure. Focusing that journey on the quest for a once-great man now fallen on evil ways, it makes use of Conrad's central concept and central figure, even retaining many of that character's qualities—his baldness, the introduction of him as disembodied "voice," and, of course, his name. Many of its other characters also have roots in Conrad: Dennis Hopper's nutty photojournalist is patently a version of Conrad's Russian "harlequin"; the black pilot of the boat is a reincarnation of Conrad's black helmsman. Much of the film's imagery also has its source in Conrad: the "snake"-like quality of the river; the heavy fog that gathers immediately prior to the entry into Kurtz's compound; the film's chiaroscuro lighting as a whole. The film even borrows some of the story's specific language: in film as in tale, we are told that Kurtz's "methods" are "unsound"; that though he is sane in mind, his "soul is mad." And the movie certainly reiterates many of the story's themes. In *Apocalypse Now* just as in *Heart of Darkness*, the central journey is both a literal and a metaphoric one: a revelation of the destructive impulses beneath the civilized veneer of Western imperialism, a voyage of discovery into the dark heart of man, and an encounter with his capacity for evil.

In short, *Apocalypse Now* is very much an adaptation and one that holds implicit a reading of *Heart of Darkness* as relevant to the American experience in Vietnam. To the film's most sympathetic critics, it is precisely this interpretation (or better, reinterpretation) of Conrad that accounts for its brilliance—both in itself and as a model of adaptation. As one of these critics suggests, Coppola's approach to adaptation—if not quite as fully realized in *Apocalypse Now* as in the infinitely less ambitious *The Godfather*—nevertheless illustrates the extent to which "the adaptive auteur," by absorbing, expanding, and transforming the works of another into his own unique vision, can prove himself "just as personally expressive as a Bergman, Fellini, or Buñuel."

Though this writer probably values "personal expressiveness" a good deal more than I do, the point is very well taken. *Apocalypse Now* certainly could have served (in the manner of *The French Lieutenant's Woman*) as an illustration of adaptation's possibilities—had it only been successful in its own terms. But whatever the views of its defenders, the movie is highly problematic—a film that, though brilliant in much of its imagery (the cinematographer here is Vittorio Storaro) and filled with sequences that have a touch of greatness about them, ultimately disintegrates into dramatic and thematic confusion.

In fact, what the movie serves to illustrate (to my mind, at least) is less the possibilities of adaptation than its pitfalls. For if such brilliance as there is in *Apocalypse Now* rests, as some critics argue, chiefly in Coppola's updating of Conrad, it's also true that its problems derive from the very same source: from its failure to update Conrad consistently; from its muddled treatment of Kurtz; from the extent to which Conrad seems to have encouraged a considerable pretentiousness in Coppola; and most important of all, from the apparent failure of Coppola and Milius to read Conrad wisely and well. And the inadequacy of their reading is reflected in nothing so much as their failure to grasp the function of the novella's distinctive point of view both as a thematic and a structural device.

In Conrad, our guide into the heart of the darkness is the author's ubiquitous storyteller, Charlie Marlow. Introduced to us by an unnamed narrator as he and Marlow and a group of friends sit about at dusk on the deck of "a cruising yawl" anchored in the Thames, Marlow proceeds to relate what the narrator calls one of his friend's "inconclusive experiences." This took place in Africa where, as a young man, Marlow was employed by a European trading company as captain of a Congo steamboat and where, journeying up river to the heart of darkness, he encountered the monstrous ivory trader, "Mr. Kurtz."

Much has been made of this intricate introduction to the story and of the manner in which it distances us from Marlow's tale. Yet, it seems to me that any "distance" beyond that which Marlow himself provides by his telling of the tale in flashback is neither particularly crucial to *Heart of Darkness* nor particularly relevant to the problems of *Apocalypse Now*. More to the point is that Marlow is established through this framework as a man who may have encountered darkness, who may have known "the fascination of abomination," but who has returned to civilization to tell the tale. Friendly not only with the narrator but with such steadfast types as a lawyer and an accountant—the other listeners on the deck that evening—he has also evidently returned with his sanity and moral perspective intact. And though he's a man who may push a bit too hard at times (as the narrator himself indicates) for the inconclusiveness of experience—his vocabulary is sprinkled with such adjectives as "incomprehensible," "insoluble," "indefinable," "impossible," "inscrutable," "unfathomable," "unearthly," "incredible," "uncanny"—we still have faith in his perceptions and observations. In other words, Marlow is a man who proves wise enough (and even witty enough) to invite our trust and identification.

In *Apocalypse Now*, we are given as narrator and companion a different sort of man altogether. He is one Benjamin Willard, a regular army captain whose various special assignments have included that of hired assassin. ("How many people had I already killed?" he muses. "There were six that I knew about for sure.") Willard is also, in contrast to Marlow, a man estranged from civilization, a man whom we meet, significantly enough, not in peaceful London but in war-torn Saigon. Nor is he at home in the jungle either. Having served time in Vietnam, having been to the States and back again, he tells us: "When I was here I wanted to be there. When I was there, all I could think of was getting back into the jungle." Thus, though his tale of Kurtz is, like Marlow's, told to us in flashback, it begins at a point when he has already known a measure of darkness, evil, and horror and has already, it would seem, been devastated by the knowledge. Indeed, the film's opening sequence—reportedly not in John Milius's script—suggests that Willard, having internalized much of the madness of Vietnam, is himself most likely mad.

The very first shot itself—an enormous upside-down close-up of Willard's glazed eyes and perspiring face—makes the point, emphasizing the skewed nature of his perceptions. So does the series of fragmented images of helicopters, smoke and jungle fires, and a Buddha-like head that follow. Mounted in superimpositions and slow dissolves, which characterize the film's style as a whole, these images also express the instability of Willard's vision—and by extension of his entire personality. And if all this weren't enough to cast doubt on his sanity, Coppola also supplies us with the sight of a semi-nude Willard in his liquor-soaked hotel room, going through a weird, ritualistic dance that climaxes with his smashing his hand into a mirror.

One might argue that in substituting Willard for Marlow, a madman for a sane one, Coppola is working out a meaningful inversion of Conrad, suggesting that in contrast to Conrad's world, a sanity such as Marlow's is not possible in our own. Or, since the film never takes us outside Vietnam, at least suggesting that no one can live through the Vietnam experience and still come out sane. But even if the position were tenable, wouldn't it be more persuasively argued *after* Willard has met with Kurtz, rather than before? Similarly, though the images that constitute his perceptions are clearly flashforwards (we will see that Buddha head later at Kurtz's compound), wouldn't it make more sense if they were flashbacks instead—that is, if Willard's madness were a function of his meeting with Kurtz and not of some previous experience? In any case, Coppola's choice of unbalanced Willard as narrator/protagonist has ended up depriving the viewer of a point of entry or identification—especially considering that no one else in the film is sane either. Doing away with Conrad's frame, Coppola's film attempts to bring us closer to its narrator, while his subjective camera angles try to bring us closer still. But the treatment of character makes all of this beside the point; emotionally, we couldn't be further away.

This emotional gap is widened, moreover, by the strangely impassive performance of Martin Sheen in the role, as well as by the texture of his voice-over narration. Spoken in an unrelenting monotone, these commentaries are couched in an emphatically hard-boiled style that seems (as many observed at the time of the film's release) more appropriate to Raymond Chandler's Marlowe than to even a stand-in for Conrad's. Hardly a wise and careful observer, this man speaks in tough-guy banalities: "I was going to the worst place in the world and I didn't even know it yet"; "It was a real choice mission and when it was over, I never wanted another"; and, after entering Kurtz's compound, seeing bodiless heads lying about, and studying Kurtz's incriminating dossier, the ultimate understatement— "Everything I saw told me that Kurtz had gone insane." How can such a man serve as the viewer's surrogate? How can he convey any shock of recognition? How can he register his discovery of evil? How can he even know evil when he sees it? Well, he can't. Thus the film, having altered the story's central consciousness, is left not only without a point of entry, but without a moral center as well.

There are also insufficient possibilities for progressive development. In Conrad, the tale's narrative stance serves as more than point of sanity—it is the means by which the entire tale is structured. Marlow, for all his repetitions, for all his circular language, still tells his tale in such a way that it builds slowly, cumulatively, toward a climactic revelation. As we travel up the river with him, seeing everything through his civilized eyes, the disintegration and disorder of civilized values builds and intensifies. Further, he begins his journey upriver believing in Kurtz as a man of exceptional gifts and moral fiber, of genius and eloquence, unaware of Kurtz's fall into darkness. Marlow's voyage, then, becomes emphatically one of discovery.

In *Apocalypse Now*, everything works to undermine such progression and revelation. Willard embarks on his search not only already acquainted with horror and darkness, but already knowing that the once-great Colonel Kurtz has fallen—indeed, the whole point of the voyage is the special assignment to "terminate" Kurtz "with extreme prejudice." Moreover, the drama itself, rather than building from lesser horrors to greater ones, reaches it high point at dead-center of the journey, in Willard's encounter with Captain Kilgore. A manic cavalry officer (brilliantly played by Robert Duvall) who has traded in his horses for helicopters but nonetheless struts about in a cavalry hat and yellow ascot, Kilgore has a passion for Wagner (his helicopter is equipped with a tape recorder that blasts "Ride of the Valkyries" during attacks), for napalm (he tells us it "smells like victory"), and, finally, for surfing (he ruthlessly assaults an enemy village for the chief purpose of clearing a neighboring beach and riding waves). Still, like Colonel Kurtz, he is (as we are told) a good soldier—a commander who loves his men and whose men love him in turn—though, like Kurtz too, he is the good soldier driven mad. Critic Michael Wood goes so far as to suggest that Kilgore is more than merely like Kurtz: he *is* Kurtz, or at least should have been. Perhaps. (I, however, tend to agree with the view that Kilgore lacks sufficient moral stature and is too absurd a creation to carry such a burden.) But whatever the case, the fact is that the film has nowhere to go after this encounter—at least in the way of revealing the pervasive madness and horrors of the Vietnam experience.

And so, in some sort of desperation to find something more terrible yet than murder and insanity, some greater and more horrendous depths of corruption, Coppola suddenly turns away from "personal expressiveness" and back to *Heart of Darkness*. At the point where Willard and the young soldiers who man the riverboat on which he has been traveling come close to Kurtz's compound, Coppola even seems to leave both Vietnam and the twentieth century. Arrows—not bullets—fly; the boat pilot is impaled on a spear; and out of nowhere, ancient temples and statuary appear, as does a horde of savages decorated with war paint. And the problem isn't only that all of this is totally inconsistent with the rest of the film. It's also that Conrad's imagery seems to have been filtered through a sensibility weaned on old Tarzan movies. As for the figure of Kurtz, though closer in conception to Conrad than any of the other figures in the film, he seems to be Conrad interpreted by a college freshman who has just taken a course in T. S. Eliot and discovered Jungian archetypes in the process. The movie's Kurtz (as played by Marlon Brando) is not only, as in Conrad, an exemplar of a great man corrupted by power and solitude, of civilization gone wild in the face of savagery, of the depths of evil possible only to those with an extreme commitment to idealism, of a man who has faced up to his own heart of darkness and recognized the horror of it all. He is here a totally mythic figure and one who knows he is a myth. He sits about reading (as the camera pedantically informs us) Frazer's *Golden Bough* and Jessie Weston's *From Ritual to Romance*. He recites T. S. Eliot's "The Hollow Men"—whose epigraph is "Mistah Kurtz—he dead." He self-consciously awaits his own rit-ual slaughter, which the film supplies, even underscoring the symbolic na-ture of the act by intercutting shots of natives killing a carabao with those of Willard hacking up Kurtz. Worst of all, he is given to uttering such mumbo-jumbo as: "Horror has a face and you must make a friend of hor-ror . . . and moral terror. If they are not your friends, then they are ene-mies to be feared."

Nonetheless, as in Conrad, where Marlow sees in Kurtz his "secret sharer" and comes to admire him (despite his extremism and "unsound methods") because he has looked upon the darkness so steadily, had the courage to choose his nightmare and to "pronounce a judgment upon the adventures of the soul," so too does Willard presumably see himself in the inflated figure of Colonel Walter E. Kurtz. But though the recognition has a greater inevitability in Coppola than in Conrad—Marlow has revealed nothing about himself that would truly align him with Kurtz, whereas Willard and Colonel Kurtz are both mired in soldiery and murder—it also seems a good deal more pointless. After all, for a man like Marlow to dis-cover the darkness at the heart of man is truly a discovery, whereas for someone like Willard—a murderer confronting a murder, a madman face to face with madness—it amounts only to a tautology. What's more, identi-fying with the sensible and sane Marlow and seeing the world from his civi-lized point of view, we share his shock of recognition, perceiving the darkness he uncovers as something uncovered in ourselves. In contrast, since we are alienated from the unbalanced Willard, we remain alienated from his discovery. Thus, we also remain alienated from the film's apoca-lyptic vision as a whole—finding it, for all its spectacular images, for all its stunning set pieces, more hollow than all those hollow men Colonel Kurtz so solemnly intones.

Postscript

Back in the late thirties, Orson Welles had plans for making a film of *Heart of Darkness*—which was to be his very first Hollywood production. Significantly, Welles (unlike Coppola) was highly sensitive to the role of point of view in the tale, insisting so much on the identification of the viewer with Marlow, in fact, that the movie was to be shot in first person.

Like Robert Montgomery's Marlowe in *Lady in the Lake,* Welles's Marlow was to appear primarily as a narrative voice, seen on screen only reflected in mirrors or in the framing episodes of the film where, back on a boat in New York harbor (Welles also had updated Conrad and shifted his locale), he would be shown telling his story. Welles even went so far as to include a prologue to the film which, in his own words, was "intended to instruct and acquaint the audience as amusingly as possible with the [movie's] special technique" and in which Welles announced to the audience: *"You're not going to see this picture—this picture is going to happen to you."* Welles— whose design also underscored the secret-sharer theme—was also to play both key roles.

No doubt but that these devices are extremely self-conscious ones. And so, had Welles's *Heart of Darkness* actually made it to the screen, the chances are it would have emerged an equally self-conscious movie. But then again, who knows. Given Welles's insightful understanding of the importance of Conrad's rhetoric and his evident willingness to explore and expand the rhetorical possibilities of his own medium, his movie just might have ended up not simply a classic of adaptation but a classic exemplar of the imaginative adaptation of point of view.

6

Style and Tone

No element of fiction seems more difficult to translate from page to screen than style. No aspect of fiction is in fact more difficult to define. Is style manner, as opposed to matter, or is it a function of both? Is it something detachable from content or isn't it? In Strunk and White's *Elements of Style*—the slim little book that has instructed countless of us in "good writing"—style is defined as an "increment of writing," that is, as something we add to expression and that implicitly, then, is separate from ideas or content. Such a view of style has considerable historical precedent: "Expression is the dress of thought," Alexander Pope wrote in the eighteenth century. "It is not enough to know what to say, but it is necessary also to know how to say it," Aristotle noted 2,000 years earlier.

Nowadays, however, such a view of style has gone out of style itself, at least in the higher reaches of aesthetic discussion. Style and content are here viewed as inseparable, as part of an organic whole that constitutes any given writer's individuality, any given work's distinctive features. "To speak of style," writes Susan Sontag, "is one way of speaking about the totality of a work of art." And in her essay "On Style," this is the way Sontag herself broaches the matter. "The mask *is* the face," she tells us. "In almost every case, our manner of appearing *is* our manner of being."

That "in almost every case" somewhat undermines her argument, and Sontag is aware of the fact. Thus, she goes on to explain: in some works, style does indeed seem to be a separable element, though in such cases, style is no longer quite style, but what she calls "stylization."

> "Stylization" is what is present in a work of art precisely when an artist does make the by no means inevitable distinction between matter and manner, theme and form. When that happens, when style and subject are so distinguished, that is, played off against each other, one can legitimately speak of subjects being treated (or mistreated) in a certain style. Creative mistreatment is more the rule.

Divide style into "style" and "stylization," see the separation of style and subject as a clue to one work's lesser quality and their unity as a key to the success of another—we are still placed in the paradoxical position of maintaining a view of style as something inseparable from subject on the one hand and separable from it on the other. To make matters even more difficult, our experience tells us that we often perceive style as both separable and inseparable from substance at the same time—in the same work, that is. Not that Sontag isn't very much to the point when she notes that lesser artists tend to reveal a disjunction of form and content more strongly than do greater ones. We tend to speak of a writer like Truman Capote as an exquisite "stylist"—suggesting by the phrase that his style is decidedly more noteworthy than his content—whereas, although her style is also exquisite, we would be highly unlikely to refer to Virginia Woolf in such terms. Or to take the opposite extreme, consider a writer like Theodore Dreiser, whose "content" is usually admired but who is often said to have no style at all—meaning that his expression is flat and dull. We don't, however, make the same remark about Dostoyevsky, even though to most of us who have read him in stultifying translations, he would seem to have even less style than Dreiser.

Still, the fact of the matter is that even in the most fully realized works where style (in Sontag's terms) seems seamless, inevitable, and totally in harmony with substance, we find ourselves somehow capable of making a distinction between these two elements. Reading a work like Virginia Woolf's *Mrs. Dalloway*, we may feel that style *is* substance, that the manner in which Woolf orders her events and presents her characters is inseparable from her novel's vision, constituting a salient aspect of its themes. But at the very same time, we also remain aware of that *style* as *style*, of the *substance* of the novel as *substance*. We remain capable, that is, of distinguishing between the particular method that Woolf uses to render Clarissa Dalloway's world and Clarissa Dalloway's world in itself.

How is this possible? How is it that we can perceive style as both fused with and separable from substance at the very same time? Quite simply, I suspect (although of course it isn't simple at all), because any given work (indeed, any given statement) exists simultaneously on various strata and has various, albeit interrelated, levels of meaning. And whereas on certain of these levels, substance (or, put another way, theme) exists independent of style, on others it remains inextricably bound up with it. As a fairly simple example, take the phrases "I haven't any" and "I ain't got none," which on a connotative level carry very different charges but on a denotative one communicate the very same thing. A more complex instance is again *Mrs. Dalloway*. We can say that on one level, the novel is about middle age and death—a thematic strand which has little connection with its style. However, we can also say that on another level, it is a novel about perception that suggests the way in which we perceive events is more significant than those events themselves—a thematic strand that has everything to do with *Mrs. Dalloway*'s style, something expressed through its style above all.

But all of this notwithstanding, just what constitutes style anyway? Sometimes, style is a local concept, seen as situated just about exclusively in the verbal particulars of any given work: in a given writer's diction (flowery or plain; abstract or concrete; heavy or light in its use of adjectives and/or its use of tropes) and in his manner of constructing sentences (periodic or loose, long or short, rhythmic or stilted). Other times, style is a global concept, perceived as encompassing everything in a work—everything, that is, except "content." Used to refer to the total sum of an artist's decisions about how to present his materials, it includes not only such matters as language (or "verbal style") but the various narrative elements of a work that are, at other times, separated out into "structure." These are the point of view from which a story is told (first person, third person, omniscient); the organization of the plot (chronological or achronological, ordered according to time or according to space); and even the type of plot itself (epistolary like that of *Pamela*; episodic like that of *Moll Flanders* or any other picaresque tale). In this usage, style also includes modes of characterization (flat or round; through interior views or exterior ones) and, if not content itself, at least an author's selection of type of content (the "realistic" material of everyday life; the "romantic" material of high adventure and fantasy).

Global or local, however, there is one matter of style on which there tends to be general consensus: that "tone" is always crucial in determining it, indeed is sometimes synonymous with it. Consider the terms in which we tend to describe various styles: not simply ornate or plain, convoluted or straightforward, but passionate or unemotional, sentimental or ironic, or to borrow the terms used by one theorist of style, "tough, sweet," or "stuffy." Each of these terms, of course, carries with it a description of attitude, which is generally what is meant by "tone"—though it should come as no surprise by now (given the widespread disagreement on the meaning of just about any literary term) that not all theorists concur as to precisely what type of attitude tone embodies.

Thus, tone is sometimes used to refer to a writer's attitude towards his audience, to his sense of his relationship to those he is addressing. ("If you really want to hear about it, the first thing you'll probably want to know is where I was born, and what my lousy childhood was like, and how my parents were occupied and all before they had me, and all that David Copperfield kind of crap . . .," writes J. D. Salinger, setting up with direct address and highly colloquial language an informal, even intimate relationship, if not quite between himself and his audience, at least between his audience and his surrogate speaker, Holden Caulfield.) The more usual usage of tone, however, makes reference to an author's attitude not only toward his audience, but toward his material as well. ("NOTICE: Persons attempting to find a motive in this narrative will be prosecuted; persons attempting to find a moral in it will be banished; persons attempting to find a plot in it will be shot," writes Mark Twain at the outset of *Huckleberry Finn*—the striking incongruity between the official language and the decidedly unofficial content, and between crimes and punishment as well, establishing the author's wry attitude *both* toward his readers and toward the novel to follow.) Whichever, tone is always a matter of emotional stance. Moreover, as certain theorists of style have demonstrated forcefully, and as the examples by Twain and Salinger should suggest, it is also (whatever else it might be) always very much a function of language.

It is, of course, because of their seemingly inextricable bond with language that style and tone seem so elusive to the moviemaker who adapts a work of fiction to the screen. The language of fiction and the language of film being so different in nature, style in film must be constructed out of totally different elements: pictorial decor and composition; camera movement and editing; transitional devices and lighting; score and sound effects, and so on. There's the flamboyant style of Fellini, made up of the carnival-like atmosphere of his settings, the grotesque faces and figures of the actors who populate them, the swirling camera movements, the exaggerated contrasts of both lighting and color, the insistently bittersweet scores inevitably provided by Nino Rota. There's the "spiritual" or "transcendental" style of a filmmaker like Robert Bresson which is a function of (among other things) his penchant for long-held shots and close-ups, for spartan imagery (such as a face shown against a dark and undistinguished background), for carefully modulated editing in which the characteristic transition is the slow fade rather than the direct cut.

But if the specific techniques by which one mounts style in film differ from those by which one creates style in fiction, this still doesn't quite explain just why translation should be considered so difficult. To begin with, since the same varying definitions apply, style can be seen not simply as a function of the specific properties of the medium—of its distinctive language and techniques; it can also be seen as a function of other elements besides—structure, modes of characterization, content itself, all of which are much more easily transferred from one medium to another than are qualities of language. Additionally, if style is, as some would claim, the expression of an artist's individuality (and thus resistant to adaptation, where another artist's individuality intercedes), style is also often the expression of quite the opposite: of an artist's tie with other artists, of his link with an entire period. We don't only speak of the Romantic style of Byron; we speak of the style of the Romantic poets. In fact, we tend to speak of Romanticism as a whole—as the style of an entire period which permeates not just the work of a single artist, or even the work of a group of artists or a single art, but the arts as a whole. We find reflections of Romanticism, of Mannerism, of Realism in all of the humanities. (The Neo-Classical style, for example,—with its emphasis on formal precision, its characteristic balance and symmetry, its ideals of common sense, reason, restraint—is found reflected in painting, sculpture, music, literature, architecture, even the arrangement of gardens.)

Because of this, it would seem evident that, as Wylie Sypher puts it, "styles have a life of their own," separate from any individual expression of them. What's more, whatever the differences in medium and content found in the various arts, a particular style can still find expression in them. There are analogous modes of organization, analogous techniques as well. Indeed, the techniques of one art may even penetrate another, causing what Sypher terms "ambiguous transformations of style." Thus, he explains, "the medium of music is not the medium of painting or literature; but the tone poem in music uses techniques that are pictorial and narrative. . . ."

We even think of style as being sufficiently unified in any given period (although, of course, it's more unified in some than others) to serve as an expression of the values, the sensibility, the entire vision of that time. In his study of existentialism, philosopher William Barrett calls up "the testimony of modern art," isolating certain of modern art's stylistic features as reflective of the same break with tradition that characterizes existentialist philosophy. And significantly, he finds this "flattening out of all planes" (either spatial or temporal), "flattening out of climaxes," and "flattening out of values" equally as characteristic of modern literature as of modern painting.

Clearly, if we can find analogous stylistic features and analogous techniques in paintings and plays, in buildings and gardens and poems, we can also find them in fiction and film. And we can find them both in the general style of any given period (parallels, for example, between the styles of much early silent film and Victorian melodrama) and in the individual style of any particular artist. Wipes and freezes and pans may be cinematic techniques; hyperbole and apostrophe and personification may be linguistic ones; but in Tony Richardson's *Tom Jones*, the one set of techniques works analogously with the other in creating similar stylistic effects. Richardson, moreover, has managed to find cinematic equivalents not simply for the global elements of Fielding's style—for his loose episodic structure, his pervasive strategy of characterization by caricature—but for his verbal style as well.

What is it then that makes style so difficult to translate from fiction to film? (And all evidence suggests that, the likes of *Tom Jones* notwithstanding, it is.) Partly, it's the imaginative challenge of finding those analogous techniques. An even greater problem, however, lies in grasping any given piece of fiction's style in the first place. Style, as we've seen, is embodied in so many elements, in so many different aspects of any work—in its structure, language, content, vision—and comes in so many varieties and types (sincere, artificial, dignified, comic, original, imitative, dull or vivid, not to mention the categories of style cited earlier, like "tough, sweet, and stuffy") that it often requires extraordinary sensitivity on the part of the reader to detect and define it. In life as well as in art, we often don't pick up on the emotional tenor of a given speaker's statements. (Is he joking? Is he being ironic? Or does he intend us to take what he's saying straight?) Yet, if we don't, in art as in life once again, we totally miss the point. Style in some instances then doesn't simply constitute one level of meaning; it totally controls all other levels as well. Moreover, the fault doesn't always lie with the listener, reader, or viewer. If detecting tone is now and then enormously difficult for an audience, controlling it is often very difficult for the artist.

And there's a further problem. Many styles, linked not simply to individual artists but to entire periods, have a tendency to date. They belong to a certain point in history, to a certain set of values, to a certain way of seeing the world. (Susan Sontag in fact suggests that the notion of style, "generically considered, has a specific historical meaning," and that "visibility of styles is itself a product of historical consciousness.") Encountering a work of another period that consequently belongs to a stylistic tradition different from our own, we will frequently (if it has other qualities to make up for the fact) forgive it certain of its stylistic and tonal tendencies. We will forgive Dickens, let's say, both his Victorian sentimentality and his manner of constructing plot via coincidental contrivances. Of course, we don't forgive the style completely—you'd have to have a heart of stone, Oscar Wilde reminded us, not to laugh at the death of Little Nell. But to adapt *The Old Curiosity Shop* to film, to show us the death of Little Nell, that is, in the context of a *contemporary* work of art, would seem even more unacceptable. There would simply have to be some major tonal modulation, some reordering of values and vision. And sometimes, the failure of an adaptation will lie precisely in the failure of the filmmaker in turn to make such adjustments, to make the style and tone of his adaptation analogous to those of the original yet still appropriate and acceptable to the present.

Thus, once again, the issue is above all one of interpretation—only here, quite specifically, of the interpretation of style: the extent to which a filmmaker who would adapt fiction to film has been able to distinguish the original's structural strategies, verbal patterns, and tonal qualities and has also understood the relevance of all of this to the work's total effect. For though no piece of fiction (and no work of art, in fact) is ever without any style at all, style is still more crucial to the total experience and ultimate scheme of some works than it is to others. In the discussions that follow, then, each of the films in question—*Women in Love, Ragtime, Tess,* and *Daisy Miller*—is based on a piece of fiction in which style and tone are of very special importance to the texture of the whole. In each instance, too, the relative success or failure of the film emerges as a matter of whether or not the filmmaker has been able to discover analogous strategies for rendering that tone and style—though what that success depends on even more is the quality of the filmmaker's insight into their nature and significance in the first place.

Women in Love: Style as Daring

Richard Aldington called his biography of D. H. Lawrence *Portrait of a Genius, But. . . .* That "but," of course, not only hovers over Lawrence's life, it also hovers over all of his works—and over none so much perhaps as *Women in Love,* the novel considered to be his masterpiece. Even its most passionate defender, F. R. Leavis, admits that the novel is a troubling one: "I have not always thought *Women in Love* one of the most striking works of creative originality that fiction has to show." But though Leavis goes on to state that he has formed a higher opinion of the novel at each rereading—other critics make similar points, and the novel is indeed one of those curiously flavored works that, like champagne and caviar, you probably have to develop a taste for—he also concedes that there's no way around its faults.

What makes this especially true is that those faults—the mysteriousness of the relationships at the novel's center, the elusiveness of some of its characterizations, the wild absurdities of many of its actions (Gudrun dancing in front of cattle, Birkin rolling naked in the grass), the overinsistence and repetitiousness of its language, the references to the likes of "blood knowledge" and "mystic union," or, as Leavis puts it, the endless "jargon"—are at the very same time a crucial source of the novel's power. They carry its sensuality, they give it its oddly mesmerizing quality, they account for its peculiar grandeur. In other words, *Women in Love* isn't a novel that achieves greatness in spite of its problems, as some have argued; it's a novel whose greatness derives in large part from those very problems themselves.

The same might be said about Ken Russell's adaptation. As its numerous detractors have pointed out, the movie is overwrought and overstated, extravagant and excessive; it might even be rightly dubbed "purple." And it's easy to argue with many of its choices: from its frequently bizarre camera angles and editing, to its selection of materials and its various interpolations, to its casting. (The dark Oliver Reed, for example, appears in the role of the nordic Gerald.) Yet Ken Russell's *Women in Love* (based on a script by Larry Kramer) is a film which, like Lawrence's novel, has an insistent, inescapable power. Far from equal to Lawrence—indeed, the movie makes clear Russell's conscious and adamant refusal to subscribe to Lawrence totally—it still manages to bring us extraordinarily close to the novelist, creating effects strikingly similar to those found in his work. The film accomplishes this not by fidelity to the letter of the novel, not by repeating particular novelistic strategies, but by its own kind of fidelity to the Lawrentian spirit and by mounting a series of original and daring strategies that capture much of Lawrence's distinctive style and tone.

In plot and structure, the film follows the novel fairly closely—it is built out of a series of parallels and contrasts, at the center of which are two intense and intensely polarized, highly symbolic relationships. On the one hand, there's that of Midlands schoolteacher Ursula Bragwen and Lawrence stand-in Rupert Birkin, a relationship with an ultimate pull toward life and affirmation; and on the other, that of her painter sister Gudrun and industrial magnate Gerald Crich, which climaxes in death and destruction. As in the novel, these central relationships are mirrored by various subsidiary ones: those between the two women and between the two men; between Rupert and the wealthy art patroness Hermione Roddice; between Gudrun and the grotesque German sculptor Loerke.

Where the film differs from the novel is in the inevitable omission of various of these minor strands and characters (the novel, after all, goes on for nearly 500 leisurely pages; the film is only two and a half hours in length), and in the equally inevitable compression of the strands it does retain—though some of the compression is so masterly that it minimizes the loss. For example, the film conveys in only a few brief minutes of flashback much of the sensual suggestiveness of the chapter-length scene of Birkin discoursing in the classroom on catkins; while, though omitting Gerald's entire relationship with Pusette and thus the novel's means of dramatizing Gerald's promiscuity, it makes a very similar point with only a single shot of him walking out of a bar one evening, a lady of the night on each of his arms.

Unlike the novel, too, where Lawrence's pattern of counterpoint is quite oblique, the film makes these parallels and oppositions more insistent and more apparent. Although this is partly a function of the film's compression, and the change in medium as well, it is also clearly a conscious decision on the filmmakers' part. Take the cinematography (by Billy Williams) as evidence. The scenes between Rupert and Ursula tend to be brightly lit, situated in daytime and frequently outdoors. The scenes between Gerald and Gudrun, in contrast, tend to be set in interiors and most often at night—with the pervading darkness serving both to comment on the texture of their relationship and to provide an ironic contrast with the later climactic scenes of that relationship's ultimate destruction which, as in Lawrence, takes place in the glaring whiteness of the snowy Alps.

The design of the individual shots frequently serves a similar end. The film, for example, makes considerable use of mirrors, most notably in the scene where Birkin expounds to Gerald his view that authentic love between man and man is as essential as love between man and woman. As Birkin puts forth his belief and as Gerald haltingly expresses doubt, we keep seeing first one man and then the reflection of the other, then the other man and the reflection of the other in turn, our vision continually doubled and disoriented. Thus, the contrasts between these two men and their views are underscored, as is—even more pointedly—the elusiveness of their relationship.

Russell's editing also follows the principle of contrast and commentary—as when during the party at the Crich home, he selects to intercut Ursula and Birkin's first unhappy attempt at making love with shots of a drowned bride and groom, both couples revealed in nearly identical positions. In the novel, the event takes a different form, and some critics have therefore taken exception to the film's treatment. (In the novel, it isn't Gerald's newly married sister but an unmarried one who drowns, and it isn't her husband she drags down to death, but a doctor who attempts to rescue her. Also, Ursula and Birkin don't make love at this point in the novel but merely declare their affection.) Still, whatever the changes, the thrust is very much the same: in both, a woman throws her arms about a man and ends up killing him; in both, love is inextricably entwined with death.

The film also manages to duplicate, frequently through analogy, the novel's rich fund of suggestive imagery. And it is precisely this imagery that goes a long way in explaining what makes the novel seem so blatant and yet so strangely elusive at the same time. For in Lawrence's pages, there's hardly a descriptive line that doesn't carry some thematic import. There's also rarely a single gesture that doesn't make more sense as an emblematic, and often puzzlingly so, expression of Lawrentian views than as an ordinary human action—whether it's Birkin throwing pebbles at the moon's reflection in a pond, or Gerald and Gudrun being attacked by the same violent rabbit, or Hermione staging a "little ballet" in Russian style at a party in her home.

It's Russell's parallel technique of investing imagery with symbolic import that makes the film also seem dense and overrich, with some of the most heavily packed images of all derived directly from the novel. There's the extraordinarily dramatic image of Gerald cruelly subduing a mare that reflects what Lawrence himself might term Gerald's "will to domination" and that also excites in Gudrun the desire to rise to the challenge. There's the equally startling one of Birkin and Gerald wrestling nude in an attempt at confirmation of a *Blutbruderschaft*. Other images come, if not from *Women in Love*, at least from other works of Lawrence—such as Birkin's lecture on the appropriate way to eat a fig, inspired by a Lawrence poem. Still others, however, are strictly the film's invention. These include Gudrun lying on a gravestone when, as in the novel, she and Ursula watch the Crich wedding—but, unlike the novel, from the vantage point of the church cemetery; Gerald and his father, captured in a dramatic crane shot while driving home from the mines in a huge Rolls Royce whose whiteness contrasts brilliantly with the gray, dusty workers surrounding it; Gudrun and Ursula passing a couple who are sourly pushing a baby carriage precisely at the moment that the two sisters are discussing the negative aspects of marriage.

Some critics have found such images obvious, facile and/or sensational. John Simon complained about both the exposure of male genitalia and the homosexual coloration of the wrestling scene—as if it would have been possible to play the scene dressed without changing its sense entirely, or as if that coloration wasn't precisely Lawrence's. But though it's not very difficult to demonstrate the aptness of Russell's choices in conveying the texture and sense of the Lawrence original or the rightness of his interpolations, either—in the novel, for example, there's sufficient prefiguring and linking of death and love to justify the film's image of Gudrun lying on a gravestone immediately after witnessing a marriage—it's a good deal more of a challenge to defend them from charges of overstatement. The simple fact is, however, that it's equally hard to so defend Lawrence. All one can really suggest is that if that nude wrestling scene, those mad dances, and those sensual figs are taken away, you simply no longer have *Women in Love*—whether it's on page or screen.

So it is with Lawrence's overheated prose style and Russell's hyperbolic cinematic one. Both stand not only as instances of the inseparability of flaws from flavor in both book and film, but also very much in analogous relationship. Abstract in diction, loaded with metaphor, heavily cadenced, highly repetitious, often periodic and intricate in structure, and overrun with so much parallelism that it frequently sounds almost Biblical, Lawrence's prose breaks every rule in the book. Take the following almost incantatory passage:

> There was a pause of strange enmity between the two men, that was very near to love. It was always the same between them; always their talk brought them into a deadly nearness of contact, a strange, perilous intimacy which was either hate or love, or both. They parted with apparent unconcern, as if their going apart were a trivial occurrence. And they really kept it to the level of trivial occurrence. Yet the heart of each burned from the other. They burned with each other, inwardly.

Or this one, in which Lawrence builds a typically Lawrentian metaphor:

> And all the while his wife [Mrs. Crich] had opposed him like one of the great demons of hell. Strange, like a bird of prey with the fascinating beauty and abstraction of a hawk, she had beat against the bars of his philanthropy, and like a hawk in a cage, she had sunk into silence. By force of circumstance, because all the world combined to make the cage unbreakable, he had been

too strong for her, he had kept her prisoner. And because she was his prisoner, his passion for her had always remained keen as death. He had always
loved her, loved her with intensity.

Prose is prose and film is film; nonetheless, there is a similarity of effect
in Russell's strategies: in the rapid series of overlapping dissolves which
capture the sight of Gudrun rolling about in the grass before Gerald, immediately after her weird dance in front of the cattle; in the brief
intercutting of shots of Gudrun laughing as Gerald treks through the
snow to his death at the end, or of his mother hysterical at his father's
funeral during an early scene of the two making love; in the presentation
of horizontal images from a vertical perspective during the scene in which
Ursula and Birkin first successfully consummate their love; in the series of
pulsating zooms which punctuate the final and brutal lovemaking of Gudrun and Gerald; in the use of slow motion during Birkin's wild nude run
through the forest; and in the film's lavish decor and luxuriant cinematography. If, as in Lawrence, we find ourselves overwhelmed, it seems to me
that's precisely the point.

What is decidedly less the point is that some of these strategies are intended to create comic effects. One critic argues that the turning of the
camera on its side is intended as satiric commentary on Birkin and
Ursula's lovemaking; another suggests that a comic aura pervades their
first unsuccessful love scene, the one intercut with the drowning. I
couldn't disagree more; still, such readings can't be totally ignored. For
they exemplify the danger involved in the overstatement Russell is prone
to both in his editing and in his camera angles, and the ease with which
the ecstatic and passionate can quickly become absurd. Lawrence too has
always struck many readers as somewhat ludicrous, and like Lawrence,
Russell has frequently been mocked as well. Not that this apparent failure
to control tone is in any way to be lauded, either in Lawrence or Russell.
And not that Russell is to be praised, either, for translating Lawrence's
faults together with his intensity. It's rather that it seems impossible to
capture one extreme and not the other. To replicate Lawrence's effects—to try to create a similar hecticness, a comparable insistence, a
sense of the rhythmical force of his language which, despite all those references to "loins" and "blood knowledge" and "mystic union," manages
to carry you along with it—is also to take Lawrence's risks. This, it seems
to me, is very much what Russell has done.

Still, if the film parallels the novel in many ways, it also departs from it radically—especially in its characterizations. And though at first glance, it might seem that such departure is most extreme in the treatment of Gerald, this isn't really the case. We may not be able to see in Oliver Reed's Gerald, Lawrence's "nordic god," nor do we find embodied in him either much of Lawrence's ambitious critique of European industrial civilization. (The film generally dismisses the novel's sociopolitical themes altogether in fact, implying, I think, that its strength tends to lie instead in its immediate view of male/female relations.) But Reed does convey—and powerfully—the brooding darkness of the man, the sense of disconnected sensuality, the overwhelming force of his will to dominate, and the pathological attraction he feels toward death. Glenda Jackson's Gudrun, while somewhat altered from Lawrence's original, also retains much of what is essential to her. Many of the changes in the character seem chiefly a matter of adjustment for period. For what was regarded as the New Woman in Lawrence's day isn't quite what might be the New Woman in ours, and to deliver a sense of Gudrun's "difference," certain qualities had to be intensified. Thus, Gudrun on film is harder, stronger, more explicitly sexual than she is in the novel, and as such, she is a perfect complement and adversary to Gerald. This again seems unmistakably Lawrence's point, because the failure of these two to achieve a perfect union is above all a failure to bend their wills to one another, to submit to one another, and so, to truly love.

Moreover, where Gerald literally chooses death in the end, Gudrun chooses a kind of death too—a Lawrentian darkness or death-in-life, embodied in her choice to go away with the sculptor Loerke. Many of the film's critics found much to complain about in the treatment of this figure. He was, they said, more sinister on film than in the novel, more perverse, he was even, as John Simon asserted, turned into a homosexual! But one can only wonder at the Loerke these critics imagined. Not only is he described in the novel as traveling with a companion who just happens to be "a large fair young man," not only is he dubbed by Birkin "a little obscene monster of the darkness," but at one point Lawrence goes so far as to write that Gudrun chooses him because for her ". . . there were no new worlds, there were no more men, there were only creatures, little, ultimate *creatures* like Loerke." Is it really either so farfetched or such a "vulgarization," then, to dramatize Loerke as a decadent homosexual?

Where the film does go against the novel's grain is in its handling of Birkin and Ursula, or rather—since Ursula (inspired by Frieda Lawrence) doesn't really come across in the novel as quite the earth mother she's evidently supposed to be, but as a character very much of a piece with Jennie Linden's often simple, puzzled, though deeply loving woman—chiefly in its handling of Birkin. The film may allow him his moments of passionate conviction: his communion with nature, his authentic sorrow at Gerald's death. It may take him and his now-and-then-mad ideas a good deal more seriously than it does Hermione and her pretentious Bohemian world, which can look quite silly, even without Russell's exaggeration, from the present-day vantage point. But unlike the novel, the film distances itself from this Lawrentian self-portrait, and in Alan Bates's performance, Birkin emerges lighter, less mysteriously agonized, much less of a thinker to be reckoned with than his novelistic counterpart. At certain moments the film even regards him with a degree of irony, going so far as to give a tinge of the absurd to many of his disquisitions about women, love, and relationship. Consider for example that during his speech about the fig, Russell pans the listeners at the table, registering their bemused and/or embarrassed responses—responses which the camera seems to invite us to share.

In other words, though the film isn't truly harsh on Birkin/Lawrence, it does tend to call certain of his views into question, and it isn't all that difficult to understand just why. Birkin is, after all, the novel's most troubling, most unrealized character. He is also the often strident spokesman for the most extreme of Lawrence's views: views about transcendent maleness, mystical union, love that goes beyond love, about the need of men for both the love of women and the world of men, and that of women for love alone—views for which many have attacked Lawrence violently and that strike even the most sympathetic of us as discomforting. It is these views, moreover, and not (as some have argued) his "purple prose" that truly make for what is "bad" in Lawrence. They are certainly what we have to allow for in order to appreciate his genius.

Does Russell's implicit criticism, then, constitute a betrayal of Lawrence? That's one way of viewing it. Yet, one also must remember how much of Lawrence Russell has managed to capture, how richly he's grasped his tone and style—which is in Lawrence what really counts—and how involving and suggestive a film he has made in the process. Thus, in the end, Russell's *Women in Love* seems to me less a betrayal than an appreciation of Lawrence, and an adaptation that (whatever its flaws) emerges an ideal instance of its kind—an adaptation, that is, which manages to be a commentary on one work of art by another, a celebration of one artist by another, and a work of art in its own right, all at the very same time.

Ragtime: Missing the Beat

If there was any contemporary novel that seemed destined for the screen, it was E. L. Doctorow's *Ragtime.* Witty and elegant, wry and nostalgic, it was a runaway bestseller, earning the highest paperback reprint sale as of that date in publishing history. It was also highly respected for its technical innovation and thematic resonance and considered serious and substantial enough to warrant discussion in academic quarterlies. Populated with a variety of colorful characters, it was set in a picturesque past characterized by dynamic social change—America in the pre-World War I years, America in her not-so-innocent age of innocence.

What's more, it has something in it for everyone. Telling the separate but intertwined tales of three representative families—one immigrant and Jewish, another WASP and middle class, still another black—*Ragtime* gives nearly all of us a chance to identify with our roots. And introducing another layer of narrative featuring actual figures—from anarchist/feminist Emma Goldman, to escape artist Harry Houdini, to industrial wizard Henry Ford and financier J. P. Morgan—it offers the recognition of meeting up with people and events familiar to us from history. Moreover, it gives these actual figures fictional life. Daring to penetrate consciousness, it reveals their thoughts; daring to play around with history, it places them in imaginary situations: Emma Goldman meets modern-day courtesan Evelyn Nesbit; Evelyn Nesbit has an affair with a member of the fictional WASP family, Mother's Younger Brother. Paralleling this technique, it then situates its imaginary characters in the midst of actual historical happenings. Tateh, the Jewish socialist immigrant, gets involved in the famous Lawrence textile strike; Father, head of the WASP household, travels with Admiral Peary to the Pole; and black pianist Coalhouse Walker, Jr., meets with Booker T. Washington. The result? An expansive, textured vision of American life and suggestive teasing of our assumptions about history, fiction, and reality itself.

But though the novel provides the wide-ranging appeal for which movies characteristically aim, it wasn't only content that made *Ragtime* seem so apt for film. It was also, and more importantly, the novel's form. Its broad-based, sweeping perspective is suggestive of the panoramic camera eye. Its fluid series of rapidly shifting episodes are reminiscent of movie sequences.

Its sharply etched images—J. P. Morgan shivering in the King's Chamber of the Great Pyramid at Giza, Freud and Jung on their visit to America riding through Coney Island's Tunnel of Love—have the staying power of freeze-frames. Its manner of making character inhere in action and appearance—so that Theodore Dreiser's sense of failure and frustration is encased in his crazy gesture of endlessly moving his chair in circles through an entire sleepless night, so that Stanford White's joviality is reflected in his burliness—also has a cinematic quality. And the novel's prose style, frequently said to be music-like and thereby reflective of the metaphor implicit in the novel's title, can also be seen as characterized by a strongly cinematic quality.

Consider a passage like the following:

> Women were stouter then. They visited the fleet carrying white parasols. Everyone wore white in summer. Tennis racquets were hefty and the racquet faces elliptical. There was a lot of sexual fainting. There were no Negroes. There were no immigrants. On Sunday afternoon, after dinner, Father and Mother went upstairs and closed the bedroom door.

Musical in texture or not, the clipped sentences and rapid rhythms also have the feel of movie shots, while the piling of image on image has the inescapable resonance of rapid editing, of the tension and conflict of montage. And if the book's counterpointed narrative strands are reminiscent of the counterpointed themes of ragtime, if in the manner of ragtime music "the left hand provides a bass line of historical events . . . [while] the right hand furnishes repetitions, improvisations and call-and-answer figures," that same syncopation and simultaneity of effect once again have parallels in cinematic strategies: in crosscutting, in multi-exposure, in asynchronous sound.

How was it then that the multi-million-dollar production of *Ragtime* managed to end up such a disappointment—a work that managed both to betray its source and to emerge stiff and stolid in itself? How especially did it fail, given not only the cinematic potential of the novel, but the impressive gifts of all those involved? The director was Milos Forman, who had done so well by Ken Kesey's *One Flew Over the Cuckoo's Nest* and had even managed to give life to his version of the then-dated *Hair*. The screenplay was by noted playwright Michael Weller, author of the widely praised play *Moonchildren*. Its cinematographer was Forman's previous collaborator Miroslav Ondricek, who had provided the distinctive visual quality of *Hair*, Lindsay Anderson's *If . . .* , and George Roy Hill's *Slaughterhouse-Five*. Its music was by highly original pop composer Randy Newman. And its casting seemed extremely apt. Paralleling the novel's mixture of the real and the fictional, of the known and unknown, the film included familiar old-timers like James Cagney, Pat O'Brien, and Donald O'Connor, together with a host of less familiar stars: Brad Dourif as Younger Brother, Elizabeth McGovern as Evelyn Nesbit, James Olson as Father, Mandy Patinkin as Tateh, Howard E. Rollins as Coalhouse Walker, Jr., Mary Steenburgen as Mother.

Was it that the filmmakers changed the narrative? Did they interpolate too much? Did they omit and compress too much? Or did they do both at once? Was it that they altered the characters in very significant ways? Was it that, appearances to the contrary, the casting missed the mark? Or was it that what seemed cinematic on page didn't turn out to be cinematic on screen? It was all of these, and still none of them. For the most crucial reason for *Ragtime*'s peculiarly flawed and flat realization on screen was the filmmakers' implicit failure to grasp the significance of the novel's structure and style—their failure to perceive that it is the novel's style that accounts for its special appeal, that makes for its distinctive texture, that carries the burden of its themes. And the result—and evidence—of that implicit failure in interpretation was their failure in turn to render anything equivalent to that style on screen.

Consider the filmmakers' choice to replace the novel's unusual narrative design with a much more traditional structure. Narrowing its multiple focus, they concentrated heavily and lengthily on but one of its several stories: that of black pianist Coalhouse Walker who, after the desecration of his Model T by racist fire chief Willy Conklin, is incited to lay siege to the Morgan Library and whose tale constitutes nearly half of the film—with the last half of that in turn given over to the Morgan Library sequence alone. True, Doctorow too gave the tale more space than any other of his plot elements, making Coalhouse the novel's main personality. But Coalhouse didn't exist in the novel, as he does in the film, at the expense of dissipating the story of immigrant Tateh to the extent that it becomes near cliché; or of so reducing middle-class Father and Mother that the characters fail to go through any of the changes which made them and their story matter; or, in other words, of drastically reducing *Ragtime*'s scope.

Consider, too, the filmmakers' even more damaging choice to do away with almost all of the novel's rich fund of historical materials—once again, it would seem, in order to make the narrative more traditional. (What other reason could there be? Certainly not length. At 305 generously spaced pages, *Ragtime* the novel is fairly short; whereas at 2 hours and 35 minutes, *Ragtime* the movie is relatively long.) Gone is Emma Goldman; gone are Freud and Jung; gone is Henry Ford; gone except for a brief glimpse is Harry Houdini; gone except for an even briefer one is J. P. Morgan. And as with character, so with event. Gone is the Lawrence textile strike in which Tateh participated (and with it, the fact that Tateh was a socialist); gone are Father's voyage to the Pole, his ironic death carrying munitions to Europe on the *Lusitania*, and the sad end of Younger Brother as Mexican revolutionary and follower of Emiliano Zapata. And gone with them are the novel's political thrust and radical sentiments, its historical vision of the pre–World War I period, and nearly all of its vision of history itself.

What is also gone is the novel's amusingly suggestive game of illusion and reality—a game Doctorow played with us not simply through his inclusion of historical materials but through his precise manner of working them into his text. Moving from fact to fiction to fact again in the space of a few pages, sometimes in the space of a single sentence—"As it happened, Houdini's visit had interrupted Father and Mother's coitus"—Doctorow is continually breaking down the boundaries between the real and imaginary. He also creates a simultaneity of effect in such instances as when the firebombing of the fictitious Emerald Isle Fire Engine Company is heard during one of Houdini's performances. The film, in contrast, opts for a much more conventional strategy in handling the few historical materials left to it: that of giving us pieces of period atmosphere and glimpses of period personalities in the form of a series of black-and-white, under-cranked images simulating newsreels. Ostensibly clever, the device is in fact misconceived—or at least misused. For, except in a single telling instance when Harry K. Thaw's mother is shown in a black-and-white "newsreel" only to have her image flush into color and into the main action of the film, the device serves—in diametric opposition to Doctorow—to set history at a careful distance from fiction.

Not that other images in the newsreels aren't also brought into the fictional strand. Booker T. Washington, shown in an early newsreel having dinner with the President, is later sent into the Morgan Library to try to reason with Coalhouse; while Sarah, the mother of Coalhouse's baby, shows up at the New Rochelle campaign stop of Vice President Sherman, also shown earlier in a newsreel. But both the brevity of the first glimpse and the time lapse between the black-and-white "factional" shot and the "fictional" one tend, in each case, to weaken the link. And the device certainly doesn't work, as do the much more complex and suggestive ones of the novel, to put quotation marks around historical reality and to call our sense of "fact" into question.

The film's editing also belies the novel's methods. Typically, the novel moves from scene to scene according to the principle of association, going from the funeral of Sarah to Harry Houdini at his mother's graveside; or from Tateh and the Little Girl riding the trolley to Massachusetts, to a celebration of "Tracks! Tracks!" and a rumination on methods of transportation, to an accident that occurred during the building of the Brooklyn Battery Tunnel. The novel's organization, then, tends to be spatial, expansive, ironic. Not so the film. It moves from sequence to sequence in a totally linear and chronological fashion. We go from Evelyn Nesbit testifying at Harry K. Thaw's trial, to Evelyn riding about the Lower East Side and meeting up with Tateh and the Little Girl, to Tateh and the Little Girl (some time later) in Philadelphia, back to Evelyn (sometime later, again) looking for them on the Lower East Side. The film even manages to provide a logical link between the newsreels and the main action by making Coalhouse the movie pianist—doing away with the newsreels, significantly enough, at the point when he changes jobs. Indeed, the only time the film tries for the kind of striking juxtaposition we find in the novel is when it cuts from Sarah and Coalhouse discussing their upcoming wedding to Sarah lying bridelike on her bier—an effect that is nonetheless so blatant as to convey nothing resembling the novel's sharp ironies.

But director Forman doesn't only fail to replicate Doctorow's narrative style; he also fails to grasp the novel's tone. The jaunty rhythms, the lyric lilt of its sentences find no expression here at all. To the contrary, there's hardly a shot (save for those in the newsreels) which isn't held long; not a sequence which isn't played out slowly, even langorously. The upshot is that the film's rhythm, rather than duplicating the snappy, syncopated feeling of ragtime, is a good deal closer to ritardando.

The film also finds no equivalent for the startling, blackly comic quality of many of the novel's images. Admittedly, Doctorow's most shocking "shots" would have been nearly impossible to translate to screen: Harry Thaw dangling his penis through his prison cell's bars; Younger Brother spewing his lust over Evelyn Nesbit and Emma Goldman. But this doesn't explain why the film fails to come up with anything more askew or daring than Evelyn Nesbit sitting shamelessly nude while negotiating with the Thaw detectives—why, for the most part, it doesn't seem to try for anything unusual at all. Its images tend to be soft-edged and bathed in gentle light, nostalgic, even pretty. Moreover, the film does more than clean up the novel sexually, it also cleans it up socially. Omitting the Lawrence strike, it deletes the strike's political violence; cutting Father's trip to the Arctic, it does away with the exploratory voyage's oppressive atmosphere; while, even where it does preserve one of the novel's potentially charged social settings—such as New York's turn-of-the-century Lower East Side—it has a way of altering it completely. In the novel, the Lower East Side is ugly and odor-infested; on film, it's picturesque. The characters, too, are cleansed, sweetened, deprived of their edge, and none more so than Coalhouse, who's ultimately turned to mush. The Coalhouse of the novel—older, more staid, more likely to mount a revolution—would never go ga-ga over his baby as he does in the film or go dancing out of the house when Sarah agrees to marry him. Nor would the novel's Coalhouse utter such banalities to Booker T. Washington as: "You speak like an angel, too bad we are living on earth"—a piece of prose equivalent in the flatness of its attempted irony to the cut from Sarah's wedding thoughts to her funeral. And Coalhouse certainly wouldn't be heard crying out desperately to God.

Ultimately, then, where *Ragtime* the novel is crisp and ironic, innovative and sharply critical, *Ragtime* the movie is soft, sentimental, and utterly conventional. And though structure, pace, imagery, rhythm, and characterization all contribute to the effect, nothing serves to encapsulate this radical tonal and stylistic shift—which constitutes, in turn, a shift in themes, in impact, in quality—more than the movie's score. For mind-boggling as it may seem, that score doesn't call up the sound of Scott Joplin or any other ragtime musician. Thoroughly pedestrian, it's made up nearly exclusively of traditional movie mood music: ethnic lilt for the Lower East Side, heavy chords for the Morgan Library siege, tinkly playground tunes for Tateh's happy visit to Philadelphia, band music for Atlantic City, and a piece of slow and sweetly romantic fluff for the final credits, immediately before which Evelyn Nesbit and unidentified partner sweep about in a ballroom dance. (They have been similarly seen at the outset of the movie.) Thus, the most obvious evidence for the film's total misconception—for its betrayal of its source and its inadequacy in its own right—is also the most obvious explanation for the startling failure to translate to screen this most cinematic of novels: the filmmakers' inability to recognize that you simply can't have *Ragtime* without "ragtime" and certainly not without its distinctive style.

Tess: Romantic Strains and Tragic Rhythms

No marriage could have seemed more unlikely than that between director Roman Polanski and novelist Thomas Hardy. Here was an intensely
modern sensibility, with a penchant for the grotesque and explicit, tackling
an eminent Victorian; here was a Polish-born filmmaker, using a German-
born star, and, by force of circumstance, the Normandy countryside as setting, while attempting to translate to film that most regional of British
novelists; here was a fugitive from American justice, accused of having had
sexual relations with a thirteen-year-old girl, attempting to bring to screen,
of all Hardy's novels, *Tess of the d'Urbervilles*—the tale of a young woman
seduced by an older man. And if all of this weren't enough to make
Polanski's efforts seem unpromising, there was the prior history of the several failed and unrealized attempts to adapt both this particular novel and
other works of the author as well*—a history suggesting that if there was
any marriage more unlikely than the one between Polanski and Hardy, it
just may have been that between Hardy and the screen itself.

What is it about Hardy that has made him so resistant to adaptation—
despite his much-vaunted pictorialism, his event-laden plots, and his larger-
than-life characters? The obvious explanation is that Hardy is much more
dated than almost any other of the great English novelists. His plots strike
contemporary taste as melodramatic, overly schematic, and discomfortingly didactic, even as the stuff of a penny-dreadful. (Tess is not only seduced and/or possibly raped by a villainous rake, but in the course of the
novel, suffers the loss of her illegitimate child, abandonment by her beloved

---

*In fact, the only noteworthy attempt to adapt Hardy during the sound era (prior to
Polanski's *Tess*) was John Schlesinger's 1967 *Far from the Madding Crowd*. As for *Tess of the
d'Urbevilles*—of which there had been at least two silent versions, one in 1913 with Minnie
Maddern Fiske, another in 1924 starring Blanche Sweet and with a dual ending, one happy,
one unhappy, from which exhibitors could choose—it had frustrated no less ambitious a
producer than David O. Selznick, who had overseen such adaptations as *Anna Karenina* and
A Tale of Two Cities. Selznick had hoped to have his wife Jennifer Jones star and to make the
film an epic on the order of his *Gone with the Wind*, but he never got any further with the
project than a hundred pages of detailed notes. It was from Selznick's estate that Polanski
obtained the rights.

husband, and the extremes of poverty before she is ultimately forced back to the bed of her hated seducer, whereupon she plunges a knife into his heart.) Many of his characters, too, seem absurdly old-fashioned, improbable types—take the instance of Tess's seducer, Alec, who with his curling moustache, his "bold rolling eye," and opening address to our heroine ("Well, my beauty . . .") seems a dead ringer for the stock villain of Victorian melodrama. As for Hardy's themes—the hypocrisies of the Victorian cult of chastity, the tension between Evangelical Christianity and the Church of England, the plight of the peasant caught between two worlds, all of which are central to *Tess*—they've hardly remained burning issues.

But Dickens too makes use of melodramatic contrivances; Fielding too gives us characters who are conceived in terms other than our own; and each author also touches on social issues that are no longer relevant. Still both Dickens and Fielding have been translated to film quite successfully and more than once. Is it simply that the works of Dickens and Fielding have retained greater force than Hardy's? This is partially the case. Or is it that Hardy's characterizations and conflicts are more internalized than theirs? This is also true to some extent—though Hardy's view is certainly less interiorized than that of most modern novelists, some of whom have also been adapted to screen quite effectively. (D. H. Lawrence is one example.) Ultimately, then, we must look elsewhere for the key to Hardy's traditional resistance to adaptation; we must look to the matter of tone. Recall that Dickens and Fielding are essentially comic novelists whose work creates the kind of distance that allows not only for laughter but for a certain degree of exaggeration and stylization. (We don't question the reality of Miss Havisham—we know she's an intentional overstatement, part of a universe which, though surely not offered to us for laughs, is still rendered with considerable comic license.) Hardy, by contrast, writes tragedy, and tragedy by its very nature permits no such comforting means of standing apart from figures or action. His works are permeated by a fierce, dark pessimism, a sense of savage and terrible gloom. As one critic notes, tragic emotion "broods like a thundercloud" over his bleak landscapes and hapless characters, as does a dreadful fatalism, an aura of the cosmic "complicity of doom."

Because of this, Hardy then is as much a Romantic as he is a Victorian—a writer whose work is permeated by the Gothic texture, the primitivism, the almost sentimental involvement with the past, and the passion for the "natural," the wild, the untamed and untrammeled, itself typical of a period even earlier than the Victorian. Hardy stands at still a fur-

ther remove from us in sensibility. No dark and mysterious stains of hered-
ity taint character and shape destiny in our world as they do in that of Tess.
No ghostly d'Urberville coaches haunt our landscapes, as they do those of
the novel. No insistent "President of the Immortals" is included in our
scheme of things, "making sport" with us as, Hardy tells us, he does with
Tess. Such pessimism as rules our lives takes another shape altogether—that
of perceiving the utter indifference of the universe.

Yet, take that troublesome tone away from Hardy, take away that rich
metaphoric style, the dense symbolic texture of his descriptions and characterizations, and one takes away what gives Hardy his value: that is, the very
genius that transforms such threadbare stuff as *Tess* is built of into the matter of art. Consider Hardy's descriptions of Flintcomb-Ash, the desolate
place where Tess suffers her greatest degradation. Here, in some of his most
suggestive and passionate prose, Hardy creates what critic Irving Howe
calls no less than a "vision of hell."

> The swede-field in which she and her companion were set hacking was . . .
> in colour a desolate drab; it was a complexion without features, as if a face,
> from chin to brow, should be only an expanse of skin. The sky wore, in an-
> other colour, the same likeness; a white vacuity of countenance with the lin-
> eaments gone. So these two upper and nether visages confronted each other
> all day long, the white face looking down on the brown face, and the brown
> face looking up at the white face, without anything standing between them
> but the two girls crawling over the surface of the former like flies. . . .

Now into this dread landscape comes a host of "strange birds":

> . . . gaunt-spectral creatures with tragical eyes—eyes which had witnessed
> scenes of cataclysmal horror in inaccessible polar regions of a magnitude such
> as no human being had ever conceived. . . .

It is with such descriptions as these that Hardy manages to invest the
world of his novel with a symbolic resonance that carries it beyond its time
and place. So also with his handling of Tess. Passage after passage serves to
transform her from the stereotypical innocent-betrayed into a towering
image of feminine fortitude and resilience, and to present her as a being inextricably bound to and symbolic of nature at its best. Take the following,
in which Hardy identifies Tess's love for Angel with the summer season, as
both part and parcel of nature's inevitable cycles:

> Amid the oozing fatness and warm ferments of the Froom Vale, at a season
> when the rush of juices could almost be heard below the hiss of fertilization,

it was impossible that the most fanciful love should not grow passionate. The ready bosoms existing there [those, of course, of Tess and Angel] were impregnated by their surroundings. . . .

Such passages are overwhelmingly lush and in this, as well as in their sensuality, their intense emotionalism, their melodramatic thrust even, they are—dare one say it?—decidedly un-British. Indeed, it is this curiously foreign flavor in Hardy that helps explain why, if troubling to us, he was also disturbing to his contemporaries. Grouping him with Continental writers such as Dostoyevsky, Zola, and Maupassant, who had a "consciousness of the misery in the world" so piercing that to read them was "about as gay as to read the daily papers," one Hardy contemporary went so far as to state that he intended never again to even speak of Hardy.

It may be just this Continental quality that also explains why—appearances to the contrary—the marriage between Polanski and Hardy turned out to be such a strikingly compatible one. The distance in time, the difference in background notwithstanding, there is in Polanski's work—from *Knife in the Water* to *Cul de Sac* and *Rosemary's Baby* to *Chinatown*—much that allies him with Hardy: the sense of impasse and hopelessness, the fatalism and claustrophobia, the feeling of intense passion, the shadowy texture, the Gothic strain. Whatever the explanation, Polanski in his *Tess* has gone a long way toward capturing Hardy and, most remarkably, in capturing Hardy's tone. Not that he hasn't worked certain modulations on it—Hardy could never be transferred from the protectively dated context of his novels to the modern screen without some adjustment for the contemporary sensibility. And it's precisely in those careful modulations that Polanski's genius lies—in the manner in which he has managed to subtly shift the key so as to retain a sufficient portion of Hardy's tone (and thus much of the power and point of the original) and yet at the same time, to make the film harmonious with the present.

Polanski's handling of the plot itself reveals his methods. Allowing Hardy to serve as his chief scenarist, he follows the novel with a fidelity that is almost startling—in fact, there isn't a single interpolated sequence in the entire film and not much interpolated dialogue either. And though Polanski and his co-writers (Gerald Brach and John Brownjohn) have also cut a great deal—only a television series, after all, can give us the lengthy Victorian novel whole—they've cut a good deal less than one might have imagined. For here Polanski proves a master at compression: pages of description of the milk-and-honey paradise of the Talbothays' dairy where

Angel and Tess meet are condensed into a single idyllic shot of a luxuriant, sun-soaked valley. And so it is also with pages of description of subsidiary characters. One glimpse of smiling, rotund, pink-faced Dairyman Crick, and we are immediately acquainted with his kindness and warmth; while a cut from Alec saying to Tess, "Goodbye, my four months' cousin," to a shot of Tess working in the wheatfields, her sister standing nearby with a baby in her arms, and then giving her that baby to nurse, condenses nearly a year into a single transition.

Not everything in the novel has been so compacted. Certain materials are quite intentionally cut, and not simply in the interests of length. (Consider that Polanski has dared, in the manner of the novel, to set an extremely leisurely pace. Filled with long-held shots, the film depends above all on contrast and editing to provide a sense of motion and rhythm, with Polanski characteristically setting a nighttime scene against a daylight one, a shorter sequence against a longer one.) In any case, Polanski's omissions include Angel's somnambulistic stroll to the crypt, Alec's religious conversion and lapse, the horrible death of the Durbeyfield horse, Tess's hanging and Angel's subsequent marriage to her sister. The principle at work here is evident. Polanski has chosen to delete from the novel its most melodramatic materials, which is to say those most unacceptable to contemporary taste. No question but that he has in this way softened Hardy; still, he hasn't done any damage to the deliberateness of the novel's overall design, to its inexorable movement toward tragedy, to its overwhelming sense of Tess's entrapment. What he has done instead is to remove Hardy's Gothic edge and, while carefully retaining his romanticism, to root the film more firmly than the novel in an acceptable reality. He has also—by removing Hardy's most obvious manipulations—somewhat lightened the heavy hand of fate, but retained enough of the novelist's sense of coincidence and destiny to keep its shadow in view. In short, Polanski has managed to work an extraordinary balance.

A similar discernment is apparent in his handling of the novel's imagery. Not as heavily emblematic (or as harsh) as in the novel, the film's imagery nonetheless retains a great deal of suggestiveness and certainly captures much of the novel's sensuality and lushness. The cinematography—the work of Ghislain Cloquet and Geoffrey Unsworth (who suffered a heart attack in the midst of the shooting)—is radiant and luminous, and shot after exquisite shot seems rendered precisely according to Hardy's instructions. There's the early, misty Mayday sequence in which, dressed all in white, Tess and friends dance at dusk on the village green; there's the sensuous scene of the tempter Alec feeding Tess ripe red strawberries; there's the climactic sequence in which Tess is captured by the police as she lies sleeping in the ruins of Stonehenge, the sun rising in a blaze behind her. Where the film does take its own course is in its choice to turn to nineteenth-century visual artists for inspiration. These images, however, instead of interpolating their own themes, carry those of Hardy. The shimmering landscapes according to Constable are in tune with Hardy's celebratory view of nature; the haymakers seen according to Millet reflect the socially conscious tinge of his vision; the imposing beauty of the film itself serves to embody Hardy's passionate romanticism.

So the film is never simply painterly, never simply picturesque. Its visual texture is instead critical to its design, central to its effects, and serves above all, as does the language and imagery of Hardy's novel, to establish tone. (The music, credited to Philip Sarde, also contributes immeasurably, carrying the lovely and plaintive strains of old English ballads even into its most full-bodied orchestrations.) And though shorn of Hardy's most blatant effects—Angel no longer has his harp, Alec no longer appears with devilish pitchfork in the threshing scene, even the ghoulish birds of Flintcomb-Ash have been deleted—the visual texture also manages to carry considerable symbolic value. As in Hardy, where the world of the dairy implies purity, so does it here; where in Hardy, the dark ominous tomb of the d'Urbervilles echoes the drear force of destiny, it does the same in the film as well; and if Hardy's clouds and mists carry a tinge of sensuality, so too do Polanski's. The difference is primarily that, as with the narrative, all the symbolic images seem a good deal more real, their emblematic texture emerging comfortably from their inherent nature. Take Polanski's most obvious symbol—the road. The place where, in the film's stunning opening sequence, we first see Tess and where her father meets up with the Parson whose information on the family's ancestry sparks the tragedy that is to come, the road is also the setting for Tess's various journeys toward the realization of her awful destiny and where that destiny itself is fulfilled. But if the road is suggestive of fate, it's never self-consciously so; it retains the realness of an actual road, with such symbolic import as it carries inevitable rather than imposed.

The characters too have been made more real, and in the case of Alec and Angel, this is an unarguable gain. Alec as the Evil One, Angel as the Fallen and Hypocritical One, are hopelessly melodramatic conceptions in the novel. Polanski has toned them down and fleshed them out. Alec especially, very well played by Leigh Lawson and given to us without his religious conversion, comes across on film as a surprisingly credible character. He is also more sympathetic than in the novel. (However, one can't be all that hard on Hardy's Alec either. After all, he doesn't desert Tess, Tess deserts him, keeping him uninformed about the baby, as well as her other troubles; while when he does discover her tragic circumstances, he ends up suffering very real remorse and supporting her entire starving family to boot.) Polanski is somewhat less successful in his treatment of Angel. The problem is chiefly one of casting—Peter Firth simply isn't appealing enough to persuade us that all those girls would fall head over heels in love with him. But he does do well at conveying Angel's limitations and even manages to make credible that decisive moment which is vaguely incredible in the novel—when, after asking Tess's forgiveness for his checkered past, he refuses to grant her any forgiveness of his own. It's interesting, too, that though deprived of much of their symbolic overlay, both characters still bear much of the thematic weight Hardy assigned them. Both embody extremes of human hypocrisy and cruelty; each represents a contrasting form of violation—the one ravishing Tess physically, the other abusing her spiritually; and in this way they also suggest opposing varieties of masculine limitation, standing in bold contrast to the feminine possibilities Tess embodies.

Polanski's greatest achievement, however, lies in his treatment of Tess herself—though it is also here that he has had the most help from Hardy. For Tess is more than the novel's dramatic center: she is also its most fully realized and convincing character, the one who demands the least apologies and adjustment. And Polanski has remained in this case strikingly faithful to Hardy's conception. As played by the seventeen-year-old Nastassia Kinski, Polanski's Tess even looks like Hardy's: "She was a fine and handsome girl—not handsomer than some others, possibly—but her mobile peony mouth and large innocent eyes, added eloquence to colour and shape." And if, as several critics noted at the time, she seems in her slimness and delicacy not quite sufficiently rooted in the earth, not completely the "natural" country lass Hardy imagined, it's significant that Hardy's country lass was not totally convincing in that role either. "Is not her sensitiveness a little false?" asks one Hardy critic. Would she really be capable, as Hardy implies she is, "of brooding so formidably" on Wordsworth's poetry? asks another. Simply put, given her history, her background, her social situation, would Tess actually have had the insight, the pride, the nobility that Hardy grants her? Not likely. It's the strength of Nastassia Kinski that—if not quite as earthy as her novelistic counterpart—she still emerges both credible as an ordinary country girl and stunningly convincing in her more exceptional qualities. She has a marked intelligence, an evident sensitivity, and a resilient quality that certainly allows us to believe in her as the bearer

An ambiguous gaze from Flora in *The Innocents*. Is Miss Jessell's ghost across the lake or isn't it?

On the quay at Lime Regis—a misty seascape from the romantic film within the film in *The French Lieutenant's Woman*.

Tadzio (and friend) in *Death in Venice*. Object of art or object of lust?

Gatsby and Daisy. But seen from whose point of view? Certainly not Nick Carraway's.

A shaven-headed Brando stands in for Conrad's Kurtz in
Apocalypse Now.

Slaughterhouse-Five—the moving march through doomed
Dresden begins.

Ragtime's Lower East Side—on film a picturesque tableau.

Desperate for contact, *Wise Blood*'s Enoch Emery shakes the hand of Gonga the Gorilla.

Looking inward—
the single most
effective shot in
Under the Volcano.

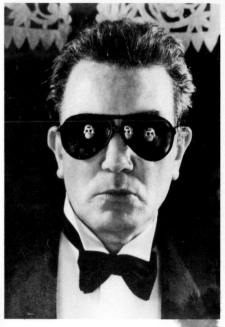

The human scream
dominates in the
climactic scene of
The Day of the Locust.

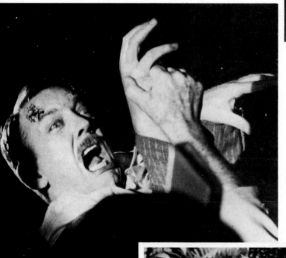

Simon's meeting
with the
Pig's Head in
Lord of the Flies:
a symbolic
encounter
deprived of
its symbolism
on film.

The Mayday dance in *Tess* captured in rich, romantic tones.

The magnificent staircase as emblem of familial relationships in *The Magnificent Ambersons*. COURTESY OF RKO PICTURES INC.

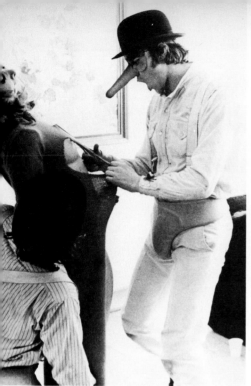

Rape to the tune of "Singing in the Rain" in *A Clockwork Orange*.

Whose Sophie? Yours or mine? From the film, *Sophie's Choice*.

Birkin (Alan Bates) communing with nature in *Women in Love*— an instance of Russell's visual translation of Lawrence's impassioned style.

Henry James made broadly comic—Winterbourne and Aunt taking tea and the waters in *Daisy Miller.*

Scenic detail substitutes for sensibility in Swann's world on film.

of the noble lineaments of the d'Urbervilles. She also manages to achieve the delicate balance between passivity and willfulness, between innocence and sensuality, creating a Tess who is at once responsible for her own downfall and a pure victim of fate.

In his perceptive book on Hardy, Irving Howe suggests that it's in his treatment of Tess that Hardy makes his authorial presence most felt—that "he hovers and watches over Tess . . . [that] he is as tender to Tess as Tess is to the world." Significantly, it's in his handling of Tess that Polanski, too, makes his directorial presence felt most fully. His camera lavishes extraordinary attention on her, revealing her in various angles, against various backdrops, and in long-held shot after long-held shot. (In several interviews given at the time of the film's release, Kinski described the amount of effort Polanski put into shaping her performance—determining every gesture, the enunciation of every line. "I see a lot of Roman in Tess, he is very much like her," Kinski was quoted as saying by way of explanation for Polanski's intense involvement with Tess's character. It helped of course that Polanski was also, at the time, intensely involved with Kinski herself.) And in so doing, Polanski has certainly assigned Tess a tonal value very much in keeping with Hardy's own, giving her the extraordinary stature, immense empathy, and tragic grandeur that he has given his film as a whole.

It's startling in this context that some have so overlooked the film's emotional texture that they have seen it as a feminist tract—but then again, some have found in Hardy no more than his case against Victorian mores. Polanski's film, like Hardy's novel, is about much more than the mistreatment of women. It's about the reaches of pain; the ennobling force of suffering; the destructiveness—and redemptive power—of love. Like Hardy's novel, Polanski's film is passionately felt and achieves a measure of greatness. And whether or not it has managed to give us Hardy precisely and totally, the film is greatly in debt to Hardy for its accomplishment—which is justification enough for the attempt to bring that strange and moving Victorian novelist to the modern screen.

Daisy Miller: The Loss of Innocence

In *Daisy Miller*, Henry James created an authentic American archetype: the innocent girl abroad. He also created a figure who, at once amusing and offensive, charmed and outraged readers in her own time and still excites argument even today. Clearly James, with his extraordinary insight, hit on a fundamental aspect of the American character—its mythic or "radical" innocence whose destructive conflict with experience makes for the archetypal American drama. But there's something else about Daisy's character that explains her sustained provocative power: a certain ambiguity that derives from James's filtering of his innocent American heroine, and her European experience as well, through the double-edged vision of irony.

In certain of her qualities, there's no doubt but that James invites us to admire Daisy. A spirited and pretty young woman from Schenectady, New York, who when in Rome simply will not do as the Romans do, she embodies much that is positive in the American sensibility: its openness, its freedom, its candor. Walking about on the Pincio unchaperoned with her Italian suitor, Giovanelli, she adamantly refuses to be bound by the rigid conventions of expatriate American society—a society which in its cruel narrow-mindedness and utter lack of comprehension mistakes her innocence for experience and ultimately does her in. Not even Winterbourne—the young American-in-residence in Geneva from whose angle of vision we see her and who is the most sympathetic to her of all the expatriates—fully understands the nature and depth of her all-American purity. He has, as he himself admits at the end of the tale, "lived too long in foreign parts," and so "was booked to make a mistake."

Yet, if Daisy commands James's sympathy, she still doesn't escape his censure. She may be frank and spirited; she may even be perceived as a fresh, wild flower who, as her death from malaria or Roman "bad air" suggests, must wither and die when transplanted to ancient and corrupt European soil. But she is also uncultivated, vulgar, an empty chatterer and hopeless flirt. In fact, as F. R. Leavis has noted, "no intelligent man could stand her for long since there could be no possible exchange of speech with her." Leavis's emphatically British view seems a trifle harsh. (Europeans from the outset have condescended to poor Daisy, whereas Americans have tended to see her as brave and indomitable.) Still, one has to acknowledge that James, who leaves no one and nothing free from his satirical touch here, tends to reserve his sharpest barbs of all for the Miller family—of which Daisy is the unmistakable product. Prototypical ugly Americans, weak Mrs. Miller and her wild son Randolph (who like Daisy has evidently been pampered, petted, and raised with total permissiveness) are nouveau riche types, traveling through Europe blind to its art, immune to its charms, and finding everything American the best—whether it be doctors or candy.

And though Daisy is certainly more appealing than either, she shares in much of their obtuseness.

Daisy's "innocence," then, doesn't simply lie in her essential purity; it is compounded equally of her ignorance. She has no insight into the significance of the conventions she flouts, no grasp of what her endless flirting signals to the Europeanized Americans around her, and her behavior is in many ways, often downright wrong. Consequently, she emerges as more than merely an exemplar of the American girl abroad; she serves as an embodiment of still another, and decidedly more tantalizing, all-American archetype: in Leslie Fiedler's description, the paradoxical "Good Bad Girl".

Given all this—the fascination of its central character and the deep-rooted nature of her appeal, not to mention its picturesque European settings—it's hardly surprising that *Daisy Miller* should have proved tempting to filmmakers.* And all the more so in that, as an early James tale (it was first published in 1879) written well before what is sometimes known as James's "period of the involved manner" (usually dated 1896–1916), it doesn't confront the filmmaker with the kind of challenges presented by such works as *The Ambassadors* and *The Golden Bowl.* It doesn't demand, that is, that he discover stylistic equivalents for James's superinvolved syntax or structural means for conveying his highly complex inner views—we see Daisy exclusively from the outside here, and though we are made privy to Winterbourne's thoughts, the story never takes us very deeply inside them. Where the trick of adapting the tale lies instead is in maintaining careful control of our attitudes: in keeping us convinced of Daisy's essential innocence, on the one hand, and of her complicity in her fate, on the other; in making her appealing and off-putting at the very same time; in balancing the satire of Winterbourne and his circle with that of Daisy and her family. In short, the challenge facing the filmmaker is that of rendering the story's delicately modulated tone.

And it is precisely this tone which Peter Bogdanovich's 1974 adaptation of *Daisy Miller* totally fails to grasp. A pity, too, since whatever the early

---

*Actually, James's work as a whole has proved enormously appealing to film (and to theatre, opera, and television as well). Aside from *The Innocents* and *Daisy Miller*, other James-inspired movies which, whatever their considerable limitations, remain worthy of study for what they can reveal about the process of adaptation are: *The Heiress* (which won Olivia de Havilland an Academy Award); and the Merchant-Ivory productions of *The Europeans* and *The Bostonians*, the latter of which was extremely well received and, for a film of its kind, remarkably successful at the box office.

(and mostly negative) reviews of the film might lead one to believe, the adaptation is far from an unintelligent one. Given the brevity of the tale, it follows that there would be several interpolations—as indeed there are. But these three or four added scenes aside, the film is strikingly faithful to James's design. It not only replicates the story's structure; it reconstructs both its events and their sequence. It even retains the story's dialogue—the script, in fact, hardly contains a word that isn't authentic James.* And, trusting the author as fully as it has, it reflects considerable insight on the part of the filmmakers into James's very distinctive power as dramatist, as well as marked appreciation of his extraordinary ear for spoken language.

The look of the film is quite marvelous too. The cinematography, credited to Alberto Spagnoli, seems perceptively guided by James's own often painterly descriptive techniques throughout. The shots of the Castle of Chillon, for example, have a strong impressionist texture, especially the lovely final one where, as Daisy glances wistfully back at the retreating sight of the castle, the image seems to carry with it, as one critic aptly puts it, a sense of "fading romantic possibility." There's also the odd low-angle shot of the Colosseum, whose distorted perspective delivers an appropriate sense of ominousness. It is here that Winterbourne, spying Daisy and Giovanelli together unchaperoned at night, finds evidence (albeit misleading) for the very worst of his fears about her. And again, the film's imagery here—its vision of Daisy in a bridelike white gown both contrasted with and shadowed by the deep blues of the surrounding darkness—goes a long way in conveying the emotional texture of the moment. ("It was as if a sudden illumination had been flashed upon the ambiguity of Daisy's behavior, and the riddle had become easy to read," thinks Winterbourne at this point in the tale. "She was a young lady whom a gentleman need no longer be at pains to respect.")

Some of the film's dramatic sequences are also very well mounted. There's the one in which Winterbourne discovers that Daisy has died—a piece of information that James, importantly, tosses off in a single line—and which Bogdanovich, in turn, narrates in long shot, keeping us at a discreet distance, then, from the revelation. With the camera situated behind the

*Reportedly, it was Bogdanovich, rather than scenarist Frederic Raphael, who insisted on using James's own language and in fact replaced Raphael's dialogue so extensively with the dialogue of the story that writer and director went into arbitration at the Writers Guild to determine whether or not Bogdanovich should share credit on the screenplay.

lacy curtains of the glass doors at the entrance to the Millers' hotel, we see Winterbourne who, carrying a bouquet of flowers and evidently en route to pay a visit to the ailing Daisy, starts up the hotel staircase only to stop midway. He has evidently been addressed by the desk clerk, whose words we cannot hear. Now we see Winterbourne turn, lower the bouquet, descend the stairs, and leave the hotel, the entire scene informing us of what has occurred, slightly, obliquely, and with an exquisitely apt reserve. Also extremely effective is the film's final scene at Daisy's graveside. Here, the other mourners having left, Winterbourne is shown standing alone, the camera slowly moving farther and farther away from him. Thus Bogdanovich emphasizes both his physical and emotional isolation, further underscoring the total emptiness of both man and moment by bleaching the image before us to a blank and jarring white.

Point of view is also well rendered in this film and quite consistent with that of the story. Not that all commentators agree: some have argued that whereas James's tale is presented from Winterbourne's angle of vision, in the film the vantage point is an objective one. But what these critics overlook is that whether or not Winterbourne's perspective prevails, there's still a narrator standing behind him in the story—an unnamed speaker who sets the scene before Winterbourne enters and who offers a brief concluding summary after his exit. ("Nevertheless, he went back to live at Geneva, whence there continue to come the most contradictory accounts of his motives of sojourn: a report that he is 'studying' hard—an intimation that he is much interested in a very clever foreign lady.") Bogdanovich's precise details may differ, but he structures his film similarly. Opening with shots of the hotel and of Randolph playing pranks in the corridor, he asserts the camera as objective narrator at the outset. Once Winterbourne has been introduced, however, it's his perspective that dominates: we stay with him throughout and, though distanced from him at times (as in the aforementioned scene where he discovers Daisy's death), we see Daisy only when he is present and therefore implicitly from his vantage point.

The film's casting, visually at least, is also very much on the mark. Cybill Shepherd is surely the all-American beauty whose face, according to James, "was not at all insipid, but . . . was not exactly expressive"; whose features, though "eminently delicate," were also characterized by a certain "want of finish"; while moustachioed, starchily attired, and somewhat awkward Barry Brown (in the role of Winterbourne) appears precisely the stiff and Europeanized American who might well (as both Randolph and Daisy suggest) be mistaken for a German.

All these elements, however much they speak on the film's behalf, ultimately amount to little. For whether because he believed it impossible for twentieth-century audiences to take Daisy's conflicts very seriously, or because he was more influenced by earlier filmmakers in his stylistic choices than he was by James,* or, though less likely, because he managed to misconstrue the author's tone, Bogdanovich made the decision to play out the film as an extremely broad comedy of manners rather than as a subtle satire. His mise-en-scène itself is telling. Take the sequence in which Winterbourne goes to visit his snobbish aunt, Mrs. Costello, in order to arrange an introduction to Daisy. Where James places the exchange between nephew and aunt in a Vevey hotel room, Bogdanovich sets the encounter in a steaming mineral bath. Now, the idea of the two meeting in such a place may be historically and atmospherically accurate, and it certainly allows for more potential visual interest than a hotel room. But Bogdanovich has mounted the scene so bizarrely and in such baroque terms that it could almost be an outtake from a movie by Fellini, whose extravagant sensibility couldn't be further from that of the fastidious James. And Winterbourne and Mrs. Costello aren't simply sitting about chatting chest deep in healing waters; they are also sipping tea with archly raised pinkies—tea served, moreover, from a floating silver set, while other trays carrying bowls of flowers slowly drift by. Outrageous? Certainly, but apparently not outrageous enough. For Bogdanovich adds to the scene two similarly immersed men playing chess on a floating board that Winterbourne—as he hurriedly follows his aunt out of the water—manages to splash, to the comically flustered dismay of the bathing gentlemen.

*Orson Welles has been seen (and correctly, I think) to have exercised the greatest influence. Indeed, it was suggested at the time of *Daisy Miller*'s release that it may have been Welles's example, in having adapted Tarkington's *The Magnificent Ambersons*, which prompted Bogdanovich to tackle James in the first place. All the more so given that the tale did seem an odd choice of materials for him. Bogdanovich in 1974 was enjoying enormous prestige, having just completed two films which had been very successful at the box office (*What's Up, Doc?* and *Paper Moon*), and *Daisy Miller*, at least in contrast to these works, seemed a decidedly uncommercial project. Andrew Sarris, in answer to just why Bogdanovich may have attempted the adaptation, went so far as to suggest that perhaps the filmmaker was "acting upon a subconscious impulse to fail beautifully as an hommage to 'Ambersons'." Sarris evidently means "fail" commercially, not aesthetically, *Ambersons* standing among cineastes as one of the all-time greats. (See concluding discussion.) Still, the notion is less farfetched than it might seem given the curiously Welles-like, self-destructive pattern Bogdanovich's career assumed in the years subsequent to *Daisy Miller*.

We come across a similar type of visual horseplay everywhere in this world—whether it's the sight of a silly, sleepy, shrugging old guard at the Castle of Chillon, or a quick shot of a grossly fat singer at the opera in Rome, or whether it's the sight (and sound as well) of Daisy's admirer Giovanelli standing at the piano and singing, to Daisy's rapid accompaniment, "Pop-Goes-the-Way-zel." It's true that James saw his world with considerable humor. But where Bogdanovich continually opts for overstatement, James tends toward ironical understatement. (As an instance, take his remark that "one of the hotels at Vevey . . . is famous, even classical, being distinguished from many of its upstart neighbors by an air both of luxury and of maturity.")

More significant yet, however, is Bogdanovich's manner of broadly caricaturing all of the players in his drama. Again, much of this has its source in James. Randolph's gesture of displaying the teeth he claims to have lost because of his travels as if they were precious souvenirs derives directly from the story; Mrs. Miller's silly and vulgar complaints about her "dyspepsia" and her goings-on about Schenectady's "Dr. Davis," as if he were one of the world's most famous and brilliant physicians, do too; and so does Daisy's relentless chatter. But there's no precedent in James for Bogdanovich to have advised Cloris Leachman to play the role of Mrs. Miller with constant sniffles and whines or to have encouraged Mildred Natwick to play Mrs. Costello as if she were a supercilious snob conceived by Oscar Wilde. Nor is there any precedent either for Eileen Brennan's performance as Mrs. Walker, the expatriate American who turns her back on Daisy at her party—a performance so sneering that it's out of kilter with the whole. (If everyone else is overly comic, Brennan is overly cruel.) In the case of Giovanelli, Bogdanovich worked a total transformation, giving us in place of James's shady and suspicious Italian a silly (if sweet and sincere) fellow who is constantly getting his "nevers" and "evers" confused. (In the novella, Giovanelli speaks "English very cleverly.") This Giovenelli is so much the gentle clown (with his "Pop-Goes-the-Way-zel") that Roman society's view of him as fortune hunter and possible seducer seems sillier than he is. As for Winterbourne, who throughout has his nostrils flared (as if sniffing something offensive to his delicacy) and enunciates his lines with undisguised affectation, he emerges too much the fop and the lightweight for us to think he ever could have properly understood Daisy, or to truly believe in his affection for her. If this Winterbourne is "booked to make a mistake," it isn't because he's "lived too long in foreign parts." It's because this pretentious pseudosophisticate (who's always tripping on Daisy's train) can't see beyond his upturned nose.

This is the key to why Bogdanovich's broad effects are so misguided. They destroy all possible irony and all possible tension as well, with the European community coming across as so absurd that no one could be expected to go along with its manners and mores, not even a good girl, and much less a good bad one. What's more, though this Europe is a bizarre place, it simply isn't one whose "bad air" is potent enough to kill a poor Daisy. James, in contrast, was careful to give it precisely such power. As William Dean Howells suggested, though "many of his people are humorously imagined, or rather humorously *seen* . . . these do not give dominant color; the business in hand is commonly serious and the droll people are subordinated." In Bogdanovich it's the other way around—so much so that Daisy's death, for all the artfulness of its announcement, seems all wrong in this comic context, a thoroughly unconvincing contrivance which consequently carries little emotional or thematic weight.

Bogdanovich goes even more astray in his portrayal of Daisy herself. And the problem isn't merely that, evidently encouraged to rattle her lines at the pace of speeded-up phonograph record, Cybill Shepherd sacrifices all of the character's tragic texture to comic effect, or that in her endless posing and flirting and chattering, she loses almost all sense of Daisy's charm and all potential for sympathy as well. Nor is it only that because of this, we are presented with a conflict, neither side of which can command the least commitment, and with a set of characters, none of whom offers a chance for identification. It is that in her highly mannered and self-conscious performance, Shepherd gives us a Daisy Miller who, far from ignorant, far from an instinctual free spirit, is a thoroughly cultivated creature—a young woman who knows what she is doing every moment she's on screen. Her defiance of curfews and chaperones seems scrupulously controlled; her gaiety and chatter seem forced and designed; and her teasing of Winterbourne is full of supersubtle sexual innuendoes. No wonder both he and his society make the mistake of believing her "guilty"—if mistake it is. For despite her nineteenth-century white flounces and frills Daisy is, if pure anything, pure twentieth century, a "Good Bad Girl" of a time other than James's, and that later period's peculiar invention—the professional virgin.

What Bogdanovich has done, then, is more than wrench Daisy out of her time, more even than deprive her of her complexity and double-edged nature. He has taken away her innocence, and thus the very quality that made her matter in the first place. Interestingly, where James's tale was (and has remained) among the most popular of his creations, Bogdanovich's adaptation ranks among his most unpopular works. The notorious unreliability of popular taste notwithstanding, this still makes for pretty strong evidence of the archetypal power of American innocence. What it also tends to testify to—considering that so much else of the screen's *Daisy Miller* follows the *Daisy Miller* we meet on the page—is the decisive role of tone in shaping the meaning and effect of a work of fiction, and, of course, of its adaptation in turn.

7

Metaphor, Symbol, Allegory

It's a critical commonplace that film has difficulty with metaphor—that given the literalness and persuasive realism of the photographic image, it's almost inescapable that on screen a rose is a rose is a rose. But what's generally ignored by those who press the point is that metaphor presents literature with a considerable challenge as well—and especially when considered from the point of view of the reader. In his classic study *Practical Criticism*, in which he asked his students at Cambridge to respond to a series of unidentified poems in order to isolate problems in reading, I. A. Richards discovered that figurative language was a chief source of interpretive confusion. His students quite typically submitted overly literal readings, failing to recognize the metaphors. In literature too, then, often a rose is a rose is a rose—however a given work might attempt to suggest that it's something else.

The other of "the twin dangers" presented by figurative language—or, as Richards phrases it, "the 'justling rock' between which too many ventures into poetry are wrecked"—is that of overinterpretation, of discovering all kinds of meanings which derive less from the metaphor itself than from some association it happens to set off in the reader. And though one usually traces the cause to either the reader's overactive imagination or his total lack of one, he isn't the only source of confusion. The very nature of figurative expression—saying one thing and meaning another, in Robert Frost's formulation—itself invites misreading; and not all figurative expression achieves an equal measure of success. A writer can construct a metaphor either too weak or stale to adequately assert its figurative force or too unclear or strained in its associations to sufficiently limit its meanings. And it's more than merely lesser writers who face such difficulties. Melville,

Hawthorne, Conrad, Faulkner, Kafka, and Beckett—to name just a few—
have all been variously accused of creating cloudy and unstable metaphors.

But certain of the problems metaphor presents to literature are much
more basic than how we recognize one when we see it or how we resolve it
once we do. The bottom line is determining just what we mean by the term
in the first place. For metaphor (like style) is one of those slippery entries in
the critical vocabulary that have various applications. Metaphor, in different contexts, may refer to very different kinds of structures and sometimes
to very different kinds of mental processes. The most common use of the
term, of course, is in reference to a particular kind of literary trope: an implicit comparison between two unlike entities; a simile from which the
"like" or "as" has been omitted—to cite the definitions most of us learned
in school. Metaphor, when used in this sense, tends to be distinguished
from the image and from other kinds of tropes—the simile, the symbol, and
so on. Neat and simple? So it may at first seem. But even on this basic level,
we tend to run into difficulties, since—whatever the appearances to the
contrary—these definitions and distinctions turn out to be extremely elusive.

Take the following from Laurence Perrine's widely used poetry text,
Sound and Sense: "In general . . . an image means only what it is; a metaphor means something more too." How, given such definitions, can we
possibly sort out one verbal structure from another? How are we even to
distinguish between extremes—between the rose as image, where, despite
Perrine, it never only means what it is, since it carries with it all sorts of
"symbolic" connotations (beauty, delicacy, the brevity of life), and the rose
as symbol, where, whatever its emblematic value, it also remains a literal
rose, meaning "what is it" at the very same time? Or consider this from another popular text, Brooks and Warren's *Understanding Poetry:* "A symbol
may be regarded as a metaphor from which the first term has been
omitted." In other words, Brooks and Warren explain, a "rose" is transformed into a symbol when the Poet, summoning up the "image" of a rose
and calling into play various of its connotations, rather than state, "My luv
is like a red, red rose" (as in a simile) or "My luv is a rose" (as in a metaphor), chooses to talk about the rose as if it were his love, without making
the "metaphorical framework" explicit. That's fine, insofar as this way of
distinguishing "image" from "simile" from "metaphor" from "symbol" at
least admits to the continuities among them and stresses that whatever the
form of the trope, it derives from literature's image-making tendency and in
turn from imagery's connotative powers. Yet, this mode of definition also

proves inadequate. For, whatever Brooks and Warren suggest, we often come across symbols where the "first term" hasn't been omitted at all, where the "metaphorical framework" has been made abundantly clear. ("Then die—that she / The common fate of all things rare / May read in thee," Edmund Waller instructs still another famous rose—a rose whose meaning and value are stated outright and that emerges as symbol nonetheless.) Some theorists attempt to get at the distinctions from another angle altogether—by suggesting that in metaphor we are making an implicit *comparison* between two entities, whereas in the symbol we are merely *substituting* one for the other. But this approach doesn't really help matters either, since almost invariably, there is some point of comparison in the substitution itself. (Hawks don't serve as symbols for dovelike qualities or doves for hawklike ones.)

Quite simply, image, metaphor, and symbol are inextricably entwined, all shading one into the other and often overlapping. And recognizing the difficulty of making hard-and-fast distinctions, literary theorists tend more and more to use these terms interchangeably, even synonymously. Most contemporary theorists, that is, no longer use the term "metaphor" to refer to a particular kind of figure, but to figurative language in general and even to extended figurative structures like allegory. What makes this somewhat tricky is that allegory itself is an elusive term which can be used to point to very different types of literary structures. Sometimes "allegory" refers exclusively to "formal allegory"—to works in which the extended metaphor or allegorical structure resolves into neat and orderly equivalencies. (For example, *The Pilgrim's Progress* or *The Fairie Queene.*) Other times, "allegory" is used to refer to works that merely have an intricate symbolic overlay (Melville's *Bartleby* and *Billy Budd*, let's say). We even find reference to the allegorical character of works less blatantly metaphoric than these, and Northrup Frye, proposing that all commentary on literary works is basically "allegorical interpretation," goes so far as to imply that all poems, plays, and novels are allegorical in nature—which in a certain sense they are. Certainly, it's the nature of literature that its characters, actions, and images point to abstractions beyond themselves, to meanings beyond the literal.

The term "metaphor" can in effect serve as a metaphor for the entire literary process, or indeed for all language itself. (Others enlarge the usage further still, perceiving metaphor as more than merely a linguistic phenomenon, but as a mode of thought. After all, the ability to detect resemblances and to sustain a simultaneity of perception—both of which are central to the creation of all figurative statement,—are hardly capacities exclusive to literature and language alone.) But one has to limit the sense of the term somewhere, and though it seems to me that in the context of prose fiction, not to mention that of film, it doesn't help to limit it too much and certainly not to a particular kind of linguistic trope, it does make sense to restrict its application to the various modes of figurative or nonliteral expression.

All of this has been by way not only of suggesting that metaphor, symbol, and allegory are shifting and often interchangeable categories but of underscoring the fact that literature has many modes of metaphoric expression. As true as this is of literature, it is also true of film, which consequently turns out to have less difficulty with metaphor than is generally assumed. (It also, paradoxically, turns out to have more difficulties, but more of this later.) For once one accepts imagery and connotation as the grounds on which metaphoric expression is built and widens one's concept of metaphor in the process, it becomes evident that film—given the sheer variety, range, and force of its image-making and connotative powers* —has extraordinary possibility for figurative statement, more perhaps than literature.

It also becomes clear that the widely held notion of editing as constituting film's most distinctive and peculiarly cinematic means of rendering tropes may be a limited, even downright erroneous one, and largely because it's embedded in the equally limited concept of the trope as a figure of explicit comparison. Not only isn't editing film's exclusive means for creating metaphor, it just may be one of its least effective means. To cut from the murder of Kurtz to that of a carabao as Coppola does in *Apocalypse Now,* or from the killing of Trotsky to that of a bull as Joseph Losey does in *The Assassination of Trotsky,* or—in the instance that obviously influenced both—from a shot of the slaughter of workers to one of the slaughter of a steer, as Eisenstein does in *Strike,* may be to use a metaphoric strategy available only to film, but there's something just a bit too obvious about the effect all the same. Similarly with a technique like that used by Karel Reisz in *Morgan,* when a slow dissolve from our erstwhile hero to a loping giraffe (one of the wild animals with which he identifies) works to briefly superimpose one image upon another, thus equating man and animal.

Film, however, has countless other ways of expressing itself figuratively.

*See Chapter Two.

It's capable of replicating many of the figurative modes of the other arts and transforming them in the process into distinctively cinematic devices. It characteristically makes use of the type of visual symbolism we associate with painting and the sound symbolism of music, while like literature it establishes the meanings and values of such symbols through narrative and context. (A burning sled can mean many things, but in *Citizen Kane* the image serves as a visual symbol of the unraveled mystery of its owner's life; while Fritz Lang's *M* takes a phrase from Grieg's *Peer Gynt* and, by having it frequently whistled by child-killer Peter Lorre, makes it an emblem of his pathological tendencies.) Also characteristic of film is the use of strategies equivalent to tropes such as metonymy and synechdoche. It's almost a natural tendency of the medium, in fact, to express the part through the whole (synechdoche)—offering us a close-up of a ring on a man's finger to suggest that he is married, a crown to tell us that a man is king—or to use one related idea to suggest another (metonymy)—a shot of a speeding train to suggest travel, of hovering vultures to suggest death, to cite a couple of standards.

Movies can also invest perfectly naturalistic imagery with figurative force. Stanley Kauffmann contends that this particular capacity of film contributes to its special power. Film "manages to make poetry out of doorknobs, breakfasts, furniture. Trivial details, of which everyone's universe is made, can once again be transmuted into metaphor, contributing to the imaginative act." And film effects this transmutation not only through various dramatic and contextual means, but also through numerous technical ones. In an essay on cinematic metaphors, Louis Gianetti, arguing that most discussions of cinematic tropes are limited by being "content-oriented," submits an entire catalogue of such technical means—a catalogue so extensive it ends up suggesting that just about every cinematic strategy there is can be used for the creation of metaphor. And so every cinematic strategy can: from variations in camera speed (slow motion to suggest the dreamlike quality of an experience, as in the pillow-fight sequence in Jean Vigo's *Zéro de Conduit;* fast motion, as in Chaplin's *Modern Times*, to liken man to machine; stop motion, as in Truffaut's *The Four Hundred Blows*, where the final freeze-frame serves as a metaphor for Antoine Doinel's sense of entrapment) through composition and lighting (as in the diving sequence from Leni Riefenstahl's *Olympiad* where, eliminating both diving board and pool from our view and focusing only on the diver, his arms extended winglike, his body outlined in dramatic contrast against a richly shadowed sky, Riefenstahl creates a figurative vision of man as bird or, better yet, as angel).

In short, film's only distinctively cinematic difficulty with metaphor—the only difficulty, that is, that derives quite specifically from the nature of the medium—is with metaphor in its most limited, most purely linguistic sense. (Film simply has no way, other than the use of language itself, of expressing something on the order of Tennyson's "I will drink / Life to the lees." The abstraction, life, eludes it, as does the particular analogy. A glass of wine, drunk to the lees or not, would on film tend to be simply a glass of wine.) But otherwise, film's problems with metaphor, symbol, and allegory are very much those of literature—different in degree, perhaps, but not really very different in kind. For like literature, film finds itself forced to steer a careful course between the two dangers that figurative statement inevitably confronts: that of lending itself to overly literal interpretation, on the one hand; that of emerging so vague as to make any precise meaning impossible to ascertain, on the other.

These dangers, however, are greater in film and, in the case of the threat of literalism, also follow quite naturally from the medium's photographic surface—a surface that gives images, actions, and characters a presentness and concreteness that tend to work against the assertion of figurative value. And though various theorists rightly remind us that this literalness is merely an illusion, that the film image always distorts perception, that it's never precisely real, the truth is that we nonetheless tend to see it that way. Because of this, one might argue that the loss of symbolic value in Huston's *Moby Dick* isn't merely a matter of Huston's choices. On film, one might say, the whale seems so inescapably a whale, the adventure so emphatically an adventure, that they have a way of distracting us from whatever larger meanings they are intended to carry. Not that it isn't possible to be similarly absorbed by the adventure itself in Melville's novel. Generally, however, film pulls more intensely in the direction of the matter-of-fact and so has to work harder to counter these literalizing tendencies. But it's a difficult problem, because despite the fact that many of literature's traditional means of asserting symbolic value translate easily to screen—insistent repetition, unusual stress, the sudden violation of the naturalistic context—those means, enlarged both literally and figuratively in the cinematic context, have a habit of becoming heavy-handed. In movies, as Raymond Durgnat suggests, metaphors that do not rise naturally from the context, that come in the form of "props," often seem less an enrichment than an "impoverishment," even in fact something "cheapening." (Durgnat doesn't give examples, but it's not difficult to summon them up. The crucifix in *Rocky* which, having no persuasive role in the plot, seemed discomfortingly obtrusive; in *Gremlins*, the highly unlikely coincidence that *The Invasion of the Body Snatchers*, which commented on the characters' current situation, just happened to be playing on television.)

Film's difficulties in focusing the meaning of its sights and sounds are somewhat harder to explain—though Durgnat's suggestion that film's inherent tendency is to "disguise metaphors" in natural surroundings may provide us with a clue. If film's metaphors are disguised, not only can we hunt for them all over the place, we can find them all over the place too. For instance, in her essay "Trash, Art, and the Movies," Pauline Kael reprints a letter to a Boston paper in which a college student argues that *The Thomas Crown Affair* is, appearances to the contrary, an updated "fable" which explores "the allegorical problem of human faith." Since *The Thomas Crown Affair* is to Kael (and I concur) a straightforward action melodrama, she cites this as an instance of a growing tendency "to try to place trash within the acceptable academic tradition." But it's an instance of something else as well. For the ease with which this student could find allegorical implications in such literal-minded "trash," the ease with which others find similar resonance in the simplest of westerns (John Ford's films as myths of the West) or in the most commercial of thrillers (Hitchcock's movies as Catholic allegories) tells us as much about the very special openness of film to what I. A. Richards might call "careless, 'intuitive' reading," as it does about our efforts to transform "trash" into "art." If the figurative language in a poem or the allegorical implications of a story can set off a host of private reminiscences and mnemonic irrelevancies, clearly film—overwhelmed with connotative suggestiveness, its every image and sound packed with the opportunity for erratic associations—carries even greater possibilities for interpretive mayhem.

What aggravates such tendencies is that though metaphoric value is inevitably established by context, whether in fiction or film, this is even more so in the case of film. That's one of the reasons it's so much more difficult to generalize about cinematic metaphors than poetic ones. In literature, certain techniques must inevitably create tropes, as, for example, the comparison of two unlike entities. But in film, a technique (noncontinuous editing, let's say) which makes for metaphor in one instance, simply may not in another. There's also the relative speed with which film must, of necessity, mount its narrative, present its images, and establish its context and symbolic values. One of the points that Richards makes by way of explaining the various failures of his Cambridge students to deal adequately with figurative language is that poetry in general and figurative statement in particular demand the kind of rereading, close reading, and *slow* reading that his students simply failed to bring to bear. We can hardly be expected to modify our pace in the reading of a novel in the same way we do for poetry. But we do have the opportunity to stop along the way if a detail catches our attention, if an image puzzles us, and in this way to perhaps uncover a metaphor we might otherwise have overlooked. Film, however, must keep moving and our perceptions right along with it. In movies, moreover, there's an operative assumption that once should be enough, and that such symbolic import or metaphoric value as a filmmaker wishes his film to carry must make its presence and meaning felt immediately. The viewer of a film is rarely prepared to bring the same effort to bear on film as he is to a poem or a work of fiction.

In other words, many of the problems film has in the handling of symbol and metaphor lie less in the nature of the medium itself than in our habits of perception—though not all of them, of course. Sometimes, the filmmaker will ground his work too fully in the medium's naturalistic surface to allow its symbolic texture to adequately assert itself; other times, he will fail to sufficiently control a work's allegorical implications so that its meanings emerge muddled and vague. And though, as suggested, novelists and poets too fall prey to these extremes, they are simply more likely to occur in film.

The particular significance of all this to adaptation is clear, especially regarding the problems a filmmaker confronts in attempting to adapt a fiction whose materials are highly metaphoric in nature. Most obviously, there's the fact that a loss of that work's symbolic thrust is, in most instances, a loss of the very quality that gives that work significance. Then, for another thing, given the inappropriateness to film of many of the devices a novelist may traditionally use to signal the presence and value of his symbolism (repetition and emphasis, for example), metaphoric fiction tends to challenge the filmmaker to come up with strategies of his own in a way that few other types of fiction do. And for still another thing, metaphoric fiction, by its very nature, places an especially heavy burden on the filmmaker's powers of interpretation; while if such fiction itself has risked falling into either literalism or vagueness, so too (but even more so) must its adaptation.

The discussions that follow, then, are of films that illustrate varying degrees of success in rising to the challenges of metaphor, symbol, and allegory. These are also films that not only make use of a variety of symbolic strategies but that, significantly, traffic in different levels of reality: *A Clock-*

work Orange and *Lord of the Flies* both bring us into worlds that are unquestionably allegorical, demonstrating in each case a very different degree of control over those allegorical implications; while *Wise Blood* and *Death in Venice* both take us into worlds that are acceptably real, each reflecting in turn vastly differing capabilities for transmuting that reality into metaphor. But they are all instances of adaptations that either foundered on one or another of the "justling rocks" of metaphoric disaster or have managed, and often through uniquely cinematic means, to steer a successful course between them.

A Clockwork Orange: Viddying Metaphor

Anthony Burgess's *A Clockwork Orange* may be a stunning novel, but it's also a startlingly savage one—a darkly ironic fable that in its pessimistic view of man and society, in the extreme horror of its materials, and in the scatological nature of its vision would have done Jonathan Swift proud. Its setting is a socialized England in the not-very-distant future where law and order no longer exist, where sex has been transformed into pornography, and politics has become a mere struggle for power. Garbage litters the streets, graffiti decorates building walls, and in the guise of vicious guerillas of the night, gangs of teenagers wander about robbing, beating, and raping anyone foolish enough to leave his home after dark or to unlock his doors.

The novel's protagonist is one of these teens—a fourteen-year-old gang leader named Alex who divides his time between playing at what he dubs the "old ultra-violence" and indulging in violent sexual fantasies to music by the likes of "glorious Ludwig van." Alex is a wry and merry sadist until, after murdering a helpless old woman, he is sent to jail and rehabilitated by the state through the "Ludovico treatment." A newly developed conditioning process, this treatment manages to make violence repugnant to Alex, but only at the cost of making sex and art repugnant too. Worse, it turns him into a mechanized creature—in Burgess's phrase, into "a clockwork orange." A subsequent suicide attempt, however, restores him to his former self, though in regaining his humanity, he also, of course, regains his passion for ultra-violence.

Direct in its themes and schematic in its construction—its essentially Christian allegory is divided into three fairly neat sections: before the fall, after the fall, the resurrection—the novel presents few problems in interpretation. Its central thesis is clear: a man deprived of free will is no longer truly a man, and so even if he chooses evil, that choice is still better than no choice at all. The novel's difficulties lie instead in making its thesis palatable. For readers must not only be persuaded to accept the novel's criticism of society's dehumanizing institutions and their threat to human individuality, they must also be able to entertain the truly unsettling materials that carry these views—the rapes, the murders, the deconditioning process itself. And they must also be willing to share in the novel's affirmation of the vicious Alex, without which its central argument loses all force.

That Burgess does in fact manage to impose his disconcerting vision on us is testimony to his novelistic powers, just as it also is to the truly dazzling quality of his chief device for reaching this end: having Alex tell his own story in his distinctive teenage argot, Nadsat. A brilliant Joycean creation, Nadsat is constructed essentially out of Slavic roots that Burgess has anglicized, often turning them into quite marvelous puns. The Russian *khorosho* meaning "good" or "well," for example, is transformed into "horrorshow," which is precisely what "good" means to Alex; the Russian *ludi* (people) is transmuted into "lewdies," which is again what people are to our hero. Nadsat is also made up of bits of slang ("cancer" for "cigarette"), archaisms (the use of "thou" and "thee" and "O, my brothers"), and what Stanley Edgar Hyman calls "amputations" ("pee and em" for "pop and mom"). Nadsat then serves as the key source of the novel's wild, black humor, while it also provides Alex with much of his bizarre appeal. Those thees and thous, coupled with his passion for Ludwig van, give him a curious mock-courtliness; those puns seem his own creation, giving him an engaging wit. Nadsat is also the novel's central method of conveying its ironic tone and expressing many of its themes: certainly, the disintegration and confusion of language it embodies works to reflect something of the same disintegration in the society that surrounds it.

The most important function of Nadsat, however, is that of muffling the novel's horror. Often difficult to comprehend, demanding continual translation, distracting the reader's attention from what is being said to the manner of its statement, it creates a buffer between the reader and the unrelenting violence before him. (It's one thing to read "loose zooblies, dripping krovvy, and poogly glazzies," and quite another to come upon "loose teeth, dripping blood, and frightened eyes.") Finally, Nadsat is the novel's most cogent method of conveying its unreality, of reminding us throughout that it is a fable and that like other works of its kind, it's here to tell us something—however disturbing—about human nature.

The problems of bringing such a novel to the screen couldn't be more evident. How find an equivalent for this stunning linguistic creation? How find a means for eliciting sympathy with the sadistic Alex? How assert the unreality and allegorical nature of the action being laid before us? How persuade the viewer to accept its vision? Above all, how protect him from the violence of the materials—a violence that, if intolerable without some sort of distancing effect on the page, would become even more intolerable on the screen without considerable softening?

Given all this, perhaps the most remarkable thing about Stanley Kubrick's adaptation of *A Clockwork Orange* is that he attempted it in the first place. But then again, one can understand the novel's special appeal. The "What's it going to be then, eh?" with which Alex begins his narrative was more or less the question Kubrick had been asking (and answering) in the two films he had made immediately prior to *A Clockwork Orange*—*Dr. Strangelove* and *2001*; and, as these films also suggest, Kubrick clearly shared with Burgess a concern with the effects of machines on man. *Dr. Strangelove*, whose arm, like the mechanism of a cuckoo clock, shoots out at intervals in the Nazi salute and HAL, the man-cum-computer, are both close cousins to Alex, the clockwork orange. Like him too, they are emblematic figures situated in allegorical worlds.

Whatever tempted Kubrick to adapt the novel and deal with its extraordinary difficulties, his methods of rising to their challenges were equally extraordinary in themselves—so much so that he ended up creating a film that is richer than its source in texture and, in its extension and development of certain thematic implications, more resonant as well. Nevertheless, Kubrick also managed to treat the novel with such careful respect that Burgess himself found the film the most faithful adaptation he had ever seen. And Kubrick in fact followed the novel's story line, used its structure, remained close to its characterizations, and even retained its first-person narration, with Nadsat itself reappearing in the form of voice-over commentary. Using an entire aresenal of boldly imaginative and highly suggestive cinematic strategies, he also managed to replicate much of that language's effect: he distanced the viewer from the film's violence; established an ironic tone; granted Alex considerable sympathy; strongly asserted his film's unreality; and, most crucially, transformed the whole into metaphor, making his movie a vehicle for expressing meanings beyond the literal.

As in the novel, everything in the film is highly stylized, especially its virtuoso opening sequence which serves as an exquisitely compressed introduction to its methods. Here, with Beethoven's Ninth on the soundtrack, we are shown Alex in extreme close-up, the angle of vision made all the more jarring, first, by the sardonic expression he wears, then by his bizarre makeup—one of his eyes but not the other is ringed by a heavy fringe of false eyelashes—and also by the fact that Kubrick holds the shot just that much longer than we might have expected. And when he finally does move the camera, he moves it so slowly, dollying back away from Alex at a pace seemingly dictated by the largo rhythms of the Ninth itself, that our sense of disorientation is only increased. So is it too by the visual revelation which follows: including as it does the sight of the outlandish costumes (bowler hats, white jumpsuits, and codpieces) of Alex and his three cronies, as well as that of the garish, grotesque, and neon-lit decor of the Korova Milkbar itself, featuring sculpted tables in the form of naked women in obscene postures before which Alex, droogs, and all the bar's other inhabitants sit as if sculpted themselves—stiff, immobile, posed into groups, almost into set pieces. Meanwhile, in voice-over, Alex himself speaks to us in a modified version of Nadsat: "That was me, that is Alex, and my three droogs . . . trying to make up our rassoodocks what to do with the evening." Clearly, this is no world like we've ever seen before; yet, it's one about which we already know a great deal. In just moments of screen time, it has already asserted its unreality, its lethargy, its vulgarity, violence, and pornographic texture; and though language, music, and camera movements have contributed to some degree, most of this has been communicated through the film's *look* alone.

Costume, decor, and mise-en-scène are only a few of the means, however, that Kubrick uses to effect the dislocation of both the viewer and the film's world. In subsequent scenes, he calls up other stylizing effects to distort our visual perspective and our sense of temporal and spatial relationships. He uses eerily dramatic backlighting in the sequence where Alex and his droogs beat up the "drunkie"; a distorting fish-eye lens in the scene where Alex rapes writer F. Alexander's wife; speeded-up motion during Alex's orgy with the two teenage girls; slow motion when Alex battles with his own droogs; and a hand-held camera and bizarre point-of-view angles during the murder of the cat lady.

Editing also contributes to our sense of disorientation, with Kubrick choosing, at several points during the film, to mount an explosively rapid montage. He punctuates Alex's masturbation scene with a series of close-up shots of his curious sculpture of four linked Jesus Christs, one shot following the other so quickly as to create the illusion of movement, thus enforcing our sense of the figures as chorus line; and also with a series of intercut shots of an explosion, falling rubble, Alex in vampire makeup, and cavemen attempting to escape from the falling rocks—all of which works in turn to carry us with appropriate violence into the violent nature of Alex's fantasies. Elsewhere, during the murder of the cat woman, we are shown (in place of the woman's own implicitly bloody face) a number of rapidly mounted and unnerving close-ups of parts of one of her abstract yet erotic paintings—a vision that manages to capture the feel of the murder and yet to aestheticize it at the very same time.

Kubrick also uses music to distance us from the action, setting up a continual ironic counterpoint that stands in the way of direct and immediate involvement. Inspired by the novel, Kubrick chooses to have Alex masturbate to the glorious sounds of Ludwig van (a coupling enforced in the film by still another set of quickly intercut images—these of Beethoven himself, whose famous, grimacing portrait hangs in Alex's room). It's strictly Kubrick's own invention, though, to choreograph a bloody fight to Rossini's *The Thieving Magpie*; to set the teenage orgy to the *William Tell Overture*; and to juxtapose the vicious beating of the writer and rape of his wife with Alex's hearty rendition of the cheery American classic, "Singin' in the Rain."

But the effect of Kubrick's many strategies is not simply to disorient us, creating a sense of the unreal and signaling the film's allegorical nature in the process. Nor is it only to establish the movie's darkly comic tone. Nor is it either merely a way of helping to undercut the force of Alex's sadism and thus allow us a certain sympathy. (Kubrick, in any case, relies most heavily on the extraordinary charisma of actor Malcolm McDowell to elicit our concern for Alex, as well as on the contrast between Alex and everyone else in his world—all of whom, as in the novel but only more so, tend to be even more repellent than he.) The most significant effect is to invest the visual texture of the film with emblematic value, to transmute the individual details of decor, costume, setting, lighting, and cinematography, and ultimately the film as a whole, into varieties of metaphor.

Most obviously, there's the way in which the stylization of Alex's most vicious acts serves to comment on Alex's own view of violence. The music here, for example, helps us understand that to Alex, violence is as cheering and exhilarating as "Singin' in the Rain," as grand as Beethoven's Ninth. The dramatic lighting and bold, primary colors act to flatten all the characters of the film, revealing them thus as two-dimensional figures reminiscent of those in a comic strip, as people equally limited in their humanity as cartoon characters. The decor, and the peculiar art objects in particular that are so major a part of it, works to communicate the total decadence of Alex's world; while these objects also indicate the extent to which this world has debased art itself. Transformed into a weapon at one point (when Alex kills the cat lady with her sculpture of a huge penis), part of the Ludovico treatment at another (where the enforced witnessing of horrifying movies becomes a crucial means of transforming Alex into *a clockwork orange),* an inspiration for violence at still another (as when Beethoven's music summons up ugly fantasies), "art objects" here, as one *Sight and Sound* article puts it, are inevitably "abused to serve base, selfish ends. They are cogs in the conditioning process."

While this writer attributes such a view of art quite specifically to Kubrick and finds it expressed in other of his films, especially *Barry Lyndon,* the view is also Burgess's. Indeed, developing the point somewhat further in his novel, Burgess not only suggests that art can be perverted to inspire violence, he even goes so far as to imply that art and violence spring from the very same roots— from man's individuality, from his will and imagination. Kubrick concurs here, too, encasing the theme once again in the emblematic texture of his film's decor. For significantly enough, as several critics have perceptively observed, once Alex enters the cleansed and sanitized institutional world—the world where man is turned into a "clockwork orange" and deprived of his humanity—all art disappears, except for religious art which, in the form of the Bible, inspires fantasies in Alex (with no small irony) nearly as violent as those inspired by Beethoven. But no statuary is seen, no paintings: the walls are barren in the prison, empty in the institute where Alex undergoes the Ludovico treatment, and coldly white washed in the hospital. Given that Alex's most vicious acts and fantasies occur in environments that, by contrast, are strongly aestheticized—from the cat lady's art-laden studio to the writer's book-lined home to Alex's own Beethoven-adorned bedroom—the implications are unmistakable and, since presented to us so immediately and directly on film, more unmistakable than in the novel: Deprive man of his potential for violence and you deprive him of his impulse for creation, of his capacity for individual expression, ultimately then of his art.

In addition, you also deprive him of his sexual potency—a fact that further underscores the perception of Alex as more thoroughly human when freely vicious. And though once again, this is a thematic stand that has its source in the novel, where (as in the film) the Ludovico treatment turns Alex into gelding as well as lamb—or at least into an emotional eunuch repelled by displays of sexuality—it's one that also emerges more strongly on film. Included among Kubrick's rich fund of visual metaphors are a striking series of phallic images, all of which are associated in one way or another with Alex. There are the phallic masks that Alex and droogs wear while performing violent acts. There's the penis sculpture with which he does in the cat lady. There's Alex's pet snake and his codpieces. A fascinating (though basically unsympathetic) analysis of the film puts forth the notion that these images can be taken as Kubrick's means of both translating and transforming Burgess's scatological vision—scatological motifs obviously being a good deal more resistant to cinematic expression than phallic ones. But if these phallic images are in fact stand-ins, Kubrick still hasn't used them merely as means for expressing the inexpressible. Where Burgess's scatology is little more than a further expression of his Swiftian disgust and despair, Kubrick makes his phallicism an expression of a more richly suggestive theme. Associating Alex with the phallus, Kubrick quite pointedly defines the various "institutional" men in other terms—making all of them either blatantly and gratingly homosexual (like social worker Deltoid) or prissily effeminate (like the mechanical prison guard) or bitterly impotent (like Patrick Magee's wheelchair-confined writer). What's more, these figures are also revealed as less than fully human themselves. Thus, potency (as embodied in the phallus) becomes another of the terrifying but nonetheless distinctively humanizing qualities that, together with art and violence, society's institutions risk crushing.

It's clear that, in *A Clockwork Orange*, Kubrick has made use of film's capabilities for the creation of metaphor to an extraordinary degree while also managing to discover striking cinematic analogies for Burgess's emphatically linguistic devices. But he's also done something else: he has ended up making a work that, whether or not more powerful than its source, is at least more powerfully disturbing and which, because of this, creates more intense conflicts in its audience.

Consider our feelings about Alex. As played by Malcolm McDowell, he may be more sympathetic and charming on screen than he is in the novel. (Indeed, several critics have complained of the fact.) But since on film we are immediate witnesses to his sadism and violence, no matter how framed and stylized his acts may be, he is also that much more despicable. Similarly, though the others in Alex's world (his victims, especially) emerge on screen as more repellent than in the book, thus in some ways justifying Alex, or at least letting him off the hook, they are played by living actors (no matter how mannered their performances), and so are that much more human. And if, in the novel, art and violence are distressingly linked, what can we say of their connection in the film, where they appear together over and over again in a single frame? No wonder the film provoked so much controversy. No wonder its experience is so difficult to resolve. For like the novel, only more so, it traps us in a terrible dilemma. And not simply the dilemma of choosing between dehumanizing order on the one hand and violent freedom on the other, with which its metaphoric surface so boldly confronts us, but a dilemma that is in itself a metaphor for that very conflict—that of either accepting a savage vision or rejecting a savagely brilliant work of art.

Lord of the Flies: Boys Will Be Boys

William Golding's *Lord of the Flies* was to the 1960s what J. D. Salinger's *The Catcher in the Rye* was to the 1950s: the youth book of the decade, the novel widely assigned in college and high school classrooms, the one that nearly every undergraduate around seemed to have read. Why was it so popular? Most of the explanations were somewhat cynical—for though the novel had been very well received by the literary establishment (on its original publication in England in 1954, E. M. Forster himself had selected it as the "Outstanding Novel of the Year"), as with any work that achieves such phenomenal success, a certain critical backlash had set in.

Some suggested that *Lord of the Flies* was popular for the same decidedly extraliterary reasons that *The Catcher in the Rye* had also been: both books expressed the kind of adolescent despair for which youth traditionally has a considerable weakness. Others felt the novel's cachet lay in something very much its own: the extent to which it addressed (or even pandered to) the spirit of its time. A few commentators even went so far as to propose that the difference between the sentimental view of Salinger and the bitter vision of Golding could serve as the very emblem of the difference between the sensibilities of the fifties and sixties. Still others felt that the popularity of the novel lay in its peculiar quality of being both "ultra-simple and grandoise" at the very same time. Its allegory was so obvious, its symbolism so obtrusive, that young readers could easily resolve it. They felt comfortable with *Lord of the Flies;* the novel gave them a feeling of knowingness, a sense of control.

And certainly, there *is* little that is particularly subtle about Golding's fable concerning a group of English schoolboys who, sometime in the midst of a future atomic war, find themselves marooned on an uninhabited tropical island where, little by little, the society they attempt to construct falls into anarchy and violence. It can easily be read as a political parable, with Ralph, the good and just boy, embodying the principles of democracy; Jack, the evil and violent one, representing those of demagoguery; and Piggy, the bespectacled, asthmatic advice-giver, symbolizing the "brain trust" who tries to bring balance to their power struggle. It can also be viewed without much difficulty in Freudian terms, with Jack read as reflective of our wild and violent inner natures (the "id"); Ralph as suggesting the standards of civilization (the "ego"); and Piggy as implying the conscience of the adult world (the "superego").

It can also be seen, perhaps most persuasively, as a religious allegory. In this scheme, Ralph emerges as Adam or Everyman; Jack as Satan or fallen angel; little Simon, the strange boy who is murdered, as a kind of sacrificial Christ figure; and the rotting pig's head (or "lord of the flies") that the boys leave in the jungle to appease the imaginary beast they believe is threatening them as synonymous with the Biblical Beelzebub, an embodiment of pure evil. And there's still another possible way of viewing the book—as an inversion and commentary on the classic Victorian tale *Coral Island*, by R. M. Ballantyne, which is referred to several times in the text and which posits a situation similar to that in Golding's novel. In *Coral Island*, however, placing a group of boys alone on a desert island serves as a dramatic device to express the Victorian belief in childhood purity and innocence, as well as the then-current faith in the empire, in social standards, and in the essential goodness of man. Golding, of course, uses the situation to express precisely the opposite.

But whether the book is read in political, psychological, or religious terms, or as a local satire on British customs and values, or even as all at once, its point is more or less the same: that man is innately cruel and violent, that without the constraints of civilization, he will revert to his natural savage state. Moreover, it's a point that has seemed to many just a bit too simplistic in its vision, just a bit too facile in its pessimism, just a mite too neat and schematic in expression.

Still, the negative criticism the novel elicited is minor compared to that which greeted Peter Brook's 1963 film adaptation. Not that the movie didn't have its defenders, or even its followers. But mostly the critics rejected it, with Bosley Crowther of *The New York Times* speaking for the majority of his colleagues when he noted that the movie had "a strangely perfunctory, almost listless flow of narrative," that it was "a curiously flat and fragmentary visualization of the original." Few revisionist views came along to rescue the film, either. In fact quite the opposite occurred. Discussing the movie some half dozen years after its release, one film text referred to it as no less than a "disaster," adding that the writer had "attended the film with two educated and sensitive adults, neither of whom could figure out what the film was about or, most of the time, what was happening."

More than excessively harsh, this view seems to me downright unfair. Over the years, I've shown Brook's *Lord of the Flies* to several different classes, each of which inevitably included a number of students who hadn't read the book, and I've never found that even these had major difficulty in following it. Nor has the film ever struck me as anything close to a total "disaster." Far from being "perfunctory," many of its implicit choices reflect careful consideration; it also seems to me to possess a much stronger sense of narrative than some critics have credited it with.

There's the film's opening montage, for example, where behind the titles we are shown a series of grainy stills—a shot of an ivy-covered English college, a class picture of a group of young students, a glimpse of a row of choir boys, another of men playing cricket. Suddenly, we cut to a series of shots of Big Ben with planes behind it, of an evacuation sign, of missiles and a mushroom cloud, of an airplane, a cloudy sky, an explosion, a map of the Pacific, and a series of spinning images suggesting a crash. The soundtrack supplies further details, bringing the stills alive: the boy's choir can be heard singing, the sound of polite clapping can be heard during the cricket match; Big Ben can be heard tolling, and behind the spinning shots is the sound of the crash itself. Thus, in mere moments and much more efficiently (and even more clearly) than the novel, the film establishes its time frame and situation and its world as a real yet unreal one, in which England has suffered an atomic attack and in which a group of evacuated boys have crashed somewhere in the Pacific.

There's also something very right about the film's often stark black-and-white cinematography (by Tom Hollyman) and about Brook's decision to use a cast of unprofessional actors—an actual group of English schoolboys, in fact—and to (reportedly) set them loose in the Puerto Rican location where the film was shot and catch them unawares while swimming or at play. For the documentary texture that results seems very much the stylistic equivalent of Golding's unadorned, philosophic prose, while the boys provide a wonderful feel for the intense Englishness of the whole and, consequently, for at least one level of the novel's import. And if Brook hasn't cast them precisely according to Golding's directions (Simon is dark in the novel, blond in the film; Ralph "might have made a boxer," according to Golding, and is somewhat slight, according to Brook), they are nonetheless effectively varied types whose looks to a considerable degree reflect their roles and personalities. The youngster who plays Simon (Tom Gaman) is appropriately fragile; the boy who plays Ralph (James Aubrey) is, as he should be, normal and healthy in appearance; while the youth who plays Jack (Tom Chapin) is lean and tall with aptly hawkish features. As for Piggy, he has been cast especially well, with pudgy, evidently nearsighted

Hugh Edwards not only looking the part but, with his hesitant, adenoidal speech, sounding it to near perfection. Edwards also is responsible for the most inspired of the film's allegedly improvised moments—one in which he tells the "littluns" (as the smaller boys are dubbed) the story of how his hometown, Camberly, got its name.

Brook also stages several powerful sequences. There's the chilling moment in which Jack and his choir, clad in dark capes and odd caps, are seen in long shot marching along the edge of the sea, *Kyrie eleison* swelling on the soundtrack; and there's the savagely rendered scene of the feast in which, the boys gone wild, Simon is killed. Aside from these choices, one might also be tempted to credit the film with having removed nearly all of the novel's attitudinizing remarks and presenting us with a straightforward and suggestive drama from which such meanings as there are arise naturally and inevitably from its situations and conflicts.

Ultimately, however, one can't credit it too much. For even when all the film's virtues are granted, it turns out that its detractors—if overstating the case and somewhat off the mark in their specific arguments—are to the point in their final evaluation. *Lord of the Flies*, the movie, doesn't fully work. A very basic problem is that Brook's implicit reading seems inconsistent. His highly literal treatment would suggest that he is taking Golding's tale above all as a commentary on British character and customs. Yet, at the very same time, he has also included—whether or not merely out of the need to justify his title—some of the novel's key symbols: the corpse of the flier, the pig's head on the stick, Simon's curious encounter with it. And he has also added (as if by way of enforcement) the frequent sound of the buzzing of flies on the soundtrack. Such symbolism doesn't fit in with a straightforward interpretation of the text, pointing instead and insistently to more metaphysical implications.

This all might still have been acceptable and even satisfactory had Brooks supplied the film with the metaphysical level needed to contain and support such implications—had he supplied his film, that is, with a multileveled texture similar to the novel's. But not only hasn't he done so, he hasn't even supplied any adequate means for clarifying his symbols in the first place. And it's here that the film becomes, if not totally unintelligible, totally ambiguous and cloudy. The point is that much as we might admire Brook's choice to rely on his drama to score its own points, he in fact has relied on it overmuch. The image of Jack and the choirboys hunting undoubtedly suggests something of man's violence; undoubtedly, too, Jack and Piggy's reliance on the conch as a means of giving its holder the right to speak suggests man's gestures toward the creation of order; and the fire the boys light in order to provide a sign of their presence quite naturally implies hope, just as the imaginary beast implies irrational fear. But all of the gestures remain little more than suggestion or, at most, reach the level of "natural" symbolism, that is, of symbolism which, rather than being determined by the particular filmic context, is inevitably part of a particular object's connotative potential. Water, for example, as an essential life-giving element, quite naturally connotes life itself; thunder, inherently frightening, often connotes danger and terror. Since "illusion and reality" is almost by definition the name of the game they play, the most commercial and mundane of thrillers or detective stories can be found to carry all sorts of epistemological overtones and metaphysical connotations. But to bring these connotations to a metaphoric level requires something else again. It is precisely this something else that Brook has failed to provide.

Admittedly, he did face a considerable challenge, especially given that Golding's text is somewhat less helpful than it might have been. Its strategies—the unusual emphasis placed on such details as the conch, and particularly the passages of internal musing on the part of Ralph and Simon—are far from easily (or comfortably) transferable to film. Indeed, considering the novel's quite considerable dose of authorial commentary, these strategies aren't necessarily the most ideal of literary devices either. For example: "Jack stood up as he said this, the bloodied knife in his hand. The two boys faced each other. There was the brilliant world of hunting, tactics, fierce exhilaration, skill; and there was the world of longing and baffled commonsense." Or, "And in the middle of them, with filthy body, matted hair, and unwiped nose, Ralph wept for the end of innocence, the darkness of man's heart. . . ." But whatever the limitations of such bald statements as fictional devices, they overwhelmingly assert the tale's allegorical nature and they also control its interpretation. And Brook simply hasn't found any effective equivalent for them. The most he seems to have come up with, aside from music—the film is quite heavily scored—are shots of turbulent skies, swaying treetops and rustling leaves, sunlight and/or moonlight dancing off the tops of waves. Not only do these verge on the trite, but, like the film's music, they work more to create mood than to carry any precise commentary.

Brook also hasn't figured out a means of giving us a sufficient sense of change, or of the passage of time. The boys' hair never grows, their clothes never become much shabbier than the rips and tears we see in them very early on. He thus tosses away an opportunity not only to intensify his drama, but to allow the imagery of the film to communicate something of its symbolic resonance. (The boys at least might have begun to *look* like savages, instead of a bunch of dirty and ragged kids.) And though Brook's nonprofessionals are, as suggested, effective in creating a sense of authenticity, they are inadequate at communicating the kind of depth of passion that might have made us see Jack as truly evil or Simon as truly spiritual. They remain, even in their war paint and screams, nothing more than English schoolboys.

Brook's greatest failure, however, lies in his handling of the novel's two chief symbols: the dead aviator whose parachute deposits him on the top of the island's mountain and, with the help of the wind, moves his corpse eerily about; and the pig's head, the "lord of the flies." In the case of the aviator, Brook's cinematography is simply too discrete. The shot of the dreaded figure comes and goes too quickly and, though obviously a dead man, he lacks the possibly distressing but still necessary detail. Thus we are left without an adequate feel either for the vision itself or for the way in which this figure, interpreted by the frightened boys as the terrifying beast, appears to them. Moreover, Brook's fleeting image carries none of the irony implicit in Golding's descriptions, as, for example, in the following passage where the man, though dead, is pictured as paying obeisance to the heavens:

> . . . the figure sat, its helmeted head between its knees, held by a complication of lines. When the breeze blew the lines would strain taut and some accident of this pull lifted the head and chest upright so that the figure seemed to peer across the brow of the mountain. Then, each time the wind dropped, the lines would slacken and the figure bow forward again, sinking its head between its knees, so as the stars moved across the sky, the figure sat on the mountain-top and bowed and sank and bowed again.

Brook does even worse, though, with Simon's meeting with pig's head. In the novel, Golding himself does something somewhat daring here: he allows Simon to hear (or at least, imagine he hears) the pig's head speaking.

> "Fancy thinking the Beast was something you could hunt and kill!" said the head. . . . "You knew, didn't you? I'm part of you? Close, close, close! I'm the reason why it's no go? Why things are what they are?"

To use the same effect on film would most likely have been too heavy-handed; yet, as in his choice to merely omit rather than translate in a meaningful manner the book's continual commentaries, Brook's solution here seems more unfortunate yet. For in this critical scene, he does no more than show us Simon staring at the head, intercutting shots of the boy's face with a series of close-ups of the pig's snout and his fly-infested mouth. These images are unpleasant, but they aren't very much more than that. They fail totally to deliver any specific meaning.

As vaguely rendered as its symbols are, and as open-ended as its connotations are as well, Brook's film is consequently stuck on the literal level—on the only level, that is, on which it fully resolves itself. It becomes, then, a movie (albeit with a few inconsistent scenes and details) about the innate viciousness of English schoolboys—schoolboys who, as Jonathan Miller put it in his *New Yorker* review, "ditch a few courtesies and reveal a full-blown version of the bullying nastiness that they [implicitly] already showed back in England's green and pleasant land." Miller, one of the few to praise the film, felt that this vision made for the movie's very "strength." One has to grant Miller his point. On a fairly direct level, *Lord of the Flies*, the movie, does have some special power. But not quite enough, and certainly nowhere near that of Golding's fable. Thus, we see not only the way in which Brook's failure to make meaningful use of his medium's potentials for metaphoric statement has diminished his film's effect and reduced its importance; we also discover something about Golding's novel—that for all the blatancy and patness of its symbolism, it probably wouldn't have amounted to very much without it.

Wise Blood: Wise Choices

If one were to accept traditional notions of what is possible for the screen, the work of Flannery O'Connor might seem utterly, unequivocally unfilmable. And not simply because of its highly emblematic nature—because of the parable-like plots and heavy overlay of metaphor that have so delighted symbol-hunters. Even more crucial are the qualities that drive us off the literal level in the first place: the grotesque surreality of O'Connor's landscapes; the often monstrous extremism of her images; the black craziness of her humor; the bizarre and frequently gruesome religiosity that makes her southern world, by her own description, a "Christ-haunted" place. All of this is certainly enough to defy a medium such as film, with its affinity for the real and its difficulty in distancing us from the dreadful. But given that it's also a medium where identification with the figures before us seems natural, inevitable, and even essential, there's still another and more problematic quality yet with adapting O'Connor: the dehumanizing freakishness of her characters. We can't read O'Connor literally because the people we encounter in her works don't seem to us fully credible, because their weirdness counters emotional involvement, denying us, as one critic puts it, a "non-ideological response" to them.

This emotional involvement is denied us with none of her characters more than with Hazel Motes, the protagonist of O'Connor's startling first novel, *Wise Blood*. The orphaned grandson of a backwoods revivalist preacher, possessed of a burning passion to deny Jesus Christ, Hazel (or Haze, as he's called in both book and film) is an absurd contradiction in terms: an atheistic evangelist. Going about spreading the gospel of his newly formed Church Without Christ where, as he proclaims, "the blind *don't* see, the lame *don't* walk, and what's dead stays that way," he is also a man who, in the process of attempting to prove that "sin don't exist" undergoes a crazy odyssey. He encounters a bevy of madmen, pariahs, and grotesques, lives through a series of equally mad adventures, and sins gratuitously. He murders an absolute stranger, a man whom a fraudulent preacher dresses up as Haze's double in order to cash in on Haze's "good idears," and at the end of the tale, immolates himself with a series of acts—including blinding himself with lime—which, however one might interpret them—as a grotesque mockery of the excesses of religious faith or as Haze's way to salvation—both shock and distress.

Nonetheless, it is precisely this hero and his weird quest that John Huston chose to bring to the screen in his 1980 O'Connor adaptation—an extraordinary film which made very clear that, whatever one might have believed beforehand, not only was O'Connor filmable but there was much about her work that transferred to the screen with remarkable ease. The screenplay, by Benedict Fitzgerald, stays astoundingly close to the novel. (Perhaps not surprisingly, given that both the scenarist and the film's producer are sons of Robert and Sally Fitzgerald, Flannery O'Connor's literary executor and the editor of her collected letters, respectively.) And many of O'Connor's scenes prove to have been imagined in strikingly visual terms: from the encounter of Hazel Motes's would-be acolyte, the moronic Enoch Emery, with movie monster Gonga the Gorilla; through Enoch's crazy theft of the Gonga costume and his nighttime excursion while wearing it; to Haze's stealthy nighttime visit to the room of the false blind preacher Asa Hawks, in order to light a match close to his face as proof that he can see.

O'Connor's written dialogue also transfers easily. Apt and convincing as spoken dialogue, it's often wonderfully amusing as well. There's the wry little monologue of Asa Hawks's daughter, Sabbath Lily, when she recites to Haze, by way of tempting him, her parodic exchange of letters with a newspaper advice-giver about her sexual yearnings. There are also the startlingly understated remarks of Haze's landlady, Mrs. Flood, who upon finding rocks in her tenant's shoes and his chest bloodied by barbed-wire wrappings, cries out: "It's not natural, Mr. Motes. It's not normal. . . . People have quit doing it."

To suggest that there's much about O'Connor that one might consider "cinematic" isn't also to claim that in *Wise Blood* the result is anything like a traditional movie. It's a thoroughly eccentric work—as eccentric as the novel itself—and as such a decidedly courageous one. (Significantly, it wasn't a Hollywood studio but an independent production company that undertook its risky financing.) Nor is it to undermine Huston's contribution or even to suggest that the film, in closely following the text, is a mere illustration of it, a film which some seemed to feel hadn't "quite made up its mind whether it wants to be a movie or a literary reading." For one thing, there's nothing about the film (aside from the nature of its source, that is) which has a "literary" feel to it. There's no extended dialogue, no voice-over narration, no lack of external movement and action. And for another, there's a good deal about the film that makes it almost as much of a piece with Huston's work as with O'Connor's, pointing to a rare congeniality between writer and filmmaker. Huston has always had a propensity for the bizarre (think of *Beat the Devil*), a sense for the mythic (think of the parable-like *The Treasure of Sierra Madre*); and his notoriously sardonic humor is to be found almost everywhere in his movies, from *The Maltese Falcon* through his adaptation from Kipling, *The Man Who Would Be King*. Moreover, if Huston's manner of bringing *Wise Blood* to the screen is insistently straightforward, in this particular case, that treatment turned out to be strikingly apt.*

The director seems to have recognized (implicitly, at least) that the somewhat paradoxical problem of bringing O'Connor's metaphorical materials to the screen isn't so much in maintaining their emblematic thrust as it is in providing them with the plausibility and human acceptability (and ultimately accessibility) they lack on the printed page.† Put another way, the

---

*For an instance in which a similar decision turned out to be anything, but see the discussion of *Under the Volcano* in Chapter Eight.

†Indeed, many see the flaw in O'Connor's work as lying exactly here—that is, in its lack of

danger in adapting a work like *Wise Blood* is that once embodied on film, O'Connor's characters might seem to us too mad, too repellent, too unbelievable to invite us to go beyond their immediate impression and search for their larger significance.

Whatever the reason, Huston has wisely chosen to ground O'Connor's grotesques in as real a world as possible. The film opens with a series of grainy black-and-white stills reminiscent of old Walker Evans photographs. We see a gravestone with "Jesus Called" scrawled in chalk across it; a Dairy Queen, on top of it a sign on which, "Repent and Be Baptized in Jesus' Name" is emblazoned in neon; a rough, splintered road sign bearing the message, evidently painted by an illiterate hand, "If You Repent, God Welcomes You." Thus, the world of the film is not only established as being steeped in theology and obsessed with the need for belief and redemption, but—with these authentic stills implying a world *glimpsed* rather than created—as situated in a "Christ-haunted" actuality. The film was shot on location in Macon, Georgia, and with the help of the low-keyed, unobtrusive cinematography of Gerald Fisher, Huston has captured the city's faded, rickety frame houses; the down-home dustiness of its streets; the authentic Southern atmosphere. Huston has also filled the film's minor roles with Georgia natives, some nonprofessionals, some local actors, and they, in turn, with their lined faces, ruined teeth, and dialect-tinged speech, provide the film's world with a further stamp of genuineness.

The major characters have also been considerably humanized, largely by having been allotted somewhat more sympathy on screen than they receive in the novel. Sometimes (though rarely), an alteration in the characterization itself effects the shift in attitude. In the story, Mrs. Flood is motivated to marry the blind Hazel by greed; in the film, it is her pathetic loneliness that drives her and also, perhaps, sexual frustration. With the help of Mary Nell Santacroce's lovely and moving performance, she emerges on screen as a much more touching figure than she is in the novel. Sometimes, it's simply a matter of the way a particular incident has been mounted. Take the scene in which Enoch—whose belief in his own intuition, or "wise blood," gives the work its title—lines up at the movie to shake Gonga the Gorilla's hand. In the novel, Enoch does so only once, O'Connor stressing the significance of the gesture by informing us that the hand was "warm and soft . . . the first hand that had been tended to Enoch in the city." In the film, Enoch goes through the line again and again, shaking Gonga's hand as

human acceptability, in the fact that her tales are too abstract.

many times as he can, making his desperation for contact more intense, his gesture that much more pathetic.

Huston has done more, however, than merely give the film an intense reality or allow the figures greater humanity and empathy. He has also managed to do all this without undermining the novel's symbolic suggestiveness. This is partly a function of the extent to which O'Connor has invested her characters and actions with such a strong and particularized symbolic value that in being transferred from page to screen they almost invariably carry that value with them. (For instance, the shriveled and shrunken mummy that Enoch steals from the zoo museum and presents to Haze as the "new Christ" for his Church Without Christ is as inevitably an ironic metaphor on film as it is in the novel; while Enoch's donning of the gorilla costume is as much a blackly comic reversal of the evolutionary process—as much an image of man-without-God as man-as-animal—on screen as it is on the page. Which is why the criticism that the film only gives us "the data of the book" and not that data's significance doesn't really make much sense. *Wise Blood* is that rare novel which has no data that doesn't have built-in significance.)

A good part of the symbolic texture, too, is generated by the effective casting and exemplary performances. Brad Dourif, with his lizard eyes, pale angular face, and passionate intensity makes Haze such an unsettling presence that, if we aren't denied an emotional and human response to him as we are in the novel—he is after all being played by a flesh-and-blood actor—we still must see him emblematically. So too in the case of both Harry Dean Stanton's ominous Asa Hawks—with his dark hat pulled down low, his dark coat buttoned high, his dark glasses and stub of a cigarette held between his thin lips—and Daniel Shor's Enoch, who even dangles his arms throughout in a manner suggesting an ape.

All of this notwithstanding, Huston's particular strategies play a significant role in pushing us away from the literal level. Consider that whereas the story begins with Haze on the train to Taulkinham (the city where the action takes place), the film opens with him returning from the army to his deserted and ruined home, and only then follow him on to Taulkinham. By thus reversing O'Connor's two opening scenes, the film tends to assert (and more explicitly than the novel) its narrative pattern as one of a journey—and a particular kind of journey, away from the burden of the past and toward self-discovery, with all of such an odyssey's mythic association. Throughout, Huston also mounts that odyssey in a sprightly, almost cheerful manner that makes for a tone somewhat lighter than O'Connor's, but which, rather than betraying her, releases and intensifies her sometimes elusive comedy. The effect of that tone is not simply to distance us sufficiently from the action so that the ugliness we must bear witness to becomes possible to contemplate. Nor is it even merely to transform the horrible into the horribly funny. The lighter tone also gives the work the feel of a comic tall tale. This may sound like a contradiction, since Huston also underscores the realism of O'Connor's materials. And so, in a sense, it is. But *Wise Blood* is a movie whose accomplishment lies very much in the extent to which it has managed to bring off such contradictory effects.

Moreover, though the film is shot in a straightforward manner—with Huston generally eschewing unusual angles and strategies of editing—he does encase Haze's memories of his childhood, at least, in surreally textured images. At first glance, these garishly colored scenes of grandpa (played by Huston himself) giving a hellfire sermon in a tent and of Haze as a child stealing a glimpse of a wriggling naked lady in a carnival sideshow might strike us as somewhat discordant with the film's texture as a whole. But the lurid quality of the cinematography has an evident purpose, serving as it does as revealing metaphor for the emotional quality of Haze's memories. Huston also introduces some highly suggestive imagery in the course of mounting the film's main narrative. Take the manner in which he has envisioned Mrs. Leora Watts (owner of "the friendliest bed in town"), whom Haze visits not out of sexual desire but simply out of the desire to sin. In the novel, she's merely described as a "big" woman; in the film, she's enormously fat—a parody figure, in fact, worthy of Fellini or Wertmuller. Reflecting on the grotesqueness of her profession, her overstated size also reflects on the grotesqueness of Haze's motives—while her marvelously comic gesture of kicking her slippers into the air with her pudgy legs serves to further caricature her sexuality.

There's also the moment in which, after Enoch has delivered to the arms of Sabbath Lily (who has finally gotten Haze to bed) the shrunken mummy he has stolen from the museum, Sabbath decides to surprise the sleeping Haze with it. Going outside the room and knocking on the door, she greets Haze (and us in turn) with a terrifically ironic sight. For standing there with a scarf around her head and shoulders, the mummy in her arms, she makes of herself not simply a mock mother, but—since that mummy is Enoch's "new Christ"—a mock Virgin and child. There's also Huston's manner of handling the demise of Haze's car, which in both novel and film bears considerable symbolic value. The immediate catalyst of Haze's choice to blind himself, the car has served as his pulpit, even for a while as his home, and has also been, as he himself makes explicit, his substitute for religion. "A man with a good car doesn't have to be justified," he tells Sabbath Lily when she informs him that her father "blinded himself for justification." In both novel and film, the car's destruction occurs when a policeman pushes it off an embankment. But whereas in O'Connor it simply turns over, landing wheels in the air, in Huston it is seen at the end sinking into a pond—a shot which, as the *Sight and Sound* review of the film pointed out, can't help but call up in this context "associations of both burial and baptism."

The film's final shot is also highly suggestive. Here, as the camera tracks further and further back from Mrs. Flood, shown to us standing watch over Haze's mutilated corpse, the realistic space of the room is violated and the entire reality of the scene undercut in turn. Thus, Huston hints both at the metaphoric nature of what is before us and also at his ultimate interpretation of O'Connor's materials. For the shot is a fairly effective equivalent of the novel's closing image, in which Haze becomes a "pinpoint of light" in Mrs. Flood's inner eye—though because she is a more sympathetic figure in the film, her evident faith in the martyred Haze becomes less ironic. Not all irony is lost, however. Haze, who was so desperate to deny Christ, becomes, as the image suggests, very much a Christ figure himself; while desperate as he was to find a convert to his atheism, he has ended up finding one to his faith instead.

Significantly, all of these connotations and metaphoric suggestions arise from the natural surface of the narrative—as much, that is, as one can call the surface "natural" here. But in any case, they do arise from plausible narrative details rather than from images thrown in for analogy's sake. Stressing the mythic or emblematic qualities carried by them, then, one obviously takes the risk of granting them a bit too much weight or, quite simply, of overreading them.

Still, the richly metaphoric context of the whole does more than make such interpretations as I've offered possible—in a very real sense, it invites them. And whether in fiction or film, context is always the final key to the validity of any interpretation. It's the key, too, as to why some of the very strategies that Huston used in this film—the documentary-like opening shots, the use of nonprofessionals—though very similar to those used by Peter Brook in *Lord of the Flies*, helped to release and even make possible the film's metaphors in the one case and served to literalize and finally deny them in the other. In his positive review of Barry Levinson's *The Natural*, much altered from Bernard Malamud's novel, Stanley Kauffmann writes: "Possibly I ought to feel guilty about not being more protective (as I often have been) of a novel by a good writer. Which underscores my chief critical dictum: criticism is less a matter of dicta than of instances." Quite clearly, metaphor is such a matter too.

Death in Venice:
The Seductiveness of the Sensual

Thomas Mann had mixed feelings about the cinema: "For me, I despise it myself, but I love it too," he wrote toward the end of the silent era. In the case of Luchino Visconti's 1971 adaptation of *Death in Venice*, one can't help but have mixed feelings about the cinema's treatment of Thomas Mann—as did the critical world at large. Vociferously condemned by some, the film was extravagantly praised by others, and went on to win several prestigious awards, including a Special Jury Prize at Cannes. The criticism itself was curiously mixed. Even the film's staunchest supporters found themselves admitting to certain of its limitations, owning that the movie didn't do justice to Mann; while its harshest critics, for their part, found themselves forced to grant its intelligence, its prodigious beauty, and the power of its Mahler-drenched score. In brief, *Death in Venice* is a film rife with contradiction. So too, in its potential for film at least, is the novella itself.

On the one hand, the tale is extraordinarily rich in imagery of the kind that must inevitably tempt the cinematic imagination. The story centers on an aging, weary, renowned German writer, Gustav von Aschenbach, who travels to Venice, where the beauty of a young Polish boy forces the belated recognition of long-rejected impulses. So there are preeminently the sights and sounds of Venice itself—as Mann describes it: "that amazing group of structures the Republic set up to meet the awe-struck eye of the approaching seafarer: the airy splendour of the palace and Bridge of Sighs, the columns of lion and saint on the shore, the glory of the projecting flank of the fairy temple, the vista of gateway and clock." There's also the luxuriousness of the grand hotel where Aschenbach stays, its beach with lovely vistas, its rooms "decorated with strong-scented flowers," filled with "subdued voices . . . speaking most of the European tongues." There are the endless sights of the exquisite boy, Tadzio. And as, in the course of the tale, Venice is gripped by a plague of cholera, there is a series of powerfully bizarre images of disease, decadence, and death: luscious but noxious strawberries; a grotesque street musician; a black-draped camera standing unattended on the beach.

On the other hand, and decidedly troublesome for film, there's the fact that the tale's plot is extremely thin. There are no events here, only incidents, with most of the story built out of thoughts, perceptions, yearnings. Of greater note, however, is the fact that everything we see, while rooted in plausible events and an actual world, is also simultaneously symbolic. What incidents there are and the imagery itself carry a heavy burden of metaphor. Sometimes, it's Mann's descriptive language that makes the point: Venice is said to be a "floating dream"; Tadzio is described as having "the head of Eros with the yellowish bloom of Parian marble," as "godlike" in his beauty, as being in fact "beauty's essence, so rare and holy it must surely have been born for his [Aschenbach's] adoration"; the gondolas are described as "black as nothing else on earth except a coffin"; the ocean is said to suggest to the artist/hero the lure "for the unorganized, the immeasurable, the eternal—in short, for nothingness."

More often, though, the metaphoric value of character, image, and atmosphere is established by long passages of exposition. Like all of Mann's works, *Death in Venice* is philosophical in texture, filled with thoughtful asides on art, beauty, and culture—there's even an imagined Socratic dialogue—which carry the novella's complex assortment of heady themes and allow for (indeed insist upon) both a symbolic and multileveled interpretation of Aschenbach's tragedy. No mere homosexual drama, *Death in Venice* is, as the story of both an artist and an *echt* German so given to discipline and moralism that he has dangerously suppressed the natural and instinctual, a replay of the classic Faust theme, the story of the inevitable downfall of the divided, unintegrated self. It is also, on other levels, a dramatization of the conflict between bourgeois values and aesthetic decadence; a tale of a world and class on the wane (the setting is in the years immediately preceding World War I); a fictional reworking of Platonic notions of beauty, desire, and virtue; a dramatization of Nietzsche's theory of culture in which man's urges toward the Apollonian (rationalism, order) are seen as at war with his impulse toward the Dionysian (the instinctual, the lawless). It has even been read, and persuasively, as metaphoric vision of the hidden perversity of the German soul.

Such metaphoric and philosophic complexities would seem hopelessly out of the reach of film. Yet Visconti has managed nonetheless to travel a daring distance in meeting the challenge they present, and he has certainly been resourceful in some of the changes he has worked on the story. Tak-

ing his cue both from Mann's admission that he modeled the character of
Aschenbach (at least in part) on Gustav Mahler and from the author's own
Dr. Faustus, Visconti (who co-authored the screenplay with Nicola
Badalucco) has transformed Aschenbach from writer to composer. Purists,
predictably, have taken issue with the change, their chief argument being,
as Geoffrey Wagner notes, that to Mann music was representative of the
Dionysiac and thus constitutes an inappropriate form of expression for the
Apollonian Aschenbach. The dramatic advantages, however, are obvious.
After all, to spend considerable time describing Aschenbach's writings as
the story does would aggravate the potentially static quality of the whole,
whereas to play the composer's music on the soundtrack intensifies and
emotionally enriches the drama. What's more, Visconti implicitly attempts
to counter the Dionysian connotations of music by having an associate of
Aschenbach comment (in a recollected sequence) on the composer's intense
commitment to form—"Pure beauty, absolute severity, purity of form . . .
the abstraction of the senses, it's all gone, nothing remains, nothing," the
friend exclaims accusingly after a disastrous performance of Aschenbach's
music.

Other critics put forth different complaints about the transformation.
Joan Mellen argues that in changing Aschenbach from writer to musician,
Visconti forfeited the advantage "of a character whose words could provide
an ironic commentary on his own behavior"—apparently ignoring the fact
that Visconti has managed to make the character's music often work to the
very same end. Indeed, in an excellent commentary on the use of music in
the movie, George P. Stein demonstrates numerous ways in which the
film's rich score functions as ironic commentary. (One evident instance is
when "the sweet nothings of Lehar's *Merry Widow,*" played by the orchestra in the Grand Hotel des Bain's lobby, reflect on the "sweet nothingness"
of the lives of the lobby's denizens; another is when the "innocent tones"
of "Für Elise" are heard both as Tadzio sits at the piano and when a prostitute does so as well, emphasizing "the co-existence in both instances of innocence and corruption.") Stein also explores music's role in the film as a
means of metaphorically expressing mood and conflict. Consider the scene
where, as Aschenbach sits on the beach mesmerized by Tadzio and overwhelmed by his destructive desires, Visconti fills the soundtrack with
Mahler's Third Symphony, its lyrics by Nietzsche speaking expressly to the
composer's situation: "Take heed! / . . . The world is deep . . . / Deep is
its pain. . . ."

Visconti has also come up with an inventive device for incorporating some of the novel's explicit philosophical commentary. Taking his cue once again from Mann's *Dr. Faustus,* he gives Aschenbach a Mephistophelean friend, Alfred, with whom he debates, in a series of flashbacks, on various questions of art and the artist's life. Admittedly, many of these debates are so dense and speed by at such a rate that they become difficult to digest. But at least they hint at the nature of some of Aschenbach's conflicts and point to the larger significance of his actions ("Beauty belongs only to the senses," proclaims Alfred. "You cannot reach the spiritual through the senses. It is only by complete domination of the senses that you can ever achieve wisdom, truth, and human dignity," asserts Aschenbach. "I reject the demonic virtues of art." "Evil," counters Alfred, "is a necessity. It is the food of genius.") The flashbacks also provide Aschenbach with motives for his journey. (The first of these shows him collapsing after a concert, a doctor asserting his need for "complete rest.") Still another courageous change that Visconti has worked on the material is to omit the first long, explanatory section of the novella and to open his film with Aschenbach's arrival in Venice. This seems to me again a well-reasoned alteration—for Visconti has in this way tightened his film's dramatic structure.

Otherwise, though, the filmmaker has stayed fairly close to the tale—translating to the screen not simply the various incidents (from the meeting with the repellently rouged and powdered man on the boat to Venice to the rouging of Aschenbach himself in the barber's chair), but the minutest details of the imagery (for example, that lone camera on the beach at the end). His visual translation, moreover, is extraordinary. There isn't a shot in *Death in Venice* (photographed by Pasquale de Santi) that isn't quite startling in its visual texture. There are the Turner-like images at the outset in which, asserting itself slowly through the mist and fog, Venice seems to take shape before our very eyes. There's the much-praised pan in the lobby of the Grand Hotel des Bains where, taking us past the giant vases of flowers, the sumptuously attired women in pearls and feathered hats chattering in many languages, Visconti in a single sustained camera movement manages to capture an entire world. (One also has to give credit here to the costumes by Piero Tosi and the settings by Ferdinando Scarfiotti, which in their almost palpable beauty are themselves works of art.) Indeed, the beauty of the whole is so ravishing as to carry, by that token alone, a certain emblematic suggestiveness. Venice here has been transformed into something not quite real; it has been quite pointedly aestheticized.

But despite all of this, Visconti's *Death in Venice* never comes close to replicating the riches of Mann's story. Nor, despite the sublimity of its visual texture, the rich suggestiveness of its music, and the emblematic feel of its imagery, does it even manage to realize its own metaphoric potential. Consciously or unconsciously, Visconti—himself a homosexual and an aging and ill one to boot at the time he made the film—evidently empathized strongly with the concrete and human drama of Aschenbach. And in mounting the film, he made a series of choices that not only testify to that fact but also, as Visconti biographer Gaia Servadio suggests, make the film, of all Visconti's works, "the most revealing of Visconti himself." More to the point, perhaps, these choices reflect an interpretation of the story which focuses so strongly on the literal that the homosexual conflict, rather than serving as a vehicle for the exploration of an aesthetic or intellectual problem—of a Faustian agony or a Nietszchean dilemma—becomes the very center and subject of the drama. Thus the film limits both its impact and significance.

Visconti's most telling (and damaging) choice lies in his casting. A gifted actor—and one especially gifted at playing intellectuals—Dirk Bogarde is, all the same, much too British for Aschenbach. (He seems especially so, of course, in the film's English-language version). His restraint and repression tend to emerge, then, as a matter much more of British fussiness than of a sternly Teutonic control and self-discipline. Moreover, though he walks about stooped and stiff, though his hair is bedraggled and thinning and his moustache gray, and though he may not in actuality be much younger than the story's Aschenbach (Mann indicates only that his protagonist is past fifty, and at the time he played the part, Bogarde was fifty-one), he still, with his boyish features, seems much too young for the role. So much so in fact that when the barber applies hair dye and makeup, rather than making him look young, he merely makes him look feminine. The point is that, accurate or not, our sense of Aschenbach in the tale is of a man well past his prime and even past his potency. Bogarde in contrast seems something else again, and thus his desire for Tadzio becomes much more explicitly sexual.

And all the more so given Visconti's casting and handling of Tadzio. Statuesque and utterly beautiful, yes. But as incarnated by Bjorn Andresen, this Tadzio is also discomfortingly androgynous. Dressed by Pietro Tosi in clinging swimsuits that reveal every contour of his young body, and standing throughout, as *Listener* critic Jan Dawson puts it, "hand on hip and buttocks discreetly pouting," he even might be seen to resemble, again to cite Dawson, "a centre fold-out for some gay magazine." To make matters worse and even more transparent, Visconti decided to characterize Tadzio as a flirt. In the film, he is continually throwing knowing and suggestive glances back at Aschenbach, glances so unequivocal that it's impossible to read them (as we might in the novella) as a function of Aschenbach's imagination.

Aside from casting and characterization, certain narrative elements also serve to literalize the film's drama. The flashbacks contain some very curious and disconcerting materials—among them a highly ambiguous scene with a prostitute. But whether the sight of the young Aschenbach standing with his head buried in his hands after his visit to the young woman is meant to reflect his guilt, his disgust, or his impotence, the general emotional import is nonetheless clear: sex with a woman is somehow unsatisfactory to him; sex itself is somehow impure. And giving the same name, Esmeralda, to both the prostitute and the boat on which Aschenbach arrives in Venice in order to meet his appointment with death, the film underscores the suggestion even further. Also revealing is the musical link between the prostitute and Tadzio when Aschenbach listens to the boy playing "Für Elise" and recalls that it was also "Für Elise" that the prostitute had played. The link may be intended to suggest continuity, or the point may be contrast instead; but in either case, the upshot is the same: to enforce not merely Tadzio's beauty but his sexuality in Aschenbach's mind and emotions.

Visconti has also intensified Aschenbach's concern with aging—certainly a theme in the story, but a much slimmer one. In Mann, the question of age is chiefly a question of death and seems only incidentally a matter of Aschenbach's desire for Tadzio. The theme asserts itself strongly, in any case, only at the point where Aschenback is driven to visit the barber. Throughout the film, however, Aschenbach is deeply concerned with growing old, reflecting what Gaia Servadio tells us was Visconti's own very particular obsession and which here takes on a very particular homosexual tinge. Aschenbach is even heard talking about the pressure of time (and implicitly the pressure of age) in an early exchange with Alfred, where he takes note of an hourglass sitting on the edge of the piano, recalling that his father also had one: "The aperture through which the sand runs is so tiny that at first sight, it seems as if the level in the upper glass never changes. To our eyes, it appears that the sand runs out only, only at the end. . . ." A philosophical concern at this point, it becomes a distinctly sexual one later on.

It's also significant, I think, that all the men we see in the film—except perhaps the officious hotel manager—tend to be either boys or old men, or grotesquely made-up men, like the passenger on the boat and the musician. In the film's world, then, men go from young to old, with no elegant or graceful middle age. Not so women who, in any case, comprise most of the Lido population, and a heavy majority of the guests at the Grand Hotel des Bains as well. The choice to heavily populate his film with women may be Visconti's means of stressing the highly feminized nature of bourgeois society, of revealing the film's world as one where women dominate—a world with which his homosexual hero is at odds but to which, since it has spawned Tadzio, he is also attracted at the very same time. Whichever, the attitude of the film itself toward women is ambiguous and toward no woman so much as Tadzio's poised and elegant mother—a silent, distant, and exquisite figure who, played by Silvana Mangano, is strangely without emotional impact.

The effect of all these specific details is, quite inevitably, to encourage a perception of the film as concrete homosexual drama, rather than as metaphoric philosophical one. But there's also something in the overall texture of the film that pulls us off the symbolic level. The whole is *so* ravishing to the eye, *so* sublime to the ear, that—for all its suggestiveness—it ultimately becomes overwhelmingly sensual, overwhelmingly immediate. There's none of the distance that would invite us to *think* while watching the film; everything about it insists that we *feel*. Thus, the film has ended up—ironically enough—illustrating Mann's very own ambivalence about cinema. He both loved and hated it, he wrote, because "compared with art's intellectual appeal its own is . . . sensational. . . . [T]he atmosphere of art is cool; it is a sphere of transmuted values; a world of style . . . preoccupied with form; a sphere of the understanding. . . ." Not so the cinema, which he felt only bathed one in emotion and sensation, which was "all raw material" that had "not been transmuted."

Visconti has indeed failed to transmute his materials—to translate, that is, the characters and images and events of his *Death in Venice* into metaphor, in the manner of Thomas Mann. Yet, he hasn't in any way suggested that metaphor itself is impossible to film. What he's done instead is to make very clear the extent to which the possibilities for metaphor and the very shape it assumes are, like all other elements in adaptation, embedded in a given filmmaker's response to, and reading of, his source. Or, put another way, in the nature and quality of his interpretation.

8

Interiors: Thought, Dream, Inner Action

To talk about thought, dream, and inner action in the novel is, to talk almost exclusively about the modern, experimental novel—the novel, that is, as deeply responsive to and influenced by the growth of modern psychology, the breakdown of traditional values, and as shaped both by the modern artist's lack of faith in the public, the objectively verifiable, the communicable even, and by certain revised notions of the nature and function of art itself. It is also, on another level, to talk about a particular permutation of the first-person or, more precisely, third-person restricted vantage point, and so to return to some of the issues broached in the chapter on point of view.

Once again, the name of Henry James looms large. For not only was James, more than any novelist preceding him, involved with the problem of restricting a given fiction's vantage point to the perspective of a single, observant character; he also made that observing consciousness the very center of the action and that action, in turn, less a matter of external event than of the development of thought and feeling. Certain of the modern novelists who followed him carried such tendencies further, turning the vision of their characters more intensely inward. In a novel like James's *The Ambassadors*, the distinction between external experience and internal perceptions *begins* to break down, whereas in Virginia Woolf's *The Waves* that breakdown is nearly total. In Woolf, the external world as such ceases to exist. All that matters, and all that we are given, is the inner world of the individual consciousness, observing nothing so much as itself.

Instrumental as Henry James was to the development of the modern novel and its emphasis on the interior view, James's brother William is widely considered to have had even more influence in this regard—as is

French philosopher Henri Bergson. It was Bergson who proposed the idea of experience as an "endless flow," of personality as continuous but ever-changing, of time as a "bottomless, bankless river, which flows without assignable force in a direction which could not be defined." Such notions, once absorbed by modern novelists (by Proust in particular, who knew Bergson's work well and at first hand), helped bring about the collapse of the novel as it had been known. Under the influence of Bergson, character emerged as a discontinuous, fragmented entity, while plot, rather than being ordered sequentially and chronologically as it once had been, moved freely from past to present and back again, with all events presented as fluid impressions of the human awareness. William James's ideas were closely related to those of Bergson, with James likewise perceiving time, experience, consciousness as continually in flux. "Consciousness," James asserted, "does not appear to itself chopped up in bits. . . . It is nothing jointed; it flows. A 'river' or a stream are the metaphors by which it is most naturally described. *In talking of it hereafter, let us call it, the stream of thought, of consciousness, of subjective life.*" Thus, the evolution of "stream of consciousness," the term most closely associated with the modern novel's journeys into thought, dream, and inner action.

As is usual with many literary terms, the meaning of "stream of consciousness" is somewhat amorphous. Sometimes used to refer to an entire set of devices with which contemporary novelists explore the internal lives of their characters, it is applied in other instances in a much more limited sense, as synonymous with a single device, otherwise known as the "interior monologue." Most frequently, though, it's used as a label for a particular kind of novel—a novel that is generally thought to have reached its apotheosis in the hands of Joyce, Woolf, and the early Faulkner, and which not a few critics believe stopped developing with them. Perhaps it's Woolf herself who offers the best description of the form, when in an early essay, "The Modern Novel," she advises the writer:

> Look within. . . . Examine for a moment an ordinary mind on an ordinary day. The mind receives a myriad of impressions—trivial, fantastic, evanescent, or engraved with the sharpness of steel. From all sides they come, an incessant shower of innumerable atoms, and as they fall, as they shape themselves into the life of Monday or Tuesday, the accent falls differently from of old; the moment of importance came not here but there, so that if a writer . . . could base his work upon his own feeling and not upon convention, there would be no plot, no comedy, no tragedy. . . . [L]ife is a luminous halo, a semi-transparent envelope surrounding us from the beginning of con-

sciousness to the end. Is it not the task of the novelist to convey this varying, this unknown and uncircumscribed spirit, whatever aberration or complexity it may display, with as little mixture of the alien and external as possible?

Woolf has here described precisely the texture of the stream-of-consciousness novel, at least in the hands of its classic practitioners. There is almost no plot in the accepted sense of the term, with such events as there are tending very much to the "ordinary." (In Woolf's own *Mrs. Dalloway*, they are nothing more than the heroine's preparations for a party over the course of a day.) The direction of the novelist's attention is decidedly "within," centered on the consciousness of a character (usually several characters, in fact) which serves as the stage on which the action is played. The patterning, whether of event or memory, is rarely causal, logical, or chronological, but associational, psychological, with any given character's consciousness flowing from one "atom" of thought to another, backward and forward in time from present experience to past association back to present again, and with the novel itself often flowing freely from one mind to another. In such novels, too, consciousness is filled with a "myriad of impressions": with endless perceptions, with all variety of recollections, many of which are summoned up by the most trivial of details, whether the smell of a flower or the taste of a madeleine.

Elusive, ambiguous, often impenetrable, no type of novel presents more challenge to the reader. (One need only cite Faulkner's choice in *The Sound and the Fury* to immerse us at the very outset in the stream of consciousness of a thirty-three-year-old idiot, making it impossible to read the beginning of his novel without first having read the end.) There is no type of novel either that presents more challenges to the screen. Indeed, there are those who would contend that the stream-of-consciousness novel—not only characterized by its inner focus and shattered narrative, but embedded in very particular linguistic devices (such as rambling sentences, intricate and extensive patterns of verbal imagery)—is essentially untranslatable. And not only from page to screen, but from English into French and from French into English, for that matter. Yet, there exists a very basic contradiction. Resistant as such novels might seem to screen adapatation, they are at the same time considered the most cinematic novels of all.

It's legend by now that no other than Sergei Eisenstein made the point about Joyce, finding in the author's "mosaic" structure and "montage" effects strategies very much akin to his own principles of "dynamic editing." Eisenstein felt that filmmakers would do well to study Joyce, and he himself wanted very much to make a movie of *Ulysses*. The plans never materialized—though Joyce reportedly had great respect for the director (they met in Paris in the thirties) and apparently wasn't averse to the notion of the novel being filmed. (Joyce didn't discourage either Stuart Gilbert or poet Louis Zukovsky from working on screenplays of *Ulysses*, nor did he totally discourage Warner Brothers' efforts to secure rights.) Unlike Virginia Woolf, Joyce loved movies. And though it's difficult to argue for any special influence—for movies having any more influence on Joyce, that is, than on other twentieth-century writers, all of whom of necessity must absorb something of the "film age" in which they live—it was surely more than his "montage" effects that made his work seem strikingly apt for filming. "It is no exaggeration to say that *Ulysses* contains equivalents for almost every conceivable film technique," stated Edward Murray in *The Cinematic Imagination*, going on to cite (and rarely with a sense of distortion or strain) strategies in Joyce "equivalent" to crosscutting, dissolves, superimpositions, fast and slow-motion effects, and the like.

Virginia Woolf's methods of moving from point to point in time within the spatial confines of a single consciousness and of moving from consciousness to consciousness within the temporal confines of a single moment are also highly suggestive of movies, and of course of their fluid movements in particular. Her technique of using certain motifs either to situate her narrative temporally at any given moment (for example, the intermittent sounding of clocks in *Jacob's Room*) or to facilitate the narrative's movement in space (like the sky-writing in *Mrs. Dalloway*, whose simultaneous perception by various characters in various places provides Woolf with a way of traveling across London) is also cinematic.

As for Faulkner, Alan Spiegel, for one, in his study of the interrelationships between film and the modern novel, finds him, of all contemporary writers, "the most elaborate and prodigious exponent of the cinematized narrative," going on to demonstrate persuasively the extent to which "retinal imagery, camera angles, and montage sequences are to be found everywhere in his [Faulkner's] novels." Certain of Faulkner's strategies are also suggestive, according to Spiegel, of film's tendency to "anatomize" motion, to give us "detailed information about how animated things and beings look when they move through time and space."

And it's more than merely the classic stream-of-consciousness novel that has been perceived as filmlike. The even more extreme and elusive novelistic excursions into consciousness that came after it—novels which suggested that if the pure stream-of-consciousness form was indeed exhausted, it was still capable of significant metamorphosis—have also been linked to film in both structure and content. The work of writers whose obscurities would seem to follow from their efforts to go beyond the dramatization of conscious internal life and to record instead the deepest reaches of the psyche, such novels have also been viewed as more profoundly, self-consciously psychological than their predecessors. And in some instances—in the work, let's say, of Djuna Barnes and John Hawkes, where the texture is both intensely surreal and poetic—such novels do seem to assume the form of nothing so much as dream itself.

Sometimes called "fabulists," sometimes "anti-realists," other times "exponents of American Gothic" (many of these novelists are in fact American), such writers as Barnes and Hawkes might strike one, at first glance, as far removed from Joyce and Faulkner. Nonetheless, the emphasis both on the inward vision and on certain dislocations of form is clearly traceable back to them, and most theoretical views of the contemporary novel would place them all on the same family tree. As for their filmlike texture, one critic, David Littlejohn, goes so far as to suggest that "the anti-realist novel—the novel of fantasy, illogicality, and absurdity . . . may be regarded as the fictional counterpart . . . of the surrealist film. . . ." Since such works tend quite typically to make use of irrational "dream" images, of superimpositions, of all types of weird visual metamorphoses, of crazy juxtapositions, of the abrupt montage of motifs—all of which are characteristic of surrealist moviemaking—the argument seems unassailable.

But whatever their affinities with film, whatever their "cinematic" qualities, the "anti-realist" novelists have tended to resist successful translation to the screen or, in many instances, any translation whatsoever. The same is true of their more accessible and, from the current-day perspective at least, more traditional predecessors. Despite intermittent announcements that someone or other was in the process of developing *Orlando* or *Mrs. Dalloway,* no major work of Virginia Woolf has ever been adapted to the large screen; while even the most highly praised of the various Faulkner adaptations—Clarence Brown's *Intruder in the Dust,* Mark Rydell's *The Reivers,* Horton Foote's *Tomorrow*—have assiduously avoided grappling either with Faulkner's interiorized vision or with finding analogous strategies for his distinctive rhetoric and style. Considerably more ambition has been brought to the three films adapted from Joyce—Joseph Strick's *Ulysses* and *A Portrait of the Artist as a Young Man* and the more daring *Passages from Finnegan's Wake,* directed by Mary Ellen Bute—and all three films have also received considerable acclaim. Still, the views of their admirers notwithstanding, all three are extremely limited works that do Joyce (or film for that matter) little justice. Among other things, all suffer from the slimness of what is sometimes called their "production values"; that is, they were made on the cheap—one of the problems that also plagues the forays into Kafka by Orson Welles in *The Trial* and Maximillian Schell in *The Castle*. In the case of the Strick films, Joyce also had the misfortune to fall into the hands of a filmmaker who, though far from lacking in sympathy and insight, betrays a good deal more sensitivity to literary values than to cinematic ones. Simply put, Strick's eye is dreadful. So poorly visualized, so amateurish in design and cinematography is his *Ulysses* that François Truffaut is said to have remarked that Strick should be banned from making movies altogether.

Given all this failure, could it be that what seems cinematic on page simply isn't cinematic on screen? It would be tempting to think so, if it weren't for the fact that both the devices found in the various anti-realist writers and the ends to which those devices have been put—the assertion of the inward vision and the exploration of the inner life—have found vital, even extraordinary expression in other cinematic contexts. Consider the films of Bergman, Godard, or Alain Resnais. Here, as in the work of the stream-of-consciousness novelists and their successors, the mind's eye is paramount and the landscapes tend to be inner ones, the screen itself becoming, in Bruce Kawin's phrase, a "mindscreen." Here, too, though some of the strategies seem overwhelmingly, untranslatably filmic (the almost blindingly bright white images in Resnais's *Last Year at Marienbad;* the blood-red fade-outs in *Cries and Whispers*), others are precisely those which characterize the anti-realist novel: the manipulation of time planes, the lack of logical continuity, the associational arrangement of sequences, the shattering of boundaries between the real and imagined and between the remembered and immediately experienced.

The movies of such filmmakers as Bergman and Resnais also make inescapable film's equally special possibilities not only for rendering subjective vantage points, but for the exploration of inner life itself—something that the efforts of surrealist filmmakers had, of course, illustrated far earlier. (Consider, among other movies, the Dali-Buñuel *Un Chien Andalou*.) Indeed, it's difficult to understand how, in the face of the work of Dali, Buñuel, and also Jean Cocteau—work with which he must have been familiar—George Bluestone could have asserted that "cinemaphotography cannot penetrate consciousness" or, as he otherwise phrased his highly influential view, that "film cannot render thought, dream or the inner life."

It's also difficult to understand how Bluestone could have held such a position in the face of other theorists' views that film's natural mode is a "dream mode," that motion pictures, as late critic R. E. Jones suggested,

> are our thoughts made visible and audible. They flow in a swift succession of images, precisely as our thoughts do, and their speed, with their flashbacks—like sudden uprushes of memory—and their abrupt transition from one subject to another, approximates very closely the speed of our thinking. They have the rhythm of the thought-stream and the same uncanny ability to move forward or backward in space or time. . . . They project pure thought, pure dream, pure inner life.

In the face of the work of Bergman and Resnais, Bluestone's contention becomes more untenable yet. Nor does it seem to me possible to even maintain, as does Edward Murray, that though film may in fact be capable of rendering inner life, "when required to penetrate the complex psyche of a character . . . it is sadly inferior to what can be done by the stream-of-consciousness novelist." For such a judgment seems based on a rather naive belief in the special privilege of language for capturing the stuff of consciousness. If thought externalized into the concrete images of film is, as some would suggest, no longer thought, why should thought encased in the medium of language be any different? Do we really, or of necessity, think in *words*? Isn't the stream-of-consciousness technique as much a convention for rendering inner experience as the dream sequence in a movie? Has Virginia Woolf really given us more insight into the inner life of Clarissa Dalloway than Ingmar Bergman has into that of the nurse Alma in *Persona*, than Fellini has into his filmmaker in *8½*, than Resnais has into his dying writer in *Providence*?

This isn't to deny the heavy burdens both the surreal and the highly internalized present to the medium of film. The filmmaker must maintain control of the import of his materials and avoid total amorphousness; while the viewer must bring intense attentiveness to bear in order to simply make sense of what is put before him. Like the stream-of-consciousness novel itself, films like *The Blood of the Poet, Cries and Whispers, Belle de Jour, Two or Three Things I Know About Her* are creations of the few for the few. And though literature certainly isn't immune to the difficulties presented by such specialization—the publishing history of *Ulysses* is notorious, and Virginia Woolf ended up publishing herself—in an art like film, which by its very nature tends to be both of the many and for the many, those difficulties are inevitably compounded.

Yet despite this, certain filmmakers have managed to find the means (both aesthetic and financial) to create such minority movies—mostly Europeans, but some have been American, and a few of these have even found support from Hollywood studios. We've had films like Henry Jaglom's "mindscreen" movie *A Safe Place*, endorsed by the New York Film Festival (where it had its premiere back in 1971) and highly praised by no less a literary modernist than Anais Nin. We've also had the "dream films" of Robert Altman—*Images* and *Three Women*—the latter of which was extremely well received. Thus, if the classic stream-of-consciousness novel has eluded filmmakers up to this point, as have most of the novels of the second and third generation of anti-realists that followed them, it isn't because their strategies or even they themselves are inherently antithetical to the medium. The problem would seem to lie instead in such extra-aesthetic matters as money and rights and above all, I suspect, courage—the courage to take risks, the courage to come up with new forms, the courage to tackle genius. Besides, other, less intimidating works which share in their concerns and structures have in fact been translated to screen. And if not with consistent success, at least with a good deal less failure than precedent might have led one to expect—as the following discussions of *Slaughterhouse-Five*, *Under the Volcano*, *The Day of the Locust*, and *Swann in Love* should demonstrate.

A note of explanation is perhaps in order regarding my somewhat unusual choice of adaptations. It may seem that in grouping and implicitly contrasting the likes of *Slaughterhouse-Five*, *Under the Volcano*, *The Day of the Locust*, and Volker Schlöndorff's *Swann in Love*, I'm mixing up apples and oranges. In fact, I am. But whatever the differences in quality of the source novels in question—and, no doubt about it, they are vast—and whatever the difference in the degree of internalization as well, all nevertheless confront the filmmaker with the types of problems that concern us here: dealing with dislocations in time and space; confronting the breakdown between external experience and inner life; finding means for mounting surreal experience and for capturing the texture of memory and dream. And the simple fact is that the solutions open to the filmmaker in adapting a lesser work in the stream-of-consciousness or anti-realist mode are also open to the filmmaker adapting a greater one.

I'm aware that some of the positions I've taken here (the particular films I've elected to defend, that is) are decidedly minority ones. More important, I also know that in setting failed attempts at the translation of truly towering works against successful adaptations of decidedly lesser ones, I'm taking the risk of illustrating a principle to which I don't subscribe: that when an adaptation succeeds, it's an indication that the original novel was less than first-rate, that "if it's worth doing, it can't be done; if it can be done, it wasn't worth it" (or as it's sometimes known, "Simon's Law"). Thus, my selection of the Proust adaptation rather than those of Faulkner or Joyce (which have the advantage of being based on English-language works) or of Kafka (which have the advantage of being based on novels better known to English-language readers than the formidable *Remembrance of Things Past*). For in dealing with Schlöndorff's adaptation of Proust, I at least had the opportunity of calling up the Pinter screenplay, which, though admittedly only a blueprint for a movie and not a movie itself, seems to me in its spectacular promise and accomplishment to mitigate that risk considerably.

Slaughterhouse-Five: Pilgrim's Progress through Time and Space

Critics have always been skeptical about Kurt Vonnegut, Jr., and it's not difficult to understand why. Fame and fashionableness have a way of making any artist suspect, and especially one like Vonnegut whose work is so simple in style as to make it also seem shallow. His curious brand of humor—"gallows" rather than "black," according to critic and novelist Vance Bourjaily, since it consistently tempers its bleakness with kindness—has also encouraged some critics to see him as "coy," "cute," and "precious." His tone of quiet resignation before the horrors he so frequently describes has led others to perceive him as an apostle of apathy. Playwright Jack Richardson sums up the anti-Vonnegut position perhaps best and certainly most forcefully: "[a] too easily understood parabolist . . . "a soft sentimental satirist . . . a popularizer of naughty whimsey, a compiler of easy-to-read truisms about society who allows everyone's heart to be in the right place."

Yet, Vonnegut, as we know, also has his supporters. And though both critics and academics certainly number among them, Vonnegut's greatest following has always been the young, with college students his most passionate devotees of all. (When Vonnegut guest taught at Harvard in the fall of 1970, there were no fewer than fifteen applicants for every place in his class.) His most popular work is, of course, *Slaughterhouse-Five or the Children's Crusade*. First published in 1969, it may have been the novel that inspired Richardson's attack, but—exciting enormous praise elsewhere—it was also key to establishing Vonnegut's critical reputation.

It's a highly autobiographical work, and Vonnegut makes the fact explicit. The first chapter establishes the author himself as character, asserts that "all of this happened, more or less," and deals with the difficulty of writing the very novel in hand ("I would hate to tell you what this lousy little book cost me in money and anxiety and time"). As Vonnegut also makes clear, the novel is based on his own devastating World War II experiences. As a German prisoner of war, he had been witness to the firebombing of Dresden by American and British pilots—the controversial raid in which 135,000 German civilians were incinerated and a city that had been an architectural wonder destroyed. Vonnegut elects to present the event, however, not through his own eyes but through those of Billy Pilgrim. An optometrist from Ilium, New York, Billy has a rich fat wife whose pancakes he loves, a married daughter, and a reformed son. (Once a junior Hell's Angel, Robert is now a member of the Green Berets.) Billy also has a dog named Spot and is an upstanding member of the Lion's Club. A modern American Everyman, it would seem—if it weren't for the fact that Billy is also, as he himself puts it, "a spastic in time," a man who travels outside chronology and without control through the absurd comedy that is his life. At one moment, we share with him a vision of his death in an inevitable future; at another, his absurd near-drowning as a child in an unalterable past; at still another, a moment from a less distant past—his youthful experience in World War II, or the Children's Crusade. Billy, moreover, doesn't only travel through time: he also travels through space, going back and forth to the distant planet of Tralfamadore, where little green fourth-dimensional creatures teach him that everything in the cosmos is timeless, ever-present, and predetermined and that only on earth, of the thirty-one inhabited planets in the universe, "is there any talk of free will."

Given the novel's unusual form, the presence of the Tralfamadorians, and Vonnegut's previous reputation as a science-fiction writer, it's no surprise that on its original publication, many were led to situate *Slaughterhouse-Five* within that genre. The *New Republic*, tellingly, gave the novel for review to J. Michael Crichton, the science fiction novelist (and filmmaker-to-be). But as Crichton himself observed, though Vonnegut's "science-fiction heritage is clear . . . his purposes are very different"; while

Vonnegut's seemingly "naive, effortless, almost childlike style" is, as Crichton recognized too, similarly misleading.

Vonnegut, in other words, is a more purposeful and intelligent artist than all the intentional simplicities of his manner would suggest. I may not adhere to the view of Robert Scholes who, in his front-page *New York Times Review* celebration of *Slaughterhouse-Five,* declared Vonnegut "among the best writers of his generation," but I do consider the novel a substantial achievement and a work that—however transparent—is very much within the mainstream of serious contemporary writing. Both a powerful antiwar novel and a wry updating of *The Pilgrim's Progress* where, as in John Bunyan's great Christian allegory, a good and gentle man with the mixed blessing of second sight journeys from the City of Destruction (read Dresden) to the Celestial City (read Tralfamadore), it's also a poignant exploration of the burden of time—a concern it shares with the most ambitious of contemporary novels. Its central theme is inescapably Faulknerian: as Jean-Paul Sartre phrases it, that "man's misfortune lies in his being time-bound." And its manner of mounting that theme—of deliriously scrambling past, present, and future and giving each of these time planes equal reality—clearly derives from the stream-of-consciousness technique, just as it also constitutes a latter-day variation on it. It may be perfectly possible to read Billy's time travels quite literally as science-fiction, but they are perhaps read more perceptively and meaningfully as mental voyages—as the expression of a benign schizophrenia and of the need of "time-bound" man to escape his "misfortune," while simultaneously attempting to exorcise past pain.

That director George Roy Hill saw *Slaughterhouse-Five* very much in these psychological terms is evident: his adaptation—based on a screenplay by Stephen Geller—plays down the science-fiction elements throughout. Not that Tralfamadore doesn't remain; or that Billy isn't encased there in a Buckminster Fuller–type geodesic dome; or that he doesn't share his celestial paradise with movie starlet Montana Wildback. But gone (or at least reduced to voices and sound effects) are the Tralfamadorians themselves; gone and replaced by a beam of light is the novel's extravagant spaceship; and gone too—at the risk of alienating Vonnegut's great following, which was great indeed at the time of the film's release in 1971—is the character of Kilgore Trout, the science-fiction writer whose books Billy has devoured and who first introduces him to the concept of Tralfamadore.

Some would argue that all of this constitutes a major betrayal of the text—among them, quite naturally, readers who remain committed to the view of the novel as sci-fi and also to those little green Tralfamadorians as well—creatures which, to my mind, with their "plumber's helper" bodies and their eyes stuck in their hands-as-heads, are the novel's weakest conception. Those who bemoan Hill's choice to delete both the framing opening chapter and Vonnegut's intermittent interruptions of his story, and therewith the author as a character, have a somewhat stronger case. Vonnegut's wry and compassionate voice is admittedly a crucial aspect of the novel's appeal. One commentator on the film also argues that since the self-reflexiveness of the novel—the fact that it is a book about the writing of a book— constitutes a major theme, its omission in the film is in turn a major loss. But it seems to me that Vonnegut's purposes in including the writer himself in his work are very different from those of other authors who do the same. Unlike Durrell in *The Alexandria Quartet* and Cortazar in *Hopscotch* (the critic's examples), Vonnegut isn't broaching merely an aesthetic question. The issue is an emotional one instead, his point being—in telling us how long it took him to get this novel written, for example—to underscore the intense painfulness of his Dresden experience. This is something the film also manages to express—though paradoxically perhaps, very much as a function of these very omissions. For without the author, his distancing voice, and the various interruptions, both the illusion of reality and the immediacy of the experience are heightened, and the film, by that token, makes the implicit despair of the whole more deeply felt.

Of course, the inherent qualities of the film medium also do their share in contributing to this effect. On the page, Vonnegut's characters are very flat and their emotional import thus diminished. And though Hill has simulated this caricatured effect to some degree by encouraging several of his actors to underplay, others to do just the opposite, each figure is nonetheless given a greater humanity on screen simply by being embodied. The casting too helps here. Michael Sacks, whose childlike, ingenuous looks couldn't be more perfect for Billy, and Eugene Roche, who is appropriately avuncular as the almost equally naive Edgar Derby, both bring a sweetly touching edge to their characters; while Ron Leibman's inventive rendition of Paul Lazzaro and Valerie Perrine's delightfully unself-conscious Montana temper any potential sentiment by making their already amusing characters just that much more comic.

But the movie's true distinction lies elsewhere—and in matters a good deal less arguable than those of theme or tone. It lies in the extent to which the film has managed to retain the novel's fractured structure, and not only without confusing the viewer but in fact with a lucidity reminiscent of the novel's own. So clear and in fact clarifying is the film's structure that *Slaughterhouse-Five* emerges the first adaptation which allows one to sense the authentically cinematic quality of the temporal and spatial dislocations of the stream-of-consciousness method—dislocations that, as suggested earlier, have always seemed so movielike on the page and yet so elusive to the screen. (I've had students who have seen the movie without having read the book express amazement that such filmic devices could ever have been realized in a novel.)

One way Hill and Geller managed to accomplish this double feat of transferring structural complexity and clarity simultaneously is by imposing a greater degree of chronology on the material than did Vonnegut—at least within the film's three different space-time planes. Billy's wartime experiences especially, though consistently intercut with both fragments of his peacetime Ilium life and bits of his existence on Tralfamadore, proceed in a logical temporal sequence. The film's first shot of Billy on this time plane—the remarkable pre-credit one which shows him wandering through the snow, a blanket thrown about him suggesting a cowl and enforcing our perception of him as Pilgrim—introduces him to us immediately prior to his capture by the Germans, and so at the outset of his Dresden experience; the last we see of him during the war is after the bombing. And while his life in Ilium is somewhat more scrambled, it's still a good deal more sequential than in the novel.

Thus the film maintains the sense of disoriented time without totally disorienting the viewer; in this way too, it both undercuts Vonnegut's (to my mind, often unnecessary and distracting) foreshadowing techniques and increases dramatic tension. On screen, in contrast to the novel, we don't see or even know of Billy's death until very near the end. And although the film does contain some early offhand allusions to Edgar Derby's execution (in the manner of the novel), it still comes as much more of a shock. It's important, however, that in presenting the execution, the film still manages to duplicate some of the novel's unsettling detachment: the event takes place with startling rapidity and is photographed at an extreme distance, as if it were mere background action.

Another strategy the film uses to avoid potential confusion, one that, importantly, also enforces its implicit psychological reading, is that of supplying somewhat clearer and more plausible explanations for Billy's time travels and their content than does the novel. In the film, Billy sees Montana Wildback both in a *Playboy* spread and in a drive-in movie *before* she is brought to Tralfamadore, allowing us to understand her as his fantasy. Not so in the novel, where it's only well into their long-standing Tralfamadorian relationship than an aged Billy catches sight of her real-life counterpart in the decidedly more prurient context of a movie shown in a New York porn shop. (Reality here, then, serves to *confirm* Billy's Tralfamadorian experiences rather than to *inspire* them, granting those experiences—and, of course, Montana—considerable reality in turn.) In the film, too, the first glimpse we are offered of Billy—once the movie proper begins, that is—is as an old man, allowing us to perceive almost everything that follows as flashback. But not quite. For Hill has also included a sequence or two which works against too facile a reading: the flashforward to Billy's death; Billy's chilling (and discomfortingly surreal) glimpse of the men in ski-masks that signals the imminence of the plane crash. (More humanly than in the novel, too, Billy doesn't simply accept the inevitability of it all—he panics at the sight.)

But important as all these devices are, it's the film's editing that constitutes its most powerful means for easing the shifts from time plane to time plane, and also for asserting the emotional and thematic importance of time itself. Much less abrupt in manner than the novel, the film often slides from past to present to past again, through visual parallels, sound bridges, and emotional associations. We move from a photographer taking pictures in the past, to one taking pictures in the present; from Billy-as-older-man walking up the stairs in his Ilium home to Billy-as-a-young-man walking up the steps of the meat locker in which he's spent the Dresden bombing. We move via a darkened screen from Billy covering his head with a blanket during the war to Billy hiding under a blanket in peacetime; via the shriek of a train whistle from Billy receiving electric shock treatments in an Ilium hospital to Billy on a train during the war; via a matching overlapping shot from the halls of "Slaughterhouse-Five" to those of the hospital where Billy is recovering from the plane crash. We cut from the feeble applause that accompanies Edgar Derby's election as "leader" during the war to the loud applause that greets Billy when elected Lion's Club president, and from Derby's fond reminiscences of his son to Billy's comically sad ones of his own. Making for an astounding technical accomplishment—the genius at work here is film editor Dede Allen—all of this also results in a rich fund of ironic counterpoint.

The film, too, adds some of its own playful toying with time. There's a wonderful sequence in which a stationary camera shows us Billy's house in long shot, as we watch the newly married young man first play with his puppy Spot and then walk off the screen out of our range of vision. The camera holds the shot, but the light shifts, and when Billy and Spot wander back into the frame, the two are just that much older. The device is repeated—accompanied by the sound of pudgy Valencia (the obsessive I'll-lose-weight-for-you wife) calling him in for lunch, dinner, a piece of cake—still another time. There's also the scene toward the close of the Dresden sequence where, as Billy and two other soldiers carry a huge grandfather clock out of a ruined building, Billy finds himself suddenly flattened to the ground by the weight of the clock—or, put another way, trapped under the burden of time.

And Billy is trapped by that burden in Dresden, where he is witness to a nightmare that he can never, no more than can Vonnegut, drive out of his memory—a vision of horror so extreme as to demand a revised perspective on human experience, and also perhaps the positing of the unearthly paradise of Tralfamadore. The film's handling of the Dresden nightmare is extraordinary, in both its reticence and its emotional power. The city is first glimpsed from a distance, taking exquisite and almost unearthly shape out of the morning mist—the impressive cinematography here is by Miroslave Ondricek, the skyline in reality that of Prague. Then, in the company of an aged German officer and his boy soldiers—thus Hill informs us this is indeed a "children's crusade," and on both sides of the battle line—we follow Billy and the other prisoners on their march through the city. And with a Bach Brandenburg concerto (played by Glenn Gould) on the soundtrack, we share Billy's wonder at the baroque magnificence around him, the camera offering us shot after shot of cherubs and angels carved on the sides of buildings, of the old winding streets, of the meandering river, of the cathedral in the background. We see, too, that (as was historically the case) the city is populated mostly by children and the aged. And because the future annihilation is implicit in these present images, our sense of grief is boundless.

Significantly, that grief is stronger in these earlier scenes of Dresden than in later ones, since Hill selects to show us little of the actual devastation. We simply see some smoldering ruins, a distant corpse here and there, with the film undercutting the effect of even these brief glimpses by having us simultaneously hear Billy in voice-over describing the event to the Tralfamadorians—"It looked like the end of the world"—and the Tralfamadorians, in turn, offering their stoic comforts. Critics complained of the understatement. Stephen Farber, for one, noted that:

. . . at a time when everyone is squealing about excessive violence in movies, *Slaughterhouse-Five* is one film that really needs more violence. . . . The

camera . . . reveals none of the terrible facts about Dresden—that, for example, the huge fire-storm produced hurricane-strength winds which sucked
fleeing civilians back into the center of the inferno, while most of those who
thought they were safe in underground shelters were baked alive or suffo-
cated by poisonous flames.

The film doesn't show us any of this, but I don't believe it could have
without either shattering us completely or violating the implicit intention
of the whole. For Vonnegut's point here is that there is no way to contemplate such a horror except from either the distancing vantage point of comedy, or without imposing on it some sense of relief, some dash of hope and
optimism, however desperate. Thus, the book ends in springtime, the war
over, with the sound of a bird singing "Poo-tee-weet"; thus, the film ends
with Billy, Montana, and their newborn babe being applauded by the Tralfamadorians. Critics complained, too, that the film confused the moral issues, making the Germans somehow blameless by focusing not on the
greater and more extensive atrocities they themselves committed but on
Dresden instead. But certainly that's the point here too. For what makes
Dresden even more horrible in a sense than Auschwitz and Buchenwald—
and the film a more devastating antiwar statement in the process—is that
the atrocity was committed not by the aggressors, not by those whom we
perceive as evil, but by the innocent defenders of justice, right, and freedom, by us. (It hardly seems coincidental that a similar point is made in *The
Pilgrim's Progress*, where it is never vice pure and simple that excites Bunyan's outrage, but apparent virtue instead.)

In short, the film was attacked not so much for being different from the
novel—as is usually the case in adaptations—but rather for being too much
like it. And it was also, then, attacked on similar grounds. Accessible and
direct, it was accused of being simpleminded; looking at horror from the
vantage point of comic resignation, it was accused of moral apathy; impli-
cating the values of justice and right in death and destruction, it was accused
of moral ambivalence. But the most interesting and most ironic criticism
was that centered on the film's form: it was too chic and fashionable; it was
derived from a novel that, rather than being too literary, was too filmlike.
As Andrew Sarris put it:

"Slaughterhouse-Five" leaves me unmoved and unimpressed. . . . Kurt
Vonnegut bothers me. Perhaps his books are too cinematic for my
taste. . . . The movie is very pretty to look at, and George Roy Hill must be

conceded a flair for fantasy, but the digestive after-effect is decidedly low-protein Resnais.

Perhaps. Perhaps, one might rather say "low-protein Faulkner" or concede that even low-protein Resnais might be more nourishing than countless high-sugar movies instead. But regardless of whether one is appreciative of *Slaughterhouse-Five* or not, it's one adaptation that emerges eminently cinematic nonetheless and that in so doing suggests in turn the eminently cinematic nature of stream-of-consciousness.

Under the Volcano: Looking Outward

Malcolm Lowry's *Under the Volcano* has often been called a "cult classic"—and I suppose rightly so, if by the term we mean a work of unusual quality passionately supported by a few. Some see it as the last literary masterpiece, others as a work on a par with Joyce's *Ulysses*, still others as even greater. At least, this is what the *Times Literary Supplement* suggests when it states that *Under the Volcano* is not only as "rich and humorous" as Joyce's masterpiece, but also "far more poetic"—something on the order of "a prose *Waste Land.*" Yet, if Lowry's 1947 novel enjoys such an astounding reputation, it is this reputation that is known much more than the novel itself. For whatever else *Under the Volcano* may be, it is also a dense and difficult work that has defeated the efforts of many a reader to get through it. (Having taught the novel several times—and to graduate students in English, I should add—I can testify to this first-hand. I can hardly remember assigning a novel that was more resisted.)

What makes *Under the Volcano* so troubling? Just about everything, it seems. To begin with, it's one of the few quite rigorous stream-of-consciousness novels we have—one in which the interior view is asserted almost entirely throughout. Moreover, we are continually challenged to slide from a given character's responses to his immediate present to memories of the past with very little clarification as to where we are at any given moment. The novel's opening chapter itself makes the point. More of an epilogue than a prologue, it is set precisely one year after the novel's main action—on the Mexican Day of the Dead in November of 1939. Here, in the fictional, volcano-shadowed town of Quauhnahuac (Lowry's thinly disguised stand-in for Cuernavaca), we follow the thoughts of one of the novel's more peripheral characters, ex–film director Jacques Laruelle who, in the course of his ruminations, introduces us to all the novel's major figures, places, and themes. The problem is that most of this only clarifies itself to the reader after he has read the whole.

To a large extent, the same difficulty confronts the reader in all of the following chapters where, moving back a year, we are made witness to the last day in the life of the novel's main character—alcoholic ex–British Consul Geoffrey Firmin who, together with his adored ex-wife, Yvonne, and his journalist half-brother, Hugh (sometime revolutionary and onetime lover of Yvonne), goes on a fateful outing to the nearby town of Parian. Sometimes immersed in the Consul's alcohol-drenched sensibility, sometimes in the more sober ones of Yvonne and Hugh—each chapter alternating the vantage point—we are given a kaleidoscopic vision of the present and a series of mental journeys into these characters' individual pasts. They are journeys, moreover, made especially complex not simply by being filled—in the manner of the Laruelle section—with numerous elusive private associations and memories. It's also that, like Lowry himself, both the Consul and Hugh (the Consul's *doppelganger* and, together with him, bearer of Lowry's biography and obsessions) are enormously learned and literary men, and their thoughts are woven out of a dazzling skein of references to politics, history, and especially literature— including the likes of Marlowe's *Dr. Faustus,* Dante's *The Divine Comedy,* Cocteau's *The Infernal Machine,* Zorilla's *Don Juan Tenorio,* the stories of Poe and the poems of Shelley, all of which demand for their identification and understanding considerable erudition on the reader's part. Their interior monologues are also expressed in highly metaphoric language, while the entire novel is packed full of suggestive imagery—the chocolate skulls and skeletons ever-present on this Day of the Dead; the twin volcanoes, Popcatepetl and Ixtaccihuatl, suggestive of perfect marriage; the constant parade of emblematic animals, from a pariah dog through a burrowing armadillo to a runaway horse; the *barranca* or great ravine edging the town and called, after Dante, the Malebolge (one of the circles of the Inferno); the continual references to the Peter Lorre film *The Hands of Orlac,* or as it's put in the novel, *Las Manos de Orlac;* the uprooted sign in the Consul's once-paradisiacal garden: *Le Gusta este jardin? Que es suyo? Evite que sus hijos lo destruyan.** And if, together with the

---

*The Consul translates the sign as follows: "You like this garden? Why is it yours? We evict those who destroy!" However, a closer translation would be: "Do you like this garden? What is yours? Keep your children from destroying it."

literary and political allusions, these images serve to transform the novel from a mere study of a particular man in decline into one of larger and more universal implications—we are variously asked to see the Consul as an Adam, a Faust, a Dante-esque figure weaving his way through an Inferno—they also confront the reader with the far from mean task of resolving and unifying them.

But more even than the symbols, the references, the rich and suggestive language, or even the interior vision itself, what seems to make the novel so troubling to readers is its stifling, doom-laden atmosphere, its overwhelming and all-encompassing vision of decay, despair and self-destructiveness. As Hugh puts it at one point: " 'Good God, if our civilization were to sober up for a couple of days it'd die of remorse on the third—.' " Still, it is also the intensity of this vision that, together with the novel's overall richness—a richness which makes it a work that insists, in the manner of poem, on being read again and again—constitutes its genius. It is also all this, of course, that makes it a work so challenging to the screen.

All the same, *Under the Volcano* has tempted many a filmmaker—partly, one can assume, because of the passionate devotion it has aroused in some of its followers; partly because whatever its difficulties the novel's external action follows the classic dramatic unities of time and place; partly because of its intensely romantic characters (the drunken ex-consul, the beautiful actress, the handsome revolutionary); and partly too because its imagery provides the whole with a richly visual texture. One rumor has it that no fewer than sixty different screenwriters have tried their hand at adapting it. Luis Buñuel noted in his autobiography that he himself had read as many as eight treatments of the novel, ultimately coming to the conclusion that it was simply much too internalized to be filmed. John Huston, for his part, reports that over the years, he read some twenty treatments, but unlike Buñuel, kept faith in the novel's cinematic possibilities. Huston is a director who has, in any case, always displayed enormous courage in the works he has chosen to bring to the screen— daring to take on, if with markedly varying degrees of success, not only such idiosyncratic works as *Wise Blood* and *Reflections in a Golden Eye*, but also resistant classics like *The Red Badge of Courage* and *Moby Dick*. Interestingly enough, the script that finally inspired Huston to make the film of *Under the Volcano* was that of a first-time screenwriter, Guy Gallo—though from all reports, Huston strongly imposed his vision on Gallo's scenario, as he did on the finished film as a whole.

The result? A movie that, given the difficulties of the novel, is in many ways admirably courageous and in certain of its aspects, quite effective too. One has to credit Huston and Gallo with their solid grasp of the book and—at least, from a dramatic point of view—with an intelligent selection from Lowry's more-than-400-page supply of materials. They culled whatever action there is from an essentially actionless novel; and by getting rid of both the flashback frame and Laruelle—surely the most superfluous and ill-defined of the novel's characters—and deleting all flashbacks within the story proper they made the whole tighter and more accessible. They also chose to concentrate more heavily on the Consul than does the novel, thus sharpening the story's focus.

The film also manages to release a good deal of Lowry's humor, so often lost on readers immersed in the novel's overall sense of despair and in their sheer struggle with the material. Lowry's wry scene in which the Consul is discovered lying face down in the road by an archetypal Britisher with his characteristically understated response ("Well, cheerio. Cheerio man. Don't go lying down in roads") is preserved almost intact. And the film makes of the bathroom scene—in which, as in the novel, the shaking Consul screams for help and gulps down some hair tonic as protection against the sight of "galloping cockroaches"—a wonderfully comic (yet simultaneously, deeply touching) sequence. The screenplay is also remarkably faithful to Lowry's dialogue which, by the way, works very well as spoken language and even manages here and there to retain some of his puns and playfulness with words. ("Who's there? Cat? Cat who? Catastrophe? Catastrophe who? Catastrophysicist"—goes an exchange between the Consul and Yvonne, transposed from one of the Consul's inner musings.)

The film is strongest, however, in its characterization of the Consul himself, with no small help from Albert Finney's superb performance. Conveying a good deal of the man's sensibility and intelligence, the intensity of his agony, and his tragic self-awareness above all, Finney makes inescapable—and inescapably painful—the Consul's knowledge of the depths of his own degradation and his ability at the same time to recognize its utter ridiculousness. Otherwise put, he sees (and we see too) the absurdity in his own pathos. The film does much less well with Yvonne—but then again, so does the novel. And Jacqueline Bisset must be credited with granting Yvonne's actions a plausibility on screen they don't always have on the page. In the film we understand, in a way we don't quite in the novel, the intensity of feeling—the mixture of guilt and love—that has driven Yvonne to return to this wreck of a man, a man just mad and self-destructive enough to greet the woman who has left him because of his drinking with an offer of a drink. As for Hugh, though Anthony Andrews doesn't seem quite up to the role, he does manage to capture something of the character's curious ambivalence.

But if the film does all this, there's still much it doesn't do. And where it fails most pointedly is in the assertion of the inner view—with Huston having resisted throughout the incorporation not simply of the novel's flashbacks, but of the Consul's mescal-drenched, often hallucinatory perspective. The cinematography (by Gabriel Figueroa) is insistently straightforward, so that everything is shown to us realistically, naturally, normally. Even the most obvious opportunies for subjective vision are excluded—as in the sequence where the Consul, driven by his desire to avoid a group of begging children at the fair, finds himself on a kind of ferris wheel. Never mind that in the film the "infernal machine" doesn't get stuck as it does in the novel. It's more important that Huston, unlike Lowry, refuses to show us the world from the Consul's upside-down point of view, either during the ride or after it. ("On terra firma, the world continued to spin madly around; houses, whirligigs, hotels, cathedrals, cantinas, volcanoes: it was difficult to stand up at all.") Huston's only concession to the wildness of the experience is the use of a fish-eye lens during the ride to distort the Consul's appearance. Importantly, however, and one might argue illogically, too, that distortion is directed objectively at the Consul himself, rather than directed subjectively at the world around him.

And gone with the inner view is nearly all of the novel's symbolic imagery—almost of necessity, since much of the symbolic value is established by associations in the mind of the consul and in the minds of the other characters. But even images which are inherently suggestive have been dropped from the film (the *barranca* or Malebolge, for example), while such images as have been retained are presented in so literal a fashion as to deny them symbolic value. The pariah dog which, in the film, is shown only in the opening scenes remains merely a wandering dog and far from a distorted emblem of the Consul. And except for a single, extremely effective shot at the outset of the film where, as the Consul wanders through a street fair, we see the chocolate skulls being sold at a stand reflected in his dark glasses, even the ever-present death images remain quite literal, not really much more than part of the general Mexican and holiday atmosphere. As for the final scene in the decadent cantina, El Farolito, it is played not, as in the novel, for its emblematic value, but—what with Huston's much-publicized use of actual whores, a salacious dwarf, and the overstated performances of the Mexican villains—strictly for melodrama.

Huston has also chosen to exclude much of the novel's emphasis on the theme of time. The past may "haunt this novel" (as one critic puts it), but it doesn't haunt this film. Or, allowing that the characters in the movie are shown to one extent or another bearing the guilt of past actions, they are haunted by the past in a much less metaphysical sense. The film's structure itself reflects the change in emphasis, since in the process of tightening the novel, the filmmakers have also imposed on the whole a strict chronological order, even to the extent of reversing the sequence of Lowry's two final scenes. In the novel, though it occurs later in time, we witness Yvonne's death before the Consul's, not quite grasping its point or knowing what to make of the sudden appearance of the runaway horse. It's only later we find out that the horse has been frightened by the shooting of the Consul, thus making him inadvertently and ironically responsible for the horrible event. The film's reversal undercuts this irony nearly completely, while it also, by betraying the novel's intricate manner of suspending time, equally undermines time's own thematic significance.

The upshot of all this rearranging, literalizing, and externalizing of the novel's materials has been taken by some critics (Stanley Kauffmann, for one) as proof that such a subjective, poetic novel simply cannot be filmed. Others (for example, Janet Maslin) see Huston's choices as following from the necessity of not overly bewildering the audience. But, as Maslin also perceptively notes, Huston "appears to have made exactly the film he wanted to"—a film that not only, as she suggests, reflects few commercial concessions but that in fact retains and even intensifies the novel's most troubling quality: its devastating depiction of addiction, its overwhelming aura of melancholy and despair.

It is also a film whose implicit choices seem to follow less from any concern with overcoming the density of the text than from a very particular reading of it. As Huston himself has stated, and as the film itself makes clear, the director had little patience with Lowry's stream-of-consciousness technique and its esoteric references and symbolism. "Lowry was rather indiscriminate with his symbols," Huston told one interviewer. "They were too many and too lush. We could very well have betrayed the author—or rather let him betray himself—by keeping all the symbols in." There's a certain irony here in that Huston also noted that "a motion picture resembles a poem more than it resembles a book"—despite the fact that it's precisely the poetry (or "symbolic images") that he has chosen to delete from his adaptation. Indeed, rather than an internalized, multileveled, and emphatically poetic allegory, what Huston implicitly saw in the novel was a fairly literal tale of a man who decides to drink himself to death for reasons which, significantly enough, come through in the film with considerably more clarity than they do in the novel. Lowry quite purposefully keeps the causes of the Consul's alcoholism cloudy, making impossible any facile psychological reading: his addiction follows from his metaphysical fall from grace; from a self-destructive temptation to live in the Inferno itself; from his Faustian urges; from the fact that, as the novel puts it, *"No se puede vivir sin amar"* ("One cannot live without love"); and above all, perhaps, from his existential angst. In Huston's view, however, the Consul's drinking seems to follow in large part from his guilt over the "Good Samaritan" incident—the incident in which, while the Consul served as commander, the remains of seven captured German officers were found in his ship's furnace.*

Certainly, Huston is careful not only to preserve (in contrast to all he has chosen to omit) the references to what in the novel is a fairly minor incident; he also has the Consul tell the story at length near the outset of the film and mention it again later. In the film, the Consul also makes explicit the extent to which it is this particular guilt that makes him identify with the murderer played by Peter Lorre in *Las Manos de Orlac.* "These very hands. The hands of Firmin. Flung seven German officers into her fiery furnace . . .," he announces to Yvonne and Hugh. But Huston hasn't only chosen to retain and emphasize the "Good Samaritan" incident; he has also selected to do the same with the novel's other political referents. (Among other things, he has Hugh perform a Spanish Civil War song.) Thus, the incident declares itself part of an overall reading of the novel that is more than simply literal but distinctly sociopolitical—a reading that seems to me extremely reductive. And it's not only because as some critics contend, in stressing the novel's political concerns, Huston has stressed its weakest elements. It's also because Huston has, at the very same time, selected to delete the aspect of the novel that gives those politics significance—Hugh's memories and inner musings on the meaning and end of political action, on the nature of social responsibility, or in other words, his stream of consciousness.

Huston's adaptation, then, whatever its particular virtues—its serious-

---

*It's noteworthy that Huston explicitly addressed himself to this interpretation, only to emphatically deny it. ("Someone asked me the other day, 'Why was the Consul a drunk?' Of course, this question had come up during the writing of the picture, and it refused to be answered in an expository way. I mean, had he turned to drink because he'd killed those men on the ship, and the memory of that haunted him and so on? Well, obviously not. . . .") But as D. H. Lawrence admonished, trust the tale and not the teller, and the tale (or film) suggests that Huston's interpretation was other than he claims.

ness, its unsettling depiction of alcoholism, the power of its leading performance, its courage in attempting to make the film in the first place—
emerges a work much less satisfying than it might have been. As such, it's a
film that illustrates not (as some have claimed) the impossibility of bringing
a novel like *Under the Volcano* to the screen but simply the inadequacy of
Huston's approach. And it also reveals something else: that though it's possible to bring a highly internalized novel to the screen by imposing an externalized view upon it, and even end up with a fairly good film in the process,
one is unlikely to come up with a great film—and certainly not with a film
that has anywhere near the poetry, power, or point of its source.

The Day of the Locust:
Hollywood as a State of Mind

Nathanael West never liked to think of himself as a surrealist. But
though his work has more recognizable reality than the work of an André
Breton, let's say, there's much about it that's surreal all the same: the grotesque distortions; the hallucinatory images; the jarring dislocations; the
creation of the aura of dream or, more precisely, of nightmare. Leslie
Fiedler, I think, best describes the experience of reading a West novel:

> Putting down a book by West, a reader is not sure whether he has been pre-
> sented with a nightmare endowed with the conviction of actuality or with
> actuality distorted in the semblance of a nightmare; but in either case, he has
> the sense that he has been presented with a view of a world in which, incred-
> ibly, he lives!

It is this final and, as Fiedler suggests, quite incredible sensation that goes
a long way in explaining the frequent descriptions of West's *The Day of the
Locust* as the best novel about Hollywood there is, although the Hollywood it presents us with is less an actual place than a state of mind. The
actions in the novel aren't representative instances of Hollywood's vulgarity, perversion, and violence; nor are they particularly symbolic. Their texture is much more that of monstrous projections of the deformed inner
lives of the novel's various characters—characters who are both pathetic
losers living on the fringe of glamor and, on another, more significant level,
bizarre and contorted images of humanity. In a word, they are grotesques.

"Who can believe that Homer Simpson, the toadying mass man from the Midwest, knows only one song—'Oh, say can you see'? Who can believe in that chaste blob Homer on any level?" asks Pauline Kael of West's novel. And though, of course, she's right that no one can believe in Homer—or for the matter, in Faye Greener, the affected movie extra/call girl/sexpot with fantasies of becoming a star; her father Harry, the laughing clown now making a meager living as a Miracle Solvent salesman; the salacious dwarf, Abe Kusich; or the cowboy-movie extra, Earle Shoop, with his "two-dimensional face that a talented child might have drawn with a ruler and compass"—not believing is the very point or, at least, a clue to the essential surreality of the novel's vision.

That a perceptive reader like Kael can ask such a question in the first place, however—and that readers in general are never quite sure whether to see the characters as real or unreal—is a clue to something else altogether: to the novel's limitations, to West's ultimate lack of control. As Leslie Fiedler puts it: "West does not seem finally a really achieved writer; certainly, no one of his books is thoroughly satisfactory, though there are astonishing local successes in all of them."

By these "astonishing local successes," Fiedler means, I expect, the startling images, the extraordinary strokes of characterization, the sudden and devastating insights into human desperation, the sharply satirical descriptions which in a mere paragraph capture a total ambiance. It is all of this that not only accounts for West's enduring reputation but also explains the appeal of his novels to filmmakers—though in the case of *The Day of the Locust*, it's also clearly a matter of the Hollywood subject matter. Still, that troubling mixture of surreality and reality (or of nightmare and actuality) remains, explaining in turn the extraordinary difficulty of adapting a work like *The Day of the Locust* to the screen.

The novel presents other, less central problems as well. There's the fragmented, discontinuous nature of its story, which is hardly much of a story at all and actually little more than a series of sketches centered around the yearnings of young painter Tod Hackett for his neighbor in the San Bernardino Arms, Faye Greener. There's the extreme violence of the novel's—cockfight, the climactic scene in which Homer's insane stomping to death of would-be child star Adore Loomis turns fans at a Hollywood premiere into a mob of vicious rioters. There's the odd division of focus whereby the novel establishes Tod as central consciousness and then more or less drops him in order to shift its attention to Homer. Also, the story is finally centered on none of these characters but rather on an abstraction—

the pathetic need of mankind for glamor and romance and the ugly betrayal of that need by society in general and the dream factory in particular. The curious quality of the novel's tone is also problematic—it's an odd combination of cruel irony and pathos, which many feel is insufficiently balanced. The irony is so strong, the comedy so bitter, the narrative stance so cool and distant, that we tend to lose sympathy with the characters—and that works against the novel's implicit intention of revealing them as the sadly betrayed and "the cheated." (This last was West's original title for the novel.) It's this lack of compassion, this tinge of superiority to its own materials that gives the novel its off-putting quality. "Readable and, in a certain sense, a literary achievement," goes Pauline Kael's evaluation, "but I don't find it likeable."

It's hardly any surprise that Kael (and numerous others) didn't find John Schlesinger's film of *The Day of the Locust* particularly likeable either. And it isn't, in any meaningful sense of the term. But though I know I'm submitting a minority opinion—and one that even the filmmakers themselves don't quite agree with (scenarist Waldo Salt, especially, has expressed dissatisfaction with his work here)—*The Day of the Locust* seems to me both a thoughtful and a sensitive adaptation and a finely realized film in itself. Its particular virtue lies in the extent to which it has surpassed the novel in achieving precisely that delicate balance between cruel irony and pathos and, more importantly, between the real and the surreal. Pulling its materials in two apparently contradictory directions at once, it asserts more explicitly than does the novel the subjective, hallucinatory nature of its experience, while at the same time, it makes its characters more human than West's and by that token, more sympathetic and moving.

Schlesinger's casting is crucial to the characters' humanity and, as even the film's detractors have admitted, superb in the case of androgynous Adore (Jackie Haley), the dwarf Abe (Billy Barty), and above all in those of Harry the clown (Burgess Meredith) and Tod (William Atherton). Meredith, for example, makes of Harry not only a second-rate performer who has made his life a hackneyed act, but a desperate old man whose hysterical laughter at the poverty of his fate absolutely chills us into compassion; while Atherton grants Tod a clarity and psychological consistency the somewhat obscure character-cum-voyeur doesn't quite have in the novel. Atherton also brings to bear on his character an inherently unsettling quality that tends both to belie his Ivy League looks and to make credible his violent near-rape of Faye.

Schlesinger's casting of Faye, however, turned out to be somewhat controversial, since in giving the role to Karen Black, he had (among other things) made Faye decidedly older than the seventeen she is in the novel. To some critics, the alteration was a total betrayal, making Faye more self-conscious, neurotic, and even more perverse in her refusal to grant Tod her sexual favors. Perhaps. But considering her brief stint as call girl, Faye's refusal is quite perverse in the novel as well, and the change in age serves to make her fantasies more desperate and futile, her affectations—the facade she has constructed, that is, out of fragments of movies and movie stars and gossip columns—even flimsier. Black also, though admittedly an uneven actress, has always been expert at conveying the very quality that is key to Faye as character: her mannered and hollow eroticism. The choice of Donald Sutherland as Homer was equally disturbing to some. But Sutherland not only seems physically apt—oversized, awkward, bizarrely featured, able with the help of the camera to make his huge hands seem as self-willed and weirdly seriocomic as they are in the novel—he also manages to bring a certain humanizing tenderness to this most extreme of West's grotesques.

Much as these actors contribute, Schlesinger hasn't relied on them exclusively to grant West's freakish types credibility and sympathy. He has also interpolated several scenes that work very much to this end as well. There's the one in which Homer and Faye are shown dancing (or more precisely, clinging to one another) to the tune of "Dancing on a Dime," the tears streaming down both their "cheated" faces, indicating their pathetic self-awareness and earning them a poignant dimensionality; and there's the early montage in which Faye and Tod are shown driving around Hollywood, taking in all the glamor, making visible the fantasies peddled by Locustland and also giving more substance to Tod's desires. Similarly, the added scene of Tod's attempt to rape Faye gives those desires dramatic form, while serving at the same time to indicate their essentially violent nature. There's also the sequence in which Adore performs a cruel imitation of Harry for Faye's benefit, with Homer as witness. While making Adore all that more hateful, the scene also gives more psychological conviction to Homer's extreme response to the child in the climactic scene.

But our concern here is less with Schlesinger's accomplishment in giving his characters human acceptability than with his somewhat paradoxical one of investing their world and thus the film as a whole with a surreal, dream-like texture. Partly, this is a function of the very look of the film. The work of Conrad Hall, the cinematography is sleepily atmospheric and bathed in an almost startling brightness which in itself works to create an aura of unreality. So, too, to a certain extent, do the film's (admittedly somewhat ob-

vious, but nonetheless emphatically Westian) under-the-credits shots—
beginning with the abrupt opening (out of darkness) of the huge door of a
sound stage and a series of overlit glimpses of extras on the set of a costume
film. More important, however, is the way in which Schlesinger, once he
identifies the film's point of view as essentially that of the painter Tod,
makes the camera's eye the artist's eye, granting it the artist's acute powers
of observation, as well as his ability to suspend a perception in time and
space and encase it in a painterly image. In one early sequence, for example,
the camera focuses on a man seated on a bench while waiting for a bus. A
vehicle passes by and another man abruptly joins him—too abruptly for the
vision to be real. Then another vehicle passes and still another man is added
to the scene, with the three finally frozen into a stunning sculptural composition of human isolation and unfulfilled expectation. Elsewhere, an elderly
couple, seated in their car and gazing up at the huge Hollywoodland sign,
are also briefly glimpsed and similarly held motionless, flattened into a striking still life of pathetic longing. Here and there, too, the film reverses the
perceptual process—turning art into life, just as these images have worked
to turn life into art. There's the sequence, for instance, where Tod is putting together his sketches for a movie rendition of the Battle of Waterloo
and actual sounds of battle suddenly are heard on the soundtrack.

At such moments as this one, the transforming vision is unmistakably
Tod's. At other points in the film, that vision is deprived of any realistic
source or rational explanation and so becomes the vision of the film itself—
underscoring that the world of the film, if resembling the actual world, isn't
quite equivalent to it. These perceptions moreover take us by surprise and
so both intensify their jarring surreality and often amuse us in the process.
At the point that Harry (unaccompanied by Tod) begins to go on his
rounds, or better still, into his door-to-door act, the world quite literally becomes a stage—as in moving from one shot to another, the camera makes
one image jerkily ascend above another in the manner of a rising stage curtain. At still another point, we watch Homer vacantly sitting in his garden,
the camera cutting to a huge close-up of a lizard, the creature becoming an
apt (and aptly Westian) metaphor for Homer himself.

Significantly, in this same sequence, we see (and *hear*, because the sound
has been strongly amplified) oranges fall from a nearby tree. The oranges
appear again as motif at the outset of the final apocalyptic sequence—
running wildly after Homer, Tod knocks a bag full of oranges out of a
woman's arms, sending them spilling out into the street. These oranges
serve as suggestive emblems in the film, just as they also do in the novel. Of

the "savage and bitter" crowd gathering at the movie premiere, West writes:

> Where else should they go but California, the land of sunshine and oranges? Once there, they discover that sunshine isn't enough. They get tired of oranges, even of avocado pears and passion fruit. Nothing happens. They don't know what to do with their time. They haven't the mental equipment for leisure, the money nor the physical equipment for pleasure. . . . Their boredom becomes more and more terrible. They realize that they've been tricked and burn with resentment. Every day of their lives they read the newspapers and went to the movies. Both fed them on lynchings, murder, sex crimes, explosions, wrecks, love nests, fires, miracles, revolutions, war The daily diet made sophisticates of them. The sun is a joke. Oranges can t titillate their jaded palates. Nothing can ever be violent enough to make taut their slack minds and bodies.

In both novel and film, that resentment and inner violence finally explode. And it is here, in the film's final riot that, more extensively than anywhere else, the camera takes that awful reality and transforms it into images of fantasy. Here, too, Tod's point of view once again clearly dominates, the imagery drawn largely both from the huge mural he's been working on, "The Burning of Los Angeles," and from his Goya-esque sketches for the Waterloo film. Thus, as the crowd breaks into frenzy, as they turn over cars and trample one another, as they seemingly rip Homer himself apart, we suddenly see among them figures with masked faces out of such Expressionist painters as Nolde, Ensor, and Munch, and compositions out of Goya. Figures and images which are oddly, discomfortingly beautiful, ghastly and gorgeous at once, they tend to work on us much in the manner of all grotesque art and certainly in the manner of the particular paintings from which they derive—that is, they encase horror in such magnificence that we tolerate its contemplation.

Some critics have complained that this penultimate, emphatically surreal sequence comes out of nowhere. But to the contrary, it seems to me that throughout, the film carefully prepares us for it. The various events have been prefigured in small before being dramatized in large all through the film, as they are also in the novel. The lack of concern of the people at Harry's funeral—they are driven from the service by a rumor that Gable is nearby—prefigures the polite apathy of movie executives when the set of Waterloo collapses. Tod's drunken frenzy when Faye tempts him beyond endurance foreshadows Homer's more extreme hysteria when driven mad by Faye's rejection and infidelity. The film's bloody cockfight readies us for the bloodier deaths of both Adore and Homer. And the riot itself comes after the smaller-scale havoc of the party at Homer's house the night before. What's more, the visual texture of that sequence has also been established—not only, as suggested, by Tod's paintings and his work on the Waterloo film, but also by the film's earlier painterly shots. And the image that both pervades the riot and that perhaps most fully contains and expresses the film's themes—the human scream—has also been foreshadowed for us. Earlier, making his sketches for Waterloo, Tod has pretended a cry of anguish, drawing his own contrived image as reflected in a mirror. During the riot, he is trampled by the crowd and his scream becomes an actual one, its intensity and universality reflected this time not in a literal drawing but in a terrifying series of visual abstractions in which the human face is transformed on screen into a contorted, agonized death mask.

Admittedly, the scene *is* in some ways overstated—despite its extreme stylization, it's clearly very difficult to take. And it's clear, too, that the film as a whole isn't flawless. It may be possible to mount a defense (as one critic does) of the sequence featuring the Aimee Semple McPherson–type evangelist, by situating its source both in West's "nearly epic catalogue of Hollywood houses of worship" and in Homer's "incessant 'Here's the Church' hand gesture," but the sequence is trite all the same. Moreover, though I can understand Schlesinger's resistance to overplaying the technique of freezing his frames into stylized images—the device overused would most likely have lost both its surprise and force—I agree with the view that the film would have benefited by a stronger assertion of Tod's perspective. It may also be true that, as Pauline Kael suggests, in trusting the book's sensibility too much the film repeated the novel's flaws. Like the novel, the film suffers from the lack of a strong central character and a character with whom we can identify; like the novel, it is also often both cruel and painful, even if to a lesser degree; while, like the novel too, it's a work that is ultimately more successful in its parts than as a whole.

Nonetheless, as in the case of the novel as well, those local successes are indeed "astonishing." For whether or not Schlesinger was fully aware of the book's limitations, he well understood the source of its power: in its dreamlike texture, in the phantasmagoric nature of its vision. And keeping faith with that vision while at the same time making use of his own medium's potential for surreal effects, he managed to give us, whether it be "actuality distorted into the semblance of a nightmare" or "nightmare endowed with the conviction of actuality," nightmare all the same. Or, otherwise put, a truly Westian film whose action is played out not on the plane of external reality but somewhere in the inner world of dream.

Swann in Love and *The Proust Screenplay:* Proust Outside and In

"Life is too short and Proust is too long," Anatole France is said to have remarked when asked why he had never read his fellow countryman's masterpiece. And the more than 3,000 densely packed pages of complex metaphor and paragraph-long sentences that make up the seven volumes of *Remembrance of Things Past* have led most readers to concur. Indeed, more than a literary monument, *Remembrance of Things Past* stands—to use the metaphor most usually applied to it—as a variety of literary Everest.

Proust has long been an Everest to filmmakers too—yet, a surprisingly tempting one. For despite the length and intricacy of his work, not to mention its intense subjectivity—nearly its entirety is devoted to the musings, memories, and associations of the first-person narrator as he makes his supreme effort to triumph over time by freezing some forty years of past experience into a work of art—it is also considered to be among the most cinematic of novels in style. In a 1935 essay entitled "The Proustian Camera Eye," Paul Goodman offers a point-by-point comparison between Proustian techniques and those of the cinema. He identifies "the Proustian free-association with the dissolving flow of cinema, the Proustian *idée fixe* [the obsessive return to a single idea, image, or sensation] with the focusing of the camera, the Proustian revelation [or sudden flash of memory, usually set off by a sensation—for example, the taste of Proust's famous madeleine dipped in a cup of tea which brings back to him his entire childhood at Combray] with the unexpected juxtapositions of the cutting-room, and the passivity of the Proustian narrator [the ultimate "voyeur"] with the 'photographic' quality of the newsreel." Extensive as are Goodman's claims for Proust's cinematic quality, French critic Jacques Bourgeois makes even greater ones. Putting forth the notion that, as a writer committed to visualizing sensation and to the image above all, Proust had "invented" all variety of cinematic techniques, Bourgeois goes on to suggest that these techniques hold within them the promise of a "cinema of tomorrow"—a claim that turned out to be prophetic. For the Proustian or subjective cinema Bourgeois envisioned in his 1946 essay is precisely the type of "first-person" cinema that has been realized in the work of Resnais and Bergman, among others.

But there are other qualities, aside from its technique, that make *Remembrance of Things Past* tempting to film. For the very vastness which makes it a literary Everest also makes it potentially all things to all men. A Bergsonian meditation on the fluidity of time and consciousness, on the ever-changing nature of personality, on the power of art and memory to recover experience past, it is also a richly populated novel of manners—a study of mores and fashions, of snobbery and *déclassement*, of the decay of the aristocratic society of the nineteenth century and the ushering in of the triumphant bourgeois one of the twentieth. It is also an exploration of the idealization and impermanence of love, of the destructive obsessiveness of jealousy, of what in the homosexual eyes of Proust was the "vice" of homosexuality. It is also a study of the growth of an artist and especially of the nature of perception. All of this may boggle and intimidate the would-be adaptor, seeming so utterly, totally untranslatable; yet, the novel also offers endless materials and possibilities. As scenarist Jean-Claude Carrière puts it: "*Remembrance of Things Past* is one of the great works of literature, and there is no reason why it should not be used as a source like Shakespeare or Balzac. Everyone should feel free to glean there whatever interests him or affects him. Great works of art are bountiful."

Carrière is, of course, explaining and justifying his own approach—the approach, that is, which he and his co-scenarists, Peter Brook and Marie-Hélène Estienne, have taken in the screenplay that forms the basis of Volker Schlöndorff's Proust adaptation, *Swann in Love*. Rather than tackle the whole, they have chosen precisely to "glean" from it, basing their film on a fragment of a fragment, on one of the several parts that make up the first volume of the whole novel cycle. In itself, it's a well-reasoned choice. For one thing, the "Swann in Love" segment of *Swann's Way* is probably more self-contained than any of the other sections of the great *roman fleuve*. For another, its central subject—the obsessive passion of wealthy and elegant aesthete Charles Swann for demimondaine Odette de Crécy—would seem to lend itself very well to dramatization, as would the various milieux in which Swann finds himself while pursuing her. Following Swann from the "little clan" of the vulgar nouveau riche Madame Verdurin to the elegant salons of the Faubourg Saint-Germain, the section (set some years before the others in the novel, in the 1880s) is filled with telling glimpses of French society and broad social satire. Most important of all, focusing exclusively on Swann with very few authorial intrusions on the part of "Marcel", our narrator, "Swann in Love" is also—in contrast to the rest of the novel cycle—essentially told in the third person.

And not only have the filmmakers selected reasonably, they have also made some intelligent dramatic choices. They have, for example, decided to compress the action into a manageable time span, following Swann's obsessive pursuit of Odette through a single twenty-four-hour period, relying on intermittent flashbacks to provide background information. They have also added a coda, derived from a later section of the novel, that helps bring the tale to completion by showing us Swann finally married to Odette; by dramatizing the discomforting exclusion of their daughter Gilberte (as well as Odette herself) from the social world in which Swann himself once comfortably traveled; and by giving us both knowledge of Swann's impending death and a glimpse of the vast changes that have occurred over the intervening years. (In the final scene, automobiles now honk their way past carriages on the Paris boulevards.) The filmmakers have also, while doing away with Marcel as narrator, attempted to make Swann stand in for him to a certain extent. For they have framed the tale with Swann's voice-over commentary and opened the film with a shot of Swann writing in bed, an image clearly intended to suggest Proust himself.

The film has also been cast thoughtfully, if surprisingly, considering that neither of the leads is French, which required that their roles be dubbed. (Of course, on the other hand the choice clearly helped with international financing and distribution.) Jeremy Irons, with his lean, pale face and elegant demeanor, certainly looks right as Swann and brings to the role the experience of having played a similarly obsessed lover in *The French Lieutenant's Woman*. (He also, to his credit, took the trouble to redub his own voice in French for the print released in America—though several found his accent wanting.) As for Ornella Muti, her Playboy-bunny sensuality may seem somewhat off-key and perhaps overly celebrated by the camera as well—as one critic suggested, "the camera lingers so fondly upon her back, breasts, eyes and teeth that Proust's anxious eroticism of the half-said and the half-seen is swamped and simplified"—but she still manages to convey something of the character's coarseness, duplicity, and sexual ambivalence. (It's telling that Luchino Visconti, who had started work on an adaptation of *Remembrance of Things Past* in the seventies, had planned on giving the role of his past-her-prime Odette to a not dissimilar type, Brigitte Bardot.) And in one instance, at least—that of Alain Delon as the Baron de Charlus—the casting turned out to be brilliant, the only problem being that we don't see enough of Delon's exquisitely comic and knowing rendition of Proust's outrageous homosexual aristocrat. (In Visconti's version, Delon was to play the narrator, Marcel.) What's more, Hans Werner Henze's music, suggesting both Franck and Fauré, very much follows Proust's directions—as do the opulent and carefully researched decor and costumes, rendered with appropriate lushness by Sven Nykvist's cinematography.

But though all of this has resulted in a film that's far from unintelligent and certainly not a total failure—indeed it was quite well received abroad, though the praise tended to be somewhat guarded—it's also a film that ultimately doesn't satisfy. It's an oddly unfeeling and unexciting work—dry and even, at stretches, quite dull. The faults are quite evident: the distant and vaguely mannered quality of Jeremy Irons's performance, Carrière et al.'s "faithful" but uncourageous screenplay, and the uninspired nature of Volker Schlöndorff's direction. Still, the problem that underlies all others is the film's failure to bring us inside Swann's sensibility, to capture the particular texture of his obsession or perspective.

For what the filmmakers have failed either to note or, more likely, to find sufficiently important is that though the "Swann in Love" section of the novel is narrated in the third person, it still makes us privy to the subtlest calibrations of Swann's feelings. It follows the vacillations of his attitudes, traces the patterns of his associations, and describes in minutest detail the nature of his perceptions of music, of paintings, and, above all, of Odette. Moreover, much as the section can stand alone, its distinction and richness still derive from the extent to which it shares in the style of the whole—a style which, in its fluid movements from present to past and in the evocative power of its images and metaphors, attempts to simulate thought and convey the nature of aesthetic perception. In short, in the "Swann in Love" segment as in the novel as a whole, the emphasis is on internal experience.

But the film gives us none of this. The voice-over at the outset may suggest the first-person perspective, but the device is not only too conventional for Proust, it isn't even sustained. The flashbacks also are neither sufficient in number nor mounted in a way to catch the distinctive nature of Proustian memory. Only at one point in the film does a reminiscence assert itself in a manner that comes close to suggesting the fluid nature of thought, or to giving the past the peculiar immediacy it has in Proust's novel: when Swann, having returned to his apartment after Odette has set off for the opera without him, is shown pacing the halls agonized, distracted, clearly obsessed, and the camera cuts so abruptly to Odette walking the very same space in the very same place that we are momentarily disoriented, our sense of past and present confused.

Otherwise, the flashbacks are traditional in style, without the Proustian feeling of the associative power of objects, places, and sensations or of the intensity of moments of heightened awareness. Most of the flashbacks even have an almost obligatory feel to them, as if they were thrown in merely to oblige the viewer familiar with Proust or to clarify the situation in some small way for the viewer who isn't. (For example, the almost perfunctory flashback at the outset when, as Swann is writing in bed, the camera cuts briefly to the cattleya scene—the moment, that is, in which Swann adjusts the cattleya orchids in Odette's dress and makes physical contact with her for the first time. Conveying almost nothing of the enormous significance of the moment to Swann, it seems included only in the way of obeisance to the potential Proustian in the audience. What, no cattleyas?)

Nor does the film try to get at the quality of inwardness in any other meaningful way. Take that extraordinary scene in the novel where, at Madame de Saint-Euverte's, Swann is moved to such sublime emotions while listening to the Vinteuil sonata. Mounting it on screen, Schlöndorff depends on the expression of his actors alone to convey the depths of the experience. And even if mere facial (or even bodily) expression were able to communicate in this way, Schlöndorff doesn't stay with Jeremy Irons long enough to truly give the actor a chance—the way, let's say, Bergman has often allowed his camera to linger on the face of Liv Ullmann or Bibi Andersson. Instead, the director cuts away to the Duchesse de Guermantes (Fanny Ardant) staring at Swann, as if in an attempt to give us a sense of the intensity of *his* emotions from *her* perceptions of them. The choice is telling, since it indicates to what extent the film has adopted the external view, not only at this point but throughout.

One commentator, in praising the film, noted that "Swann's midnight carriage chase after the elusive Odette, social receptions, supper parties, haut monde tittle-tattle and military parades [are] all captured with the pathos of distance. . . ." I'm not sure about the "pathos," but the critic is right about the "distance." The problem is that such distance is totally at odds with Proust, who shows us almost nothing from a distance and just about everything in extreme close-up. Proust also shows us everything from a particular, individualizing perspective, whether it be that of his narrator, "Marcel," or of Swann—the man whom "Marcel," in any case, identifies with so fully. The film, in contrast, completely eschews the establishment of such a distinctive point of view. It may give us a glimpse of

Botticelli's *Jethro's Daughter*, the figure with whom art connoisseur Swann identifies Odette. But, as in the cattleya scene, the shot seems merely to be paying obeisance to the text, since it never manages (or even really tries) to give us a feeling for what this image signifies—the camera never even hinting at the way in which Swann's association of the Botticelli with Odette reflects on his manner of idealizing and aestheticizing his real-life love object and of thus linking love and art. And as with this shot, so with the imagery throughout, which, opulent as it may be, is also thoroughly conventional and unrevealing. We may see the extravagant dresses, the feathered hats, the oriental rugs, the brocaded walls, the glistening chandeliers. We may see Paris life—the elegant restaurants, the baroque decor of the brothels. All of it, however is glimpsed as it might be in a coffee-table book.

In short, this film has "gleaned" from Proust not his inner explorations, but his external ones: his observations on fashions and decor and social mores. And though the external is clearly a part of Proust, it's a very limited part indeed and a part that touches only very lightly on the distinctive nature of his genius. Moreover, it's not only "scenic" Proust or "postcard" Proust—as some reviewers have noted—it's also fairly banal Proust which does not differentiate his vision of obsessive passion from any other.

One generous critic said of Schlöndorff's film that it is "at best, the sort of adaptation that honours its author without claiming the all-embracing ambition to which he aspired" and "at worst, Proust for middle-brows." Part of me wants to go along with this critic and even say that such a Proust is better than no Proust at all, since what we have here is Proust at last made available, a Proust for whom, as another reviewer put it, "no esoteric knowledge [is] required." But another part of me bristles at the thought. For the truth of the matter is that Schlöndorff's Proust, a Proust "for middle-brows," isn't Proust at all. And what's worse, it isn't even a very good movie.

Expectations play an enormous role in our response to adaptations: we tend to approve a film that meshes with certain of the preconceptions we bring with us and whose implicit reading of its source coincides in some significant way with our own. But in the particular case of *Swann in Love*, the problem for me, at least, isn't simply that Schlöndorff's Proust isn't my Proust, that the movie I've made in my mind bears little resemblance to his. It's also that I bring to it an awareness of yet another cinematic conception of Proust—and one that is everything Schlöndorff's isn't. I'm speaking, of course, of Harold Pinter's *The Proust Screenplay,* a work so audacious and brilliant in its conception that it seems to me presumptuous to say that it coincides with my own vision. Let me say rather that it made me see Proust in some ways more clearly than I ever had before and understand more fully and completely, too, what is meant by the description of Proust as "cinematic."

Tackling—in contrast to Schlöndorff's film—not one novel but all seven, *The Proust Screenplay* manages, astoundingly enough, to capture much of the thrust and movement of the entire novel cycle: its circularity, its pattern of motifs, its texture as a series of experiences that both inspire the creation of a work of art and constitute a work of art themselves. Astoundingly too, it touches on almost all of the major Proustian themes. But what Pinter grasps and emphasizes most of all is that central Proustian concern with inner states, with the subjective nature of experience, with the fluidity of time and consciousness.

Establishing "Marcel" as central consciousness, the screenplay presents the experience of the whole exclusively from his point of view—though, unlike the novel where he is essentially both invisible and passive, he appears here also as participant. We meet him first in a scene taken from the final volume of the series, as a middle-aged man en route to a musicale at the Guermantes mansion. In Proust, the narrator stumbles on an uneven flagstone in that scene, setting off a series of memories which are further intensified as he sits in the Guermantes library. Similarly, in Pinter, Marcel also stumbles, also sits in the library, and we move via his thoughts back to his childhood; we then proceed chronologically from that point forward in time. As in the novel, however, that forward movement is often interrupted—sometimes with a flashforward, other times with an associative montage.

Pinter carries us, moreover, through just about every major dramatic event in the novel, introduces us to most of its major characters as well, and compresses it all with breathtaking skill. He summarizes the "Swann in Love" segment to which Schlöndorff devoted his entire film in a mere eight pages of the scenario—approximately ten or fifteen minutes of screen time—scoring in that space just about all of the same points about obsessive passion that Schlöndorff does and, in addition, suggesting something of its larger significance to the whole. The screenplay also moves into the segment with an exquisitely Proustian flow of the camera. Walking together with his parents near the hedge at Tansonville, past Swann's Combray home, the child Marcel glimpses Odette, and Pinter's directions are as follows:

75. C.U. ODETTE, SEEN THROUGH LEAVES.
76. C.U. ODETTE, FOURTEEN YEARS YOUNGER.
77. INT. THE VERDURINS' HOUSE, PARIS 1879.
> Over ODETTE'S face, the voice of MME. VERDURIN.

> MME. VERDURIN (V.O.)
> She's just a little tiny piece of
> perfection. Aren't you?. . .

And the last shot in the Odette/Swann sequence moves us out of it with a similar flow, returning us to the place where it all began. Again, there is a voice-over, this time Swann's, musing on Odette's confession to him about her possible lesbian relationships:

90. EXT. SWANN'S PARK AND HOUSE AT
> TANSONVILLE. DAY.
> No one in sight.

> SWANN (V.O. with fatigue)
> Perhaps two or three times.

> Bird song.

> I knew quite well what she was after.

In an excellent analysis of the Pinter screenplay in *Literature/Film Quarterly*, Mark Graham suggests that there are, of course, no parallels in the novel for the kind of rapid juxtapositions of both events and images found in the screenplay. Cinematic as Proust's techniques may be, Proust is nothing if not leisurely. He is so leisurely, in fact, that we often lose sight of his total design. This isn't true of the Pinter adaptation which, as Graham points out, has the virtue of making that design—the thematic unity of the whole, the analogies between the various phases of Marcel's experience, the echoes, the repetitions, the sustained motifs—more strongly evident.

Pinter also gives us a sense of the decisive role of what in Proust sometimes goes by the term "involuntary memory"—of the way, that is, in which a perception, a sensation, a sound can set off memories, carry us back on a journey through time. Consider the moment in which Marcel trips on the cobblestone. Repeating it toward the end of the screenplay, Pinter cuts from the scene to:

396. Very dim quick flash of Venice.
397. MARCEL'S face.
398. EXT. PRINCE DE GUERMANTES'S HOUSE.
       MARCEL stands still.
       He sways back again and forward.
       He remains still.
       He sways back again and forward.
       In background chauffeurs regarding him curiously, with amusement.
       MARCEL sways back.
399. Blue glow.
400. Chauffeurs.
401. Blue mosaics in Saint Mark's Church.
402. MARCEL's face.

Also present in the screenplay are sequences that convey the Proustian stress on the importance of perception, on the shifting nature of point of view. And Pinter has chosen to preserve the two scenes in the novel most crucial to expressing Proust's vision: Marcel's glimpse of the church steeples and his sight of the trees on the road to Hudimesnil. Pinter's description in both instances emphasizes (as does that of Proust) the continual alteration of Marcel's perspective and of his perception in turn.

What all of this should make clear is the extent to which Pinter—in contrast to Schlöndorff—has chosen to center his film on Marcel's subjectivity. What's fascinating is that Pinter manages this while at the same time omitting the entire opening section of the novel where the narrator, lying sleepless in bed, recalls his past, just as Pinter also leaves out any reference to Proust's famous madeleine. What he gives us instead is a montage of images which, much more immediately cinematic in nature, works quite exquisitely to the same end. That is like the madeleine and the section devoted to the narrator musing, these images both assert the film's inner focus and establish the various motifs which will be developed later. The film begins:

1. Yellow screen. Sound of a garden gate bell.
2. Open countryside, a line of trees, seen from a railway carriage.
       The train is still.
       No sound. Quick fade out.
3. Momentary yellow screen.
4. The sea, seen from a high window, a towel hanging on a towel
       rack in foreground. No sound. Quick fade out.

5. Momentary yellow screen.
6. Venice. A window in a palazzo, seen from a gondola.
   No sound. Quick fade out.
7. Momentary yellow screen.
8. The dining room at Balbec. No sound. Empty.
9. EXT. THE HOUSE OF THE PRINCE DE GUERMANTES.
   PARIS. 1921. AFTERNOON.
   In long shot a middle-aged man (MARCEL) walks towards
   the PRINCE DE GUERMANTES'S house.
   His posture is hunched, his demeanor one of defeat.
   Many carriages, a few cars, a crowd of chauffeurs. Realistic sound.
10. INT. LIBRARY. THE PRINCE DE GUERMANTES'S HOUSE.
    1921.
    A waiter inadvertently knocks a spoon against a plate.
    MARCEL, large in foreground, looks up.
11. INT. DRAWING ROOM. THE PRINCE DE GUERMANTES'S
    HOUSE. 1921.
    The drawing room doors open.
    The camera enters with MARCEL, who hesitates.
    Hundreds of faces, some of which turn towards him,
    grotesquely made up, grotesquely old.
    A tumult of voices.

Confusing at first, perhaps, but completely, inescapably Proustian. Besides, whatever the immediate dislocation, there are significant clues to what is going on and what it all means. We sense, for example, from the camera's focus on the "middle-aged man" and from the distorted nature of the scene at which he is present—the drawing room with its hundreds of "grotesquely made up, grotesquely old" faces—that we are seeing the scene from that man's subjective vantage point. We also assume that the stream of images before us most likely constitutes his "stream of consciousness"— and all the more so because certain of the shots, such as the one through the open window, imply an observer.

In the course of the film, moreover, each of these images clarifies itself, the yellow screen almost immediately. For in Shot 22, the camera pulls back to reveal that the yellow screen is actually a portion of Vermeer's *View of Delft*, the painting which Marcel will tell us later is "the most beautiful painting in the world." Stanley Kauffmann has written that when he read that camera direction and "saw how this *visual* motif had been brought forward to underlie a new sensory-mnemonic-emotional system in a different medium," he "felt a cold shiver of excitement. The book had been *transformed*." I don't think that description can be bettered.

The Proust Screenplay is, of course, a screenplay and not a movie, and who knows, it may never be. (Pinter and the late Joseph Losey, who originally hired Pinter to do the adaptation and was to direct the film, were never able to raise the money.) And who knows either what the film would finally look like once the screenplay was translated to the screen. (Its visual and editing challenges are enormous, as are the demands the film would place on the actor chosen to play "Marcel.") Still, even in this tentative form, Pinter's work contrasts tellingly with Volker Schlöndorff's. It implies that when an adaptation fails it isn't because of any inherent limitations in the film medium or because a novel simply can't be put on screen; it suggests that the cause lies instead in a very individual failure of either courage or imagination on the part of the filmmaker. What's more, offering a glimpse, at least, of the kind of extraordinary cinematic life that might be given to that most impossible, intractable of literary works, *Remembrance of Things Past*, *The Proust Screenplay* says a great deal about the possibilities of adaptation. Above all, though, my reason for including it here is that I can think of no work that better embodies what I've tried to suggest throughout this book: that the finest adaptation is centered on the most sensitive reading of its source and that it consequently exists not simply as art but as significant commentary; and that rather than diminishing film, the contact with literature tends to enrich it. And do more than enrich it. For what *The Proust Screenplay* illustrates most pointedly of all is that in its collaboration with literary greatness, film may produce greatness itself.

The Magnificent Ambersons: Reversing the Bias

Tess, Women in Love, Death in Venice, Apocalypse Now, Under the Volcano, Swann in Love—the adaptations discussed in the foregoing chapters have not only been drawn from literary works which in the intricacy of their rhetorical strategies and in the distinctive nature of their structure and style have challenged the film medium; they have also been based, for the most part, on works of towering stature. Most novels, as we know, are neither so fully achieved nor anywhere so complex. Whether "a good read" like Mario Puzo's *The Godfather*, a prestigious bestseller like Somerset Maugham's *Of Human Bondage*, a Pulitzer Prize winner like Margaret Mitchell's *Gone with the Wind*, or even the work of a Nobel laureate like Pearl S. Buck's *The Good Earth*, the greater part of fiction tends to the conventional. And it is such works as these—neither masterworks nor pulp, but middle-ground novels—that have provided the inspiration for the bulk of adaptations. Thus, though significantly different in kind from the type of adaptation that has concerned us up to now, a word about such films is in order.

Predictably, such adaptations tend to excite little in the way of critical controversy and are generally greeted with greater generosity than those which tread on more hallowed ground. Not only do readers simply bring less commitment to novels like *How Green Was My Valley* or *The Informer* than they do to time-honored classics, but such straightforward works also transfer to the screen with a good deal more ease as well. Still, the praise hasn't been without its qualifications nor the response without its share of bias either. High-culture enthusiasts, for example, have often seen the success of these adaptations—of a film like *From Here to Eternity*, let's say, or even an *Elmer Gantry*—as only further proof of the source novel's limited quality. Recall Simon's Law—that when an adaptation succeeds, it's an indication that the original is less than first-rate. The success of these movies has also been taken as testimony to the inferior status of film itself. What better evidence of the medium's limitations, detractors of film have suggested, than precisely its propensity for the accessible and simplistic, for the melodramatic and sentimental. (That the novel has always shared a similar propensity—managing to produce masterworks all the same—is something these critics somehow overlook. It's true that had Emma Bovary lived in the twentieth century, she probably would have fallen prey to Hollywood-manufactured fantasies; but let's not forget that as it is, she suffered from reading novels.)

Defenders of film, quite naturally, take a somewhat different tack and especially when an adaptation based on middling stuff achieves a rank in cinema higher than its comparable rank in literature. Either they ignore the fact that the film is an adaptation altogether, dismissing the novelist's contribution and crediting all to the filmmaker alone or, more frequently yet, they regard the adaptation as a triumph of style over substance.

Such a work is Orson Welles's adaptation of Booth Tarkington's *The Magnificent Ambersons*'s—a film to which cineastes bring so much commitment that they reverse the traditional book/film bias. Regarding the film as vastly superior to the book, they grant the Tarkington novel little value, crediting Welles with all of *Ambersons's* virtues and blaming Tarkington for all its faults. Not that there isn't a small degree of truth in this—at least, insofar as the film is in fact superior to the novel; and not that the tendency to credit Welles overmuch isn't also understandable. There are few films indeed that warrant such defense and protection as *The Magnificent Ambersons*, the movie having suffered in the manner of Erich von Stroheim's *Greed*—significantly perhaps, also an adaptation—gross indignities and mutilation at the hands of studio powers. After holding several reportedly disastrous previews, RKO cut the film from 131 minutes to its present 88-minute length, and ordered several sequences reshot, including the movie's final one, all without the director's approval. (Welles was in South America at the time, shooting the ill-fated *It's All True*.) The missing footage has yet to be found. Still, sufficient evidence remains in the form of the final draft of Welles's script, the cutting continuity of the original release print, and testimony from those who worked on the film to enable us to reconstruct Welles's intentions; while the movie itself survived its alterations to the degree that even in its present, approximate form it has emerged as one of cinema's most prestigious works. "If Flaubert re-read

Don Quixote each year, why can't we re-see *The Ambersons* every year?"
François Truffaut remarked; and evidence of the extent to which others
share in his appreciation can be found in the fact that for the past two decades, *The Magnificent Ambersons* has been ranked among the Top Ten
films of all time in *Sight and Sound*'s international critics poll—along, of
course, with that other Welles achievement, the front-running *Citizen
Kane.*

The Magnificent Ambersons is a remarkable film, and it's also—though
very few have approached it in these terms—a remarkable adaptation. That
isn't the only reason, however, that I've chosen it to conclude this book.
An instance in which a minor and conventional novel has been transformed
into a major and unconventional film, it has the particular virtue of allowing us to approach the film/book relationship from a somewhat different angle than those assumed in earlier discussions; while, in the special
nature of its achievements and in certain of its shortcomings as well, it allows at the very same time for both the reconsideration and reinforcement
of many of the principles put forth in those discussions.

To begin with, whatever the oblivion to which current critical opinion
may have assigned Booth Tarkington, he was in his own lifetime
(1869–1946) an enormously popular writer. In fact, the problems his fiction presents are implicit in that very popularity and in popular fiction as a
whole—its lack of originality and daring and its self-conscious manipulations and adjustments for the reader—though given that Tarkington was
not only more popular than most but that he determinedly and
unashamedly courted that popularity, those problems are compounded.
"The laurel," he remarked, "is bestowed by the people," who in the long
run "recommend a work of art to the pompous critic." Unashamedly, he
identified himself with the "middle-brows," making clear his lack of patience both with the avant-garde experimentations of many of his fellow
writers and with their questionable subject matter as well. (Consider that
Joyce and Lawrence were his contemporaries and that he outlived F. Scott
Fitzgerald and Nathanael West.)

At one point in the novel *The Magnificent Ambersons*, young Georgie
Amberson expresses his literary preferences: "My theory of literature is an
author who does not indulge in trashiness—writes about people you could
introduce into your own home. I agree with my Uncle Sydney, as I once
heard him say he did not care to a read a book or go to a play about people
he would not care to meet at his own dinner table." Generally,
Tarkington's stance toward Georgie is critical; but in this case, it seems

fairly clear that Georgie is speaking for Tarkington himself. For Tarkington aligned himself with just such literature—with conservative Howellsian realism and the genteel tradition, that is. He was also given to an old-fashioned mode of narrative: to the heavily plotted story; to authorial intrusion and the omniscient point of view; to fairly uncomplicated characterizations; to equally obvious symbolism, where he indulged in symbolism at all; and above all, to the sentimental, upbeat conclusion. And though all of this may have helped to endear him to the general reader, such an approach had already long gone out of style in serious literary circles.

Still, whatever his failings, Tarkington did receive—along with the approval of the public—numerous literary distinctions, including the Pulitzer Prize twice—first for *The Magnificent Ambersons* (1918) and then for *Alice Adams* (1921). Moreover, however otherwise limited in his art, Tarkington certainly had his charms—his humor, his appealing "light touch," his strong sense of place and atmosphere, and intermittently (especially in *Ambersons*), his sharp social vision. He was also, as even his detractors had to admit, an extremely skillful storyteller and one who displayed a decided dramatic flair. Not only did he write plays himself, but his works were widely adapted by others to stage, to radio, and to film.

Chief among those others was Orson Welles who, it's important to note, thought very highly of the author. It helped, of course, that Tarkington was a friend of Welles's family, that Welles came from the same Midwestern background that is the setting for the author's emphatically regional works, and that Welles's father apparently served as the model for Eugene Morgan, the spirited and affectionate inventor and manufacturer of automobiles who is one of *Ambersons*'s central characters. But even without Welles's quite explicit statement that he made *The Magnificent Ambersons* because he loved the novel and believed Tarkington a "hugely underrated" writer—Welles's respect for the author is evident. During his Mercury Theatre radio days, he had adapted *Penrod, Seventeen,* and *Ambersons* itself; while the extraordinary fidelity of his film to its source certainly testifies to his equally extraordinary trust in it.

And it isn't simply a matter of the extent to which Welles has followed Tarkington's plot, kept faith with his characterizations, and even repeated the novel's sequence of events. (Like the novel, the film follows the fall of a proud and aristocratic family, the Ambersons, paralleling their turn-of-the-century decline with that of their Midwestern city and contrasting it with the rise of the industrious and industrial Morgans. Ultimately, both families are united and so, too, old and new with the projected marriage of rehabilitated Amberson grandson Georgie and forgiving Morgan daughter Lucy.) It's that there's hardly a scene or even a line of dialogue in the film that doesn't derive directly from the novel. And similarly with the film's overall method and structure—its movement back and forth from the panoramic and generalized to the immediately dramatic and particular—and its point of view as well. *Ambersons,* the novel, comes to us through an often chatty storyteller, an omniscient narrator who describes, summarizes, and passes judgment, and who can take us anywhere and inside any mind he wishes. And though that narrator is less insistently with us in the film, he's present nonetheless in the form of Welles's off-screen voice, which is heard at the outset of the film and intermittently toward the end: both at the point that Welles makes us privy to the thoughts of the dying Major Amberson and when he speaks to us concerning the sad ironies of proud George's final "come-uppance."

Welles even relies on Tarkington for his most celebrated and most emphatically "cinematic" effects. Consider the film's opening series of insets—the image of the trolley politely waiting for a passenger, accompanied by Welles's voice-over commentaries establishing the flavor of the period and the themes of time and change ("In those days, they had time for everything"); the summary of changing fashions in which an as-yet-unidentified Eugene Morgan (Joseph Cotton) appears and reappears before a full-length mirror, modeling hats and coats and trousers; the chatter of the choruslike townspeople about the Ambersons' fabulous mansion and about the Ambersons themselves. All of this—every word, just about every image, and the montage effect itself—is drawn directly from the novel. "In that town, in those days, all the women who wore silk or velvet knew all the other women who wore silk or velvet," writes Tarkington, and also announces Welles. "The long contagion of the 'Derby' hat arrived: one season the crown of this hat would be a bucket; the next it would be a spoon," writes Tarkington, with Welles both telling and showing us the same.

And the rest of the film follows in kind with effect after effect, and sequence after sequence—from the strategy of summarizing young George's history and personality through his two reckless rides through the town in a horse-drawn cart, one as a child and another as a young man; through the choice of the Amberson ball as dramatic setting for the reunion of ex-lovers Isabel Amberson Minafer and Eugene Morgan and the first meeting and attraction of their children George and Lucy; to the ironic counterpointing of George and Lucy's romantic ride in an old-fashioned sleigh with that of the older generation in Eugene's newfangled automobile; to George's stubborn and cruel decision to keep his now-widowed mother and Eugene apart, signaled through his shutting the door in Eugene's face; right down through George's final, devastating walk as humiliated scion of a ruined and forgotten family through a brutally altered town—all this so closely parallels the novel that the novel has the feel (at least, when read after seeing the film) of being not merely the film's inspiration, but its very scenario.

It follows, too, that the film's much-praised historical vision also has its source in Tarkington. What makes *The Magnificent Ambersons* a "remarkable movie," critic Michael Wood contends, is its "sense of historical change as tangled and relentless, of the passing of personal time and time of the city, of the intransigence of desire and the uselessness of hindsight." Film historian David A. Cook, for his part, finds the movie strikingly "prophetic," suggesting as it does "in 1942, and in a story set in 1905 . . . that the quality of American life will ultimately be destroyed by the automobile and urbanization." Both critics are on the mark regarding the film's virtues. The problem is that Wood who, significantly, doesn't fail to situate the film's "rudimentary psychology" in its literary source, somehow manages to gloss over the fact that the "sense of historical change" and that sense of the "uselessness of hindsight," too, also derive from Tarkington. As for Cook—if he can laud Welles for being "prophetic" in 1942, what can we say of Tarkington, who made the point in 1918?

Similarly, it's also Tarkington who has provided the basis, at least, for the film's much-analyzed and much-praised complexities of tone. Certainly, a great deal of the film's appealing humor—which serves to balance and lighten the essentially tragic drama laid before us—is taken directly from the author. For example, George's absurd response to Lucy's question of what he intends to be—"a yachtsman" (and this after his intense criticism of lawyers and bankers and politicians, all of whom, in his view, waste their lives)—is Tarkington verbatim; while the film's self-conscious use and witty mockery of the word "come-uppance"—though linked by some of the film's commentators to Welles's similar mockery of the rosebud motif in *Kane*—also has its origin in Tarkington who figuratively, at least, places quotations about the term whenever it appears. The film's curious mixture of nostalgia and criticism also is found in the novel. "One has the strong impression," writes Maurice Bessy of the movie, "that his [Welles's] head prefers the industrialist family of the North that finds itself in full ascension, while his heart is in complicity with the traditionalist family that is slowly disappearing. He surrounds the past with a sort of baroque tenderness that irony is scarcely able to mask. He remains unreasoningly attached to those good old days 'which he knows ought never to return.' And he does not even completely condemn George Minafer, the proud Amberson heir. . . ." To anyone who has read the novel, this hardly comes as a surprise given that in Tarkington too—as one of his critics suggests—"the reader is swept into a maze of mixed loyalties."

Clearly, *The Magnificent Ambersons* as film owes considerably more to *The Magnificent Ambersons* as novel than is generally conceded—and not only its complex vision of historical change; its strikingly prophetic view of the effect of the automobile on men's lives; its rich tonal mixture of the sentimental and ironic. The film is also beholden to the novel for its sharply observed dramatization of family life. The tensions between Georgie and maiden Aunt Fanny Minafer; Fanny's desperate, unrequited love for Eugene; even the basis for the brilliant kitchen scene—all are found in the novel. The film is indebted to the novel, too, for the strand of economic themes to be found in Welles's final script and evidently present in the original version of the film, but sadly excised by RKO.

Still, in the manner of the finest adaptations, the film is far from a mere illustration of Tarkington's text. It's an appreciative and intelligent reading of its source that ultimately puts on screen its interpretation of the novel rather than the novel itself. Welles may only have made one major change—his alteration of Tarkington's ending which RKO, unfortunately, "corrected" and which also makes clear that whatever Welles's love for the novel he wasn't totally blind to its limitations. But throughout, he has worked subtle and careful modulations on Tarkington's materials which, without betraying the author, not only consistently invite us to see him freshly, distinctively, but which also deepen and enrich the novel's import.

For one thing, implicitly seeing the strength of the novel as lying in its vision of the family as a whole and in its broad, epic quality, rather than in its individual characterizations, Welles tends to keep us at a greater distance from the various figures than does Tarkington. Despite the omniscient narrator, we are only rarely made privy to any of the characters' thoughts and we rarely see anyone alone either. Characters tend to be viewed as couples, in groups, and more often than not set against a moving, busy backdrop— whether it's George and Lucy exchanging their strained farewells on a bustling street or the dying Isabel returning to the town, with oddly distorted images of stores and buildings shown through the carriage windows. The effect is primarily to strengthen our sense of the family and drama as representative, emblematic even, and to give us a film, then, that is more clearly and directly a social parable than its source. But it's also to make Georgie himself less central than he is the novel. The film, in fact, allots all of the main characters—Eugene, Isabel, Georgie, Fanny—equal status. And since Georgie is not simply an unpleasant, off-putting character, but also a problematic one—given, among other things, his not very convincing transformation from absurdly proud aristocrat to contrite and self-sacrificing manual worker—this is a matter of unarguable gain.

For another thing, Welles evidently saw in Tarkington a greater sense of despair than is generally granted him and which, though clearly to be found in the novel, tends to be somewhat obscured by the author's proverbial "light touch." So the film emerges (even in its present shortened form) a considerably more pessimistic work than its source. Partly, this is a matter of simple selection, of what Welles has chosen to preserve from Tarkington and what he has chosen to omit; even more significant, though, is the manner of Welles's presentation. The look of the film—the exquisitely shadowy, expressionistic texture provided by Stanley Cortez's cinematography—itself deepens and darkens the whole; while there's also the heightened tragic effect of several of its key moments, such as the close-up of the dying Major Amberson, firelight playing on his ancient face as he weakly utters, "The sun. It must be sun," or the brief but intensely moving sequence signaling Isabel's death when Fanny, abruptly rushing into the shot, throws her arms around George to moan, "She loved you, she loved you."

The film also gains greater emotional and thematic gravity through the increased sense of nostalgia (and consequently, of loss) which runs through the early scenes, an effect to which Bernard Herrmann's score adds immeasurably, with its tinkly music-box sound immediately preceding the ball, its medley of lovely yet vaguely discordant sleigh bells during the sleigh-ride scene. There's also the extraordinary poignancy Welles brings to the reading of some of Tarkington's lines, such as his final description of the changing city: "It was heaving up in the middle incredibly; it was spreading incredibly; and as it heaved and spread, it befouled itself and darkened its sky." And Welles's ending (had it been preserved) would have served to underscore the point. As described by Bernard Herrmann, the conclusion had Eugene visiting Fanny in the boardinghouse where she now lives. Having reconciled with George after the accident in which George has been hit by a car, and with the young man's marriage to Lucy imminent, Eugene now asks Fanny to come and live with him in order to look after him. She declines his offer and leads him to the door, at which point the boardinghouse is revealed as the Amberson mansion, its once countrified surroundings now so dramatically urbanized as to be filled with the shrill sound of traffic—traffic that Morgan, an inventor of automobiles, has himself ironically helped to create. The sound gets louder and louder until, as Hermann puts it, "it finally smothers the whole screen. . . ." How does one compare this to RKO's conclusion, in which Eugene is shown standing with Fanny in the hospital corridor, murmuring to her sentimentally about being "true at last" to his own "true love" as she looks beatifically toward the heavens? RKO may be closer than Welles to the novel, but that's hardly a virtue since the ending of the novel is dreadful.

But the effectiveness of Welles's adaptation doesn't lie only in its implicit reading of its source—in the extent to which it has managed to both build on Tarkington's strengths and underplay his weaknesses. It also lies, of course, in its manner of mounting that interpretation, in its peculiarly cinematic means of narrating Tarkington's story. Welles, for example, may have borrowed Tarkington's language and even his montage effects when putting together his own montage of changing fashions; but the visual equivalent of Tarkington's jaunty and amusing catalogue—Eugene's comic stream of appearances before the mirror—is strictly his own invention. He may have been inspired by Tarkington, too, in making the Amberson mansion a symbol of the family's changes of fortune; but again it is Welles and not Tarkington who makes the staircase an imposing emblem of the house and who, playing out key dramatic scenes on it, also makes it a symbol of altering relationships. As for the nostalgia carried by many of Tarkington's descriptions and commentaries, Welles expresses it in numerous distinctively cinematic ways—through the film's score; through the texture of much of its cinematography, often suggestive, as Joseph McBride points out, of period daguerrotypes; and through such techniques as the old-fashioned iris used to close the scene of the sleigh ride.

Tarkington's highly formal and often ornamental language can also be said to have its equivalent in the film—in the baroque trappings of its settings, in the decorative quality of its costumes, and in certain elements of its mise-en-scène. (For example, in the highly formalized, highly artificial, almost painterly shot of the seated Amberson family, their estate in the background, questioning Georgie in the foreground about his bad behavior.) Yet, one can't really push the matter too far. For the truth is that in the process of adapting a novel like *The Magnificent Ambersons*, analogy is a good deal less the key than it would be if one were translating a work more deeply and richly embedded in intricate literary strategies. Much of *Ambersons* seems to almost slide onto the screen, almost as if it had been conceived for it in the first place—which is, of course, one of the reasons that Welles had to tamper so little with the novel's essential design and why, in so many ways, it reads like a scenario as well.

What's more, rather than being one of its virtues, the novel's style—for all its dramatic and cinematic potential—is basic to its limitations. That formality of texture may be amusing for a single shot, that ornateness for a bit of decor, but permeating the work as a whole, as it does in this "genteel" novel, it makes for flatness, dullness, even prissiness. Welles's challenge then was less in finding equivalents for the novel's style than in going beyond it, in creating a style that would prove somehow more appropriate and enriching to *Ambersons's* structure and substance than Tarkington's own. And it's the extraordinary way in which he has met this challenge that—along with his manner of shifting Tarkington's emphasis and modulating his tone—goes a long way in explaining the film's greater power. Proving himself a more courageous and innovative artist than Tarkington, Welles also makes clear his greater understanding and command of his medium. Indeed his film is so rich in cinematic strategies and in strategies for which there are not only few equivalents in Tarkington, but few literary equivalents at all, that *The Magnificent Ambersons* emerges more than mere testimony to Welles's own quite stunning gifts as cinematic storyteller. It can serve as testimony to the narrative possibilities of film itself.

One of the obvious virtues of the film, for example, lies in its powers of compression—though admittedly, that power has often been unduly strained here by RKO's cutting. Still, in the opening montage and in the ballroom sequence, among others, the film has an economy and energy that any novel would have considerable difficulty equaling—not to mention a novel by the prolix Tarkington. Consider, too, how much the film gains from the simultaneity of effect possible to that medium alone and especially from the complex orchestration of the deep-focus cinematography to which Welles was so partial. There are the contrasts and parallels contained in that exquisitely rendered shot of Eugene and Isabel dancing romantically in the shadowed foreground while the more brightly lit George and Lucy are shown in the background watching them; there's the dramatic interplay of response and expression in the film's various meal scenes—in the kitchen when Fanny bursts into tears, at the dining-room table where George insults Eugene—or the simultaneous vision of old and new, of carriages and cars in the various shots of George, his mother, his grandfather riding through the town. Or think of the powerful ironies created by the medium's very special fund of transitions: the old-fashioned iris device mentioned earlier, which closes in not on the sight of a sleigh but on that of an automobile; or a dissolve such as the one in the final montage sequence where a shot of a house gives way to a shot of a factory, both momentarily held before us at once. There's also the emotional force the film derives from its distinctive ability to combine sound and image—the traffic sounds that Welles would have had us hear at the close; the combination of chatter, song, and the rattling of the automobile with the pastoral vision of the snowy countryside in the sleigh-ride scene.

There's also the dramatic power that comes from other possibilities special to the medium: the overlapping dialogue and sound bridges that Welles uses throughout that make for both realism and fluidity; the low-angle shots of the gossiping townspeople or of the mourners at Wilbur's funeral that give special weight to their statements and expressions; or the jarring close-up of the bathtub spigot, water bursting from it, that—following the scene in which George is told to leave Mrs. Johnson's house and opening the one with his uncle in the bathtub—makes the cut seem even more abrupt than it is, the moment even more decisive. The film also gains enormously by dint of the medium's simple ability to make objects, places, its entire past world, palpable for us. Because we *see* that house, because we are brought inside the ball, because we move to the rhythms of the music too, we come to feel their loss more intensely, to long for them all the more.

At several points, I've noted how a figure who is thinly sketched and unconvincing on the printed page will, when transferred to screen, sometimes gain in dimension and reality merely by being embodied. Tarkington's characterization being far from his strong point, this is true to some extent in *The Magnificent Ambersons* too—though of no character so much as Aunt Fanny. She may be more richly conceived than others in the novel to begin with; certainly she has more texture than the passive Eugene, the saccharine and pallid Isabel, the shadowy Major, and the vaguely drawn older George Amberson (known as Jack in the film). But this doesn't really detract from actress Agnes Moorehead's screen presence, a presence much more intense than that of the others in the cast. (Dolores Costello is beautiful, but dull; Joseph Cotton has always been competent but unexciting.) It's Moorehead's extraordinary performance above all that works to make Fanny the memorable, complex, and moving character she is and to furnish every scene to which she's central with a strong and edgy realism. Tim Holt as George has a much more thankless role; but given that in each of Fanny's key scenes, he serves her as effective foil, he deserves more credit than is usually granted him. Besides, he does manage to give the unlikely George some credibility and appeal.

All the same, even made more vivid and immediate on film than they are on the printed page, these characterizations remain a crucial flaw, finally making *The Magnificent Ambersons* as movie (whatever its reputation) something a good deal less than a masterpiece. For all the suggestiveness of Tarkington's broad social vision and for all the dramatic potential of his materials—or, in short, for all his unsung contributions to Welles's film—his text still remains limited not simply in its style but in its human core. Committed to creating characters who might be welcome in the drawing-room, to conflicts appropriate to the canons of the genteel tradition, and to leaving his readers comforted by a happy ending and a prevailing optimism, Tarkington doesn't only emasculate his figures but trivializes both them and their story. In their individual psychologies and in their relationships, they emerge genteel to the point of artificiality; while the Oedipal drama in which they are involved is so politely played out, so lacking in sexual charge and significance, as to emerge naive and simplistic.

Moreover, such limitations as these can't be overcome merely by strong performances or by alterations in emphasis, and they certainly can't be corrected by style alone which, whatever the views to the contrary, is unable to truly triumph over substance. What these limitations demand instead is a drastic revision of story, of characters, of flavor—of the text as a whole—something Welles obviously had no intention of doing. Earlier in these pages, I suggested that, aside from the ease of its translation, lesser fiction has only one authentic advantage for film—the fact that we will tend to bring to the adaptation less in the way of expectations. I also suggested that all things being equal, the more substantial the novel on which an adaptation is based, the more substantial a film that adaptation is likely to be.* *The Magnificent Ambersons* serves as proof. All things being equal, had Tarkington's novel only been greater, Welles's film would have been greater too.

But whatever its ultimate limitations. *The Magnificent Ambersons* re-

---

*As I write this I can hear the countering argument—that when Welles attempted in *The Trial* to adapt a greater novel than *Ambersons* he ended up with a lesser film. But the simple fact is that all things weren't equal in that case. Welles brought much less in the way of insight and imaginativeness and sheer cinematic skill to *The Trial.* He also brought much less sympathy. As suggested earlier, he loved Tarkington—perhaps in fact overmuch. It's evident from *The Trial* that he felt less attraction to Kafka.

mains an exemplary adaptation all the same. It's an intelligent and appreciative interpretation of its source; it makes use to an extraordinary degree of its medium's possibilities and reflects great imaginativeness in the discovery both of analogous strategies and of strategies all its own; it mirrors and even enlarges the symbolic texture of the original; it remains consistent with its point of view; and if it modulates the tone of the novel somewhat, it doesn't falsify it. It's also a film that, if limited by its source in some ways, is also deeply indebted to it for many of its most crucial accomplishments.

Most important of all, however, *The Magnificent Ambersons* is a film that serves to totally undermine the long-received view that "the book is always better than the movie," or in its more sophisticated form, that film must of necessity simplify, belittle, and do untold damage to fiction. It speaks eloquently to the fact that whatever theorists have held in the past, literary forms do not by their very nature resist conversion to the screen; to the contrary, they often both invite and flourish from it—as does film from that conversion in turn. And what better argument both for the continuity of literature and film and for the art of adaptation itself.

Bibliography

Note: It would have been impossible to list all the sources which have contributed to the writing of this book. In a very real sense, they constitute a lifetime of reading. Thus, for the most part, I have restricted the bibliography to works to which I make specific reference in the text. Here and there, however, I have included a work not cited in the notes which I found particularly valuable as background reading.

For the convenience of the reader, I have tried throughout to make reference to the anthology in which sources that have been widely reprinted are most readily available. I have also omitted from the bibliography all newspaper and magazine articles for which publishing information has already been supplied in the notes.

I. General References

Adler, Renata. "Polemic and the New Reviewers." In Adler, *Toward a Radical Middle*. New York: Random House, 1969.

Affron, Charles. *Cinema and Sentiment*. Chicago: University of Chicago Press, 1982.

Andrew, Dudley. *Concepts in Film Theory*. New York: Oxford University Press, 1984.

Arendt, Hannah. "Society and Culture." *Daedalus*, Spring, 1960.

Armes, Roy. *French Cinema Since 1946, Volume Two: The Personal Style*. London: Zwemmer, 1966. Reprint, N. J.: A. S. Barnes & Co.

Arnheim, Rudolph. *Visual Thinking*. Berkeley: University of California Press, 1971.

Barrett, Gerald R., and Thomas L. Erskine. *From Fiction to Film: D. H. Lawrence,*

"The Rocking Horse Winner." Encino, Calif.: Dickenson Publishing Company, 1974.

Barrett, William. *Irrational Man: A Study in Existential Philosophy.* New York: Doubleday Anchor Books, 1962.

Barthes, Roland. *Mythologies.* Annette Lavers, trans. New York: Hill and Wang, 1972.

Battestin, Martin C. "Osborne's *Tom Jones:* Adapting a Classic." In W. R. Robinson, ed., *Man and the Movies.* Baltimore: Penguin Books, 1967.

Bazin, André. *What Is Cinema?* Hugh Gray, trans. and ed. 2 vols. Berkeley: University of California Press, 1967.

Beach, Joseph Warren. *The Twentieth Century Novel: Studies in Technique.* New York: D. Appleton-Century Co., 1932.

Bergman, Ingmar. "Introduction." In *Four Screen Plays of Ingmar Bergman,* Lars Malmstrom and David Kushner, trans. New York: Simon and Schuster, 1960. Passages reprinted as "Film Has Nothing to Do with Literature." In Richard Dyer MacCann, ed., *Film: A Montage of Theories.* New York: E. P. Dutton, 1960.

Bergson, Henri. *Creative Evolution,* Arthur Mitchell, trans. New York: The Modern Library, 1911, 1944. Passages reprinted in Ellmann and Feidelson. (See below.)

Black, Max. *Models and Metaphors: Studies in Language and Philosophy.* Ithaca, N.Y.: Cornell University Press, 1962.

Bluestone, George. *Novels into Film.* Baltimore: John Hopkins Press, 1957.

Booth, Wayne C. "Distance and Point-of-View: An Essay in Classification." In *Essays in Criticism: A Quarterly Journal of Literary Criticism,* January, 1961.

————. *The Rhetoric of Fiction.* Chicago and London: University of Chicago Press, 1961.

Braudy, Leo. *The World in a Frame: What We See in Films.* New York: Anchor Books, 1977.

Brooks, Cleanth, and Robert Penn Warren. *Understanding Fiction.* New York: Appleton-Century-Crofts, 1959.

————. *Understanding Poetry.* 3rd ed. New York: Holt, Rinehart and Winston, 1960.

Burchard, John E. "Doubts." In David C. Stewart, ed., *Film Study in Higher Education.* Washington, D.C.: American Council on Education, 1966.

Carpenter, Edmund. "The New Languages." In Edmund Carpenter and Marshall

McLuhan, eds., *Explorations in Communication: An Anthology.* Boston: Beacon Press, 1960.

Cavell, Stanley. *The World Viewed: Reflections on the Ontology of Film.* New York: Viking Press, 1971.

Chatman, Seymour. *Story and Discourse: Narrative Structure in Fiction and Film.* Ithaca, N.Y. and London: Cornell University Press, 1978.

_____. "What Novels Can Do That Films Can't (and Vice Versa)." In W. J. T. Mitchell, ed., *On Narrative.* Chicago and London: University of Chicago Press, 1981.

Cohen, Keith. *Film and Fiction: The Dynamics of Exchange.* New Haven, Conn.: Yale University Press, 1979.

Conger, Syndy M., and Janice R. Welsch, eds. *Narrative Strategies: Original Essays in Film and Prose Fiction.* Macomb, Western Ill.: University Press, 1980.

Cook, David A. *A History of Narrative Film.* New York: W. W. Norton, 1981.

Culler, Jonathan. *Structuralist Poetics.* Ithaca, N.Y.: Cornell University Press, 1975.

Davidson, Donald. "What Metaphors Mean." In Sheldon Sacks, ed., *On Metaphor.* Chicago and London: University of Chicago Press, 1978.

Dryden, John. *Of Dramatic Poesy and Other Critical Essays,* George Watson, ed. Vol. 1. London: J. M. Dent and Sons, 1962.

Durgnat, Raymond. *Films and Feelings.* Cambridge, Mass.: M.I.T. Press, 1967.

Eco, Umberto. *A Theory of Semiotics.* London and Bloomington: Indiana University Press, 1976.

Eidsvick, Charles. "Soft Edges: The Art of Literature, The Medium of Film." *Literature/Film Quarterly,* Winter, 1974. Reprinted in Harrington. (See below.)

_____. "Toward a *Politique des Adaptations.*" *Literature/Film Quarterly,* Summer, 1975. Reprinted in Harrington. (See below.)

Eisenstein, Sergei. *Film Form and the Film Sense,* Jay Leyda, trans. Cleveland and New York: World Publishing Company, 1957.

Ellmann, Richard. *James Joyce.* New York: Oxford University Press, 1959.

_____. and Charles Feidelson, eds. *The Modern Tradition: Backgrounds of Modern Literature.* New York: Oxford University Press, 1965.

Fiedler, Leslie. *Love and Death in the American Novel.* New York: Criterion Books, 1960.

Fish, Stanley. *Is There a Text in This Class?* Cambridge, Mass.: Harvard University Press, 1980.

Forster, E. M. *Aspects of the Novel.* New York: Harcourt Brace, 1927. Reprinted 1954.

Frank, Joseph. "Spatial Form in the Modern Novel." *Sewanee Review,* Spring, Summer, and Autumn, 1945. Reprinted in John W. Aldridge, ed., *Critiques and Essays in Modern Fiction: 1920–1951.* New York: Ronald Press, 1952.

French, Brandon. "Lost at Sea." In Peary and Shatzkin, eds., *The Classic American Novel and the Movies.* (See below.)

Friedman, Melvin. *Stream of Consciousness.* New Haven, Conn.: Yale University Press, 1955.

Friedman, Norman. "Point of View in Fiction: The Development of a Critical Concept." *PMLA,* December, 1955.

Frye, Northrup. *Anatomy of Criticism.* New York: Atheneum, 1965.

Garrett, George. "Don't Make Waves." In W. R. Robinson, ed., *Man and the Movies.* Baltimore: Penguin Books, 1960.

Geduld, Harry M., ed. *Authors on Film.* Bloomington: Indiana University Press, 1972.

Gianetti, Louis. "Cinematic Metaphors." *Journal of Aesthetic Education,* October, 1972.

Gibson, Walker. "Authors, Speakers, Readers, and Mock Readers." *College English,* February, 1950. Reprinted in Tompkins. (See below.)

———. *Persona: A Style Study for Readers and Writers.* New York: Random House, 1969.

———. *Tough, Sweet, and Stuffy: An Essay on Modern American Prose Styles.* Bloomington: Indiana University Press, 1966.

Gregory, R. L. *Eye and Brain: The Psychology of Seeing.* New York: McGraw-Hill, 1966.

Hardison, O. B., Jr. *Aristotle's Poetics.* Englewood Cliffs, N.J.: Prentice-Hall, 1968.

Harrington, John, ed. *Film and/as Literature.* Englewood Cliffs, N.J.: Prentice-Hall, 1977.

Hauser, Arnold. *The Social History of Art.* Vol. 4. New York: Vintage Books, 1958.

Horton, Andrew S., and Joan Margretta, eds. *Modern European Filmmakers and the Art of Adaptation.* New York: Frederick Ungar, 1981.

Humphrey, Robert. *Stream of Consciousness in the Modern Novel.* Berkeley: University of California Press, 1955.

Iser, Wolfgang. *The Act of Reading: A Theory of Aesthetic Response.* Baltimore and London: John Hopkins University Press, 1978.

_____. *The Implied Reader: Patterns in Communication in Prose Fiction from Bunyan to Beckett.* Baltimore: John Hopkins University Press, 1974.

James, Henry. *The Art of the Novel: Critical Prefaces.* New York: Charles Scribner's Sons, 1934.

James, William. *The Principles of Psychology.* Cambridge, Mass.: Harvard University Press, 1981 (originally published 1890). Passages reprinted in Ellmann and Feidelson. (See above.)

Jinks, William. *The Celluloid Literature.* Beverly Hills, Calif.: Glencoe Press, 1971.

Kael, Pauline. "Trash, Art, and the Movies." *Harper's Magazine,* February, 1969. Reprinted in Kael, *Going Steady.* New York: Bantam Books, 1971.

Kauffmann, Stanley. "The Film Generation." In Kauffmann, *A World on Film.* New York: Delta Books, 1966.

_____, with Bruce Henstell, eds. *American Film Criticism.* New York: Liveright, 1972.

Kawin, Bruce F. *Mindscreen: Bergman, Godard, and First-Person Cinema.* Princeton, N.J.: Princeton University Press, 1978.

Kermode, Frank. *The Classic: Literary Images of Permanence and Change.* New York: Viking Press, 1975.

Klein, Michael, and Gillian Parker, eds. *The English Novel and the Movies.* New York: Frederick Ungar, 1981.

Kracauer, Siegfried. *Theory of Film: The Redemption of Physical Reality.* New York: Oxford University Press, 1965.

Langer, Susanne K. *Feeling and Form.* New York: Charles Scribner, 1953.

_____. *Philosophy in a New Key.* 3rd ed. Cambridge, Mass.: Harvard University Press, 1942. Reprint 1980.

Leavis, F. R. *The Great Tradition.* New York: Anchor Books/Doubleday, 1954.

Levinson, André. "The Nature of Cinema." *Theatre Arts Monthly,* September, 1929. Reprinted in Lewis Jacobs, ed., *Introduction to the Art of the Movies.* New York: Noonday Press, 1960.

Linden, George W. *Reflections on the Screen.* Belmont, Calif.: Wadsworth, 1970.

Lindsay, Vachel. *The Art of the Moving Picture.* New York: Macmillan, 1915. Reprint New York: Liveright, 1970.

Littlejohn, David. "The Anti-Realists." *Daedalus,* Spring, 1963.

Lubbock, Percy. *The Craft of Fiction*. New York: The Viking Press, 1957 (originally published 1921).

McBride, Joseph. *Orson Welles*. London: Secker and Warburg, 1972.

Mann, Thomas. "On the Film." In Mann, *Past Masters*, H. T. Lowe-Porter, trans. New York: Alfred A. Knopf, 1933. Reprinted in Geduld. (See above.)

Mast, Gerald. "Literature and Film." In Jean-Pierre Barricelli and Joseph Gibaldi, eds., *Interrelations of Literature*. New York: Modern Language Association of America, 1982.

_____. "What Isn't Cinema?" *Critical Inquiry*, December, 1974.

_____, and Marshall Cohen, eds. *Film Theory and Criticism*. 2nd ed. New York: Oxford University Press, 1979.

Metz, Christian. *Film Language: A Semiotics of the Cinema*, Michael Taylor, trans. New York: Oxford University Press, 1974.

Mitry, Jean. "Remarks on the Problem of Cinematic Adaptation," Richard Dyer MacCann, trans. *MMLA Bulletin*, Spring, 1971.

Monaco, James. *How to Read a Film*. Rev. ed. New York: Oxford University Press, 1981.

Morin, Edgar. *Le Cinéma ou l'Homme Imaginaire*. Paris: Editions de Minuit, 1956.

Murray, Edward. *The Cinematic Imagination: Writers and the Motion Pictures*. New York: Frederick Ungar, 1972.

Nichols, Bill, ed. *Movies and Methods*. Berkeley: University of California Press, 1976.

Nicoll, Allardyce. *Film and Theatre*. New York: Thomas Y. Crowell, 1936.

Panofsky, Erwin. "Style and Medium in the Motion Pictures." *Critique*, January–February, 1947. Reprinted in Mast and Cohen. (See above.)

Peary, Gerald, and Roger Shatzkin, eds. *The Classic American Novel and the Movies*. New York: Frederick Ungar, 1977.

_____. *The Modern American Novel and the Movies*. New York: Frederick Ungar, 1978.

Perrine, Laurence. *Sound and Sense: An Introduction to Poetry*. 2nd ed. New York: Harcourt, Brace and World, 1963.

Plimpton, George. "Ernest Hemingway." In *Writers at Work: The Paris Review Interviews*. 2nd series. New York: Viking Press, 1965.

Ricardou, Jean. *Problèmes du Nouveau Roman*. Paris: Editions du Seuil, 1967.

Richards, I. A. *The Philosophy of Rhetoric.* New York: Oxford University Press, 1936.

_____. *Practical Criticism.* New York: Harcourt Brace, 1929. Reprint New York: Harvest Books, no date.

____. *Principles of Literary Criticism.* New York: Harcourt Brace, 1925.

Richardson, Robert. *Literature and Film.* Bloomington: Indiana University Press, 1969.

Rosen, Marjorie. *Popcorn Venus: Women, Movies, and the American Dream.* New York: Coward, McCann & Geoghegan, 1973.

Rosenblatt, Louise M. *The Reader, the Text, the Poem: The Transactional Theory of the Literary Work.* Carbondale: Southern Illinois University Press, 1978.

Sartre, Jean-Paul. *What Is Literature?* Bernard Frechtman, trans. New York: Washington Square Press, 1966.

_____. *The Words,* Bernard Frechtman, trans. New York: George Braziller, 1964.

Scholes, Robert. "Narration and Narrativity in Film." *Quarterly Review of Film Studies,* August, 1976. Reprinted in Mast and Cohen. (See above.)

_____, and Robert Kellogg. *The Nature of Narrative.* New York: Oxford University Press, 1966.

Seton, Marie. *Sergei M. Eisenstein: A Biography.* New York: A. A. Wyn, 1952.

Simon, John. "Adaptations." In Simon, *Movies into Film: Film Criticism 1967–70.* New York: Delta Books, 1971.

Sontag, Susan. *Against Interpretation.* New York: Farrar, Straus & Giroux, 1966.

_____. *Styles of Radical Will.* New York: Delta Books, 1970.

Spiegel, Alan. *Fiction and the Camera Eye: Visual Consciousness in Film and the Modern Novel.* Charlottesville: University Press of Virginia, 1976.

Strunk, William, Jr. *The Elements of Style: With Revisions, and Introduction, and a New Chapter on Writing by E. B. White.* New York: Macmillan Company, 1959.

Suleiman, Susan, and Inge Crossman, eds. *The Reader in the Text: Essays on Audience and Interpretation.* Princeton, N.J.: Princeton University Press, 1980.

Sypher, Wylie. *Four Stages of Renaissance Style: Transformations in Art and Literature 1400–1700.* New York: Anchor Books/Doubleday, 1955.

Thorpe, Margaret Farrand. *America at the Movies.* New Haven, Conn.: Yale University Press, 1939.

Tompkins, Jane P., ed. *Reader-Response Criticism: From Formalism to Post-Structuralism.* Baltimore: Johns Hopkins University Press, 1980.

Truffaut, François. "A Certain Tendency of the French Cinema." In Bill Nichols, ed., *Movies and Methods.* Berkeley: University of California Press, 1976.

van Ghent, Dorothy. *The English Novel: Form and Function.* New York: Harper and Row, 1953.

Wagner, Geoffrey. *The Novel and the Cinema.* Rutherford, N. J.: Fairleigh Dickinson University Press, 1975.

Wellek, René, and Austin Warren. *Theory of Literature.* New York: Harcourt, Brace and Company, 1942.

Wimsatt, W. K., Jr. *The Verbal Icon: Studies in the Meaning of Poetry.* New York: Farrar, Straus, & Cudahy, 1960.

Woolf, Virginia. *The Common Reader.* 1st Series. London: Hogarth Press, 1925. Selections reprinted in *Collected Essays.* Vol. 2. New York: Harcourt, Brace & World, 1967.

_____. "The Movies and Reality." *New Republic,* August 4, 1926. Reprinted in Geduld. (See above.)

II. References to the Specific Adaptations Discussed

Baumbach, Jonathan. *The Landscape of Nightmare: Studies in the Contemporary American Novel.* New York: New York University Press, 1965.

Bessy, Maurice. *Orson Welles,* Ciba Vaughan, trans. New York: Crown Publishers, 1971, (originally published in French, 1963).

Cecil, Lord David. "The Elizabethan Tradition and Hardy's Talent." In Scott Elledge, ed. *The Norton Critical Edition of "Tess of the d'Urbervilles."* 2nd ed. New York: W. W. Norton, 1979.

de Beauvoir, Simone. *The Second Sex,* H. M. Parshley, trans. New York: Alfred A. Knopf, 1953.

Dimeo, Steven. "Reconciliation: *Slaughterhouse-Five*—The Film and the Novel." *Film Heritage,* Winter, 1972–73.

Fennimore, Keith J. *Booth Tarkington.* New York: Twayne Publishers, 1974.

Fowles, John. "Foreword." In Harold Pinter, *The French Lieutenant's Woman: A Screenplay.* Boston-Toronto: Little, Brown and Co., 1981.

Ginden, James. " 'Gimmick' and Metaphor in the Novels of William Golding." *Modern Fiction Studies*, Spring, 1960.

Gomez, Joseph A. "Russell's Images of Lawrence's Vision." In Klein and Parker. (See above.)

Goodman, Paul. "The Proustian Camera Eye." *Trend*, January/February, 1935. Reprinted in Kauffmann with Henstell. (See above.)

Gottlieb, Sidney. "The Madding Crowd at the Movies." In Peary and Shatzkin, eds. *The Modern American Novel and the Movies*. (See above.)

Graham, Mark. "The Proust Screenplay: *Temps perdu* for Harold Pinter?" *Literature/Film Quarterly*, 1982.

Gumenik, Arthur. "*A Clockwork Orange:* Novel into Film." *Film Heritage*, Summer, 1972.

Hagopian, John V. "Bad Faith in *The French Lieutenant's Woman*." *Contemporary Literature*, Spring, 1982.

Hassan, Ihab. *Radical Innocence: Studies in the Contemporary Novel*. Princeton, N. J.: Princeton University Press, 1961.

Higham, Charles. *The Films of Orson Welles*. Berkeley: University of California Press, 1970.

Hough, Graham. *The Dark Sun: A Study of D. H. Lawrence*. New York: Capricorn Books, 1956.

Howe, Irving. *Thomas Hardy*. New York: Macmillan, 1967.

Hutchison, Alexander. "Luchino Visconti's *Death in Venice*." *Literature/Film Quarterly*, Winter, 1974.

Hyman, Stanley Edgar. "Afterword." In Anthony Burgess, *A Clockwork Orange*. New York: Ballantine Books, 1965.

Isaacs, Neil D. "Unstuck in Time: *A Clockwork Orange* and *Slaughterhouse-Five*." *Literature/Film Quarterly*, Spring, 1978.

Jones, Edward T. "That's Wormword: *The Day of the Locust*." *Literature/Film Quarterly*, Summer, 1978.

Jones, Howard Mumford, Ernest E. Leisy, and Richard M. Ludvig, eds. *Major American Writers*. 3rd ed. Vol. 2. New York and Burlingame: Harcourt, Brace and World, 1952.

Kael, Pauline. "The Darned." *New Yorker*, May 12, 1975. Reprinted in Kael, *Reeling*. New York: Warner Books, 1976.

———. "The Innocents." In Kael, *I Lost It At the Movies*. Boston: Little, Brown and Co., 1965.

————. "Lust for 'Art.' " *New Yorker,* March 28, 1970. Reprinted in Kael, *Deeper into Movies.* New York: Bantam Books, 1974.

Kauffmann, Stanley. "A la Recherche du Temps Perdu: The Proust Screenplay." *New Republic,* December 24, 31, 1977. Reprinted in Kauffmann, *Before My Eyes.* New York: Da Capo, 1980.

Kettle, Arnold. *An Introduction to the English Novel, Volume Two: Henry James to the Present.* New York and Evanston, Ill.: Harper Torchbooks, 1960.

Kimbrough, Robert, ed. *The Norton Critical Edition of "The Turn of the Screw."* New York: W. W. Norton, 1966.

Kinder, Marsha. "The Power of Adaptation in *Apocalypse Now.*" *Film Quarterly,* Winter, 1979–80.

Leaming, Barbara. *Polanski: A Biography: The Filmmaker as Voyeur.* New York: Simon and Schuster, 1981.

Leavis, F. R. *D. H. Lawrence: Novelist.* Chicago: University of Chicago Press, 1979 (originally published 1955).

Liggera, J. J. " 'She Would Have Appreciated One's Esteem': Peter Bogdanovich's *Daisy Miller.*" *Literature/Film Quarterly,* Vol. XI, No. 1, 1981.

McCarthy, Todd. "Cracking the Volcano." *Film Comment,* August, 1984.

Mellen, Joan. "Death in Venice." *Film Quarterly,* Fall, 1971.

Menides, Laura Jehn. "John Huston's *Wise Blood* and the Myth of the Sacred Quest." *Literature/Film Quarterly,* Vol. IX, No. 4, 1981.

Millet, Kate. *Sexual Politics.* Garden City: Doubleday & Co., 1970.

Moskowitz, Ken. "Clockwork Violence." *Sight and Sound,* Winter, 1976/77.

Naremore, James. *The Magic World of Orson Welles.* New York: Oxford University Press, 1978.

O'Connor, Flannery. *The Habit of Being,* Sally Fitzgerald, ed. New York: Farrar, Straus & Giroux, 1979.

Palmer, James W. "Cinematic Ambiguity: James' *Turn of the Screw* and Clayton's *The Innocents.*" *Literature/Film Quarterly,* Summer, 1977.

Parrington, Vernon Louis. *Main Currents in American Thought.* Vol. 3. New York and Burlingame: Harcourt, Brace, and World, 1930, 1958.

Peter, John. "The Fables of William Golding." *Kenyon Review,* Autumn, 1957.

Pinter, Harold. *The Proust Screenplay.* New York: Grove Press, 1977.

Pullene, Tom. *"Wise Blood."* *Sight and Sound,* Winter, 1979/80.

Rackham, Jeff. "John Fowles: The Existentialist Labyrinth." *Critique: Studies in Modern Fiction*, Vol. XIII, 1972.

Rankin, Elizabeth D. "Cryptic Coloration in *The French Lieutenant's Woman.*" *Journal of Narrative Technique*, September, 1973.

Rapf, Joanna E. " 'Human Need' in *The Day of the Locust:* Problems of Adaptation." *Literature/Film Quarterly*, Vol. IX, No. 1, 1981.

Rodgers, Bernard F. "A Novelist's Revenge." *Chicago Review*, Winter, 1975/76.

Rosenbaum, Jonathan. "The Voice and the Eye: A Commentary on the 'Heart of Darkness' Script." *Film Comment*, November–December, 1972.

Rubinstein, Anne T. *The Great Tradition in English Literature from Shakespeare to Shaw, Volume Two: Robert Burns to Bernard Shaw.* New York and London: Modern Reader Paperbacks, 1953.

Sartre, Jean-Paul. "Time in the Work of Faulkner." In Sartre, *Literary and Philosophical Essays,* Annette Michelson, trans. New York: Criterion Books, 1955.

Servadio, Gaia. *Luchino Visconti: A Biography.* London: Weidenfeld & Nicholson, 1981.

Shields, John C. "*Daisy Miller:* Bogdanovich's Film and James's Nouvelle." *Literature/Film Quarterly*, 1983.

Simon, John. *"Women in Love."* In *Movies into Film.* (See above.)

Sobchack, Vivian C. "Decor as Theme: *A Clockwork Orange.*" *Literature/Film Quarterly*, 1981.

Stallman, R. W. "Gatsby and the Hole in Time." *Modern Fiction Studies*, November, 1955.

Stein, George P. "*Death in Venice:* From Literature to Film." *The Journal of Aesthetic Education*, Fall, 1982.

Stephens, Martha. *The Question of Flannery O'Connor.* Baton Rouge: Louisiana State University Press, 1973.

Wood, Michael. "Parade's End: The Past in Movies." *American Film*, March, 1976.

Zambrano, Ana Laura. *"Women in Love:* Counterpoint on Film." *Literature/Film Quarterly*, Winter, 1973.

Notes

Chapter One

Page 4   Bush's view: reprinted in Kauffmann with Henstell, 58.

6   Woolf's views: reprinted in Geduld, 86–91.

6   "The filmmaker . . . is . . . the equal of the novelist": Bazin, I, 40.

7   "The entertainment industry": Arendt, 283–84.

8   Bluestone's work, perhaps significantly, originally served as his doctoral dissertation and drew on another, similar study—Lester Asheim's unpublished dissertation "From Book to Film."

9   "Destruction is inevitable": Bluestone, 62.

9   "Dizzy height of fidelity": Bazin, I, 68.

9   "The main works of Aeschylus": Burchard, 113–14.

9   "In the same league": ibid.

10   Chester and Fiedler's remarks: quoted by Adler, 110.

10   Keeping movies at the level of "kitsch": for an example of such an argument, see Eidsvick, "Toward a *Politique des Adaptations*," reprinted in Harrington.

12   Determining the "essence" of film: for an enlightening discussion of the efforts put forth by various theorists, see Mast, "What Isn't Cinema?"

12   "Cinema is a kind of pan-art": Sontag, "A Note on Novels and Films," in *Against Interpretation*, 245.

13   Truffaut's views appeared in his essay "Un Certaine Tendance du Cinéma Français," *Cahiers du Cinéma*, January, 1954. Reprinted as "A Certain Tendency of the French Cinema," in Nichols, 224–236.

14   Linden's comments: Linden, 38.

14   Resnais: quoted by Armes, 122.

14   Godard: quoted by Walter S. Ross in "Splicing Together Jean-Luc Godard," *Esquire*, July, 1969.

16   For figures on the sales of *Wuthering Heights* and the source novels of other thirties adaptations: see Thorpe, 239–41.

16   Sartre's views: *What Is Literature?*, 169–70. His example is actually Michelle Morgan in *La Symphonie Pastorale*.

16   Taxi driver anecdote: cited by Thorpe, 241–42.

Chapter Two

Page 21 "Language in the strict sense": Langer, *Philosophy in a New Key*, 96.

21 For further discussion of icons and symbols: see Eco, 190 and passim; also Is er, *The Act of Reading*, 62–68.

22 Words and pictures as part of our complex of human communication: see Cohen, 3 and passim.

22 Film as more than a language of images: offering a similar view of the multiform nature of film's mode of communication, Gerald Mast speculates whether an old term like "biograph"—referring to the recording of life in general—wasn't a more accurate descriptor of movies than any of our current labels. Even "cinema," Mast reminds us, deriving as it does from "cinematograph, the recording of motion," tends to overstress the visual. See Mast, "Literature and Film," 301–2.

22 Garbo's face as icon: Barthes, 56–57.

22 "Sound, articulate or not": Panofsky in Mast and Cohen, 249.

24 Levinson quote: Levinson in Jacobs, 151.

25 An image pressed on the retina disintegrates: see Gregory, 43–44; cited by Eidsvick, "Soft Edges."

26 Barrett's view: Barrett and Erskine, 15.

26 Metz's view: see Metz, 108–46.

26 Bergman quote: Bergman in MacCann, 144.

27 Sontag quote: "Spiritual Style in the films of Robert Bresson," in *Against Interpretation*, 177.

29 "A dog + a mouth": Eisenstein, 30, 60.

30 "A narrative which organizes itself": Mitry, 7–8.

30 "Fictionality": Wellek and Warren, 14.

31 "The Film Age": see Hauser, 226 and passim.

32 Bazin's view: expressed in both "The Ontology of the Photographic Image" and "The Evolution of the Language of Cinema," in Bazin, I.

33 "A virtual present": Langer, *Feeling and Form*, 412.

34 "Spatialize time": Panofsky, 246.

35 "The illusion of space": Bluestone, 61.

35 For an extended analysis of the patterning of the fair scene in *Madame Bovary*, see Joseph Frank's seminal essay "Spatial Form in the Modern Novel."

35 "The king died": Forster, 86.

36 "The basic nature of character": Braudy, 184, 187.

36 Hemingway quote: in Plimpton, 235–36.

36 "All lifelike characters": Frye, 172.

37 Chatman's discussion: Chatman, "What Novels Can Do That Films Can't," in Mitchell, 117–36. Though I disagree with Chatman on this point and on several others, I still find his discussion enlightening. See also his very thorough and well-reasoned *Story and Discourse.*

38 "A logical or *continuous* use of space": Sontag, "A Note on Theatre and Film," in *Styles of Radical Will,* 108.

39 "What is given to us": Nicoll, 167.

39 Distinctions between theatre and film: for further discussion, see not only Sontag and Nicoll but also "Theatre and Cinema: Parts I and II" in Bazin, I, as well as Panofsky and Cavell on the actor. As Harrington suggests in *Film and/as Literature,* there has been much more theoretical work done on the interrelationships between theatre and film than on those between novel and film. What Harrington doesn't note that I might is that such work also tends to hold up better.

Chapter Three

Page 47 Critics sharing an emphasis on the reader and his response include, among others, Georges Poulet, Wolfgang Isr, Jonathan Culler, Stanley Fish, David Bleich, and Norman Holland. A useful introduction to their work can be found in Jane P. Tompkins, *Reader-Response Criticism,* and in Susan Suleiman and Inge Crossman, *The Reader in the Text.*

47 "A confusion between the poem": "The Affective Fallacy," in Wimsatt, 21.

48 "Memories of movies": Cavell, ix.

48 "Movies have been my landmarks": Rosen, 12.

48 "The reader has tended": Rosenblatt, 1.

48 "Ontological conditions": Cavell, 45.

48 "The passivity of the spectator": Morin, 101. Quoted also by Affron, who led me to Morin's fascinating study.

49 "Event in time": Rosenblatt, 12.

49 "Gaps": Iser, *The Implied Reader,* 274 and passim.

49 "Kinetic art": Fish, "Literature in the Reader: Affective Stylistics," in Fish, 43.

49 "Certain features of fiction": Scholes, "Narration and Narrativity in Films," in Mast and Cohen, 421.

53 "Anticipation and retrospection": Iser, loc. cit.

56 "A woman drawn": "Letter to Ernest Duplan," quoted by Ricardou, 91.

58 "Meryl Streep's work": *New Yorker*, December 27, 1982.

58 Problematic nature of Nathan's character: see, for example, Christopher Lehmann-Haupt's review of Styron's novel in the *New York Times*, May 29, 1979, in which he finds Nathan a "golem" and his insanity "the one artistic problem that Mr. Styron fails to solve."

58 "Hamlet and Macbeth": Hardison, 122.

60 "In some ways": *New Republic*, January 10–17, 1983.

Chapter Four

Page 63 "Story is": Garrett in Robinson, 246. "Big Boss " was actually Columbia's Harry Cohn, a movie mogul notorious for his vulgarity and ruthlessness.

63 All texts read in a relational manner: for further discussion of this notion of "intertextuality," see, among others, Culler, 138 and passim.

69 "First, that of metaphrase": Dryden, 268.

69 "The *transposition*": Wagner, 222–27.

69 Barrett's view: Barrett and Erskine, 19–21.

69 Validity of interpretation: there has been much debate on the issue in recent years, a good deal of it having taken place in the pages of *Critical Quarterly*. See especially Wayne Both, " 'Preserv ing the Exemplar': or, How Not to Dig Our Own Graves"; M. H. Abrams, "The Deconstructive Angel"; and J. Hillis Miller, "The Critic as Host," all in the Spring, 1977, issue; see also Fish's rebuttal in Fish, 303–71.

74 "The film *Moby Dick*": Carpenter, in Carpenter and McLuhan, 171–72.

74 "What Bradbury deleted": French, in Peary and Shatzkin, *The Classic American Novel and the Movies*, 53–54.

75 "The shape of reading": Fish, 13.

75 "No core of agreement": ibid., 342–43.

79 "Far more of the great art": Richards, *Principles*, 22 1– 2.

79 "One of the most successful": Battestin in Robinson, 32.

79 "Essential spirit and manner": ibid., 36.

80 "Analogy is the key": ibid., 37.

81 "Penetrating consciousness": Bluestone, 208. His precise phrase is "cinemaphotography cannot penetrate consciousness." See Chapter Eight for further discussion.

Chapter Five

Page 85 Analysis of point of view in fiction: Booth's *The Rhetoric of Fiction* is probably the most sustained and influential of recent works, but see also Norman Friedman, Lubbock, Beach, as well as Booth's essay, "Distance and Point-of-View."

85 "Window . . . of consciousness": James, "Preface to "The Portrait of a Lady," in *The Art of the Novel*, 46.

85 Reader's relationship with speaker: a concept, like point of view (of which it is, of course, an aspect), much discussed and analyzed by contemporary theorists. For two especially useful discussions, see Gibson, "Authors, Speakers, Readers, and Mock Readers," and his *Tough, Sweet, and Stuffy*.

88 Truffaut's views on the subjective camera: cited by McBride, 65.

90 "The cinema has had its Samuel Richardson": Sontag, "A Note on Novels and Films," in *Against Interpretation*, 242–43.

The Innocents

92 Such questions have been raised: a representative sample of the classic essays dealing with James's novella can be found in Kimbrough. See also the overview of the critical argument surrounding the tale in Booth, *The Rhetoric of Fiction*, 311–16 .

97 Kael on *The Innocents*: in *I Lost It at the Movies* , 163–72.

97 "A few readers": Kimbrough, 169.

98 "Perhaps the children": quoted by Kael, op. cit.

The Great Gatsby

100 Nick as ironic narrator and hypocritical prig: this unusual but highly influential (and to my mind, deeply mistaken) view of Nick was first put forth by Stallman.

103 "Defunct arch-priest": Stallman.

The French Lieutenant's Woman

105 Eleven years: Fowles recounts "the saga of the filming, or more accurately the non-filming of *The French Lieutenant's Woman,* " in his "Foreword" to the published edition of Pinter's screenplay.

105 As Fowles himself suggests: cited by Leslie Garis, "Translating Fowles into Film," *New York Times Magazine*, August 30, 1981.

105   Whom Pinter credits: Garis, ibid.
106   Existential themes: see, for example, Rackham.
107   "Bad faith": Hagopian, 190.
107   "Boring red herring": for a review of such criticism of the novel, see Rankin, 193 and passim.
109   Mike . . . cries out, "Sarah": according to Richard Corliss (reported by Arthur White) in "When Acting Becomes Alchemy: *The French Lieutenant's Woman*," *Time*, September 7, 1981, it was Fowles himself who suggested this ending.
109   "A love story": Garis, op. cit.
110   "Brilliant metaphor": Fowles, xii.

Apocalypse Now

111   "The adaptive auteur": Kinder, 12.
115   Kilgore as Kurtz: Michael Wood, "Bangs and Whispers ," *New York Review of Books*, October 11, 1979.
115   The view that Kilgore lacks sufficient moral stature: see Kinder, 20.
115   Welles's plans to adapt Conrad: see Rosenbaum, who also reprints the introductory sequence to the unproduced film.

Chapter Six

Page 118   "Increment of writing": Strunk and White, 53.
118   " To speak of style": Sontag, "On Style," in *Against Interpretation*, 18.
118   " 'Stylization' ": ibid., 19.
120   One theorist of style: see Gibson, *Tough, Sweet, and Stuffy*; also Gibson, *Persona*.
122   "Styles have a life of their own": Sypher, 8–9.
122   "The testimony of modern art": Barrett, 42–65.
123   Richardson's *Tom Jones*: for further discussion of analogous techniques, see Battestin.

Women in Love

124   "I have not always thought": Leavis, *D. H. Lawrence: Novelist*, 175.
125   Other critics on *Women in Love*: see Hough, 72–90.
128   Simon on *Women in Love*: in *Movies into Film*, 57 –62.

129 Tilted camera as satiric commentary: see Gomez in Klein and Parker, 254.

129 Comic aura in unsuccessful love scene: see Zambrano.

129 Mockery of Lawrence: see, for example, the late Donald Malcolm's devastating review of *Lady Chatterley's Lover* in *The New Yorker*, September 12, 1959.

131 Attack on Lawrence's views: for the most stringent of these criticisms, see Millett and de Beauvoir.

Ragtime

133 "The left hand": Rodgers, 141.

Tess

138 Rights to *Tess:* Leaming, 192–95.

139 "Broods like a thundercloud": Cecil in Elledge, 420.

139 "Complicity of doom": van Ghent, 241.

140 "Vision of hell": Howe, 454.

141 One Hardy contemporary: see remarks by Andrew Lang quoted in Rubinstein, II, 841.

144 "Is not her sensitiveness": Kettle, II, 54.

144 "Brooding so formidably": van Ghent, 239.

145 "He hovers and watches over Tess": Howe, 455.

145 Kinski: quoted by Leaming, 202.

Daisy Miller

146 "Radical innocence": the phrase is Ihab Hassan's. For his discussion of *Daisy Miller,* see Hassan, 43–44.

146 "No intelligent man": Leavis, 175.

147 "Good Bad Girl": Fiedler, 298–300.

147 "Period of the involved manner": Jones, Leisy and Ludwig, II 1405.

148 "Fading romantic possibility": Liggera, 19.

149 Point of view of film and tale: see Shields, for example, who claims moreover that Bogdanovich's alteration of point of view, rather than a flaw in the film, is one of its distinctive virtues—a means used by the filmmaker for making the tale his own. To my mind, the argument is a convoluted one.

150 Sarris on Bogdanovich: *The Village Voice,* July 11, 1974 .

152 Howells on James: quoted in Jones, Leisy, Ludwig, II, 1406.

Chapter Seven

Page 154   "The twin dangers": Richards, *Practical Criticism*, 184.

155   Success of figurative expression: for a somewhat different view see Davidson in Sacks, who argues that "there are no unsuccessful metaphors, just as there are no unfunny jokes. There are tasteless metaphors, but these are turns that nevertheless have brought something off, even if it were not worth bringing off or could have been brought off better," 29.

155   "An image means": Perrine, 69.

155   Brooks and Warren's definition: *Understanding Poetry*, 5 55 -56.

155   "Allegorical interpretation": Frye, 89.

156   Metaphor as metaphor for language: see Richards, *The Philosophy of Rhetoric*, 90.

157   Metaphor as a mode of thought: for an extremely useful taxonomy of the various modes of metaphoric statement, with a particular emphasis on the mental processes involved, see Black, 25–47 especially.

158   "Makes poetry out of doorknobs": Kauffmann, "The Film Generation," 417.

158   "Content-oriented": Gianetti, 54.

159   Metaphors in the form of "props": Durgnat, 226.

160   Student letter: Kael, "Trash, Art and the Movies," in *Going Steady*, 136–37.

160   "Careless 'intuitive' reading": Richards, *Practical Criticism*, 184.

A Clockwork Orange

163   Hyman's analysis of Nadsat: see "Afterword" to the Ballantine edition of the novel.

164   Burgess's view of Kubrick's film: cited by Arthur Bell, "A Pain in the Gulliver," *Village Voice*, January 20, 1972; see also Anthony Burgess, "Letter," *Los Angeles Times*, February 21 , 1972.

164   "Abused to serve base, selfish ends": Moskowitz, 24.

164   Critics on Kubrick's decor: see Sobchack; also Robert Hughes, "The Decor of Tomorrow's Hell," *Time*, December 27, 1971.

164   A fascinating (though basically unsympathetic) analysis: see Gumenik.

Lord of the Flies

169   Explanations for the popularity of *Lord of the Flies*: those cited are adapted primarily from a series of letters printed in the *New Republic*,

May 4, 1965. The magazine had invited faculty members at several universities to speak to the issue.

169   Judgment of Golding as simplistic: the corpus of Golding criticism—both positive and negative—is massive. But for some indication of the nature of the critical complaints concerning the novel's blatancy, see Gindin and Peter.

170   Crowther's review: *New York Times*, August 20, 1963.

170   One film text: see Linden, 46.

170   "Attended the film with": ibid.

170   "Ditch a few courtesies": Miller, *New Yorker*, August 31, 1963.

Wise Blood

175   Symbol-hunters: O'Connor herself had some amusing things to say about this. See especially her letter of May 25, 1959, in the collected letters, *The Habit of Being*; also Robert Towers, "Flannery O'Connor's Gifts," in the *New York Review of Books*, May 3, 1979, who in quoting from this letter adds some useful commentary of his own.

176   "Non-ideological response": Stephens, 73–74.

177   "Quite made up its mind": "Goings on About Town," *New Yorker*, April 16, 1984. Its reservations notwithstanding, the *New Yorker* does finally praise the film though, suggesting that it "works in the end, against all odds, because of its wild, strange humor and its sympathy for the rigors of home-fried Christian passion." I agree on both counts.

177   Criticism of O'Connor: see among others, Baumbach and Stephens.

177   "The data of the book": Kauffmann, *New Republic*, March 15, 1980.

180   Mythic associations of film's narrative pattern: several critics have also made much of the extent to which the film's opening sequence calls up John Ford, in particular the *Grapes of Wrath*. And at least one, Laura Jehn Menides, goes so far as to see the sequence as establishing certain thematic links between the two films—the contrast with the secular quest in *Grapes of Wrath* serving to stress the religious nature of that in *Wise Blood*. But this "reading" not only fails to enrich our experience of the film, it pushes matters a bit too far. So too with Roger Angell's interpretation of the image of the newspaper-wrapped mummy Enoch steals from the museum as an in-joke, referring back to Huston's *The Maltese Falcon* ("The Current Cinema," *New Yorker*, February 25, 1980). After all, O'Connor herself describes the mummy as "wrapped in newspapers," and it's hard to believe she had Huston's movie in mind.

181   "Associations of both burial": Pullene, 57.

182   "Possibly I ought to feel guilty": *New Republic*, June 11, 1984.

Death in Venice

182   "For me, I despise it": Mann in Geduld, 129.

182   "That amazing group of structures": this and all other quotations from *Death in Venice* are from the translation by H. T. Lowe-Porter. New York: Vintage Books, no date.

184   Wagner on the film's critics: Wagner, 342.

184   Mellen's view: Mellen, 41.

184   Function of music in the film: Stein, 68–69.

185   Source of Visconti's choices in *Dr. Faustus*: for an extended analysis of the debt of both the debates and the character of Alfred to this later Mann novel, see Hutchinson.

186   "The most revealing": Servadio, 198.

186   Feminizing him: this view of Bogarde is shared by Wagner, among others; see Wagner, 344.

186   "Hand on hip": Dawson, "Cooking the Books," *The Listener*, March 11, 1971.

188   "Compared with art's": Mann, loc. cit.

Chapter Eight

Page 190   "Endless flow": Bergson in Ellmann and Feidelson, 724, 729.

190   "Consciousness": James in Ellmann and Feidelson, 717.

190   "Look within": Woolf, *Collected Essays*, II, 106.

191   Eisenstein's views on Joyce: Seton, 490.

192   Joyce and the *Ulysses* screenplays: see Ellmann, 666.

192   "It is no exaggeration": Murray, 128 and passim.

192   Woolf and film: for an extended analysis of Woolf's filmic strategies see Humphrey, 51–56 especially, and Murray, 142–53.

192   "The most elaborate": Spiegel, 88, 117.

193   "The anti-realist novel": Littlejohn, 250.

194   "Mindscreen": see Kawin's study for a fascinating analysis of the various filmic strategies used by these filmmakers for the exploration of inner states.

195   "Dream-mode": Langer, *Feeling and Form*, 415.

195   Jones quote: *The Dramatic Imagination: Reflections and Speculations on*

the Art of the Theatre (New York: Duell, Sloan & Pearce, 1941), 17–18. Quoted by Langer, loc. cit.

195 "When required to penetrate the complex psyche": Murray, 134.

197 "Simon's Law": Simon, *Movies into Film*, 25.

Slaughterhouse-Five

197 Bourjaily on Vonnegut: *New York Times Book Review*, August 13, 1972.

197 Richardson on Vonnegut: *New York Review of Books*, July 2, 1970.

197 Vonnegut at Harvard: see Richard Todd, "The Masks of Kurt Vonnegut, Jr.," *New York Times Magazine*, January 24, 1971.

198 Crichton on Vonnegut: *New Republic*, April 26, 1969.

199 Scholes on *Slaughterhouse-Five: New York Times Book Review*, April 6, 1969.

199 "Man's misfortune": Sartre, *Literary and Philosophical Essays*, 79.

200 Argument concerning the novel's self-reflexiveness: Isaacs.

203 Farber quote: *New York Times*, June 11, 1972.

204 Sarris quote: *Village Voice*, June 15, 1972.

Under the Volcano

205 "Rich and humorous": *Times Literary Supplement*, January 2 6, 1967.

205 "A prose *Waste Land*": ibid., May 11, 1962.

205 Buñuel's remark: cited by Stanley Kauffmann, *New Republic*, June 18, 1984.

207 Huston's history with various scripts: cited in Universal Pictures production notes for the film.

207 Huston's contributions to Gallo's screenplay: see, among other articles suggesting the extent of Huston's control of the project, Aljean Harmetz, *New York Times*, June 14, 1984.

210 "Haunt this novel": *Times Literary Supplement*, May 11 , 1 962.

210 Maslin on *Under the Volcano: New York Times*, June 13, 1984 .

210 Huston interview: Harmetz, loc. cit.

211 Huston on the Consul's motives: McCarthy, 60.

Day of the Locust

212 "Putting down a book by West": Fiedler, 465.

212 "Who can believe": *The New Yorker*, May 12, 1974.

213 "West does not seem": Fiedler, loc. cit.

214 "Readable": Kael, loc. cit.

214 Salt's views: quoted by Rapf, 24.

218 Defense of the Aimee Semple McPherson sequence: see Edward T. Jones, 225.

218 Need for strong assertion of Tod's perspective: see Gottlieb's in Peary and Shatzkin, *The Modern American Novel and the Movies*, 95–106.

Swann in Love and The Proust Screenplay

219 Goodman on Proust: in Kauffmann and Henstell, 311–14.

219 Bourgeois on Proust: "Le cinéma à la recherche du temps perdu," *La Revue du Cinéma*, Numéro 3G, 1946; quoted in *Le Monde*, February 23, 1984.

220 Carrière's statement: quoted by David Robinson, "Magical Fragment of Remembrance," *Times* (London), April 6, 1984.

220 "The camera lingers": Malcolm Bowie, "Sexually Scenic," *Times Literary Supplement*, April 27, 1984.

221 Visconti's casting of Proust: Servadio, 200.

223 "Swann's midnight carriage chase": Thomas Quinn Curtiss, "Schlöndorff's Way with Proust's Swann," *International Herald Tribune*, February 22, 1984.

224 "At best, the sort of adaptation": Derek Malcolm, "Coming Home to Proust," *Manchester Guardian*, April 5, 1984.

224 "No esoterie knowledge": Judy Stone, "Splendid 'Translation' of Proust," *San Francisco Chronicle*, April 13, 1984.

226 All quotations are from the published version of *The Proust Screenplay*.

227 Lack of parallels between novel and screenplay: see Graham, 39 and passim.

228 "Saw how this *visual* motif": Kauffmann, *Before My Eyes*, 396–97.

Afterword

Page 230 Materials on *The Magnificent Ambersons* are to be found in the Lilly Library, Indiana University, and in the Film Library of the Museum of Modern Art, which has a copy of Welles's final draft of the script, dated October 7, 1941. Charles Higham's *The Films of Orson Welles* contains a summary of the missing footage, based on the cutting continuity of the original release print.

231 Truffaut's remark: quoted by McBride, 84.

232 Tarkington on popularity: Fennimore, 134. I am also indebted to Fennimore for information on Tarkington's publishing history.

233 "Light touch": Parrington, III, 375.

233 Welles on Tarkington: These remarks were made at a public seminar *Working with Welles*, hosted by the American Film Institute and held in Los Angeles, January, 1979.

235 Wood's views: Wood, 25.

235 Cook's views: Cook, 369.

235 "One has the strong impression": Bessy, 36.

236 "The reader is swept": Fennimore, 68.

237 Herrmann on *Ambersons*: quoted by Naremore, 133.

238 McBride on *Ambersons*'s cinematography: McBride, 58 and passim.

INDEX

A

Abstraction, 32
Academy Awards, 5
Actors, problems in accepting in
  roles, 56–57
Academy of Motion Pictures Arts
  and Sciences, 11
Adaptations:
  Academy Awards and, 5
  detractors of, 5–20
    Arendt, quoted, 7–8, 15
    politique des auteurs, 13–
    14
    Bluestone, views of, 8–9
    changes in films and, 18–19
    destructiveness to film and,
    16–17
    destructiveness to literature
    and, 15–16
    entertainment and, 7–10
    European films and, 8–9
    films as "art" and, 10–15
    film's relationship to literature
    and, 6, 12–17, 20
    great works of literature and,
    9–10
    Hollywood and, 14, 18
    lack of originality and, 14–15,
    17
    mass media and, 7–9
    "necessity" of adaptations
    and, 17–18
    silent films and, 6
    sound era and, 6–7
    Truffaut, views of, 13
    Woolf, quoted, 6, 15
  film as literature, *see* Film as
    literature

as mission of motion pictures, 4
"proven property" and, 4
a touch of class and, 4–5
"Affective Fallacy," 47
*AFI Guide to Courses in Film and
  Television*, 11*n*.
Agee, James, 11*n*.
Aldington, Richard, 124
Alice Adams (Tarkington), 233
Allegory, 156
  see also Metaphor, symbolism,
    and allegory
Allen, Dede, 202
Almendros, Nestor, 61
Altman, Robert, 196
Ambassadors, The, (James), 147,
  189
American Film Institute, 11
American Tragedy, An (Dreiser),
  68–69
Analogy, *see* Modes of Adaptation
Andersen, Hans Christian, 5
Anderson, Lindsay, 133
Andersson, Bibi, 23, 24, 223
Andresen, Bjorn, 186
Andrews, Anthony, 208–209
Anger, Kenneth, 12
Anna Karenina (Tolstoy), 30,
  138*n*.
"Anti-realists," 193, 194, 196
Antonioni, Michaelangelo, 14*n*.,
  17, 23
Apocalypse Now, 110–16, 157
Archibald, William, 92
Architecture, 31
Ardant, Fanny, 223
Arendt, Hannah, 7, 8, 10, 15
Aristotle, 24, 38, 118
Arnheim, Rudolph, 24

"Art films," 10–15
Arvin, Newton, 77
Asphalt Jungle, The, 14
Assassination of Trotsky, The, 157
Assommoir, L', 4
Astaire, Fred, 25
Atherton, William, 214
Attitude, *see* Style and tone
Aubrey, James, 171
Audience for films, 6–7
Austen, Jane, 30, 56, 85–86
Auteurs, 13–14, 111
Avventura, L', 17

B

Badalucco, Nicola, 184
Ballantyne, R. M., 170
Bardot, Brigitte, 221
Barnes, Djuna, 193
Barrett, Gerald, 26, 69–70
Barrett, William, 122
Barrie, Sir James, 15
Barry Lyndon, 9, 18, 33, 167
Barthes, Roland, 22
Bartholomew, Freddie, 16
Bartleby, 69, 156
Bartolini, Luigi, 15
Barty, Billy, 214
Battestin, Martin, 79–80, 110
Baxter, Warner, 98
Bazin, André, 6, 9, 31–32
Beat the Devil, 177
Beckett, Samuel, 35, 155
Belle de Jour, 70, 195
Ben-Hur, 4
Bergman, Ingmar, 9, 17, 23, 48,

111, 194, 195, 220, 223
    on word versus film, 26–27, 28
Bergson, Henri, 190
Berlin Alexanderplatz, 78
Bertolucci, 70
Bespoke Overcoat, The, 69, 99
Bessy, Maurice, 235
Bicycle Thief, The, 15
Billy Budd (Melville), 156
Birth of a Nation, The, 3, 15, 33
Bisset, Jacqueline, 208
Black, Karen, 100, 214–15
Blake, William, 72
Blood of the Poet, The, 195
Blow Up, 23, 46
Bluestone, George, 8, 9, 10, 69, 80–81, 194–95
Bogarde, Dirk, 186
Bogart, Humphrey, 22, 39, 56
Bogdonovich, Peter, 147–53
Bonnie and Clyde, 19
Book of Daniel, The (Doctorow), 15–16, 66
Bostonians, The, 19, 147n.
Boston Phoenix, The, 55n.
Bottoms, Sam, 110
Bourgeois, Jacques, 219–20
Bourjaly, Vance, 197
Brach, Gerald, 141
Bradbury, Ray, 13, 74–77
Brakhage, Stan, 12
Brando, Marlon, 115
Braudy, Leo, 36
Breathless, 90
Brennan, Eileen, 151
Bresson, Robert, 9, 27, 70, 71, 121
Breton, André, 212
Broken Blossoms, 3

Brook, Peter, 40, 170–75, 220
Brooks, Cleanth, 155–56
Brothers Karamazov, The, 15, 57
Brown, Barry, 149–50
Brown, Clarence, 193
Browning, Elizabeth Barrett, 3
Brownjohn, John, 141
Brynner, Yul, 19, 57
Bulwer-Lytton, Edgar, 4
Buñuel, Luis, 19*n*., 70, 111, 194, 207
Bunyan, John, 199, 204
Burgess, Anthony, 162–68
Burke, Thomas, 3
Bush, Stephen, 4
Bute, Mary Ellen, 193

C

Cabaret, 69
Cabinet of Dr. Caligari, The, 90
Cagney, James, 134
Cain, James M., 65
Call of Wild, The, 3
Camus, Albert, 65
Capote, Truman, 92, 119
Carpenter, Edmund, 74–77
Carrière, Jean-Claude, 220, 222
Carroll, Lewis, 32, 55
Carr-Smith, Rodney, 69
Casablanca, 22, 38–39
Castle, The, 194
Catcher in the Rye, The (Salinger), 85, 169
Catch-22, 69
Cavell, Stanley, 48
Chandler, Raymond, 88, 114

Chapin, Tom, 171
Chaplin, Charlie, 158
Character, 35–37, 55–58
Chatman, Seymour, 37
Chester, Alfred, 10
Chien Andalov, Un, 49, 194
Children of Paradise, 17
Chinatown, 141
"Chink and the Child, The," 3
Chinoise, La, 27
Chronicle of Anna Magdelena Bach, The, 27
"Cinematic" films, 13, 14, 16
Cinematic Imagination, The (Murray), 192
Citizen Kane, 9–10, 25, 33, 158, 232, 235
Clansman, The (Dixon), 3, 15
Classics of literature, 65–67, 77
Clayton, Jack, 92, 99, 104
Clockwork Orange, A, 161–68
Cloquet, Ghislain, 142
Cocteau, Jean, 194
Commentary, *see* Modes of Adaptation
Compression and selection, 78
Connotation, 26, 157
Conrad, Joseph, 9, 51, 110–17, 155
Conversation, The, 23, 99
Cook, David A., 235
Coppola, Francis, 23, 30, 33, 157
  Apocalypse Now and, 110–16
  The Great Gatsby and, 99, 102, 104
Coral Island (Ballantyne), 170
Cortez, Stanley, 237
Costello, Dolores, 240

Cotton, Joseph, 234, 240
Crichton, Michael, 198–99
Cricket on the Hearth, The, 3
Cries and Whispers, 194, 195
Crime and Punishment, 63, 70
Crowther, Bosley, 170
Cul de Sac, 141

D

Daisy Miller, 145–53
Dali, Salvador, 194
Daniel, 18, 66
Dante, 10
Dawson, Jan, 186
Day for Night, 105
Day of the Locust, The, 196, 212–19
Dean, James, 48
Death in Venice, 162, 182–88
Decoding, process of, 25
De Havilland, Olivia, 147*n.*
Delannoy, Jean, 9
Delon, Alain, 221–22
Denotation, 26
Deren, Maya, 12
Dern, Bruce, 100
De Santi, Pasquale, 185
Dairy of a Country Priest, 9
Dickens, Charles, 3, 8, 33, 55, 124, 139
Dietrich, Marlene, 36
Disney, Walt, 5, 15, 68
Divine Comedy, The, 79
Dixon, Thomas, 3, 15
Dr. Faustus, 184, 185
Doctorow, E. L., 15, 66, 132, 135, 136
Dr. Strangelove, 164

Dodeskaden, 89
Dos Passos, John, 35
Dostoyevsky, Fyodor, 15, 30, 48, 67, 70, 71, 119, 141
Double vision, 53–58, 104–10
Dourif, Brad, 134, 179
Down There (Goodis), 65
Drama, as distinct from narrative, 38
Dreams, *see* Thoughts, dreams, and interior action
Dreiser, Theodore, 119, 133
Dryden, John, 69, 70
Durgnat, Raymond, 159–60
Duvall, Robert, 114–15
Dynamic editing, *see* Editing

E

Easy Rider, 23
Editing, 157, 202
    "dynamic," 29, 191–92
    montage, 29, 192
Edwards, Hugh, 171–72
Effi Briest, 17
8½, 14*n.*, 17, 195
Eisenstein, Sergei, 6, 29, 157, 191–92
Elements of Style (Strunk and White), 118
Eliot, T. S., 66, 115
Emma (Austen), 85–86
Emotions, 26–28
Ennery, Adolph D., 3
Enoch Arden, 3
"Essence" of films, 12–15, 16

Estienne, Marie-Hélène, 220
E.T., 47
Europeans, The, 147*n.*
"Evolution of the Language of
     Cinema, The," 6

F

"Fabulists," 193
Fahrenheit 451, 13
Fallen Idol, The, 9
Farber, Stephen, 203–204
Farewell to Arms, A, 19
Far from the Madding Crowd, 138*n.*
Farrow, Mia, 100
Fassbinder, 17
Faulkner, William, 33, 91, 155
   stream of consciousness and,
        190–93, 199, 205
Fellini, Federico, 10, 14*n.*, 17, 35,
        68, 111, 121, 150, 180,
        195
Femme Coquette, Une, 14
Femme Douce, Une, 70, 71, 73
Ferguson, Otis, 11*n.*
Fiction, 58–59
Fictional narrative, 12, 30–40
Fidelity, varying notions of,
        63–81
   change in title, time, or locale
        and, 68–69, 78–79
   ideal viewer and, 63–64, 66–67
   "interpretive communities"
        and, 75–77
   major works of literature and,
        65–67, 77
   modes of adaptations and
        69–71
   point of view and, 80

pulp fiction and, 64–65
quality of implicit
     interpretation of its source
     and, 71
response and, 73–77
time factor and, 78
transformation of verbal to
     visual and, 79–80
translation and, 69, 70–71
validity and, 71–77
Fiedler, Leslie, 10, 77, 147, 212,
        213
Field, Betty, 98
Fielding, Henry, 79, 86, 87, 123,
        139
Figueroa, Gabriel, 209
Figurative expression, *see*
     Metaphor, symbolism,
     and allegory
Film and literature, 20, 21–40
   abstraction, 32
   character, 35–37
   connotation, 26
   decoding, 25
   denotation, 26
   "fictionality," 30–31
   intellect and emotions, 26–28
   language, 21–22, 28–31
   meaning, 22
   mental images, construction of,
        25
   mode of construction, 28
   narrative, 30–40
   perception, 24–25
   plot, 35
   realism, 31–32
   setting, 37–38
   sound, 22–23
   spatiality, 34–35

symbolic versus iconic signs,
      21–22, 25
syntax, 32, 34
tenses, 33–34
theater and, 38–39
thought from image versus
      image from thought and,
      24
time, 32–35
words, 22–26, 29–31, 32
Film Comment, 11
Film Criticism of Otis Ferguson,
      The, 11*n.*
Filmmaker as reader, 63–81
Film Culture, 11
Finch, John, 39
Finney, Albert, 208
First Love, 70
Firth, Peter, 144
Fish, Stanley, 49, 50, 75–76
Fisher, Gerald, 178
Fiske, Minnie Maddern, 138*n.*
Fitzgerald, Benedict, 176
Fitzgerald, F. Scott, 98–99, 104,
      232
Fitzgerald, Robert and Sally, 176
Flaubert, Gustave, 35, 55–56,
      231–32
Foot, Horton, 193
Ford, Ford Madox, 87
Ford, Henry, 132, 135
Ford, John, 13, 14*n.*, 48, 64, 65,
      90, 160
Forman, Milos, 133
Forster, E. M., 35, 169
Fort Apache, 13, 14
Fosse, Bob, 69
Four Hundred Blows, The, 158
Four Nights of a Dreamer, 71

Fowles, John, 104–105, 107, 109,
      110
France, Anatole, 219
Francis, Freddie, 94, 107
Frankenstein, 15
French, Brandon, 74–77
French Connection, The, 49
French Lieutenant's Woman, The,
      104–10, 111, 221
French New Wave, 11, 18
Freud, Sigmund, 76, 77, 95, 96,
      97, 133, 135, 169–70
Friedman, Anthony, 69
Frost, Robert, 154
Frye, Northrop, 36–37, 156
"Für Elise," 184, 187

G

Gallo, Guy, 207–208
Gaman, Tom, 171
Garbo, Greta, 22
Garson, Greer, 55, 56
Geller, Stephen, 199, 201
"Gentle Creature, The," 70, 71
Gianetti, Louis, 158
Gide, Andre, 9
Godard, Jean-Luc, 14, 27, 48, 90,
      194
Godfather, The, 17, 99, 111
Godfather, Part II, The, 33, 34
Gogol, 69
Golden Bowl, The, 147
Golding, William, 169–75
Goldman, Emma, 132, 135, 136
Gone with the Wind, 5, 56
Goodbye, Mr. Chips, 5
Goodis, David, 65
Goodman, Paul, 219

Good Soldier, The (Ford), 87
Gottlieb, Sidney, 218
Gould, Glenn, 203
Graduate, The, 90
Graham, Mark, 226
Grant, Cary, 56
Grapes of Wrath, The, 13, 14, 19, 65, 78
Great Expectations, 8, 85
Great Gatsby, The, 10, 54, 98–104, 107*n.*
Great Train Robbery, The, 17, 19
Greed, 78, 231
Green, Graham, 8
Green Room, The, 13, 65
Gregory, André, 23
Gremlins, 160
Griffith, D. W., 3, 6, 90
Guernica, 59
Guinness, Alec, 57

H

Hair, 133
Haley, Jackie, 214
Hall, Conrad, 215
Hamlet, 29
Hands of Orlac, The, 206, 211
Hardy, Thomas, 67, 138–45
Hauser, Arnold, 31
Hawkes, John, 193
Hawks, Howard, 17
Hawthorne, Nathaniel, 155
Haycock, Ernest, 64
Heart of Darkness (Conrad), 110–17
Heiress, The, 69, 147*n.*
Hemingway, Ernest, 36, 59
Henry V, 17
Henze, Hans Werner, 222

Herr, Michael, 110
Herrmann, Bernard, 237–38
High culture, 7–9, 14
Hill, George Roy, 18, 133, 199–205
His Girl Friday, 17
Hitchcock, Alfred, 14*n.*, 37–38, 48, 64, 90, 160
"Hollow Men, The," 115
Hollyman, Tom, 171
Hollywood, 14, 18
The Day of the Locust and, 212–19
Holt, Tim, 240–41
Hood, Thomas, 3
Hopkins, Gerard Manley, 28
Hopper, Dennis, 111
Houdini, Harry, 132, 135, 136
Howe, Irving, 140, 145
Howells, William Dean, 151
Huckleberry Finn (Twain), 121
Huston, John, 13–14
Moby Dick and, 74–77, 159
Under the Volcano and, 207–12
Wise Blood and, 176–81
Hutton, Timothy, 16
Hyman, Stanley Edgar, 163

I

Ideal viewer, 61, 63–64, 66–67
If . . ., 133
Illusion, creation of, 58
Imagery, 155–57
see also Metaphor, symbolism, and allegory
Images, 196
Imitation, *see* Translation
Innocents, The, 92–98, 99, 147*n.*

Intellect and emotion in film and
    literature, 26–28
  reflective art and, 27
"Interior monologue," 190
Interiors, *see* Thoughts, dreams,
    and interior action
Interpretation, 43–62
  fidelity of, *see* Fidelity
  Validity of, *see* Validity of
    Interpretation
"Interpretive communities,"
    75–77
Intruder in the Dust, 193
Invasion of the Body Snatchers, The,
    160
Irons, Jeremy, 107, 221, 222, 223
Irving, John, 56
Iser, Wolfgang, 49, 50, 53
Italian Neorealism, 11, 18
It's All True, 231

J

"Jabberwocky," 32
Jackson, Glenda, 130
Jacob's Room (Woolf), 192
Jaglom, Henry, 196
James, Henry, 13, 65, 78
  Daisy Miller and, 145–53
  point of view and, 85–86, 189
  The Turn of the Screw and,
    91–98
James, William, 189–90
*James Agee on Film: Reviews and
    Comments*, 11*n*.
Jones, Jennifer, 19, 55, 138*n*.
Jones, R. E., 195
Joyce, James, 10, 35, 48, 66, 78,
    205, 232

  stream of consciousness and,
    190–94
Jude the Obscure (Hardy), 67
Jules and Jim, 13, 17
Jung, Carl, 76, 133, 135

K

Kael, Pauline, 10, 57–58, 97,
    160, 213, 214, 218
Kafka, Franz, 155, 194, 241*n*.
Kauffmann, Stanley, 60, 158,
    181–82, 210, 228
Kawin, Bruce, 194
Kaye, Danny, 48
Kennedy Center, 11
Kerr, Deborah, 93, 95
Kesey, Ken, 133
Kidnapped, 16, 63
Killers, The (Hemingway), 85
Kinski, Nastassia, 144–45
Kipling, Rudyard, 14, 177
Kleist, Heinrich von, 17
Kline, Kevin 44, 57, 58
Knife in the Water, 141
Kracauer, Siegfried, 31
Kramer, Larry, 125
Kubrick, Stanley, 9, 23, 164–68
Kurosawa, Akira, 67, 89

L

Ladd, Alan, 39, 98
Lady in the Lake, 88, 92, 116
Lady Vanishes, The, 37–38, 64,
    90
Landri de Biciclette, 15
Lang, Fritz, 158
Langer, Susanne, 21–22, 33

Language, 21–22, 28–31, 58–60, 121
Last Days of Pompei, The (Bulwer-Lytton), 4
Last Year at Marienbad, 46, 90, 194
Lawrence, D. H., 48, 124–31, 139, 211*n*., 232
Lawson, Leigh, 143
Leachman, Cloris, 151
Lean, David, 8
Leavis, F. R., 124–25, 146
Leibman, Ron, 200
Leigh, Vivien, 56
Levison, André, 24
Levinson, Barry, 181
Lie Down in Darkness (Styron), 52
Lincoln Center, 11
Linden, George, 14–15
Linden, Jennie, 131
Lindsay, Vachel, 6, 10, 12
Listener, 186
"Literary" films, 13, 17
Literature/Film Quarterly, 226
Literature's relationship to film, 6, 12–15
  as destructive to film, 16–17
  as destructive to literature, 15–16
  film as a form of literature, *see* Film as literature
Little Caesar, 17
Littlejohn, David, 193
Lockwood, Margaret, 38
Lolita, 87
London, Jack, 3
Lord of the Flies, 162, 169–75
Lorre, Peter, 63, 158, 206, 211
Losey, Joseph, 157, 229

Lowry, Malcolm, 205–11
Lukas, Paul, 37
Lumet, Sidney, 18, 66

M

M, 158
Macbeth, 67
McBride, Joseph, 238
McDowell, Malcolm, 166, 168
McGovern, Elizabeth, 134
McLaren, Norman, 12
McLuhan, Marshall, 9, 10
MacNicol, Peter, 56, 57, 58
Madame Bovary, 8, 18, 19, 35, 69
Magee, Patrick, 168
Magnificent Ambersons, The, 150*n*., 231–42
Mahler, Gustav, 182, 184
Malamud, Bernard, 15, 64, 181
Mallarmé, Stéphane, 32
Malle, Louis, 23
Maltese Falcon, The, 34, 177
Mangano, Silvana, 188
Mankowitz, Wolf, 69
Mann, Thomas, 182–88
Man Who Would Be King, The, 14, 177
Marat/Sade, 40
Marquise of O, The, 9, 17
Maslin, Janet, 210
Mass culture, 7–9, 11
"Masterpiece Theatre," 67
Maupaussant, Guy de, 14, 141
Méliès, Georges, 3, 19
Mellen, Joan, 184
Melville, Herman, 74, 76, 154–55, 156, 159
Mépris, Le, 14

Mercury Theatre, 233
Meredith, Burgess, 214
Merry Widow, 184
Metaphor, symbolism, and
    allegory, 80, 154–88
  adaptations and, 161
  cinematic devices for, 157–59
  A Clockwork Orange, 161–68
  Death in Venice, 182–88
  definitions of, 155–57
  editing and, 157
  interpretive confusion and,
    154–55, 159
  Lord of the Flies, 169–75
  overinterpretation and, 154,
    159, 160
  poetry and, 155–56, 160–61
  cinematic difficulties with,
    154–55, 159–61
  Wise Blood, 175–82
Metaphrase, *see* Translation
Metonymy, 158
Metz, Christian, 26
Milius, John, 110, 112, 113
Miller, Jonathan, 175
Minelli, Vincente, 8, 18, 69
Mitchell, Margaret, 56
Mitry, Jean, 30
Moby Dick, 19, 56–57, 71,
    73–77, 78, 85, 159, 207
Modern novels, 85–87, 189–96
  "anti-realists" and, 193, 194,
    196
  Henry James and, 85–86, 189
  William James and, 189–90
  "stream of consciousness" and,
    190–96
Modern Times, 158
Modes of adaptation, 69–71

analogy and, 69
commentary and, 69
transposition and, 69
Moll Flanders, 120
Montgomery, Robert, 88, 98,
    116
Moorehead, Agnes, 240
Moravia, Alberto, 14
Morgan, 157
Morgan, J. P., 132, 133, 135
Morin, Edgar, 48
Moskowitz, Ken, 167
Moving Picture World, The, 4
Mrs. Dalloway (Woolf), 119–20,
    191, 192, 193, 195
Murray, Edward, 192, 195
Muti, Ornella, 221
My Dinner with Andre, 23,
My Night at Maud's, 27

N

Nanook of the North, 12
Narrative, 12, 30–40
  defined, 38
Narrative stance, *see* Point of view
Narrativity, 49
Natural, The (Malamud), 15–16,
    64, 73, 181
Natwick, Mildred, 151
Neo-Classical style, 122
Nesbit, Evelyn, 132, 134, 136,
    137
New Criticism, 47
Newman, Randy, 133
New Republic, 198
New Yorker, 175
New York Times, The, 170, 199
Nichols, Dudley, 65

Nichols, Mike, 69
Nicoll, Allardyce, 39
Nietzsche, Friedrich, 183, 184, 186
Nigger of the Narcissus, The (Conrad), 51
Nin, Anaïs, 196
1984, 19
Novel and the Cinema, The (Wagner), 9*n.*, 69
Novels into Film (Bluestone), 8, 9
Nykvist, Sven, 222

O

Oberon, Merle, 19
O'Brien, Pat, 134
Obsessione, 65
O'Connor, Donald, 134
O'Connor, Flannery, 175–81
Odd Man Out, 8–9
Oedipus, 24
Of Mice and Men, 5
Oliver Twist, 8
Olivier, Sir Lawrence, 17, 19, 29, 40, 57
Olson, James, 134
Olympiad, 158–59
Omniscience, *see* Point of view
Ondricek, Miroslav, 133, 203
One Flew Over the Cuckoo's Nest, 133
"On Style," 118
On the Waterfront, 49
Ophul, Max, 105
Originality, 14–15, 17
  lack of, 14–15
  criterion, 17
Orlando (Woolf), 193

Orphans of the Storm, 3
Osborne, John, 79
Othello, 40
Outcast of the Islands, An, 9

P

Pakula, Alan, 44, 53–62
Pamela, 120
Panofsky, Erwin, 22–23, 34
Paper Moon, 150*n.*
Paraphrase, *see* Translation
Passages from Finnegan's Wake, 193–94
Passage to India, A, 19
Passivity of viewer, 48–49
Patinkin, Mandy, 134
Patton, 99
Peck, Gregory, 19, 56–57
Peer Gynt, 158
"Penetrating consciousness," *see* Thoughts, dreams, and interior action
Perception, 24–25, 45–47, 60–62
Perrine, Laurence, 155
Perrine, Valerie, 200
Persona, 23, 26, 195
Peter Pan, 15
Pilgrims Progress, The (Bunyan), 199, 204
Pinter, Harold, 78, 105, 108, 109, 197, 225–29
Pippa Passes, 3
Place in the Sun, A, 68–69
Plot, 35
"Poem in October," 23
Poetry, 23–24, 28, 47, 72, 210
  metaphor and, 155–56, 160–61

Point of view, 80, 85–117
  Apocalypse Now, 110–17
  The French Lieutenant's Woman,
    104–10
  The Great Gatsby, 98–
    104
  The Innocents, 91–98
  omniscience, 86–87
  storytellers and, *see* Storytellers
  subjectivity, 87, 89–90
Polanski, Roman, 39, 138–45
Popcorn Venus: Women, Movies,
  and the American Dream
  (Rosen), 48
Pope, Alexander, 118
Porter, Edwin S., 19
Portrait of a Genius, But . . .
  (Aldington), 124
Portrait of the Artist as a Young
  Man, A, 193–94
Possessed, The (Dostoyevsky),
  67
Postman Always Rings Twice, The,
  65
Practical Criticism (Richards),
  154
Prevert, Jacques, 17
Pride and Prejudice (Austen), 30,
  56
Proust, Marcel, 78, 190, 197,
  219–29
"Proustian Camera Eye, The,"
  219
Proust Screenplay, The, 78,
  224–29
Providence, 90, 195
Psycho, 29
Pulitzer Prize, 233
Pulp fiction, 64–65

Q

Quo Vadis (Sienkiewicz), 4

R

Raging Bull, 49
Ragtime, 132–37
Raphael, Frederick, 148*n.*
Reader-response criticism, 47
  application to film, 47–53
  validity of, 73–77
Reality, film and, 31–32
Red Badge of Courage, The, 207
Redford, Robert, 16, 39, 98, 100,
  102, 104
Redgrave, Michael, 38, 03
Red River, 36
Reed, Carol, 8
Reed, Oliver, 125, 130
Reflections in a Golden Eye, 207
Reflections on the Screen (Linden),
  14
Reisz, Karel, 105, 107–108, 109,
  157
Reivers, The, 193
Remembrance of Things Past
  (Proust), 197, 219–29
  The Proust Screenplay, 224–29
  Swann in Love, 219–24
Renoir, Jean, 14*n.*
Resnais, Alain, 9, 14, 194, 195,
  205, 220
Response, 43–62
  validity of, *see* Reader-response
    criticism
Resymbolization, 50–52, 61
"Revolutionary films," 14–15
Richards, I. A., 79, 154, 160–61

Richardson, Jack, 197, 198
Richardson, Tony, 79, 110, 123
Riefenstahl, Leni, 158–59
Ritt, Martin, 18, 71
River, The, 12
RKO, 231, 236, 238, 239
Robbe-Grillet, Alain, 87*n*.
Roche, Eugene, 200
Roche, Henri-Pierre, 13, 17
Rocky, 160
Rogers, Ginger, 25
Rohmer, Eric, 9, 17
Rollins, Howard E., 134
Romantic style, 122
Ronde, La, 105
Room at the Top, 99
Rosemary's Baby, 141
Rosen, Marjorie, 48
Rosenblatt, Louise, 47, 49
Rota, Nino, 121
Rouge et le Noir, Le, 10
Rules of the Game, The, 14*n*.
Russell, Ken, 125–31
Ryan, Robert, 98
Rydell, Mark, 193

S

Sacks, Michael, 200
Safe Place, A, 196
Salinger, J. D., 121, 169
Salt, Waldo, 214
Santacroce, May Nell, 178
Sarde, Philip, 143
Sarris, Andrew, 150*n*., 204–205
Sartre, Jean-Paul, 16, 39, 199
Scarfiotti, Ferdinando, 185
Schell, Maximillian, 70, 194
Schlesinger, John, 138*n*., 214–19

Schlöndorff, Volker, 196, 197,
    220–25, 227, 229
Scholes, Robert, 49, 199
Searchers, The, 14*n*.
Secret Garden, The, 51–52
Selznick, David O., 138*n*.
Servadio, Gaia, 186, 187
Setting, 37–38
Seventh Seal, The, 17
Shakespeare, William, 17, 67
Shawn, Wallace, 23
Sheen, Martin, 114
Shepherd, Cybill, 149, 152
Shoot the Piano Player, 65
Shor, Daniel, 179
Sienkiewicz, Henrik, 4
Sight and Sound, 14*n*., 167, 181,
    232
Signs, 21–22, 25, 28–29
Silent films, 4, 6, 19, 22
Simon, John, 128
"Simon's Law," 197, 231
Singer, Issac Bashevis, 64
Slaughterhouse Five, 133, 196,
    197–205
Slocombe, Douglas, 102
Sociétie Film d'Art, 3–4
Song of the Shirt, The, 3
Sontag, Susan, 12, 27, 38, 90–91,
    118–19, 123
Sophie's Choice, 43–46, 50–62,
    63–64, 66, 67, 71–74,
    78, 85
Sound and Sense (Perrine), 155
Sound and the Fury, The, 18, 19,
    33, 71, 91, 191
Spaciality, 34–35
Spagnoli, Alberto, 148
Spider's Strategem, The, 70

Spiegel, Alan, 192
Stagecoach, 64, 65
Stagecoach to Lordsburg, 64
Stanton, Harry Dean, 179
Steenburgen, Mary, 134
Stein, George P., 184
Steinbeck, John, 14, 65
Stevenson, Robert Louis, 16
Storaro, Vittorio, 111
Storytellers, 85–91
   contemporary, 86–87, 189–96
   first-person, 87–88, 90, 91
   James and, 85–86, 189
   objectivity and, 87, 90–91
   omniscient, 86–87
   subjectivity and, 87, 89–90
   third-person, 89, 90
   see also Point of view
Stranger, The, 65
Straub, Jean-Marie, 27
"Stream of consciousness,"
   190–96
   see also Thoughts, dreams, and
   interior action
Streep, Meryl, 43, 44, 55*n.*,
   57–58, 106, 107
Streisand, Barbra, 64
Strick, Joseph, 66, 193, 194
Strike, 157
Stroheim, Erich von, 231
Strunk, William Jr., 118
Style and tone, 60, 80, 118–53
   adaptation and, 121–24
   attitude and, 120–21
   Daisy Miller, 145–53
   defined, 118
   elements of, 120, 123
   inseparability from substance,
   119–20

language and, 121
Ragtime, 132–37
stylization and, 118
Tess, 138–45
theme and, 119–20
tone, 120–21
Women in Love, 124–31
"Stylization," 118
Styron, William, 43, 44, 50–62,
   66
Subjectivity, 87, 89–90
   see also Thoughts, dreams, and
   interior action
Sun Also Rises, The, 69
Sunset Boulevard, 17
Surrealism, 194, 212–19
Sutherland, Donald, 215
Swann in Love, 196, 219–24
Swann's Way (Proust), 196, 220
Sweet, Blanch, 138*n.*
Symbolism, *see* Metaphor,
   symbolism, and allegory
Symphonie Pastorale, 9
Synechdoche, 158
Syntax, 32, 34
Sypher, Wylie, 122

T

Tale of Two Cities, A, 138*n.*
Tarkington, Booth, 150*n.*,
   231–42
Television, effect on film, 11
Temporality, 32–35
   film and literature and, 32–35
   spatialized time, 34–35
Tennyson, Alfred Lord, 3
Tenses, 33–34
Tess, 54, 138–45

Thackeray, William, 86, 87
Theater and film, differences, 38–39
Theme and style, 119–20
Thieving Magpie, The, 166
Third Man, The, 9
Thomas, Dylan, 23–24, 28
Thomas Crown Affair, The, 160
Thoughts, dreams, and interior action, 80–81, 189–229
  "anti-realists" and, 193, 194, 196
  The Day of the Locust, 212–19
  modern novels and, 189–96
  "penetrating consciousness," 80–81
  The Proust Screenplay, 224–29
  Slaughterhouse Five, 197–205
  "stream of consciousness" and, 190–96
  Swann in Love, 219–24
  Under the Volcano, 205–12
Three Women, 196
Throne of Blood, 67
Thus Spake Zarathustra, 23
Time Frame, shift in, 68–69
Tolstoy, Lev, 30
Tom Jones, 79–80, 87, 110, 123
Tomorrow, 193
Tone, 120–21 *see also* Style and tone
Top Hat, 25
Tosi, Pietro, 185, 186
Totter, Audrey, 88
Translations, 69, 70–71
  imitation, 69, 70
  metaphrase, 69, 70
  paraphrase, 69, 70

Transposition, *see* Modes of Adaptation
"Trash, Art, and the Movies," 160
Treasure of Sierra Madre, 177
Trial, The, 194, 241*n.*
Trilling, Lionel, 75
Trip to the Moon, A, 3, 19
Triumph of the Will, 12
Truffaut, François, 13, 88*n.*, 105, 158, 194, 232
Turn of the Screw, The (James), 91–98
Twain, Mark, 121
Twenty Thousand Leagues under the Sea, 3
Two English Girls, 13
Two Orphans, The (Ennery), 3
Two or Three Things I Know About Her, 195
2001, 19, 23, 35, 89–90, 164

U

"Ugly Duckling, The," 5
Ullmann, Liv, 223
Ulysses, 66, 78, 192–95, 205
Understanding Poetry (Brooks and Warren), 155–56
Under the Volcano, 196, 205–12
Uniqueness of films, 12–15, 16
Unsworth, Geoffrey, 142

V

Validity of interpretation, 71–77
Vanity Fair, 87
Verne, Jules, 3
Vertigo, 14*n.*

Vietnam, 110–16
Viewer as reader, 43–62
Vigo, Jean, 158
Visconti, Luchino, 65, 182–88, 221, 222
Visualization, 50–53
Vonnegut, Kurt, Jr., 197–205
Von Sternberg, Joseph, 70
Voyeurism, 48, 49

W

Wagner, Geoffrey, 9, 69, 70, 184
Waller, Edmund, 156
War and Peace, 18
Warren, Austin, 30
Warren, Robert Penn, 155–56
Washington, Booker T., 132, 135, 137
Waste Land, The (Eliot), 66
Waterston, Sam, 100, 103
Waves, The (Woolf), 91, 189
Wayne, John, 36
Wellek, René, 30
Weller, Michael, 133
Welles, Orson, 39, 116–17, 150*n.*, 194, 231–42
Wertmuller, Lina, 180
West, Nathaniel, 212–19, 232
Whale, James, 15
What's Up, Doc?, 150*n.*
Wheel Spins, The (White), 64
White, E. B., 118
White, Ethel Lina, 64
White, Stanford, 133
"White Night," 71

Whitney, James, 12
Wild Bunch, The, 17
Wilde, Oscar, 124, 151
Wilder, Billy, 17
Williams, Billy, 126
Williams, Robin, 55, 56
William Tell Overture, 166
Wilson, Edmund, 95
Wilson, Louise, 98
"Window . . . of consciousness," 85–86
Wise Blood, 162, 175–82, 207
Wizard of Oz, The, 5
Women in Love, 124–31
Wood, Michael, 115, 235
Woolf, Virginia, 6, 7, 15, 26, 35, 48, 91, 119
  the modern novel and, 189–93, 195
Words in film, 22–26, 29–31, 32
  expressive capabilities of, 22–26
  images and, 29–31
World According to Garp, The, 18, 55, 56
World in a Frame, The (Braudy), 36
World Viewed: Reflections on the Ontology of the Film, The (Cavell), 48
"Writer's films," 13, 16–17
Wuthering Heights, 5, 8, 16, 19, 19*n.*, 69, 78, 85
Wyler, William, 8, 19*n.*, 69

Y

Yentl, 64
Yojimbo, 49

Z

Z, 49
Zanuck, Darryl, 16,
   63
Zapata, Emiliano, 135

Zéro de Conduit, 158
Zola, Émile, 4, 141
Zukovsky, Louis, 192